DORIE'S COOKIES

dorie greenspan

DORIE'S COOKIES

photography by davide luciano

food styling by claudia ficca

A RUX MARTIN BOOK   HOUGHTON MIFFLIN HARCOURT   BOSTON   NEW YORK   2016

Library of Congress Cataloging-in-Publication Data
Names: Greenspan, Dorie, author.
Title: Dorie's cookies / Dorie Greenspan.
Description: Boston : Houghton Mifflin Harcourt, [2016]
Identifiers: LCCN 2015042719 (print) | LCCN 2016000912 (ebook) | ISBN
9780547614847 (paper over board) | ISBN 9780547614854 (ebook)
Subjects: LCSH: Cookies. | LCGFT: Cookbooks.
Classification: LCC TX772 .G764 2016 (print) | LCC TX772 (ebook) |
DDC 641.86/54 — dc23
LC record available at http://lccn.loc.gov/2015042719

Book design by Melissa Lotfy

Printed in China
SCP 10 9 8 7 6 5 4 3 2 1

For Joshua,
my cookie monster

acknowledgments

With this book, I can look back at almost fifteen years of working with two extraordinary people, people who are not just the best at what they do, but are the best at being friends: David Black, my agent, and Rux Martin, my editor. I wish every writer a team as good as this one — it makes all the difference in the world to have great people at your side, and they have been the greatest. Everything I do is better because of them.

And every recipe I do is better because of Mary Dodd. When I say that a recipe works, I say it with confidence, because after I've created and tested it, Mary runs it through its paces. This is our second book together, and I never want to do another without her.

Once again, a bushel of thanks to Judith Sutton, who copyedited *Cookies*, as well as ten of my other books, for her ability to soul-search a recipe. No one does this work with more skill than Judith, no one cares about it more and no one is luckier than I to have worked with her for so long.

It is beyond a pleasure to thank Davide Luciano and Claudia Ficca for the bold beauty of this book. Davide, the photographer, and Claudia, the food stylist, are a wildly creative, dynamic, talented couple and a joy to work with. The day they walked into my former cookie shop, Beurre & Sel, I knew we'd work together some day; I just couldn't have imagined that their work would be so exceptional. And thanks to Cindi Gasparre, who assisted Claudia, and made the best-looking World Peace Cookies ever, and to my friend Ellen Madere, whose eye I always trust.

Special thanks to Laurie Woodward, the founder, and Julie Schaeffer and Stephanie Whitten, the backbones of *Tuesdays with Dorie*, the online baking club. I love you and all the TWDers, and have from the start, which is now almost a decade ago. Your enthusiasm always inspires me.

I am so fortunate to have worked again with Carrie Bachman, whose expertise in public relations is matched only by her exceedingly good humor. And thanks to HMH for adding Brittany Edwards, Jessica Gilo and Brad Parsons to the team. Once again, HMH has surrounded me with star people: Melissa Lotfy, who designed this amazing-looking book; Jacinta Monniere, the best-ever typist; Jamie Selzer, Eugenie Delaney and Chloe Foster,

who saw the book through production; Jill Lazer, who worked with the printer to ensure that it was beautiful; and Sarah Kwak, for making it all run smoothly.

A cookie jar full of cookies, mostly chocolate, to Linling Tao, for her smart and generous counsel and for being a great cookie-tasting companion. And limitless thanks to Pierre Hermé, my friend and mentor in all things sweet. Merci also to the many people who helped make Beurre & Sel so special.

As you'll soon read, Beurre & Sel was a cookie boutique that I started with my son, Joshua, who's called himself a cookie monster from just about the first day he could speak. His love of cookies hasn't diminished all these years later. I'd say I love him more for it, but it would be impossible to love him any more than I do. I am lucky to be able to once again close, as I have eleven times before, with love to him and to his father, my indescribably wonderful husband, Michael.

contents

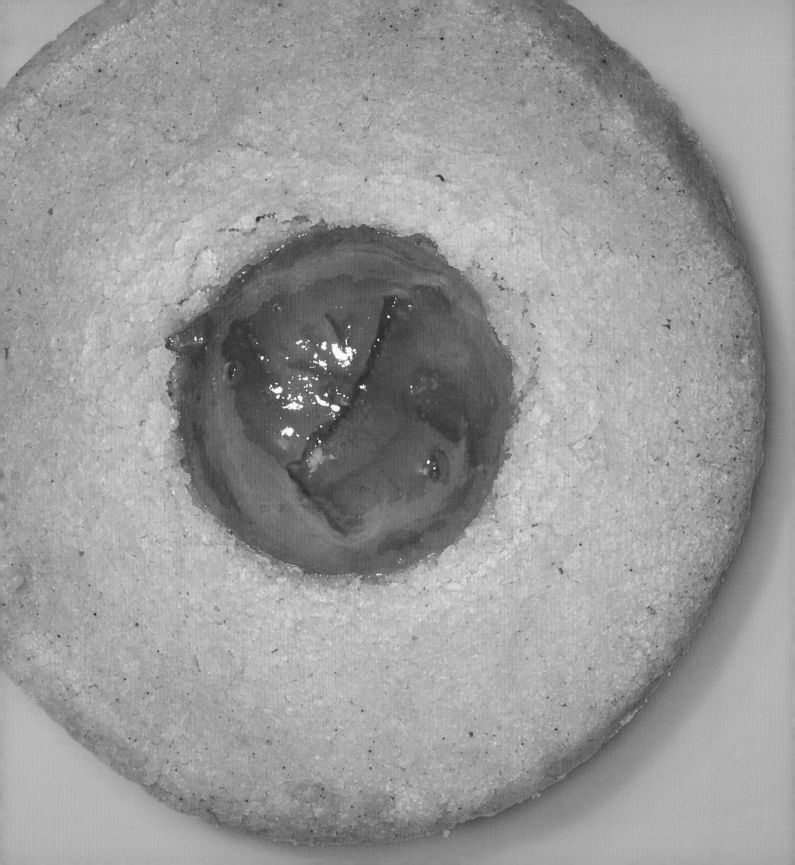

introduction

Hearing I was working on a cookie book, everyone who knew me said the same thing: "Of course you are." Cookies and I have been pals forever.

I come from a family of cookie lovers. I married into a cookie-loving family, and I created one of my own. Michael, my husband, will polish off a plate of cookies and proclaim, as though he's Superman keeping the planet safe, "Done! That temptation's out of the way!" Our son, Joshua's, Twitter bio is: "C is for Cookie." As for me, I've been known to get up in the middle of the night because I've invented a new cookie in my sleep. (Yes, I bake what I dream and sometimes it's pretty great. The Classic Jammer is the blue-ribbon winner in that category.)

My friends were right: Of course I was writing a cookie book — it's something I've wanted to do since I started writing cookbooks twenty-five years ago.

Not that I haven't already written a lot about cookies, probably enough to fill an armload of books. I've never counted, but it's likely that by now I've got at least three hundred cookie recipes to my name: recipes I dreamed; recipes I made up in the light of day; recipes I begged for and those that came to me as gifts; recipes I discovered in places near and far-flung; and recipes that re-created memories. Joshua claims that cookies are memories, and I often bake to make memories real again.

With so many recipes behind me, the question was, how many could there be ahead? Here's what I found out: If you think about cookies night and day for three years — which is what I did when writing this book — you realize that the cookie-verse is infinite. The only thing that can stop the dream machine is a deadline, and I got to mine, but not before I'd put a trio of purple stars, my code for "book it," next to more than 160 recipes. The bar for three purple stars was high. To earn it, a recipe had to be exciting enough to make me want to bake it again and again, and to make me think that it would be intriguing enough for you to want to do the same.

There was something else, and it's at the heart of why I write: Whatever I work on, I want it to make me stretch. I want to learn new things and I want to be able to pass them along to you. With this book, I wanted to get a fresh look at cookies, to see what they could be when, along with butter, sugar, eggs and flour, I added curiosity. I wanted to see if the cookies would stretch with me.

It's a lot to ask of little lumps of dough, but it worked! I had an inkling it might, because of my years at Beurre & Sel, the cookie boutique Joshua and I had in New York City. (You can read all about it on page 330.) I started the cookie stretch there, making cookies for the shop that looked unlike any we'd seen before and crossing into the world of savory cookies, calling them cocktail cookies and designing them for grown-ups. (Every recipe from the Beurre & Sel collection, sweet and salty, is included here.)

But then, I got curiouser and curiouser, and I let my curiosity lead me.

When Michael and I saw ring-shaped cookies in Barcelona's bakeries, I came home and taught myself how to make them — those are the anise-scented Rousquilles. When I read the ingredients in a cocktail and thought they'd make a great cookie, I performed a little culinary transmogrify and created nuggets with the cocktail's name, Bee's Sneeze, and its gin too. When I found a scribble in an old notebook that said, "Make a strawberry-shortcake cookie," I followed its dictum (turns out the cookie is both ethereally beautiful and delicious). When Michael tasted one of my new chocolate cookies and thought it reminded him of Melody cookies, his favorite boxed cookies from childhood (and one of mine), I went back to the kitchen and came up with a Melody that is close to memory. I wondered if I could make a savory meringue — I could and did, and it's hot and spicy and flavored with togarashi, the sweet-and-salty Japanese pepper mix. And, I wondered, if honey and Gorgonzola are so good together on a cheese plate, could they be just as good in a madeleine? Yes! And the combo is even better with champagne. I discovered that a simple dough made with yogurt rises toweringly tall and flakes like puff pastry. A sour cream dough puffs almost as much. And I faced down skepticism when I served savory rugelach and announced that the ingredient that gave the dough its light crunch and wheaty flavor was Triscuits! I won smiles, but I could tell that my husband was thinking, "I can't believe you messed with my mother's rugelach recipe!" Happily, he's known me a long time, so he thinks, but doesn't speak . . . until he's tasted. (His mom's rugelach is here too.)

And because cookies are memories, I returned to a handful of my favorites, delighted to find that they were as good as I'd recalled. Classic Madeleines remain as they were, but they've got a new sibling, Vanilla–Brown Butter Mads. Classic Brownies stay, but they keep company with Sebastian's Remarkably Wonderful Brownies, Snowy-Topped Brownie Drops, Lucky Charm Brownies and more. My Classic Best Chocolate Chip Cookie is still fabulous, but so is my slightly chewier, slightly spicier Newest Chocolate Chip Cookie and its sidekick, the Two-Bite One-Chip Cookie.

I dreamed and followed my dreams and then, when I had notebooks filled with purple stars, I panicked. I loved everything I'd baked, but had I baked a book?

When I began, I knew I wanted cookies that were quick to make; cookies that would bring out the inner tinkerer in all us project-bakers; cookies for holidays and celebrations; cookies we'd want to make on weekends; and cookies for school nights and lunch boxes and picnics and snacking at all hours on every and any day. And so I kept baking. But curiosity and impetuous midnight baking don't necessarily organize themselves into chapters.

Knowing it was too late in the game to mend my messy ways, I just crossed my fingers and made up a stack of index cards, each one marked with the name of a cookie, and I dealt them out into piles that matched the chapters I wanted (but hadn't paid attention to before). In fifteen minutes, the job was done and every cookie had a home. I took it as a miracle and proof that I was right to put my faith in the cookie elves.

This is the book I dreamed it would be, filled with the recipes I loved sharing with my family and friends, ones I want to share with you and ones I hope you'll share with the cookie monsters and lovers in your life.

"C is for Cookie." Bake them, share them and enjoy them!

xoxo Dorie

THE PERFECT-COOKIE
TECHNIQUES, INGREDIENTS AND GEAR
HANDBOOK

techniques

Of all the things we bake, cookies are among the easiest, but, like everything we bake, they need their own special brand of TLC. Because I've been baking cookies for so long, it was actually hard for me to list the little things you should be doing — they've become second nature to me. But they'll come just as naturally to you the more you bake.

Preheat your oven. A few years ago, I had my oven checked by a specialist and he told me that I shouldn't put something in to bake just after the indicator light said the oven had reached temperature. He told me to wait, and I have ever since. Here was his advice: Set your oven to temperature, wait for the beep or the light or whatever signal your oven gives you that it's ready and check the oven thermometer (the one you should keep in the oven at all times; see page 22), then let the oven continue to heat for another 10 to 15 minutes. This extra preheating period guarantees that the oven is hot and that you're not going to cause the temperature to drop drastically when you open the door to slide in your baking sheet. Having the right heat the instant your baking sheet goes in is really important with cookies, since most cookies spend only a short time in the oven.

Line your baking sheets. Lining your sheets with parchment paper or silicone baking mats makes cleanup a snap, and it also helps your cookies to bake more evenly.

Butter (or spray) your pans. Since I find buttering pans as annoying as you no doubt do, I only ask you to do it when it's absolutely necessary. To properly butter a pan, use softened butter and coat the pan using a pastry brush, the best tool, or a crumpled paper towel. (In my recipes, the butter you use to prep the pans is always separate from whatever amount of butter is listed.) If you need to flour a pan after it's buttered, put a spoonful of flour in the pan, shake the pan around so that the flour covers the entire surface and then turn the pan over a trash bin and tap it to knock out the excess flour.

Anytime a recipe calls for buttering or buttering and flouring a pan, you can use baker's spray, an oil-based spray with flour that mimics the butter-flour combo. I'm a fan of butter, but it's impossible to refute the convenience of spray, especially for muffin tins.

Measuring and measurements. No matter where I go, the question of measurements comes up, and within minutes, sides have been drawn. There are the volume (cups and spoons) versus weight people, and then the weight group splits up and you've got Team Ounces versus Team Grams. If you really want to know, here's how I'd line up: weights over volume and metric over ounces. It's not just that weights are more reliable, it's that weights, particularly metric weights, are easier to use, and faster too. I took Math for Poets in college, but even I can see the logic in the metric system, which is based on the number ten. I'd love to figure out the secret to getting everyone to adopt the system, but, failing that, I hope you'll buy a scale and give it a shot. It's especially useful if you like to fiddle with recipes, doubling them for a crowd or cutting them down for twosomes.

However, all of these recipes were tested with both volume measures and weights. Because of space limitations, I've listed volume and metric weights. If you like ounces, you can flip the switch on your scale, and all will be revealed.

Prep like a pro. *Mise en place* is French for "putting in place," and I can't encourage you enough to do this each time you bake. Measure and/or weigh your ingredients, chop what needs to be chopped, melt what needs to be melted, arrange whatever pans and gear you need and then check everything you've prepped against your recipe. It takes just minutes to get everything ready like this (think cooking show) and it will increase the pleasure of baking enormously. It will also save you from those moments we've all had, the ones where you're mixing away merrily and discover that you've forgotten to add an ingredient or don't even have the ingredient in the house. *Mise en place* spares you those "aargh" experiences.

Bring butter to room temperature. For most cookies, and all cookies that begin by beating butter and sugar together, butter should be "at room temperature," an expression that has as much to do with texture as with temperature. For the butter to blend properly with the sugar and other ingredients, it should be soft, but not so soft that it's oily. If you press the butter, your thumb should leave a shallow indentation.

If you don't have time to bring your butter to room temperature, you can bash it into spreadability with a rolling pin. Or you can break off pieces and, using the heel of your hand, smear them across the counter. Or cut the butter into small pieces so it will soften faster.

Sifting/straining. I'm a lazy baker and if I can get away with not having to sift or strain, I will. And most of the time I can. The times I can't are when confectioners' sugar or cocoa powder is involved. These ingredients are lumpy by nature and just whisking them together with the other dry ingredients is not usually enough to thoroughly de-lump them. Trust me — if I tell you to sift or strain, it's because you must. When you need to mix together flour, baking powder and/or soda and spices, though, you can just whisk them in a bowl and be done with it.

Beating butter, sugar and eggs together.

Many cookie recipes start by having you beat the butter and sugar together (I usually beat in the salt at this point) and then beat in the eggs one at a time. Whether you're beating with a stand or hand mixer, the rule is the same: Beat long enough to blend, but don't beat on high speed, because you don't want to aerate the dough. A light and fluffy butter-sugar-egg mixture is what you want for cakes, because air helps cakes rise, but you don't need that rise for cookies and, in fact, most of the time you don't want it either. Cookies bake for a short time and what often happens when they've gotten too much air is that they rise and then fall. If you're meant to aerate the dough, the recipe will tell you; if not, just set your mixer to medium (or lower) speed and blend.

Add the flour all at once.

It took me years to come to this technique, but now that I have, it's the one I use all the time. When you are ready to add the dry ingredients to the cookie dough (or batter) — a step that usually comes at the end of the process, or just before you add chips or nuts or crunchies — turn the mixer off, add the flour all at once, and pulse the mixer on and off until the risk of flying flour has passed. Then, once the flour is in,

mix on low speed only until it disappears into the dough or is incorporated. Don't mix any longer — there's no need, and more mixing will just overwork the dough. If you add the flour all at once, you're mixing less than you would if you added it in several additions. Still, there are a few times when the all-at-once method won't work. When it's not appropriate, I'll tell you. And after the dough or batter comes together, it's good to give everything a last turn by hand with a flexible spatula.

Rolling out dough.

It took me just as long to radicalize my dough-rolling technique as it did to rethink the way I added flour. Rolled dough needs a refrigerated rest — I've known that since I started baking. What I only recently discovered is that when the dough gets that rest doesn't matter much to the dough, but it makes a big difference to the dough maker (which would be you or me). Cold dough is tough to roll, and waiting around for it to reach the perfect temperature is an irritating hit-and-miss affair. And so, annoyed at being annoyed, I decided to disregard everything I'd ever been taught and roll the dough out as soon as it was made, when it was soft, supple and submissive, and to give it the big chill after the roll-out. It was a cookie-making life-changer.

I roll the dough out between pieces of parchment paper. There are several advantages to rolling dough sandwiched between parchment (it could be wax paper), among them: You don't have to add more flour to the dough. It's also easy — and magnitudes easier than the old-fashioned chill-and-then-roll technique.

Once the dough is rolled out, I put it on a baking sheet and chill it. If you have room in your freezer, freeze it. The dough chills faster, it can stay in the freezer for a long time and it can usually be cut straight from the freezer (if it can't, the recipe will tell you so).

A personal rule of thumb: I usually roll cookie dough twice and almost never more than three times. Meaning I roll the dough and cut out cookies; gather the scraps, roll, chill and cut; and then repeat one more time. (If I weren't rolling just-made dough between parchment, I'd only roll it twice and the likelihood would still be high that the second batch wouldn't be as good as the first . . . because you have to add some flour to roll it. You don't have to worry about this with my "new" technique.)

Logging dough for slice-and-bake cookies. The key to pretty slice-and-bake cookies is getting a tight log of dough. If the log has an air pocket or a hollow, you'll have a little hole in the center of your cookies. To get a sturdy, solid log, start with a tight hunk of dough — it can be any shape — and roll it into a log under your palms. Keep checking it and, as soon as you feel a hollow in the log, start over. When the log is as good as you can get it, you can do the tightening trick: Place the dough in the center of a piece of parchment or wax paper. Pull the side of the paper farthest from you over the log, then grab a ruler or a bench scraper. Hold on to the bottom paper with one hand and, with the other, place the ruler or scaper at the top of the paper-covered log. Slide the straight edge toward you, smoothing the paper against the log as you go, until you get to the bottom of the log. At this point, wedge the straight edge under the top piece of paper and the log, holding the ruler or scraper at an angle to the log, and simultaneously push the ruler or scraper under the log and pull the bottom piece of paper toward you. The push-and-pull creates the tension necessary to tighten the log. Work your way along the length of the log and then lift the top paper — you'll have a beautifully smooth, tight log, ready to be wrapped and chilled before it's sliced and baked.

Scooping dough for drop cookies. Drop cookies bake best when they're all the same size and using cookie scoops (see page 25) guarantees that. Unless otherwise directed, always use a level, not a rounded, scoopful of dough for each cookie. If you don't have scoops, you can use spoons. (I always tell you whether the spoonful should be level or rounded.)

Working with egg whites. Neatness counts when you're beating egg whites and making meringue. Egg whites won't beat properly if there's the least bit of yolk lurking or the smallest speck of fat in the mixing bowl or on the whisk. You need to start with impeccably clean, dry equipment, and you also need to pay attention to the look of the whites. You're aiming to beat enough air into the whites so that they increase in volume and stiffen enough to form peaks, but at every stage, what you want most is to have whites that are glossy. If you lose the gloss, it means you've overbeaten the whites. Overbeaten whites form clumps and clouds and won't fold into batter properly. Working with whites isn't hard as long as you pay attention to the details. When the whites have turned opaque (and in some cases have formed soft peaks), it's time to add the sugar (sugar is what changes egg whites into meringue; it serves as a tightening agent, giving structure to the whites). Add it little by little — slow and steady are the bywords.

Chilling dough. Many doughs need to be chilled before they're baked, especially rolled-out doughs. If the instructions tell you to chill the dough, please do so — I wouldn't ask you to wait for the dough if it weren't necessary. Some doughs need to chill so that they can relax — after being mixed and/or rolled, they need a cool rest to ensure that they'll be tender. Some doughs need to chill because they won't hold their shape if they're baked without a cold rest. Sometimes freezing a dough is better than refrigerating it, and sometimes it doesn't matter — I'll let you know.

Discover your oven's hot spots. If the cookies that bake in the back left-hand corner of the oven (for instance) are always darker than the others,

you've got a hot spot. To find out if your oven has hot spots and where they are, so that you can adjust for them by rotating your baking sheets, line a baking sheet with parchment paper or a silicone baking mat and spread some shredded coconut evenly over it. Pop the baking sheet into a 350-degree-F oven and bake without turning the sheet or stirring the coconut. Start looking at the coconut after 3 minutes and then check on it every minute or two to see how it's coloring. When all of the coconut is toasted, look at the sheet — you'll immediately know everything about your hot spots.

Rotating baking sheets. When you're baking cookies on two oven racks — and sometimes when you're baking just one sheet on the center rack — it's good to rotate the baking sheet(s), so that the cookies bake evenly. For the two-rack rotation, the aim is to switch the baking sheets both front to back and top to bottom. In the rare event that your oven's heat is even, meaning there are no hot spots, you don't need to rotate them, especially if the baking time is short. Actually, with very short baking times, it's better not to rotate — the unevenness is less problematic than the loss of heat that would be incurred by opening the oven door.

Cooling cookies is necessary. I think of cooling as another step in the cookie-baking process. While it's often tempting to grab a just-baked cookie, the truth is that most cookies don't come into their own until they've been allowed to cool. It's during cooling that a cookie's true texture develops. That said, there are some cookies that must be served soon after they're baked. It's one of the sweet things about the cookie family: Differences abound.

Cutting bar cookies. I don't like to cut cookies in the pan — I'm afraid of scratching the pan's surface — so I often advise you to unmold and invert a cookie slab before cutting it into bars. You can, of course, ignore my advice, but only if you promise me that you will use hard plastic spatulas or scrapers, not metal, to do the cutting. In many cases, the easiest way to cut bars is to cut the cookie slab into quarters, remove the quarters from the pan and cut each quarter into bars. If I'm not going to serve all the bars at once, I cut as I go: The cookies keep best as a block.

Freeze precut or scooped ready-to-bake dough. Almost all cut-out cookies can be frozen unbaked. Cut out the cookies, place them on lined baking sheets and freeze them. When they're solidly frozen, pack them into airtight containers, separating the layers with parchment, and freeze for up to 2 months. Then remove only as many cookies as you need and bake them directly from the freezer; add another minute or two to the baking time. You can do the same thing with scooped-out (or spooned) balls of dough; let them stand at room temperature to warm up a bit while you preheat the oven.

Thawing. Most cookies make the best transition from frozen to ready-to-eat if you allow them to defrost in their wrappers. If you have time, let them defrost overnight in the fridge; if not, just leave them on the counter. If your thawed cookies have lost their crispness and crunch, pop them into a 350-degree-F oven for a couple of minutes, then let them cool on a rack.

ingredients

Like everything else you bake or cook, the quality of your cookies will depend on the quality of your ingredients. Happily, the basic and most frequently used ingredients for cookies are easy to get and, for the most part, inexpensive. Keep these basics on hand, and you can have cookies on a whim. Good cookies.

Butter. All of these recipes were developed using unsalted butter, in part so that I could control the salt in the recipes and in part because unsalted butter has a higher butterfat content, and I wanted that extra fat for flavor and texture. If all you've got in the fridge is salted butter, use it. Your cookies will be just fine made with salted butter, but you might want to pull a pinch or two of salt out of the recipe.

When I am in Paris, I bake with high-fat cultured butter every day (culturing, a form of fermenting, gives butter a slight tang and more acidity). At home in America, I bake with a variety of butters, including Vermont Creamery (high fat, cultured); Kerrygold (high fat); Land O'Lakes (normal fat); and Cabot (normal fat). Because these recipes were tested with so many kinds of butters, you should have success using your favorite.

Volumes and weights: Equivalent measurements for 1 stick of butter are 8 tablespoons, ½ cup, 4 ounces, or 113 grams.

Storing butter: Wrapped and kept away from foods with strong odors, butter will keep for weeks in the refrigerator and for up to a year in the freezer.

All-purpose flour. You can use either bleached or unbleached all-purpose flour in these recipes. Flour should be kept in a cool, dry place. As soon as you get flour home, empty it into a bin — if you're measuring flour in cups (volume measures), you can't get an accurate measure digging the cup into a packed sack of flour.

To measure flour by volume: Use a table knife or fork to stir the flour around in the bin, lifting it and aerating it as you stir. Then scoop up enough flour to mound over the top of the measuring cup and sweep the back of a knife across the cup to level the flour, taking care not to pack the flour down in the process. Whatever you do, don't rap the cup on the counter; it's a sure way to tamp down the flour and throw off your measurements.

Volume and weight: All of my recipes are based on 1 cup of flour equaling 136 grams, or 4.8 ounces.

Whole wheat flour. I use regular whole wheat flour, not white or pastry whole wheat flour. The measurements for whole wheat flour are the same as for all-purpose: 1 cup equals 136 grams, or 4.8 ounces.

Gluten-free flour. Many of these recipes are what I refer to as "naturally gluten-free," meaning that I didn't do anything to make the recipes gluten-free — they just are. I am not an expert in gluten-free baking, but the few times I've tried to take standard recipes and make them gluten-free, I've used Cup4Cup flour and been successful.

Eggs. These recipes were developed and tested with large eggs. It's not a precise measurement, but I figure that each egg (out of the shell) weighs about 50 grams, or 1¾ ounces, with the yolk weighing 20 grams, or about ¾ ounce, and the white weighing 30 grams, or about 1 ounce.

Temperature: Eggs should be kept refrigerated. When a recipe calls for eggs at "room temperature," as many do (eggs blend best when they're not cold), pull the eggs out of the fridge about 20 minutes ahead of time. If you haven't planned ahead, pop the eggs into a bowl of very hot tap water and leave them there for 3 to 5 minutes. Using cool eggs is not fatal, although it can be ugly:

Cold eggs can make a dough look curdled before the dry ingredients are added.

Egg whites: It's easier to separate eggs when they're cold, but egg whites won't beat to the limit of their capability if they are not at room temperature, so allow enough time for this.

Raw eggs: A few of these recipes include raw eggs. I usually use organic and/or local eggs, and I make sure that that's what I use when the eggs will be raw. Raw eggs are not recommended for the very young, the very old, pregnant women or anyone with a compromised immune system. Unfortunately, pasteurized eggs are not an option when meringue is on the menu — they don't beat properly.

Granulated sugar. This is the baker's basic workhorse. (When a recipe calls for sugar, I mean granulated sugar. Please do not substitute brown sugar — the moisture content is different and the results will not be the same.) For the record: 1 cup sugar equals 200 grams, or 7 ounces.

Brown sugar. My "house" brown sugar is light brown sugar, but if all you've got is dark brown sugar, that's fine. Whether light or dark, brown sugar should be moist — if you pinch it a bit, it should hold together. There are all kinds of tricks to soften hardened sugar, but I haven't found one that's consistently reliable. Always store brown sugar in a sealed plastic bag with as much air pressed out of it as possible.

I created and tested these recipes using the following equivalents: 1 cup light or dark brown sugar equals 200 grams, or 7 ounces.

To measure brown sugar by volume: Unlike most other ingredients, brown sugar is not lightly scooped into a cup measure — it's packed. You needn't press it down with all your might, but you do want to press it into the cup enough so that when you turn it out, the sugar retains the shape of the cup.

Sanding and pearl sugars. Both of these are used for decoration. Sanding sugar is fine-grained and sparkly, and it's available in myriad colors. Pearl sugar is, as its name suggests, white and round — it looks like a box of polka dots. Sometimes called Swedish sugar, pearl sugar is crunchy and won't soften much when baked. It's available online or at Ikea stores.

Salt. When I started baking, salt was always measured in pinches; today it's measured in teaspoons and I think that sweets are better for it. As it does in savory food, salt lifts the flavors in most everything you bake, especially when you're using chocolate.

My everyday baking salt is fine sea salt. You'd think this would be easy, but beware: Not all sea salts are equally salty, so it would be good if you could do a taste test first to find the one you like best. I use Baleine fine sea salt, which comes in a blue canister and is available in most supermarkets.

I use two other kinds of salt: fleur de sel, a moist, grainy sea salt (my favorite comes from Guérande, France) that is not very salty, and Maldon sea salt, a flake salt that is quite salty that I only use to finish cookies.

Cocoa. Always use unsweetened cocoa powder (not cocoa for making drinks), and if you can, splurge on it. As with chocolate, the quality of the cocoa will seriously affect the quality of your cookies. I prefer Dutch-processed cocoa, cocoa treated with alkaline, for its flavor and color, but all of the recipes will work with non-Dutched cocoa as well. My favorite brands are Valrhona, a rich, dark French cocoa that's got hints of red; Guittard, a fine American cocoa; and Droste cocoa, from Holland.

Chocolate. My first-choice chocolate is dark — I'll always grab bittersweet. But unless the chocolate is to be melted and mixed into a dough or batter (when its color and cacao content will matter), you should choose the chocolate you love most. Just because I chop dark chocolate to fold into my chocolate-chip-cookie dough doesn't mean you can't use milk chocolate or even white. Treat yourself to a chocolate tasting so that you can decide what you like most and stock up on it.

Milk and white chocolates are a little more difficult to choose. Milk chocolate has a very low percentage of cocoa solids (the ingredient that makes chocolate chocolate) and white chocolate is a blend based on cocoa butter. The flavors, the levels of sweetness and the way the chocolates melt can vary greatly among brands. I get the best results when I use high-quality imported chocolate (such as Valrhona) or equally high-quality domestic chocolate (such as Guittard).

When a recipe calls for chopped chocolate, you're meant to chop block, bar or disk-shaped chocolate into chip-size shards — haphazard is the word here — and to scrape the shards and all the chocolate "dust" into the dough. I love the dust — it colors the dough and spreads the flavor of chocolate throughout the cookie. (Yes, you can substitute an equal amount of chips, but the chocolate you chop will almost certainly be of better quality than what you buy as chips.)

Chocolate chips: I do keep chocolate chips on hand — regular and mini chips, semisweet and milk and white chocolate too. While my preference is always for good-quality block, bar or disk chocolate, there are times when chips are the way to go.

Chocolate chips are formulated to hold their shape under heat, so they don't melt the same way as regular chocolate. This is good in some cookies and not so good in others; the recipes will point you in the right direction.

Never use chocolate chips when a recipe calls for melted chocolate. But you can use melted chips for piping a cute squiggle on a cookie or for topping a brownie — that's when their specific form of meltability shines. Again, the recipes will detail everything.

Dried fruit. I know it sounds like an oxymoron, but dried fruit should be moist and plump. Hard, shriveled fruit won't get better when it's baked — it will just ruin your cookies. To be safe, soak (or "plump," the pro term) the dried fruit before mixing it into your dough. For years, I'd just give the fruit a quick dunk and call it quits. But a recent episode of absent-mindedness — I forgot about the fruit for almost half an hour — convinced me that giving the fruit a leisurely soak improves its texture and intensifies its flavor. I usually soak fruit in very hot tap water, but you can use tea or fruit juice or an alcohol, like rum, brandy, port or a liqueur. Make sure to drain the fruit and pat it dry before adding it to the recipe.

Nuts and seeds. These add texture and flavor to cookies and, because they can take a lot of chewing, they help make the flavors of anything else last. I love this bonus! Nuts and seeds are naturally oily, so they can turn rancid and spoil whatever you are baking. Always taste them before adding them to a recipe. To keep nuts and seeds fresher longer, tightly wrap them and store them in the freezer. While untoasted nuts are the general rule in baking, if you want to increase the flavor of nuts and get a little more crunch into a recipe, toasting will do the trick.

You can toast whole nuts, chunks or pieces or chopped nuts. The same technique works for coconut.

To toast nuts, seeds and coconut: Center a rack in the oven and preheat it to 350 degrees F. Line a baking sheet with parchment paper or a silicone baking mat.

Scatter the nuts, seeds or coconut over the sheet and bake, stirring often, until fragrant — your best test for doneness — and golden brown. The amount of color will depend on your preference. (Some people like to toast nuts until they're dark down to their centers; my own preference is for a light golden color.)

Cool before using them.

Vanilla and other extracts. Pure! Pure! Pure! Please use only pure extracts. They are more expensive but worth every penny. Vanilla extract is the one you'll be using most often. Vanilla not only adds its own flavor to a cookie, but it rounds out the flavors of eggs and butter as well. My favorite vanilla extracts are made by Sonoma Syrup Co. (I love their "Crush" extract, with vanilla-bean pulp blended into it), Star Kay White (which also makes the pure rose extract I like best) and Nielsen-Massey. With orange, lemon and peppermint, you can use pure oil just as you would pure extract.

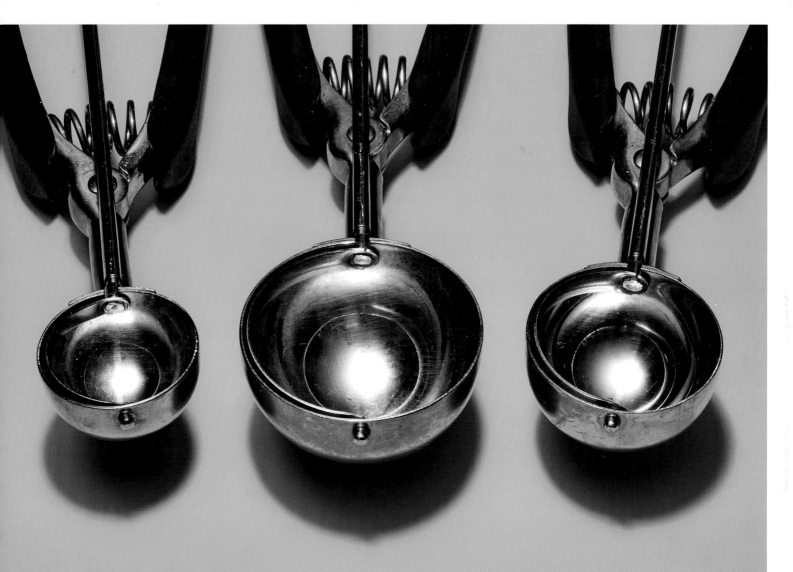

gear

When I think back to the days when I baked in a kitchen the size of a thimble and had nothing but some wooden spoons that my mother-in-law had given me and one chipped ceramic bowl, I feel as if I was the culinary equivalent of Abe Lincoln, walking miles in the snow to get to school. But somehow I managed to teach myself to bake. Not macarons and not fancy tarts, but at that point in my life, I didn't know what a macaron was and the idea of baking a tart was off in the realm of magical thinking. I could probably still turn out cookies and cakes in a kitchen like that and, if I had to, I could roll dough with a wine bottle, but I'd rather not. Having the proper tools increases the joy of baking. Good tools make baking easier and faster, of course, but for me, it's also a lot about the pleasure of having the right tool for the right job. You don't have to go overboard, but I do encourage you to buy the best tools you can afford. Do that, and you probably will never have to replace them.

Here are the tools, big and small, that I think you'd be happy owning. Treat yourself to them, put them on your wish list or hint to everyone you know.

Oven thermometer. I'm assuming that you have an oven, but I'm not assuming that it's accurate, no matter how fancy it is. Ovens cycle up and down, and the temperature you set them to is usually more an average than a constant. This is fine when you're braising beef for a couple of hours, but cookies are in the oven for a short time, so you want to be sure that your oven hits the temperature you need. (See page 9 for info on preheating your oven.)

Stand mixer. A stand mixer is a big-ticket item, but if you bake regularly, it's an investment you will be happy to have made. Buy the best, sturdiest mixer you can afford, and expect to have it for years. I have several mixers, and one of them is a KitchenAid that was given to me in the 1970s. (I'm afraid to say that it's never needed a repair for fear of jinxing it.) My favorite mixer has a 5-quart bowl, but I'm also happy using a 6-quart mixer. Anything larger seems too large for me as a home baker, but my husband, who's the bread baker in the family, likes his 7-quart bowl and is eyeing a 10-quart mixer.

Hand mixer. Most recipes in this book can be made with a hand mixer. Even if you own a stand mixer, you might want to have a hand mixer in the cupboard for those times when you've got a small quantity of something to beat, like a couple of egg whites or whipped cream.

Food processor. When I first got a food processor, I think I made every recipe that came with the handbook, and then I stopped — I realized that most of the recipes were better made with other tools or by hand. But when it comes to baking, the food processor is indispensable. It's the best tool for making doughs — pie and tart dough, of course, but also and especially shortbread. The processor works so quickly and efficiently that the butter stays cold and the flour never gets overworked. The machine also makes short work of grinding nuts into flour and making batters in which the ingredients need to be emulsified as much

as mixed — for instance, in the Lucky Charm Brownies (page 39). Most of the jobs that a processor does cannot be done by a blender; they're two very different machines.

Scale. Until I started working with chefs in France, the idea of using a scale and measuring my ingredients by weight rather than scooping and spooning them was as foreign to me as the language everyone else in the kitchen was speaking. But I became a convert and a committed fan of the metric system. You can make every recipe in this book using volume measures — the ingredients were measured both ways — but I think that once you start weighing ingredients, you'll see how quick, easy, neat and accurate it is. The "tare" button (the one that sets the scale to zero and allows you to keep adding ingredients to a bowl on the scale and weighing them) will become your best friend. Most digital scales come with switches that allow you to go from ounces to grams — look for one with that feature.

Measuring cups and spoons. Even if you're a confirmed scale user, you still need sturdy measuring cups and spoons. For measuring liquids, you want a see-through measure with a spout. I prefer glass, because there are plenty of times when I use it to measure a liquid and then to heat the liquid in the microwave. I have a couple of 1-cup and 2-cup (1-pint) measures in the cupboard; I also have a gallon measure, which I often use when I'm making ice cream or custard.

For dry ingredients, if you are using volume

measures, you need a set of measuring cups and spoons. The cup-set should include ¼-, ⅓-, ½- and 1-cup measures; if the set includes other size cups too, great, but these are the basics. For the spoons, you need ¼ teaspoon, ½ teaspoon, 1 teaspoon and 1 tablespoon. A second set of cups and spoons would be nice, but not necessary. What is necessary is that the cups and spoons be sturdy — misshapen cups (and plastic cups can become misshapen) don't measure accurately.

Baking sheets. For a long time, I bought every new baking or cookie sheet that came on the market. I bought smooth ones and ones that had a special pattern that turned out to be better at collecting grease than baking cookies. I bought sheets with rims and without. I bought shiny sheets and dull ones, light-colored and dark and even one that was gold-toned. I bought nonstick and regular, and I bought insulated sheets, which never let the cookies burn, but didn't let them brown either. (There are some recipes, though, for which insulated sheets are great, so if you have one, pull it out then. If not, you can do what I do: stack two sheets. The recipes all indicate this.)

I was late coming to what became my everyday baking sheets, and I came to it when we had to outfit the kitchen at Beurre & Sel (see page 330). We bought what just about every professional pastry chef buys: inexpensive rimmed baking sheets made from lightweight, quick-heating aluminum. Known as half sheet pans or jelly-roll pans, they

are 12½ x 17½ inches. They are perfect for cookies and, when I'm not using them for sweets, they are pressed into service to roast vegetables or chicken or make "sheet-pan suppers," aka one-pan meals.

Take care not to bang up or warp your sheets (very high heat can cause some pans to warp), and always bake with a liner, parchment paper or a silicone baking mat, for more even baking and easy cleanup. Because often you will be baking two sheets at a time, and because you will want to freeze rolled-out dough on the sheets, it would be good to have four baking sheets, though of course you can manage with fewer.

Parchment paper. I used to keep a roll of parchment from the supermarket in my kitchen, but now, because of my pro-kitchen experience at Beurre & Sel, I buy it in 1,000-sheet boxes. I line baking sheets with parchment and baking pans too. Most important, I roll dough out between pieces of parchment. The paper cuts down on the amount of flour that must be used, and it makes it easy to roll soft doughs and to turn them over so you can roll on both sides, making an otherwise difficult job a breeze. And when dough is between pieces of parchment paper, it's easy to slide it onto baking sheets so that it can chill. It's also good for wrapping cookie logs for freezing. Depending on what you use it for (chocolate can be messy), you can usually get at least a second use from a sheet of parchment.

Silicone baking mats. Sized to fit a half sheet pan, these mats make any baking sheet nonstick. They can withstand heat way above cookie-baking temperatures, and they wash clean in an instant. If anything sticks (it almost never does), the mats can go into the dishwasher and are reusable hundreds of times. I'm especially fond of silicone mats for macarons and meringues.

Baking pans. The basic pans for a cookie baker are, along with baking sheets, 8- and 9-inch square pans for bars and brownies and a 9-x-13-inch pan, which is also known as a brownie pan. A pie plate or an 8- or 9-inch round cake pan is good for fan-shaped shortbreads. For some of the cookies that I love, you will need one (preferably two) regular muffin tin(s) and a 24-cup mini-muffin tin or two 12-cup ones. And, finally, a mini and a regular madeleine pan for those incomparable shell-shaped cookies. If you're buying new baking pans, buy light-colored nonstick (they'll give you nicer-colored cookies than dark pans) and, if you can find them, pans with squared (rather than rounded) corners.

Baking rings. These metal rings, which are 2 inches in diameter and at least ¾ inch high, are often called plating, prep, forming or food rings. I baked the Beurre & Sel collection in metal rings so that they would be a uniform size and have a very particular, tailored look, but all the ringed cookies can also be baked in muffin tins. Rings are available online and at good kitchenware stores; Ateco is the best-known brand.

Cooling racks. I know that the world loves warm cookies, but even warm cookies have to cool a bit before they're munched, and many (read most) cookies have to cool a lot more — the majority of cookies only develop the texture they're meant to have when they've reached room temperature. Cookies need to cool on racks that lift them above the countertop and allow air to move around them. My rack "wardrobe" includes racks that are small enough for a 9-inch square of brownies and racks that can take a 9-x-13-inch pan. And I have a couple of big racks for big-batch cookies. Whatever size you buy, get at least two so that you can unmold and then flip the cake or cookie bars over to cool right side up.

Cookie scoops. Please, please, please buy cookie scoops and please buy three: a small scoop, with a capacity of 1½ teaspoons; a medium scoop, with a capacity of 1½ tablespoons; and a large scoop, with a capacity of 3 tablespoons. Of course you can use a spoon to drop the dough for cookies, but the scoop is so much more elegant. And more practical. When you scoop, every cookie is the same size, which means that in addition to looking nice, the cookies all bake to the same degree of doneness in the same amount of time. Unless otherwise instructed, always use a level scoop of dough. Fill the scoop, run the edge of the scoop against the rim of the mixing bowl and drop the dough onto the baking sheet. The scoops I use are made by OXO Good Grips.

Rolling pin. My favorite rolling pin for cookies is what is called a French pin. It's a straight cylinder — mine is made of nylon, but most are wood or silicone — with no handles and no tapering at the ends. It's also not very heavy. You can use any pin you've got at home and you'll be fine, but if you're looking to buy a new pin and want one that will be perfect for cookies, pie and tart shells, and small pastries, buy a French pin. Pins for cookies and pastries should be lightweight; save the heavy pins with the ball-bearing handles for bread doughs that need to be pushed around with authority.

"Cheaters" for rolling. Rolling dough to an even thickness is important, but it takes a talent I wasn't born with and have never been able to acquire, so I cheat — I use rolling rings or strips. The rings are like rubber bands of varying thicknesses that you put on the ends of your rolling pin to guide you. In fact, they don't just guide you, they make it almost impossible for you to roll the dough to anything but the right thickness. Rings are widely available, as are rolling strips (look for them online). The strips are my preferred tools. Mine are homemade: They're lengths of metal (although they could be a different material; Lucite is also great), bought at the hardware store, two strips for each thickness; I have strips for rolling dough 1/8 inch, 1/4 inch, a scant 1/2 inch and 1/2 inch thick. I put the strips on either side of my dough and just roll my pin across them until I get the precise thickness I need. If you're like me, once you know that you can always nail the thickness — and once you're committed to rolling between pieces of parchment (see page 11) — you'll think nothing of whipping up roll-out cookies on the spur of the moment. These are tools that make the cookie life the easy life.

Pizzelle and waffle makers. There are a few recipes in this collection that call for a pizzelle or waffle iron, and they're good ones, but, sadly, there is no substitute for these machines. The Three-Way Pizzelles (page 258) and Bruno's New Year's Sugar-Cone Waffles (page 253) must be made on a pizzelle iron. The Devil's Food Wafflets (page 255), which are intended for a waffle iron, can be baked in a pizzelle maker.

Candy thermometer. There are a handful of recipes, including the marshmallows (page 458), for which you'll need a candy thermometer. If you own a digital probe thermometer that you use for chickens and roasts, it will work for cooking sugar; just don't let the point of the probe touch the bottom of the saucepan. If you're buying a candy thermometer, make sure it either has feet that lift it off the bottom of the pan or, better yet, a clip that attaches it to the pan.

brownies, bars, break-ups and biscotti

SEBASTIAN'S REMARKABLY
WONDERFUL BROWNIES

1 cup plus 2 tablespoons (150 grams)
    all-purpose flour

1⅓ cups (112 grams) unsweetened cocoa
    powder (see headnote)

1 stick plus 3 tablespoons (11 tablespoons;
    5½ ounces; 156 grams) unsalted
    butter, cut into chunks, at room
    temperature

2½ cups (500 grams) sugar

½ teaspoon fine sea salt

1 teaspoon pure vanilla extract

4 large eggs, lightly beaten, at room
    temperature

As soon as I began making these brownies, friends started calling them "the best," making me sorry I hadn't started baking them years before, when Sebastian Alexander first told me about them. Sebastian, who lives in Amsterdam, and I became culinary pen pals in the early days of food forums on the Internet. We were both interested in baking, and I fell in love with his photography. Since then, we've gone from virtual to real friends, meeting when we can in the city we both love, Paris.

While Sebastian was in college, he was a barista and later a baker in an Amsterdam coffeehouse, and that's where these brownies got their start. They're unusual in the way they're made and extraordinary in how they taste. The texture is neither cakey nor fudgy, but creamy, slightly chewy at the center and slightly crunchy at the edges. The butter, sugar and eggs are beaten for almost ten minutes, and Sebastian rightly cautions not to cut the process short — it has everything to do with getting that marvelous texture. And that taste, that remarkable taste . . . so chocolatey. And so much less sweet than you'd imagine, given the amount of sugar in the mix. The secret is cocoa powder, not chocolate, which gives the brownies their deep color and flavor.

A word on cocoa: Buy the best Dutch-processed cocoa you can find — it will make all the difference. I make these with Valrhona cocoa, which might be part of the reason my friends consider them "the best." Find the cocoa you like, and I think your friends will love the brownies the way my friends do.

Makes 20 brownies

Center a rack in the oven and preheat it to 325 degrees F. Butter the sides of a 9-x-13-inch baking pan, dust the interior with cocoa powder, tap out the excess and line the bottom with parchment paper.

Sift the flour and cocoa together.

Working with a stand mixer fitted with the paddle attachment, or in a large bowl with a hand mixer, beat the butter, sugar and salt together at low speed for 3 minutes, scraping the bowl as needed. Beat in the vanilla. If you're using a stand mixer, switch to the whisk attachment. With the mixer on medium-high, pour in the eggs, then beat for about 5 minutes more, or until the mixture has at least doubled in volume. Switch to a flexible spatula and gently fold in the dry ingredients, checking the bottom of the bowl frequently for dry ingredients. Don't be discouraged when your light batter collapses — it's unavoidable. Scrape the batter into the pan and smooth the top.

Bake for about 40 minutes, rotating the pan after 20 minutes, or until the brownies have puffed — the top may crack here and there — and a tester inserted into the center comes out clean. Transfer to a rack and allow the brownies to cool until they are just slightly warm or at room temperature.

Run a table knife between the brownies and the sides of the pan, cut the brownies into quarters and carefully lift the quarters out of the pan with a broad spatula. Cut the brownies into 20 bars.

This is the Old Faithful of my brownie collection, the recipe I've turned to for years whenever I've wanted brownies straight up or needed a base on which to try out some new ideas — it was my jumping-off point for Snowy-Topped Brownie Drops (page 113). It's the recipe I always give to new bakers, knowing they'll love it — everyone does — and that they'll always be successful with it. And it's the recipe I make when I know I'll have a bunch of people at the house — it's an easy nibbler (especially if you cut it into mini squares).

Classic brownies are made with unsweetened chocolate. I used to make these with some unsweetened chocolate (2 ounces) and some bittersweet (4 ounces). These days I use all bittersweet (or sometimes all semisweet) because I prefer the roundness you get from those chocolates. Happily, the recipe accepts this change easily, and it will accept others. See Playing Around for a few ideas and then riff away.

Makes 16 brownies

Center a rack in the oven and preheat it to 325 degrees F. Line an 8-inch square baking pan with parchment paper and butter the paper and the sides of the pan.

Set a large heatproof bowl over a saucepan of simmering water (make sure the water isn't touching the bottom of the bowl), put the butter in the bowl and scatter over the chocolate. Heat just until the butter is melted and the chocolate is almost melted (residual heat will finish the job); you want to be careful not to heat the ingredients so much that they separate. Remove the bowl from the saucepan and stir until you have a thick, shiny mixture.

Working with a flexible spatula, stir in the sugar. Your beautiful chocolate will turn grainy, but keep stirring. When the sugar is incorporated, add the cold eggs one at a time, beating energetically after each one goes in. Beat, beat, and some of the gloss will return to your heavy batter. Stir in the salt, followed by the vanilla. Add the flour all at once and gently stir and fold it in. When it is almost incorporated, stir in the walnuts, if you're using them. Scrape the batter into the pan and smooth the top.

5 tablespoons (2½ ounces; 71 grams) unsalted butter, cut into chunks

6 ounces (170 grams) bittersweet or semisweet chocolate, coarsely chopped

¾ cup (150 grams) sugar

2 cold large eggs

½ teaspoon fine sea salt

1 teaspoon pure vanilla extract

⅓ cup (45 grams) all-purpose flour

1 cup (120 grams) chopped walnuts (optional)

STORING

You can keep these tightly wrapped at room temperature for about 4 days, but they're really best within 2 days of baking. They can be wrapped airtight and frozen for up to 2 months.

Rum-Raisin Brownies. Pour 2 table-spoons dark rum over ⅓ cup raisins and heat them in a saucepan or in the microwave. When the last of the flour is stirred into the brownie batter, stir in the raisins along with whatever rum is left in the bowl.

Chopped-Chocolate Brownies. When the last ingredients have been stirred into the batter, add 4 ounces finely chopped semisweet or bittersweet chocolate.

Ginger Brownies. Mix together 2 teaspoons finely minced peeled fresh ginger and 1 tablespoon sugar and let the ginger soften in the sugar for at least 10 minutes. Stir the ginger and its syrup into the brownies after you've incorpo-rated the eggs.

Orange Brownies. Grate the zest of 1 orange over the sugar and use your fingertips to rub the ingredients together until the sugar is moist and aromatic. If you'd like, add a drop (truly a drop) of orange oil to the batter.

Brownies with Other Flavors. For Cinnamon-Mocha Brownies, whisk ½ teaspoon instant espresso and ¼ teaspoon ground cinnamon into the flour. For Peppermint Brownies, add 1 teaspoon pure peppermint oil or extract to the batter.

Bake the brownies for 27 to 29 minutes, rotating the pan after 15 minutes, or until the top is uniformly dull; a tester plunged into the center will come out almost clean. Transfer the pan to a rack and cool until the brownies are just warm or reach room temperature.

Invert the brownies onto a rack and peel away the paper, then invert onto a cutting board and slice into 16 squares. Or, if you don't need the brownies all at once, cut what you need and keep the rest wrapped.

PEANUT BUTTER AND FUDGE BROWNIES

I am immune to peanut butter's common charms. If I couldn't have another peanut butter cup for the rest of my life, I'd be just fine. But add peanut butter to a cookie, a cake or these brownies, and you'll have to fight me for the last crumb. It's something about the way peanut butter blends with other ingredients that changes the game for me. Here it plays middleman to dark chocolate brownies and luscious dark chocolate glaze. It's a riff on a classic match made better with salted peanuts in the brownies and nutmeg in the frosting. These little twists and the dark chocolate — use your favorite eat-out-of-hand chocolate — make these a touch more sophisticated than the usual brownies. Think of them as strivers, working to transcend the brownie class and jump into the world of gâteaux. They'd make it, if only could they tamp down their fun factor.

Makes 32 brownies

Center a rack in the oven and preheat it to 325 degrees F. Line a 9-x-13-inch baking pan with foil: To get good coverage and an overhang on each side, use two pieces of foil, placing one the long way and one the short. Butter the foil.

TO MAKE THE BROWNIES: Put the butter in a small heavy saucepan and add the chopped chocolate. Cook the butter and chocolate over very low heat, stirring often, until they are melted and the mixture is smooth; be careful not to overheat the ingredients.

Remove the pan from the heat and whisk in the sugar, followed by the vanilla and salt. Don't worry if your once-smooth chocolate is now grainy — it's about to get better. One by one, beat in the cold eggs, whisking vigorously after each one goes in. By the time the fourth egg is in, the batter should be thick, glossy and beautiful. Switch to a flexible spatula and gently fold in the flour, then the nuts, mixing only until the dry ingredients are incorporated. Scrape the batter into the pan, making sure to get it into the corners; smooth the top.

Bake the brownies for 28 to 30 minutes, or until the top is dull all over and a tester inserted into the center comes out with only a few moist crumbs attached to it. Transfer the pan to a rack and allow the brownies to cool to room temperature before frosting.

FOR THE BROWNIES

- 1½ sticks (12 tablespoons; 6 ounces; 170 grams) unsalted butter, cut into chunks
- 10 ounces (283 grams) bittersweet chocolate, coarsely chopped
- 1½ cups (300 grams) sugar
- 1½ teaspoons pure vanilla extract
- ¼ teaspoon fine sea salt
- 4 cold large eggs
- 1 cup (136 grams) all-purpose flour
- 1 cup (146 grams) roasted salted peanuts, coarsely chopped

FOR THE FROSTING AND GLAZE

- 1 cup (256 grams) chunky peanut butter (not natural or old-fashioned)
- 1 stick (8 tablespoons; 4 ounces; 113 grams) unsalted butter, at room temperature
- ⅔ cup (80 grams) confectioners' sugar
- ¼ teaspoon fine sea salt
- ⅛ teaspoon freshly grated nutmeg
- 1 tablespoon milk (whole or skim)
- 1 teaspoon pure vanilla extract
- 7 ounces (200 grams) semisweet or bittersweet chocolate, chopped

TO MAKE THE FROSTING AND GLAZE: Working in a stand mixer fitted with the paddle attachment, or in a medium bowl with a hand mixer, beat the peanut butter and 4 tablespoons of the butter on medium speed until well blended. Beat in the confectioners' sugar, salt and nutmeg, then the milk and vanilla.

Using an offset icing spatula or a table knife, spread the frosting evenly over the top of the brownies.

Cut the remaining 4 tablespoons butter into 8 pieces and toss them into a small heavy saucepan. Add the chopped chocolate and cook, stirring constantly, over very low heat until the butter and chocolate are melted and you have a thick, smooth, shiny glaze.

Spoon the glaze over the frosting and, using an offset spatula or table knife, cover the surface evenly. Refrigerate the brownies until the frosting and ganache are set, about 90 minutes.

Use the foil overhang to help you carefully lift the brownies out of the pan. Place the brownies on a cutting board and, using a long chef's knife, cut into 32 pieces. (If you'd like, you can go even smaller with these, cutting 48 tiny squares, making them more like petits fours.) While you can eat the brownies straight from the refrigerator, they're most flavorful and have the best texture at room temperature.

LUCKY CHARM BROWNIES

Sometime, more than thirty years ago, after I got my first food processor, I made a brownie I called 15-Minute Magic, and I've been noodling with the recipe ever since. Every time I do something to it, it's great. The basic recipe (which is gluten-free, a term that wasn't in the daily lexicon three decades ago) is a mix of almonds, sugar, eggs, butter, chocolate and amaretti cookies, crackly puffs imported from Italy that manage to bundle the maximum amount of almond flavor into their dainty, featherlight shells. The ingredients are whirred and baked. That's it. And whether I bake the brownies as a cake or a torte, or I serve it plain or glazed or buried under cream, jubilation ensues. That's the reason I think of these as my lucky charm. When I decided to spice things up a bit and to dust the glaze with crushed amaretti, they quickly became another member of the magical 15-Minute Jubilation Family.

A word on the amaretti: The most famous of these cookies is the brand Lazzaroni Amaretti di Saronno. Lazzaroni amaretti come in a distinctive red-and-white box or tin, and the cookies are wrapped in colored tissue paper. Each paper holds two dome-shaped cookies, and I refer to them as double amaretti. There are many other brands available, though, and, in the thirty years that I've made these, I think I've probably used all of them, and I've had success with them all.

Makes 16 brownies

Center a rack in the oven and preheat it to 350 degrees F. Butter an 8-inch square baking pan, line the bottom with parchment paper, butter the paper and dust the pan with cocoa powder, tapping out the excess.

TO MAKE THE BROWNIES: Toss the almonds, amaretti, sugar, cocoa, cinnamon and salt into a food processor and pulse and process in short spurts until the almonds and cookies are finely ground. Add the butter and eggs and process, scraping the bowl occasionally, for 2 minutes, or until the mixture is light and homogeneous. Add the melted chocolate a little at a time, pulsing after each addition. Process for a few seconds to give everything a last go-round, then

FOR THE BROWNIES

¾ cup (75 grams) sliced or slivered almonds

6 double amaretti (about 72 grams; see headnote)

⅓ cup (67 grams) sugar

2 tablespoons unsweetened cocoa powder

½ teaspoon ground cinnamon

¼ teaspoon fine sea salt

1 stick (8 tablespoons; 4 ounces; 113 grams) unsalted butter, cut into chunks, at room temperature

3 large eggs, at room temperature

4 ounces (113 grams) bittersweet chocolate, melted (it can still be warm)

FOR THE GLAZE

2 ounces (57 grams) bittersweet chocolate, finely chopped

¼ cup (60 ml) heavy cream

1 tablespoon sugar

1 tablespoon water

2 double amaretti (about 24 grams), crushed

scrape the bowl and pour the batter into the pan. Rap the pan against the counter a few times to burst the biggest bubbles in the batter — stand back to avoid getting showered with errant cocoa powder.

Bake the brownies for 25 to 28 minutes, or until a tester or toothpick inserted into the center comes out streaky. If the top erupts in a couple of places — it happens — use a pancake turner to gently press the domes down as best as you can. Transfer the pan to a rack and let rest for 15 minutes.

Run a table knife between the sides of the pan and the brownies. Turn the brownies out onto the rack, peel away the paper, invert onto another rack and cool to room temperature.

When you're ready to glaze the brownies, line a baking sheet with foil or parchment paper and place the rack with the brownies over it.

TO MAKE THE GLAZE: Put the chopped chocolate in a heatproof bowl. Bring the cream, sugar and water to a boil in a small saucepan over medium heat, or do this in the microwave. Pour the cream over the chocolate and stir gently until you have a smooth, glossy glaze.

Pour the glaze over the brownies and use a long offset icing spatula to spread it evenly over the top. Sprinkle the crushed amaretti over the glaze. Refrigerate the brownies for at least 30 minutes to set the glaze (it will set but never harden).

When you're ready to serve, transfer the brownies to a cutting board and cut into 16 pieces. If you're not going to serve all the brownies at once, it's best to cut bars as you need them.

SALTED CHOCOLATE-CARAMEL BARS

FOR THE SHORTBREAD BASE

1 cup (136 grams) all-purpose flour

¼ cup (21 grams) unsweetened cocoa powder

1 stick (8 tablespoons; 4 ounces; 113 grams) unsalted butter, cut into chunks, at room temperature

⅓ cup (67 grams) sugar

¼ teaspoon fine sea salt

FOR THE CARAMEL TOPPING

1 cup (200 grams) sugar

2 tablespoons water

1 tablespoon light corn syrup

½ cup (120 ml) heavy cream, at room temperature (or slightly warmed in a microwave)

2 tablespoons (1 ounce; 28 grams) unsalted butter, cut into 3 pieces and very soft

¼ teaspoon fleur de sel or a good-size pinch of fine sea salt

2 ounces (57 grams) bittersweet chocolate, finely chopped

About ½ cup (60 grams) pecans, toasted and coarsely chopped

This is the kind of cookie that makes you think you should stop everything, throw over your regular life and open a fancy pastry shop just so you can have a legit excuse to bake — and eat — these every day. The base is a simple chocolate shortbread, one with just enough sugar and salt to make it delicious but not obtrusive. It's a cookie that knows that its place is to give the voluptuous star, the caramel, a foundation on which to flaunt its assets, among them its characteristic smooth, slow-melting texture; its deep flavor, which blends burnt sugar, dark chocolate and a hint of salt; and its looks, all sleek sophistication even while it's enticing you to grab it like a greedy kid. The bars are topped with toasted pecans, there for flavor and to add a bit of crunch to the lithesome caramel.

Makes 21 bars

Center a rack in the oven and preheat it to 350 degrees F. Generously butter (or spray) an 8-inch square pan.

TO MAKE THE SHORTBREAD BASE: Whisk together the flour and cocoa powder.

Working with a stand mixer fitted with the paddle attachment, or in a large bowl with a hand mixer, beat the butter, sugar and salt together on medium speed until smooth, about 2 minutes. Turn off the mixer, add the dry ingredients all at once and beat on low until the dough comes together. This will take a little longer than you might expect, so don't get discouraged. Give the dough a few last turns with a flexible spatula and scrape it out into the pan. Using your fingertips, pat the dough evenly over the bottom of the pan; press down and make sure to get the dough into the corners.

Bake the shortbread for 21 to 23 minutes, rotating the pan after 10 minutes, or until it is slightly darker around the edges and just starting to pull away from the sides of the pan; it will not feel completely firm if poked gently. Transfer the pan to a rack and allow the shortbread to cool completely.

TO MAKE THE CARAMEL TOPPING: Put a heatproof bowl close to the stovetop, along with a small bowl of cold water and a pastry brush (preferably silicone).

STORING

When the caramel is fully set, the cookies (cut or intact) can be wrapped in plastic and refrigerated for up to 5 days. Remove them from the refrigerator about 10 minutes before serving.

Put the sugar, water and corn syrup in a small saucepan or skillet and bring to a boil over medium-high heat. Allow the ingredients to bubble away, brushing down the sides of the pan with cold water if there are spatters and swirling the pan a couple of times once you start seeing some color, until the caramel turns a pale to medium amber. (Don't let it get as dark as mahogany.) Lower the heat, stand away from the pan and add the cream, followed by the butter and salt — ingredients that might cause the caramel to roil. Remove the pan from the heat, drop in the chocolate and, using a silicone spatula or wooden spoon, stir to blend.

Pour the hot caramel over the shortbread and sprinkle with the nuts. Allow to set at room temperature.

When the caramel is firm, run a table knife around the sides of the pan, carefully unmold the cookie onto a rack and turn it over onto a cutting board. Using a long thin knife, cut 21 bars (cut into 3 strips and then cut each strip into 7 bars). Alternatively, leave the cookie whole and cut individual bars as needed.

CHOCOLATE AND WALNUT BARS

These bars were built on a memory of a torte I had in Rome and a few disparate recipes given to me by friends. Are they truly Roman? Nope. But they have that pleasantly dry, sponge texture that I love in European cakes, and that full walnut flavor that I remember. And just for fun, they're also glazed (more chocolate), studded with chocolate and nuts (for additional flavor and chew), cut into bars (lots more to share) and best served cold. Would a little gelato hurt? Not at all!

The recipe requires a fair number of bowls, but I hope you'll take solace in the fact that it's delicious, keeps well and serves many.

Makes 18 bars

Center a rack in the oven and preheat it to 350 degrees F. Butter a 9-x-13-inch baking pan and line the bottom with parchment paper.

TO MAKE THE BARS: Put 1 cup (6 ounces) of the chopped chocolate in a heatproof bowl set over a pan of simmering water (make sure the water isn't touching the bottom of the bowl) and heat until the chocolate is melted; turn off the heat and leave the bowl over the pan. (Or melt the chocolate in the microwave.)

Put the remaining chocolate in a small bowl. Chop ¼ cup (30 grams) of the walnuts and add them to the chopped chocolate.

Put the remaining 1 cup (120 grams) walnuts in a food processor, add the flour and pulse and process until the walnuts are ground. Transfer to a bowl.

Put the butter, ¼ cup (50 grams) of the sugar and the salt in the processor and pulse and process until blended. With the machine whirring, add the yolks one at a time, processing after each one goes in and scraping down the sides and bottom of the bowl as needed. Then scrape the bowl and pour in the ground walnut and flour mixture, followed by the melted chocolate. Pulse and process only until blended; you'll have a thick mixture. Scrape into a large bowl and, using a sturdy flexible spatula, stir in the chopped chocolate and walnuts.

Pour the egg whites into the bowl of a stand mixer fitted with the whisk attachment, or into a large bowl in which you can use a hand mixer. Beat at high speed until the whites turn opaque and hold their shape just a bit, then slowly

FOR THE BARS

8 ounces (227 grams) bittersweet chocolate, coarsely chopped

1¼ cups (150 grams) walnuts (halves or pieces)

½ cup (68 grams) all-purpose flour

7 tablespoons (3½ ounces; 99 grams) unsalted butter, cut into chunks, at room temperature

¾ cup (150 grams) sugar

¾ teaspoon fine sea salt

8 large eggs, separated, at room temperature

FOR THE GLAZE

4 ounces (113 grams) bittersweet chocolate, finely chopped

½ cup (120 ml) heavy cream

2 tablespoons sugar

2 tablespoons water

45

add the remaining ½ cup (100 grams) sugar, 1 tablespoon at a time. Whip until the whites hold stiff, glossy peaks.

Using a flexible spatula, stir about one quarter of the whites into the chocolate mixture to lighten it. Don't worry about deflating the whites here — you're meant to. Then fold in the remaining whites in 3 additions, folding them in as gently as you can. If, after the last of the whites goes in, you've still got some white streaks in the batter, let them go. It's better to have a few streaks than to overwork the batter. Turn the batter into the pan and wiggle the pan around to even it, or smooth the top with the spatula.

Bake for 25 to 28 minutes, or until a tester inserted into the center of the bars comes out clean; the torte will have pulled away from the sides of the pan and, if you press the top, it will feel springy and firm. Transfer the pan to a rack and leave for 3 minutes, then unmold onto another rack and peel away the paper; cool completely. (Leave the torte with the smooth bottom side up — it's nicer for glazing.)

When you're ready to glaze the bars, line a baking sheet with foil or parchment paper and place the rack with the torte over it.

TO MAKE THE GLAZE: Put the chopped chocolate in a heatproof bowl. Bring the cream, sugar and water to a boil in a small saucepan over medium heat, or do this in the microwave. Pour the cream over the chocolate and stir gently until you have a smooth, glossy glaze.

Pour the glaze over the top of the torte and use a long offset icing spatula to spread it evenly over the top; some will spill over the sides, and that's fine. Refrigerate for at least 30 minutes to set the glaze (which will remain fairly soft).

When you're ready to serve, cut into 24 bars, each 1½ x 3¼ inches. (If you're not serving all the bars at once, it's better to cut them as you need them.)

FUDGY MOCHA BARS

1¾ cups (238 grams) all-purpose flour

¼ cup (21 grams) unsweetened cocoa powder

1½ tablespoons ground espresso or coffee beans (or instant)

¾ teaspoon baking powder

¼ teaspoon baking soda

1½ sticks (12 tablespoons; 6 ounces; 170 grams) unsalted butter, cut into chunks, at room temperature

1¼ cups (250 grams) packed light brown sugar

2/3 cup (134 grams) sugar

½ teaspoon fine sea salt

2 large eggs, at room temperature

2 teaspoons pure vanilla extract

1 cup (6 ounces; 170 grams) finely chopped chocolate (semisweet, bittersweet or milk)

1 cup (120 grams) finely chopped walnuts

STORING

Well wrapped, the bars can be kept at room temperature for up to 3 days. Wrapped airtight, they'll be fine in the freezer for up to 2 months.

I walked into the kitchen with blondies on my mind. An hour or so later, these dark-as-fudge bars were resting on the cooling rack. Somewhere between intention and action, they'd taken a random turn. Maybe it was the cup of coffee I was sipping that made me think I should add ground espresso or the chocolate I was nibbling that led me to the cocoa bin. By the time I finished, the blondies were nowhere to be seen. The brown sugar–caramel flavor and chewiness associated with blondies are still there, but keeping them company, and turning what would normally be a very sweet cookie into something with an edge, are the cocoa, espresso, chocolate and bits of walnuts.

Makes 16 squares

Center a rack in the oven and preheat it to 350 degrees F. Butter or spray a 9-inch square baking pan and line the bottom with parchment paper.

Whisk the flour, cocoa, espresso (or coffee), baking powder and baking soda together.

Working with a stand mixer fitted with the paddle attachment, or in a large bowl with a hand mixer, beat the butter, brown sugar, sugar and salt together on medium speed until smooth, about 2 minutes. Add the eggs one at a time, beating for 1 minute after each one goes in. Beat in the vanilla. Scrape down the bowl. Add the dry ingredients all at once and pulse the mixer a few times, then, when the risk of flying flour has passed, beat on low until almost incorporated. Add the chocolate and nuts and mix briefly; then mix by hand with a sturdy flexible spatula — you'll have a thick, heavy, sticky dough. Scrape it into the pan, pushing it into the corners and evening the top as best as you can.

Bake for 33 to 36 minutes, rotating the pan after 15 minutes, or until the top is dull, dry and wrinkled and, most important, a tester inserted into the center comes out clean. Transfer the pan to a rack and let cool for 30 minutes.

Gently run a table knife around the edges of the pan, invert the block onto the rack, carefully peel away the parchment and turn the block over onto another rack to cool.

Cut into 16 squares.

MARY'S MAINE BARS

1½ cups (204 grams) all-purpose flour

1½ cups (204 grams) whole wheat flour

1 teaspoon baking soda

1 teaspoon fine sea salt

1 teaspoon ground cinnamon

1 teaspoon freshly grated nutmeg

¾ teaspoon ground cloves

1 cup (200 grams) sugar

¾ cup (180 ml) unsulfured molasses

½ cup (120 ml) flavorless oil, such as canola

1 large egg, at room temperature

¼ cup (60 ml) buttermilk, at room temperature

Sanding or granulated sugar, for sprinkling

STORING

Wrap the bars well, and they will be fine at room temperature for at least 4 days; wrapped airtight, they can be frozen for up to 2 months.

When Mary Dodd, my wonderful recipe tester, returned from a family trip to Maine, she cooked everything Maine, from lobsters to chowders to blueberry muffins, for weeks afterward, if not earning herself honorary citizenship in the Pine Tree State, then at least making the rest of us believe she was a Down Easter. Of the things she cooked and baked, this recipe turned up most often, bringing happiness with it. Mary's first taste of the bars was in Portland, where they were called Little Cranberry Island Gingerbread. It must be some kind of Maine magic, but the combination of molasses and a hefty dose of cinnamon and cloves but no ginger, tricks you into believing you're eating old-fashioned gingerbread.

I'm the suggestible type, so when Mary told me the recipe was from Maine, the first thing I wanted with it was blueberries. Turns out that folding some blueberries into the dough is as good as you'd think it would be. Serving the bars with whipped cream and Blueberry Syrup (page 470) is also good. In fact, the full flavors of molasses and spice invite other matches. Try spooning some Mixed Citrus Curd (page 467) over the bars or go deep and swirl spiced apple butter through the dough; see Playing Around.

A word on the measuring trick: Whenever you've got something sticky like molasses (or honey or corn syrup) in a recipe, measure it in a glass measuring cup that you've buttered or oiled; the butter or oil slicks the way for the sticky stuff to just slither out. And when you've got oil in the recipe — as you do here — measure the oil first and pour it out, then measure the molasses — it'll slide out of the cup, leaving almost no residue.

Makes about 20 squares

Center a rack in the oven and preheat it to 350 degrees F. Generously butter a 9-x-13-inch baking pan or coat it with baking spray. Line it with a piece of parchment paper.

Whisk both flours, the baking soda, salt and spices together.

Maine Blueberry Bars. Once the dough is mixed, gently stir in 1 cup fresh blueberries. Or, if you're making this in any season but summer, use 1 cup dried blueberries that you've soaked in very hot tap water for about 10 minutes, drained and patted dry.

Maine Apple Butter Bars. Once the dough is spread evenly in the pan, dot the top with spoonfuls of apple butter (spiced or plain) — you'll need about ¼ cup — and use a blunt table knife to swirl it into the dough to create a nicely marbled surface.

Working with a stand mixer fitted with the paddle attachment, or in a large bowl with a hand mixer, beat the sugar, molasses, oil and egg together until smooth. Add half of the dry ingredients and pulse the mixer to start blending them in, then beat on low speed only until the flour disappears into the dough. Pour in the buttermilk and mix to combine. Add the remainder of the dry ingredients and, still working on low, beat until incorporated. You'll have a smooth, heavy, sticky dough. Scrape the dough into the pan, using a knife or offset spatula to get it into the corners and to even the top as best you can. Sprinkle with sugar.

Bake for 26 to 30 minutes, rotating the pan after 15 minutes, or until the top is dry and a tester inserted into the center comes out clean. Transfer the pan to a rack.

After 10 minutes, run a blunt table knife around the edges of the pan, invert the Maine bars onto a rack, peel away the paper, turn it over onto another rack and let cool. When you're ready, cut it into 20 bars (about 1¾ x 3¼ inches).

CAST-IRON PAN CHOCOLATE CHIP COOKIE BARS

My friend Mark Henry can do anything with steel — and does. While he's primarily a knife maker, he's also a pots-and-pans man, crafting beautiful cast-iron pans with materials from Australia, where he was born. Mark's wife, Natasha, decided to try baking in her husband's pans and chose my classic chocolate chip cookie (page 127) as her test. What she made was a gorgeous cookie-cake, something I'd never tried. Yes, I know that the back of every bag of chocolate chips suggests baking the dough in a large rectangular pan (aka a brownie pan), but that never appealed to me. And then along came the cast-iron pan cookie, and I couldn't wait to get into the kitchen. Baked this way, the good old choc-chipper becomes something completely different. The long, slow bake in cast iron causes the edges and bottom of the cookie to caramelize. The thickness makes it chewy. And the sheer size of the cookie — 9-plus inches in diameter, 1 inch high, with its surface speckled with chips and add-ins — makes it not just alluring, but dramatic, a description rarely applied to an everyday cookie.

To celebrate my conversion, I tweaked my recipe, adding lots of chopped chocolate (I like milk chocolate here), coconut and apricots. And because the coconut and apricots are sweet, I cut down the sugar.

Bake it big, cut it small (or use the recipe to make cookies; see Playing Around), get out the tea and thank Mark and Natasha for turning a standard into a standout.

A word on the pan: I use a well-seasoned cast-iron skillet that's 9½ inches in diameter and a generous 1½ inches high. If you don't have such a pan, use a 9-inch or, better yet, 10-inch round cake pan. You won't get the same caramelization, but you will get the chew and the flavor. Keep an eye on the baking time; it will be at least 10 minutes less.

Makes about 12 to 30 bars, depending on size

¾ cup (120 grams) snipped or chopped dried apricots

1½ cups (204 grams) all-purpose flour

½ teaspoon baking soda

1½ sticks (12 tablespoons; 6 ounces; 170 grams) unsalted butter, cut into chunks, at room temperature

½ cup (100 grams) sugar

½ cup (100 grams) packed light brown sugar

1 teaspoon fine sea salt

1 large egg, at room temperature

1 large egg yolk, at room temperature

2 teaspoons pure vanilla extract

2 cups (240 grams) shredded sweetened coconut

10 ounces (283 grams) milk chocolate, finely chopped (or 1½ cups chips)

STORING

Wrapped well, the bars will keep for up to 3 days at room temperature. You can freeze them, packed airtight, for up to 2 months; thaw in the wrapping.

Center a rack in the oven and preheat it to 325 degrees F. Generously butter a 9½-inch cast-iron skillet and place it on a baking sheet, which will make moving it in and out of the oven easier; or use a deep 9- to 10-inch round cake pan.

Put the apricots in a bowl of very hot tap water and leave them to plump while you make the dough. When you're ready for them, drain them well, pressing out as much liquid as you can, and pat them dry.

Whisk together the flour and baking soda.

Working with a stand mixer fitted with the paddle attachment, or in a large bowl with a hand mixer, beat the butter, both sugars and the salt together on medium speed until light and creamy, about 3 minutes; scrape down the sides and bottom of the bowl as needed. Add the egg and then the yolk, beating for 1 minute after each goes in. Beat in the vanilla. Turn off the mixer, add the dry ingredients all at once and pulse to begin the blending, then beat on low speed until the flour is only partially incorporated. Add the coconut, chocolate and apricots, pulsing after each addition and then, if necessary, beat on low to finish blending everything in. Complete the job by giving the dough a few good turns with a sturdy flexible spatula. Scrape the dough into the pan and use the spatula to coax it into the corners and to smooth the top as well as you can.

Bake the cookie-cake for about 1 hour (45 to 50 minutes if using a cake pan), rotating the pan after 30 minutes, or until the top is deeply golden brown, the edges are firmer than the center and the cake is pulling away ever so slightly from the sides of the pan. Transfer the pan to a rack, run a blunt table knife around the edges and allow the cake to cool until it is just warm or reaches room temperature.

When you're ready to serve, either cut the cake in half and transfer the pieces to a cutting board to slice or carefully (you don't want to scratch your skillet) cut the cake into large or small bars in the pan.

PLAYING AROUND

Multi-Mix-In Chocolate Chip Cookies. Use a medium cookie scoop (1½ tablespoons) or a tablespoon to portion out the dough. If you use a spoon, roll heaping tablespoons of dough into balls between your palms. Place the mounds of dough about 2 inches apart on baking sheets lined with parchment paper or silicone baking mats and press them down lightly with your fingers. Bake in a preheated 350-degree-F oven for 13 to 14 minutes, until the cookies are golden brown and set around the edges. (If you bake two sheets at a time, rotate the sheets top to bottom and front to back at the midway mark.) Lift the cookies onto racks and allow them to cool until they are just warm or they reach room temperature.

LECKERLI

FOR THE COOKIES

2/3 cup (160 ml) honey

1/2 cup (100 grams) sugar

1/2 cup (120 grams) candied orange peel, homemade (page 474) or store-bought, finely chopped

Finely grated zest of 1 lemon

2 cups plus 2 tablespoons (287 grams) all-purpose flour

1 teaspoon baking soda

1 teaspoon ground cinnamon

1 teaspoon freshly grated nutmeg

1/2 teaspoon ground cloves

1/4 teaspoon freshly ground black pepper

1 cup (100 grams) sliced almonds, unblanched or blanched

2 tablespoons kirsch, Grand Marnier or dark rum (optional)

FOR THE GLAZE

1/2 cup (60 grams) confectioners' sugar, sifted

1 1/2 tablespoons water

1 tablespoon kirsch, Grand Marnier, dark rum or water

Leckerli is a kind of spice cookie, in the gingerbread and *pain d'épices* (French spice cake) family, but with deep roots in Switzerland. In fact, even in the Alsatian region of France, where leckerli is a tradition, it's called *leckerli de Bâle*, giving recognition to its city of origin, Bâle, or Basel. The story goes that leckerli, made from a heavy dough of honey, sugar, candied zest and almonds, baked and glazed, debuted in the mid-1400s. The glaze, however, was a laggard — it didn't show up until the eighteenth century.

Like pain d'épices, leckerli, which is associated with Christmas but made all year long, can be one thing or the other. It can be somewhat hard (although it should never be dry) or it can be soft (mine is softish and chewy); it can be chockablock or lightly studded with candied orange or lemon or citron peel or a combination (I use candied orange peel and some fresh lemon zest); and it can be very spicy or just a little spicy (mine's just spicy enough). What doesn't vary is the fact that it's baked in one big piece and then glazed before it is cut into smaller pieces.

I love recipes with history, but I also love recipes with leeway, and this one's got both. Have fun with it, and if you want to make it part of your family's holiday tradition, make it your own: Decide on the spices you like best, the kind of candied peel and the size of the pieces.

And if history, fabulous flavor and a touch of exoticism aren't enough to make this a holiday stalwart, there's convenience: Lecklerli is meant to "age," so you can make it up to two weeks ahead — a joy during a busy time.

Plan Ahead! Once mixed, the dough needs to rest and develop flavor for 1 to 2 days before it's baked.

Makes about 60 cookies

Packed in a container with parchment or wax paper between the layers, the leckerli will keep for up to 2 weeks. If the cookies get hard, slide a slice of apple into the container to soften them. They can be packed airtight and frozen for up to 2 months, but the glaze won't fare all that well. Of course, you can always give them a dusting of confectioners' sugar to cover up any imperfections . . . or not.

TO MAKE THE COOKIES: Pour the honey and sugar into a medium saucepan and bring to a boil, stirring just until the sugar dissolves. Stay close — once the honey boils, it can easily bubble over. Remove the pan from the heat; stir in the candied peel and lemon zest and scrape into a large bowl. Set aside to cool to lukewarm, about 30 minutes.

While the honey is cooling, whisk together the flour, baking soda and spices.

Using a sturdy flexible spatula or a wooden spoon, stir the almonds and the kirsch (or other alcohol), if you're using it, into the honey mixture, then gradually add the dry ingredients. You're going to end up with a very heavy dough, so be prepared to put some muscle into the mixing.

Scrape the dough out onto a piece of parchment paper dusted with flour and shape it into a square. Dust the top with flour, sandwich it with another piece of parchment and roll it into a 12-inch square. Don't worry about precision, but do try to get the dough a scant ½ inch thick (I actually aim for ⅓ inch, but I don't always make it). Slide the sandwiched dough onto a baking sheet, wrap the setup in plastic wrap and refrigerate it for 2 days or keep it at room temperature for 1 day.

GETTING READY TO BAKE: Center a rack in the oven and preheat it to 400 degrees F. Line a baking sheet with parchment paper or a silicone baking mat.

Peel the parchment away from the top and bottom of the dough and place the dough on the lined baking sheet. Bake the leckerli for 13 to 15 minutes, or until it is golden and puffy; it may crack, but that's fine. Press on the dough lightly, and it will be soft. Slide the leckerli, still on its parchment or mat, onto a cooling rack.

MEANWHILE, TO MAKE THE GLAZE: Put all the ingredients in a bowl and stir until smooth.

Using a pastry brush, brush the glaze evenly over the entire surface of the warm leckerli. If some drips down the sides, that's fine. Allow the leckerli to cool to room temperature.

Carefully slide the leckerli off the parchment and onto a cutting board. Working with a chef's knife or other long knife, trim the edges and cut the leckerli into 3-inch-wide bands. Cut each band into ¾-inch-wide cookies.

CRUMB-TOPPED APPLE BARS

These bite-size bars come as close to pie as a cookie possibly can. They're a triple-decker affair: The base is a brown-sugar cookie that, once pressed into the pan, might just as well be a crust; the midsection is apples cut into chunks and tossed with a little honey (raisins and nuts are optional); and the topping is crumbs made from the same dough as the crust. It's very beautiful and very delicious.

No matter what apples I use, the cookies are always great. After you've mixed the apples with the honey, taste a piece and add a pinch or more of sugar if you'd like more sweetness, or a drop of lemon juice for bite. You can also add a smidgen of spice if you want — go for the apple-pie spices: cinnamon, nutmeg, ginger, cloves and/or allspice — but I don't.

Makes about 24 bars

Center a rack in the oven and preheat it to 375 degrees F. Butter a 9-x-13-inch baking pan and line the bottom with parchment paper.

TO MAKE THE CRUST AND CRUMBS: Put the butter, both sugars, the salt and vanilla in a food processor and whir until the ingredients are blended, scraping down the sides and bottom of the bowl as needed. Pour in the flour and pulse until the flour is fully incorporated and you have soft, moist clumps of dough. Turn the dough out and knead it gently to bring it together. Cut off one third of the dough, cover and set aside; you'll use this for the crumbs.

Break the other hunk of dough into pieces and press them evenly over the bottom of the pan, making sure to get into the corners. Prick the dough all over with a fork.

Bake the crust for 18 to 20 minutes, or until golden brown. Although you're going to bake the crust again, this is really the only opportunity you've got to get color on it and to make certain that it's baked through, so take advantage of it; well baked is better than underbaked here. Transfer the crust to a cooling rack.

TO MAKE THE FILLING AND CRUMBS: Peel and core the apples, cut them into chunks about 1 inch on a side (don't worry about precision) and put them

FOR THE CRUST AND CRUMBS

2 sticks plus 2 tablespoons (18 tablespoons; 9 ounces; 225 grams) unsalted butter, cut into chunks, at room temperature

¾ cup (150 grams) sugar

½ cup (100 grams) packed light brown sugar

¼ teaspoon fine sea salt

1½ teaspoons pure vanilla extract

2¾ cups (374 grams) all-purpose flour

FOR THE FILLING

About 1½ pounds (about 4; 680 grams) apples, such as Granny Smith or Braeburn

1½ tablespoons honey

Sugar, if needed

Freshly squeezed lemon juice, if needed

¼ cup (40 grams) plump, moist raisins (optional)

¼ cup (30 grams) coarsely chopped nuts, such as almonds, pecans or walnuts (optional)

Confectioners' sugar, for dusting (optional)

in a bowl. Drizzle the honey over the apples and toss to coat them evenly. Taste a piece of apple and decide if you'd like to stir in a pinch or two of sugar or a squirt of lemon juice. Mix in the raisins and/or nuts, if you're using them, and then spread the fruit evenly over the crust, again taking care not to neglect the corners.

Pinch off pieces of the reserved dough and scatter them over the fruit. You won't have a heavy coat of crumbs, and there'll be fruit peeking out from under the crumbs.

Bake for 50 to 55 minutes, or until the crumbs are well browned and the fruit is soft when poked with the point of a knife or a slender skewer. If your apples were juicy and they're now bubbling, you're golden. Transfer the pan to a rack and cool until just warm or at room temperature.

Put a piece of parchment paper over a rack, unmold the bars onto the rack and peel off the parchment, then turn the bars over onto a cutting board. Cut into 24 squares. These are good warm or at room temperature, and they're not at all bad chilled. If you'd like, dust with confectioners' sugar just before serving.

STORING

The crust can be made up to 8 hours ahead, cooled and kept covered at room temperature. It can also be wrapped airtight and frozen for up to 2 months; no need to defrost before using. I think that the bars are at their peak within hours of baking. The crust gets soft, ditto the crumbs, when left overnight — though this seems to be a condition preferred by some cookie lovers, notably my husband, so I leave it to you to discover what you like. The bars can be refrigerated, well wrapped, for up to 2 days or frozen for up to 2 months.

BLUEBERRY-BUTTERMILK PIE BARS

FOR THE CRUST

¾ cup (102 grams) all-purpose flour

⅓ cup (67 grams) sugar

¼ cup (33 grams) cornmeal (not coarse)

2 tablespoons cornstarch

¼ teaspoon fine sea salt

1 stick (8 tablespoons; 4 ounces; 113 grams) cold unsalted butter, cut into 8 pieces

FOR THE TOPPING

1½ tablespoons cornstarch

1½ cups (360 ml) buttermilk

4 large eggs, at room temperature

½ cup (100 grams) sugar

Pinch of fine sea salt

2 teaspoons pure vanilla extract

2 tablespoons (1 ounce; 30 grams) unsalted butter, melted and cooled

1 cup (150 grams) fresh blueberries

Except for one dream-worthy buttermilk pie that I had at Husk in Nashville, which was made by the uber-talented pastry chef Lisa Donovan, I have no connection to this Southern specialty. But I couldn't get that pie out of my head, and I couldn't stop thinking it would make a good bar cookie. It does. Both the custard top and the cornmeal crust are soft, but each holds a surprise: The crust has a bit of sandiness and the topping, all silk and velour, has the pop of beautiful berries. As for tastes, you get sweet, salty and wholesome grain flavors from the crust and a soothing mix of warmth and tang from the custard.

The pie bars are good at room temperature or chilled, served unaccompanied or brought to the table with lightly sugared blueberries, mixed berries or Blueberry Syrup (page 470). They certainly don't need it, but they're nice with whipped cream.

Makes 16 squares

TO MAKE THE CRUST: Have an 8-inch square baking pan at hand.

Put the flour, sugar, cornmeal, cornstarch and salt in a food processor and pulse a few times to blend. Drop in the chunks of butter and work in long pulses — about a dozen or so — until you have a moist dough that forms curds. Turn the dough out into the baking pan and use your fingertips to press it evenly into the pan. Put the pan in the refrigerator while you preheat the oven (it needs a short chill before baking).

Center a rack in the oven and preheat it to 350 degrees F.

Bake the crust for 23 to 25 minutes, or until it's golden brown. Even though the crust will be baked again with the topping, it needs to be thoroughly baked now, so err on the side of more golden rather than less. Transfer the pan to a rack and allow the crust to cool completely.

If you've turned off the oven, return it to 350 degrees F.

TO MAKE THE TOPPING: Spoon the cornstarch into a small bowl and pour over ¼ cup of the buttermilk. Stir until the cornstarch dissolves; this is a slurry, which will thicken the custard.

Whisk the eggs in a medium bowl until foamy. Add the sugar and immediately start whisking vigorously (you must beat sugar and eggs together quickly, or the sugar will "burn" the yolks and cause a film to form). Whisk in the salt and vanilla, then whisk in the slurry. When the slurry is fully incorporated, stir in the remaining 1¼ cups buttermilk, followed by the melted butter.

Scatter the blueberries over the crust and then pour on the topping. The blueberries will shift — they've got nothing to hold on to — so try to even them out by poking them with your fingers or a spoon, but give up if it's not happening.

Bake the bars for 42 to 45 minutes, or until the topping is puffed all the way to the center, brown around the edges and firm everywhere. Transfer the pan to a rack and cool for 20 minutes.

Carefully run a table knife around the edges of the pan, place a piece of parchment paper over the pan and unmold the bar onto a rack. Remove the pan and invert the bar onto another rack to cool to room temperature; chill if you'd like.

Just before serving, slide the bar onto a cutting board and, using a long, thin knife, cut 2-inch squares.

CABIN-FEVER CARAMEL BANANA BARS

By the time the second blizzard in six days had rolled into Connecticut, I was certifiably stir-crazy and the only path to peace and serenity was, as it almost always is, baking. Fortunately, I had a lone sad-looking, black-speckled banana in a basket sending out "save me" signals.

I was thinking banana bread, but no sooner had I grabbed the butter and eggs than the idea of banana bars took shape. I had nutmeg in mind, but when I noticed the cardamom, I had a change of heart, and I'm glad I did — it's the subtle star in the mix. The peanuts were a last-minute addition; ditto the milk chocolate glaze. I put this together with what I had on hand, and you can too. Swap the cardamom for nutmeg, cinnamon, a tiny pinch of cloves or an equally minuscule pinch of star anise; the peanuts can be any nut or none at all; and the glaze can be any shade of chocolate or just a swish of jam, marmalade, peanut butter or, dare I say it, a blizzard of confectioners' sugar.

Makes 16 bars

Center a rack in the oven and preheat it to 350 degrees F. Butter or spray an 8-inch square baking pan, dust the interior with flour and tap out the excess.

TO MAKE THE BARS: Cut the butter into pieces, toss into a small saucepan and sprinkle over the brown sugar. Set the pan over low heat and cook, stirring occasionally, until the butter and sugar are melted. Scrape the mixture into the bowl of a stand mixer or a large bowl in which you can use a hand mixer and let cool for about 10 minutes.

Meanwhile, whisk together the flour, salt, baking powder, baking soda and cardamom. In a medium bowl, mash the banana and yogurt together with a fork until you have a smooth puree.

If you're using a stand mixer, fit the bowl and paddle attachment to the stand. Add the sugar to the melted ingredients and beat on medium speed for 1 minute. Add the egg and beat for 2 minutes, then beat in the vanilla. Reduce the speed to low and beat in the banana-yogurt mixture, beating for 1 minute after it's incorporated. Turn off the mixer, add the dry ingredients all at once and

FOR THE BARS

¾ stick (6 tablespoons; 3 ounces; 85 grams) unsalted butter

⅓ cup (67 grams) packed light brown sugar

1 cup (136 grams) all-purpose flour

¼ teaspoon fine sea salt

¼ teaspoon baking powder

¼ teaspoon baking soda

¼ teaspoon ground cardamom

1 very ripe banana

2 tablespoons plain yogurt or sour cream

⅓ cup (67 grams) sugar

1 large egg, at room temperature

½ teaspoon pure vanilla extract

½ cup (73 grams) chopped salted peanuts or other nuts (optional)

FOR THE TOPPING

4 ounces (113 grams) milk chocolate, finely chopped (or ⅔ cup chips)

¼ cup (36 grams) chopped salted peanuts or other nuts (optional)

pulse to begin blending, then beat on low speed until the flour almost disappears into the batter. Add the chopped nuts, if you're using them, and mix just to blend. Scrape the batter into the pan and use a flexible or offset icing spatula to get the batter into the corners of the pan and to even the top.

Bake for 22 to 24 minutes, or until a toothpick inserted into the center of the cake comes out clean — it will have started pulling away from the sides of the pan and the top will spring back if you press it lightly in the center. Transfer the pan to a rack.

If you want the top of the bars to be smooth, run a table knife around the edges of the pan and turn the cake over onto the rack; place the rack on a baking sheet. If a bump here and there is okay with you, there's no need to unmold.

TO MAKE THE TOPPING: Sprinkle the chopped chocolate over the hot cake and slide the cake, on the baking sheet or in its pan, into the turned-off oven for 3 minutes. Remove the cake and smooth the melted chocolate with an offset icing spatula or butter knife. If you're using the nuts, sprinkle them over the icing and gently pat them into the chocolate. Cool the cake until it is only just warm or it reaches room temperature.

Using a serrated knife or a chef's knife, cut the cake into 16 bars, each 2 x 2 inches.

STORING

If you want to keep the bars, it's better to cut them as you need them. Covered, the uncut bars will keep for 3 days; the cut bars will be good for about 2 days. Wrapped airtight, the bars will keep in the freezer for up to 2 months.

SWEET POTATO PIE BARS

FOR THE CRUST

1½ cups (204 grams) all-purpose flour

½ cup (60 grams) confectioners' sugar

¼ teaspoon fine sea salt

1 stick plus 1 tablespoon (9 tablespoons; 4½ ounces; 128 grams) very cold unsalted butter, cut into small pieces

1 large egg yolk

FOR THE TOPPING

One 15-ounce can (about 1½ cups; 425 grams) sweet potato puree (or canned pumpkin puree)

2 large eggs

½ cup (120 ml) heavy cream

½ cup (100 grams) packed light brown sugar

¼ cup (60 ml) pure maple syrup

¼ cup (60 ml) buttermilk

1½ teaspoons pure vanilla extract

1 teaspoon ground cinnamon

¼ teaspoon freshly grated nutmeg

¼ teaspoon fine sea salt

Whenever I see the subject line "I officially hate you" in a message from Mary Dodd, my recipe tester, I know I've done something especially good. It's her not-so-cryptic code for "you've made something I can't stop eating." When I came up with these pie bars, I preempted her message. My subject line was: "Now you'll officially hate me more!"

While I created these with Thanksgiving and Christmas in mind, like the best holiday treats, these are too good to be tagged for holidays only. The crust is my favorite shortbread crust, the one I always use for tarts. Because it's wonderful on its own as a cookie, it does more than just hold up the topping. And the topping is everything you want in a holiday pie: custardy, perfectly spiced and perfectly sweetened with brown sugar and maple syrup. I make it with canned sweet potato puree, but you could make it with pumpkin. (Make sure to use unsweetened puree, not pie filling.) The crust and the topping are equal partners — both are full of flavor and both are the same thickness, so that every bite is half cookie, half pie.

In addition to being just what you want at the end of a feast, the bars have a stealth advantage: They're remarkably easy and quick to make (no small thing when it's holiday time). The crust is put together in the food processor, pressed (not rolled) into the pan and baked immediately (no chill time needed). The topping's made in the processor too (and no need to rinse it between jobs).

I'm not sure how much you might hate me when I suggest you top the pie bars with marshmallows (see Playing Around), but I'm willing to take the risk.

Makes 16 bars

Center a rack in the oven and preheat it to 400 degrees F. Butter a 9-inch square baking pan; also butter a piece of aluminum foil that you'll use to cover the crust.

Sweet Potato and Marshmallow Pie Bars.
If you'd like to cover the top of the bars
with toasted marshmallows (and I can't
imagine why you wouldn't), count on
about 30 full-size marshmallows or
2½ cups minis. You may even want to
make your own; see Vanilla Marshmallows
(page 458). Just before serving, preheat
the broiler. (It's really best to serve the
bars when the marshmallows are still
warm, but you can toast them up to 1 hour
ahead.) Put the bars, still in their baking
pan, on a baking sheet. If you're using
full-size marshmallows, cut them in half
or on the diagonal (they're very pretty
cut diagonally) and arrange them cut
side down on the sweet potato custard.
If you're using minis, cover the entire
surface of the pie bars with them. Broil
for 1 to 3 minutes, until the tops of the
marshmallows are golden.

STORING

Like sweet potato pie, these bars
are best enjoyed the day they're
made. You can make them up to
8 hours ahead, keep them at
room temperature and cut them
when you're ready to serve
them. Or you can make them up
to 1 day ahead and store them,
covered, in the refrigerator.
Chilled, the topping becomes
more like a velvet pudding. It's
a little different from classic pie,
but it's great.

TO MAKE THE CRUST: Put the flour, confectioners' sugar and salt in a food
processor and pulse a couple of times to blend. Scatter the pieces of butter
over the dry ingredients and pulse until the butter is cut in coarsely — don't
worry about getting it evenly mixed. Stir the yolk just to break it up and add
it a little at a time, pulsing after each addition. When the yolk is in, process in
long pulses — about 10 seconds each — until the dough forms moist clumps and
curds. Pinch a piece of the dough; it should hold together nicely.

Turn the dough out into the buttered pan. Spread it evenly and, using your
fingertips, press the dough down so that you've got a compact layer. Don't
worry if it's bumpy — it'll be fine. Prick the dough all over with a fork, cover with
the foil, buttered side down, and pour in some dried beans and/or rice for pie
weights.

Bake the crust for 15 minutes. Carefully remove the foil and weights, return
the pan to the oven and bake for another 5 minutes, or until the edges of the
crust are golden brown. Place the baking sheet on a rack and let the crust rest
while you make the topping. (Leave the oven on.)

TO MAKE THE TOPPING: If there are any stuck-on bits in the processor bowl,
wipe them out. Put all of the topping ingredients in the bowl and process, scraping down the sides of the bowl as needed, until you have a smooth mixture,
about a minute or two. Rap the bowl against the counter a few times to pop as
many of the topping's bubbles as possible, then pour the topping over the crust.

Bake for 10 minutes, then lower the oven temperature to 325 degrees F and
bake for another 25 to 30 minutes (most likely you'll need the full 30 minutes),
or until the topping is set; a tester inserted into the center should come out
clean and the topping shouldn't jiggle when the pan is tapped. Transfer the pan
to a rack and let cool until the bottom of the pan feels only just the least bit
warm or has come to room temperature. (If you're the type who likes warm pie, I
won't stop you from cutting the bars sooner.)

Carefully cut the pie bars into quarters. Lift each quarter out of the pan with
a broad spatula and cut each quarter into 4 pieces.

These bars have three components, each a knockout: The double crust is a cocoa-walnut shortbread cookie. The filling is a fresh cranberry jam, made in minutes. And then there are fresh raspberries, which are added after the bottom crust is in the pan and the jam has been spread over it. Adding the berries (preferably cold ones) just before the bars are baked gives these a bright, sweet-tart layer of flavor. They also make for a stunning look: Because the berries are lumpy and bumpy, the top crust melts as it bakes and takes on their undulating form. It's magical and beautiful, and it all happens in the oven without you doing a thing.

When all the oohing and ahing is over, the prize is the taste and texture. The dark cocoa-walnut crust is soft, buttery, just a little sweet and very flavorful, and the jam and berries are vibrant and a touch tangy. It's a very special cookie, and you'll be happy to serve it for as long as your supply of cranberries lasts.

A word on timing: You can make both the crust and the filling ahead, so that when things get hectic at holiday time, all you've got to do is assemble and bake the bars.

Makes 16 bars

TO MAKE THE CRUST: Put the flour, sugar, cocoa and salt in a food processor and whir just to blend. Scatter over the walnuts and pulse and process until pulverized; scrape the bowl as needed to make certain you haven't created a firm layer on the bottom. Add the cold butter and, working in long pulses, process until you have a grainy mix with some larger morsels. Stir the egg and water together and add to the machine a little at a time, pulsing after each addition. Then work in long pulses until the dough forms curds and large moist crumbs; squeeze it, and it should hold together.

Turn the dough out and knead it gently to bring it together. Divide it in half and shape each half into a square.

Working with one piece of dough at a time, roll the dough between pieces of parchment paper until it's about 9 inches square (you're going to cut each piece

FOR THE CRUST

1½ cups (204 grams) all-purpose flour

½ cup (100 grams) sugar

¼ cup (21 grams) unsweetened cocoa powder

¾ teaspoon fine sea salt

1 cup (120 grams) walnuts

1 stick (8 tablespoons; 4 ounces; 113 grams) very cold unsalted butter, cut into small pieces

1 cold large egg

1 tablespoon cold water

FOR THE FILLING

2 cups (198 grams) cranberries (if frozen, don't thaw)

⅔ cup (134 grams) sugar

½ cup (120 ml) orange juice

6-ounce box (1¾ to 2 cups; 177 grams) fresh raspberries, chilled

Sanding sugar, for sprinkling

into an 8-inch square, so don't worry about precise measurements and raggedy edges). Slide the dough, still between the paper, onto a baking sheet — you can stack the slabs — and freeze for at least 2 hours.

MEANWHILE, MAKE THE JAM: Stir the cranberries, sugar and orange juice together in a medium saucepan. Place the pan over medium-high heat and bring the mixture to a boil, stirring frequently with a heatproof spatula. After about 5 minutes, when the mixture starts to bubble and foam and the berries are popping, stir constantly until the jam thickens and your spatula leaves quickly disappearing tracks on the bottom of the pan. Scrape the jam into a heatproof bowl, press a piece of plastic wrap against the surface and refrigerate until chilled, at least 2 hours.

GETTING READY TO BAKE: Center a rack in the oven and preheat it to 400 degrees F. Butter an 8-inch square baking pan.

The dough gets soft quickly, so while you're working with the first piece, keep the other in the freezer. Peel away both pieces of parchment and return the dough to one piece of paper. Cut the dough into an 8-inch square. Place the dough in the baking pan, scrape the cranberry jam over it and use a small offset icing spatula or the back of a spoon to spread it evenly, making sure to get jam into the corners; you'll have a thin layer. Top with the fresh berries.

Cut the second piece of dough into an 8-inch square and place it over the berries. Pat the dough down lightly and sprinkle with sanding sugar. (You can gather the scraps together, re-roll them, chill and then cut and bake them as cookies.)

Bake for 35 to 40 minutes, or until the crust (which will have conformed to the shape of the berries) feels set and, most important, the fruit is bubbling up around the edges. Transfer the pan to a rack and let the bars cool to just warm or to room temperature. Or, if you'd like to unmold the bars, allow them to cool in the pan for 10 minutes, then run a blunt table knife between the crust and the sides of the pan. Place a piece of parchment over a rack and unmold the bars onto the rack. Quickly but gently turn the bars over onto another rack and let cool.

When you're ready to serve, cut into sixteen 2-inch squares.

CHOCOLATE-PECAN PIE COOKIE BARS

FOR THE CRUST

1½ cups (204 grams) all-purpose flour

½ cup (60 grams) confectioners' sugar

¼ teaspoon fine sea salt

1 stick plus 1 tablespoon (9 tablespoons; 4½ ounces; 128 grams) very cold unsalted butter, cut into small pieces

1 large egg yolk

FOR THE TOPPING

½ cup (120 ml) Lyle's Golden Syrup or light or dark corn syrup

¼ cup (50 grams) packed light brown sugar

2 tablespoons (1 ounce; 28 grams) unsalted butter, melted

1 large egg

1 large egg yolk

2 tablespoons dark rum or bourbon (or 1½ teaspoons additional pure vanilla extract)

1 teaspoon pure vanilla extract

½ teaspoon fine sea salt

About 6 ounces (1½ cups; 180 grams) pecan halves or pieces

3 ounces (85 grams) chopped semisweet or bittersweet chocolate (or ½ cup chips)

No matter the season, no matter the reason, if I ask Michael, my husband, what he wants me to bake, his answer is, dependably, chocolate-pecan pie. So it was no surprise that when I began working on this book, he said, "There goes pecan pie!"

Not so fast. What about Chocolate-Pecan Pie Cookie Bars? Well, they're great. They've got everything that we love about pecan pie, plus chocolate and a sweet shortbread crust, plus the fun of being able to eat them out of hand.

The topping for these bars is my favorite pecan pie filling with a couple of spoonfuls of dark rum, which is the best flavor perk-up for brown sugar and butter and a good match with chocolate.

Makes 24 bars

Center a rack in the oven and preheat it to 400 degrees F. Butter a 9-inch square baking pan, and butter a piece of aluminum foil that you'll use to cover the crust.

TO MAKE THE CRUST: Put the flour, confectioners' sugar and salt in a food processor and pulse a couple of times to blend. Scatter the pieces of butter over the dry ingredients and pulse until the butter is cut in coarsely — don't worry about getting it evenly mixed. Stir the yolk just to break it up and add it a little at a time, pulsing after each addition. Then process in long pulses — about 10 seconds each — until the dough, which will look granular soon after the egg is added, forms moist clumps and curds. Pinch a piece of the dough, and it will hold together nicely.

Turn the dough out into the buttered pan and spread it evenly. Using your fingertips, press the dough down into the pan so that you've got a compact layer. Don't worry if it's a bit hill-and-dale-ish — it'll be fine. Prick the dough all over with a fork. Cover with the foil, buttered side down, and pour in some dried beans and/or rice. Place the pan on a baking sheet.

Like pecan pie, these bars are
best the day they are baked. If
you have leftovers, you can cover
them and keep them for a day
at room temperature. Or, if you
and yours like cold pie, you can
refrigerate the bars for up to
2 days.

Bake the crust for 15 minutes. Carefully remove the foil and weights, return the pan, still on the baking sheet, to the oven and bake for another 5 minutes, or until the edges of the crust are golden brown. Place the pan on a rack and let the crust rest while you make the topping. (Leave the oven on.)

TO MAKE THE TOPPING: Working in a large bowl, whisk the syrup and brown sugar together. One by one, gently whisk in all the remaining ingredients except the nuts and chocolate. Don't whisk too energetically — you want a homogeneous topping, but you don't want bubbles. Switch to a flexible spatula and stir in the pecans and chocolate.

Pour the topping over the crust and, if the nuts seem to be unevenly distributed, use the spatula or your fingers to spread them around. Bake for about 25 minutes, or until the topping has puffed across the top and set — it won't jiggle when you tap the pan. Transfer the pan to a rack to cool until the bottom of the pan feels comfortably warm or reaches room temperature. If you want to unmold the bars, run a table knife between the bars and the sides of the pan. Invert the bars onto a rack and then turn right side up onto a cutting board. Or work in the pan (carefully, so you don't gouge it). Cut into 24 bars, each 2¼ x 1½ inches.

RAISIN BARS

I know exactly where I found this recipe, but I have no idea where it originally came from. The handwritten recipe was on page 127 of a bound recipe book that I kept early in my marriage. Not a clue as to whether Aunt Bertha gave me the cookie recipe or I swiped it from a grocery store magazine. Perfect — if cursory — instructions and nothing more. Online, I've found similar recipes, but still no attribution. Most of the recipes agree on the basics: a cooked raisin filling thickened to jammy with a bit of cornstarch (see page 79 for a Christmas variation); a bottom pressed-into-the-pan layer of oatmeal-and-nut cookie dough; and a top layer of that same dough pinched into nuggets that bake to a mix of crunchy and soft. For sure, the rum that I like to add wasn't in the original. If the recipe brings back a memory of a cookie from long ago, as it did for me, that would be lovely.

A word on the nuts: They're up for grabs here, but I'm putting in a bid for sliced almonds. They've got the right flavor for the oats and raisins, and I think they look pretty popping up here and there among the hillocks of oatmeal crumble on top.

Makes 24 bars

TO MAKE THE FILLING: Put the cornstarch in a small bowl and pour over the 2 tablespoons cold water. Stir until the cornstarch dissolves; set the slurry aside.

Put the raisins and the remaining 1⅓ cups water in a small saucepan and bring to a boil, stirring. Give the slurry a good stir, add it to the pan, along with the sugar and salt, and cook over medium heat, stirring, until the mixture thickens, about 2 minutes. Remove the pan from the heat and stir in the rum (if you're using it) and vanilla. Scrape the filling into a bowl and set it aside to cool while you make the dough.

TO MAKE THE COOKIE DOUGH: Center a rack in the oven and preheat it to 350 degrees F. Butter a 9-inch square baking pan.

Whisk the flour and baking soda together.

FOR THE RAISIN FILLING

3 tablespoons cornstarch

2 tablespoons cold water, plus 1⅓ cups (315 ml) water

2 cups (320 grams) raisins

½ cup (100 grams) sugar

⅛ teaspoon fine sea salt

1 tablespoon dark rum (optional)

1½ teaspoons pure vanilla extract

FOR THE COOKIE DOUGH

1⅓ cups (181 grams) all-purpose flour

¾ teaspoon baking soda

2 sticks (8 ounces; 226 grams) unsalted butter, cut into chunks, at room temperature

1 cup (200 grams) packed light brown sugar

½ teaspoon fine sea salt

2 teaspoons pure vanilla extract

1½ cups (120 grams) old-fashioned rolled oats (not quick-cooking)

1 cup (100 grams) sliced almonds or other chopped nuts

Working with a stand mixer fitted with the paddle attachment, or in a large bowl with a hand mixer, beat the butter, brown sugar and salt together on medium speed until smooth, about 2 minutes. Beat in the vanilla. Turn off the mixer, add the flour all at once and pulse the machine to get the blending started, then mix on low speed until the flour is almost incorporated. Add the oats and nuts and mix until the flour disappears and you have a moist dough.

Using your fingertips, press about two thirds of the dough evenly into the buttered pan. Spoon over the raisin filling, smoothing it with the back of the spoon or a small offset spatula. Finish by breaking off pieces of the remaining dough and scattering them over the filling as a kind of crumble. Press them very gently into the top of the filling.

Bake for 30 to 32 minutes, rotating the pan after 15 minutes, or until the top is deeply golden and the filling has bubbled up around the edges of the pan. Place the pan on a rack and let the cookie rest for about 15 minutes.

Run a table knife between the cookie and the sides of the pan, turn it out onto a rack and then invert onto another rack. The cookie slices best when it's cooled to room temperature or is chilled, but if it calls out to you when it's still warm, slice it; just be gentle. Transfer the cookie to a cutting board and slice it into 24 bars.

PLAYING AROUND

Mincemeat-Oatmeal Bars. When the holidays roll around, think about filling the cookies with 2½ cups mincemeat, homemade or store-bought, in place of the raisins. Do this, and you might want to swap the rum for Grand Marnier.

STORING

The filling can be made up to 1 day ahead, and refrigerated, covered. The dough can be refrigerated, covered, for up to 2 days. The cookies keep nicely at room temperature for 1 day and for up to 5 days, wrapped well, in the refrigerator (they're nice straight from the refrigerator). For longer storage, wrap them airtight and freeze for up to 2 months.

MS. CORBITT'S PECAN CAKE FINGERS

FOR THE CAKE FINGERS

¾ cup plus 2 tablespoons (120 grams)
    all-purpose flour

½ teaspoon baking powder

¼ teaspoon fine sea salt

1½ cups (180 grams) finely chopped
    pecans, preferably toasted

2 cups plus 2 tablespoons (425 grams)
    packed light brown sugar

3 large egg whites, at room temperature

2 teaspoons pure vanilla extract

FOR THE ICING

2 cups (240 grams) confectioners' sugar

1 stick (8 tablespoons; 4 ounces; 113 grams)
    unsalted butter, cut into chunks

½ teaspoon pure vanilla extract

Before there was Julia Child, there was Helen Corbitt, a woman who was born in New York but made her name as a chef, cookbook author, teacher and tastemaker in Texas, first at hotels (including the gorgeous Driskill Hotel in Austin), and then as food director for the Neiman Marcus department stores. I'd heard about Corbitt and even owned a couple of her books, but I'd never cooked or baked a recipe of hers nor, I'm embarrassed to say, had I given her her due as a culinary mover and shaker. The first recipe of hers I ever made was this one from 1957, and I made it only because my friend John Bennett, the Oklahoma chef, said I had to.

John was right. And you know what? You have to too. It not only makes elegant brown-sugar-and-chopped-pecan cookies, but it's a recipe with an unusual and wonderful construction. From the directions to whip the egg whites until they're marshmallowy, you might think you'll end up with a crispy meringue cookie, but you won't. When Ms. Corbitt put the word "cake" in the name, she knew what she was doing: Baked, cut into fingers and finished with the irresistibly good brown-butter icing, the meringue becomes chewy and cakey. Over time — and these are good keepers — the texture becomes cookie-like. At any stage, it's a gem.

Makes 39 cookies

TO MAKE THE COOKIES: Center a rack in the oven and preheat it to 275 degrees F. Put a dab of butter (it'll act like glue) in the middle of a quarter sheet pan (a rimmed baking sheet measuring 9½ x 13 inches), line the pan with parchment paper and generously butter the paper. (I like a quarter sheet pan because its sides are low, but if you don't have one, use a 9-x-13-inch baking pan.)

Whisk the flour, baking powder and salt together in a small bowl.

Put the pecans in another small bowl or on a piece of parchment paper (which will make a good funnel when it's time to add them to the batter). Measure out ¼ cup of the dry ingredients, pour them over the nuts and toss until incorporated.

Push the brown sugar through a medium strainer into a bowl or onto a piece of parchment paper; discard any lumps that remain in the strainer.

Working in a stand mixer fitted with the whisk attachment, or in a large bowl with a hand mixer, whip the egg whites on medium-high speed until they form soft peaks. With the mixer running, very gradually add the brown sugar, then raise the speed to high and whip a minute longer — you'll have a shiny, marshmallowy, café-au-lait-colored meringue. Whip in the vanilla.

Remove the bowl from the stand (if necessary) and, using a flexible spatula, gently fold the remaining flour mixture into the meringue in 3 additions. Don't worry about getting the last portion of flour thoroughly incorporated, because you've got more folding to do: Fold in the flour-dredged pecans, again adding them in 3 batches and trying to be as gentle as you can. The meringue will deflate, but its shine should have lingered on. Spread the batter evenly into the pan, making certain that you get it into the corners, and smooth the top.

Bake the cake for 50 to 55 minutes, or until the top is dry, dull and pale. Press it gently, and there'll be no spring. (With these cake-cookies, a little more time in the oven or a tad less isn't serious, so just go with your best guess.) Transfer the pan to a cooling rack and wait for about 3 minutes, then run a table knife around the edges of the pan to release the cake; turn the pan over onto the rack and unmold. If the cake doesn't release immediately, run your knife around the edges again, turn it over and give the pan and rack a little shake. Gently remove the paper, invert the cake onto another rack and allow it to cool.

When it is completely cool, transfer the cake to a cutting board and, using a long, thin knife, cut the cake into fingers, each 3 x 1 inch.

TO MAKE THE ICING: Pour the confectioners' sugar into a medium heatproof bowl.

Heat the butter in a small saucepan over medium heat until it melts and then boils. Standing close by and swirling the pan occasionally so you can see beneath the foam, cook the butter until it turns a cozy shade of brown. You'll see dark spots in the butter, and that's just fine. The more color you get, the more flavor you'll get — just don't take it so far that the butter burns.

Pour the butter (including the dark bits) over the confectioners' sugar and add the vanilla. Working with a flexible spatula, stir and mash the butter into the sugar until you have a firm mixture. It will look more like something you'd mold than spread — and that's just right.

TO ICE THE COOKIES: This is a very stiff icing, so you'll have to figure out the best way for you to handle it. I've found that a small offset icing spatula is good for the job and that using my fingers to push the icing every once in a while is helpful. Scoop up some icing, press it onto the center of a cookie and, holding the cookie firmly with one hand, spread the icing as evenly as you can over it. Once the icing starts moving, it's easier to control, so after you've got the cookie covered, you can use your spatula to smooth the top of the icing. Or not — the cookies look fine even when the icing isn't perfect. Leave the cookies at room temperature for about an hour, until the icing firms.

BABY BUCKWHEAT BARS

2⅓ cups (280 grams) buckwheat flour

1 teaspoon baking powder

2 large eggs, at room temperature

3 large egg yolks, at room temperature

2 sticks (8 ounces; 226 grams) unsalted
   butter, at room temperature

1½ teaspoons fleur de sel or 1 teaspoon
   fine sea salt

1 cup (200 grams) sugar

2 teaspoons pure vanilla extract

1½ tablespoons dark rum

6 ounces (170 grams) chocolate (choose
   your favorite; see headnote), finely
   chopped

1 large egg

Splash of cold water

Pinch of salt

Maldon sea salt or fleur de sel, for
   sprinkling (optional)

STORING

Well wrapped and at room temperature, these will be perfect
for up to 4 days and delightfully
nibble-able for another 4 days.
They can be wrapped airtight and
frozen for up to 2 months.

The people of Brittany, on the western coast of France, call the flour they mill from buckwheat *blé noir*, or black wheat — the color is that dark. The buckwheat flour we get is not always that dark (there's great variation), but it comes with the same distinctive rich, nutty flavor.

It was the color of these bars and that nut-like taste that made me want to add chocolate to them. But while I insist you fold in some great chocolate at the end of the mixing, I leave the choice of which great choc-olate to you. I've used lots of different chocolates, from milk to the darkest bittersweet. (My favorite here is a caramel milk chocolate from Valrhona, Caramelia.) And should you decide, as I often have, that you'd like to glaze the bars with chocolate, see Playing Around.

If you've never baked with buckwheat, which contains no gluten, you might be surprised by the way the flour thickens as you mix it and by the texture you get when you bake it. Because I chose to make these 100-percent buckwheat, the bars bake to a pleasantly dry and grainy texture, which is much more tempting than it sounds.

A word on mixing: The batter for these bars needs an unusually long and vigorous beating — their texture depends on it — and so a stand or electric mixer is essential.

Makes about 100 tiny bars

Center a rack in the oven and preheat it to 350 degrees F. Generously butter or spray a 9-x-13-inch baking pan. Line the bottom with a piece of parchment paper, butter or spray the paper, dust it with all-purpose flour (or buckwheat flour, for a gluten-free option) and tap out the excess.

Whisk the flour and baking powder together. In a medium bowl, lightly whisk the whole eggs and yolks together.

Working with a stand mixer fitted with the paddle attachment, or in a large bowl with a hand mixer, beat the butter and salt at medium-high speed, scraping down the bowl occasionally, for 5 minutes, or until the mixture is light

I like a bittersweet glaze (page 489) on these, but you can go for a milk chocolate ganache (page 476) if you prefer something less intense. Glaze the bars after they've cooled. Unmold them onto a rack, put a piece of parchment or foil under the rack — your drip-catcher — and pour over the glaze, using a long icing spatula to spread it evenly. Refrigerate — or freeze briefly — before you cut into bars.

and smooth and resembles mayonnaise. Switch to the whisk attachment if you're working with a stand mixer, add the sugar and beat for another 5 minutes at medium-high speed, scraping the bowl often. Reduce the speed to low and slowly but steadily incorporate the whisked eggs; the batter will look curdled, but that's okay. Scrape the bowl, then increase the speed to medium-high and beat for 3 minutes — the ugly-duckling batter will now be satiny, shiny and lovely. Scrape the bowl, then add the vanilla and rum and beat just to blend. Turn off the mixer, add the flour all at once and pulse the machine to begin incorporating it. When the risk of flying flour has passed, turn the mixer to medium and beat for 2 minutes more. (Since buckwheat has no gluten, you don't have to worry about overbeating.) Add the chocolate and mix just to distribute it.

Scrape the batter into the pan. It's heavy and sticky, so do the best that you can to spread it evenly.

Using a fork, beat the egg, water and salt together. Brush the glaze over the top of the batter and then use the fork's tines to create a crosshatch pattern. (The marks often bake away, but I always like to give them a try.) Sprinkle the top of the cake sparingly with Maldon salt or fleur de sel, if you're using it.

Bake the bars for 30 to 35 minutes, or until the top is browned and firm to the touch and a tester inserted into the center comes out clean. Transfer the pan to a rack and let the bars cool to room temperature.

To unmold, run a knife between the sides of the pan and the bars, invert the pan onto the rack and gently peel away the parchment. Turn the paper over, so that the clean side is up, and use it to line a cutting board; turn the bars over onto the board. Using a long, thin knife, cut into 1-inch squares.

SWEDISH VISITING CAKE BARS

These are a mash-up of two recipes I love: almond-meringue topping, which I usually use on fruit tarts and (a variation of the) Swedish Visiting Cake, which is usually unadorned. I can no longer remember when or why I married these two, but once I did, the knot was tied for life — the crisp almonds and chewy cake make a perfect couple.

The cake is supremely satisfying and the topping is unusual in that it bakes to a meringue finish, but there's no whipping involved. You just mix egg whites and confectioners' sugar together — I do it with my fingers — swish sliced almonds around in the mix and spread it over the batter. The oven does all the work.

Makes 9 squares or 18 triangles

Center a rack in the oven and preheat it to 350 degrees F. Lightly butter a 9-inch square baking pan and line it with parchment paper.

TO MAKE THE TOPPING: Put the sugar in a medium bowl and pour over the egg whites. Using your fingers or a fork, mix until the sugar is moistened. If there are lumps, ignore them. Toss in the almonds and stir them around until they're coated with the sugared whites. Set aside while you make the batter.

TO MAKE THE BARS: Working in a large bowl, whisk the sugar, eggs and salt together until the mixture lightens in color and thickens a little, about 2 minutes. Whisk in the vanilla and almond extracts. Switch to a flexible spatula and gently stir in the flour. When the flour is fully incorporated, gradually fold in the melted butter. You'll have a thick batter with a lovely sheen. Scrape it into the pan and use the spatula to work the batter into the corners. The layer will be very thin.

Give the topping another stir, or a run-through with your fingers, and turn it out onto the batter. Use a spatula or your fingers to spread the almonds evenly over the mixture, making sure to get nuts into the corners too.

Bake for 28 to 32 minutes, or until a tester inserted into the center of the cake comes out clean or with only a few crumbs stuck to it. The meringue

FOR THE TOPPING

1 cup (120 grams) confectioners' sugar

3 large egg whites

1½ cups (150 grams) sliced almonds, blanched or unblanched

FOR THE BARS

¾ cup (150 grams) sugar

2 large eggs, at room temperature

¼ teaspoon fine sea salt

1½ teaspoons pure vanilla extract

¼ teaspoon pure almond extract

1 cup (136 grams) all-purpose flour

1 stick (8 tablespoons; 4 ounces; 113 grams) unsalted butter, melted and cooled

Confectioners' sugar, for dusting (optional)

Wrapped, the bars will keep at room temperature for 4 to 5 days.

topping will be pale golden brown. If you'd like a deeper color on the topping, run it under the broiler until you get the shade of gold you like best.

Transfer the pan to a rack and let rest for 5 minutes, then run a knife around the edges of the cake and unmold it onto the rack. Very gently peel away the parchment and invert the cake onto another rack to cool to room temperature.

Transfer the cake to a cutting board and, using a long, thin knife, slice it into nine 3-inch squares. For smaller portions, cut each square into two triangles. If you'd like, you can dust the bars with confectioners' sugar just before you serve them.

NATASHA'S MUM'S FRUIT AND WALNUT BREAD BARS

About 1 cup (about 170 grams, but more is fine) plump, moist mixed dried fruit, such as crystallized ginger, papaya, cherries, pineapple, apricots, figs and/or other favorites, snipped, cut or chopped into bite-size pieces

1 cup (136 grams) all-purpose flour

1¼ teaspoons baking powder

3 large egg whites, at room temperature

¼ teaspoon fine sea salt

½ cup (100 grams) sugar

1 cup (120 grams) coarsely chopped walnuts

After so many years of baking and decades of "translating" recipes from home and professional bakers around the world, I've gotten pretty good at reading a recipe and imagining what it will be like. But I couldn't crack this one. First of all, I was puzzled by the word "bread" in the title. And what about the fact that there are no egg yolks or butter or oil? And all that dried fruit? I'll confess that I held out no hope for them. But the recipe came to me from my friend Natasha Johnson, whose "mum" made the bars regularly in her native Australia. Knowing how good these turned out to be, I'll never turn down a recommendation from Natasha, and I'll certainly never reject one from her mother.

Despite their name, these bars are not bready at all, although they are slightly firm. They're rich — it's all those walnuts and dried fruit, which also make the bars a little chewy and give them so much flavor. If you go heavy on the ginger in the fruit mix — and I think you should — you'll also get a little heat.

A word on the dried fruit: "Mum" made these with red and green gla-céed cherries, crystallized ginger and dried pineapple, while Natasha, who says that she thinks ginger and pineapple are the important fruits to include, suggests that dried papaya is also good. My favorite combo is ginger and apricots, but I'm with Natasha: Play around.

Makes 32 bars

Center a rack in the oven and preheat it to 350 degrees F. Butter or spray an 8-inch square baking pan.

If your fruit isn't moist, toss it into a bowl, cover with very hot tap water and let it sit and plump for about 5 minutes. Drain and pat dry.

Whisk the flour and baking powder together.

STORING

Wrapped in plastic, these will keep for at least a week at room temperature. If you'd like to freeze them, wrap them airtight, and they'll be good for up to 2 months.

Working with a stand mixer fitted with the whisk attachment, or in a bowl with a hand mixer, beat the egg whites and salt until the whites hold soft peaks. Gradually beat in the sugar and continue to beat until the peaks are firm and glossy (glossy is really important — if you lose the gloss, you've overbeaten the whites). Switch to a sturdy flexible spatula and gently fold in the flour mixture, followed by the walnuts and dried fruit. The fruit and nuts are heavy and bulky, so no matter how gentle your touch, you're bound to seriously deflate the meringue — it's fine. Turn the batter out into the buttered pan and use the spatula to smooth the top as best as you can.

Bake for 30 to 32 minutes, rotating the pan after 15 minutes, or until the bread feels set but still has some give all over; a tester inserted into the center should come out clean. The bread will not brown, because it doesn't have yolks or butter to promote color; rather, it will be a warm ivory color, like nougat. Transfer the pan to a rack and let rest for 5 minutes, then run a table knife between the bread and the sides of the pan, unmold and turn it over to cool to room temperature.

Cut into 32 bars, each about 1 x 2 inches.

TORTA SBRISOLONA

Translated from the Italian, *torta sbrisolona*, a traditional cookie that's been beguiling people since the Renaissance, means "crumbly cake," but most people think of it as a cookie and I'm voting with the majority here. You make the dough rather the way you'd make streusel, if streusel had cornmeal and almond flour, stir in chopped almonds, and then squeeze, pinch and press the dough into nubbins that you toss into the baking pan. Torta sbrisolona is crunchy, sweetened just enough (most of the sweetness comes from the cornmeal) and pleasantly dry, the way biscotti are. If you're a fan of dry, crunchy cookies — so Italian — then you, like I, will find these a constant temptation. Whether you cut the torta into neat morsels or let everyone have at the big square, you'll be happy pairing the cookies with coffee or tea or something stronger, from white or red wine to brandy to bitter digestivos. They might also be served with something grown-up, such as a hunk of cheese — I'd opt for Gruyère or a blue like Stilton or dolce Gorgonzola.

A word on the cornmeal: I have made these with gritty cornmeal for polenta and fine cornmeal for porridge, and the cookies are good either way. My own preference is for the finer-ground grain, but experiment and see what you like.

¾ cup (102 grams) all-purpose flour

½ cup (50 grams) almond flour

⅓ cup (53 grams) yellow cornmeal

⅓ cup (67 grams) sugar

½ teaspoon fleur de sel or ¼ teaspoon fine sea salt

½ teaspoon ground cinnamon

5½ tablespoons (2¾ ounces; 78 grams) cold unsalted butter, cut into small chunks

1 large egg yolk, lightly beaten

⅓ cup (50 grams) whole almonds, very coarsely chopped

Makes about 16 cookies

Center a rack in the oven and preheat it to 325 degrees F. Butter an 8-inch square baking pan.

Put all the dry ingredients in a food processor and pulse to blend. Scatter over the chunks of butter and, using long pulses, work the butter in until the mixture resembles coarse cornmeal, scraping the bottom of the bowl once or twice if needed. Again pulsing the machine, pour in the egg yolk, then process in long pulses until you've got a mixture that's moist and grainy — think wet sand. You don't want to process so long that you get big curds and clumps, but you do want the dough to hold together when you pinch it.

Turn the dough out into a bowl, stir in the almonds and use your fingers to

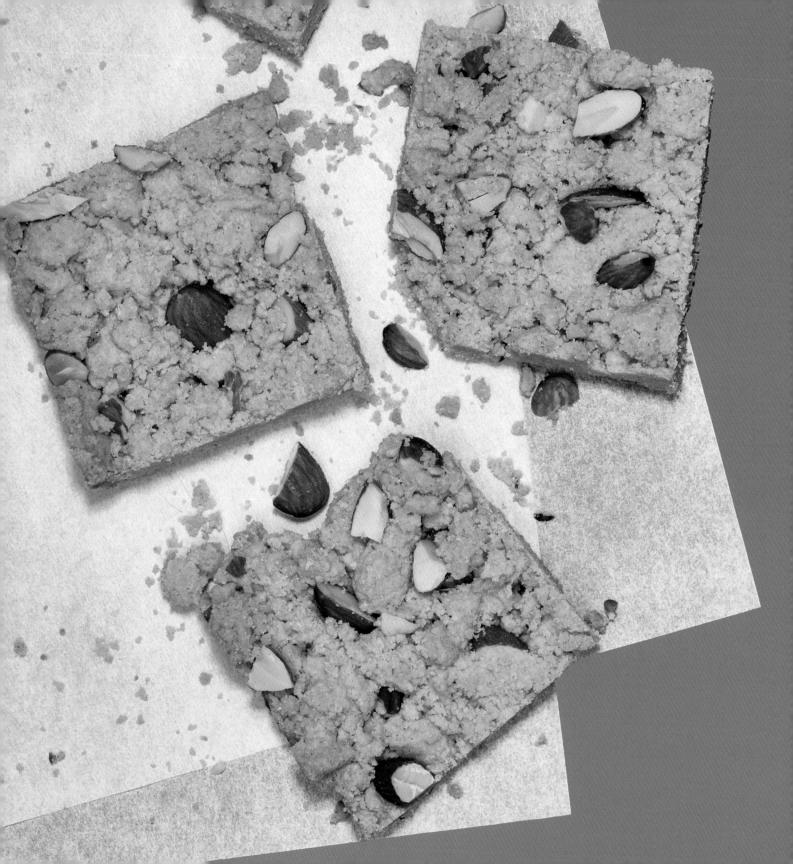

squeeze the dough into small streusel-like morsels, dropping the pieces into the buttered pan as you go. When all the dough is in, pat it down gently — "gently" being the important word. You don't want to crush the clumps, you just want to start them on the road to sticking together.

Bake the torta for 34 to 38 minutes, or until the top is deeply golden brown. Transfer the pan to a rack and wait about 3 minutes, then run a table knife between the torta and the sides of the pan and turn it out onto the rack. If you want to cut the torta into pieces, this is the moment: It cuts most easily when it's warm. Invert it, slide it onto a cutting board and cut into whatever-size pieces you'd like, using a long chef's knife. Return the pieces to the rack to cool to room temperature. If you want to serve the torta as a break-apart sweet, simply invert it and let it cool on the rack.

PLAYING AROUND

Fruit-and-Nut Sbrisolona. I don't know that I've seen an Italian do this, but after the dough is blended and you're ready to mix in the almonds, you can toss in a handful of plump, moist dried fruit. While almost any kind of dried fruit is good with the cornmeal and nuts, dried cherries or apricots (snip them into pieces) are especially good here. Likewise (snipped) dried figs or even small pieces of candied lemon or orange peel. And a handful of chopped chocolate couldn't hurt.

PECAN–BROWN SUGAR CRACK-UPS

1 cup (120 grams) pecans (whole or pieces), toasted

1 cup plus 2 tablespoons (150 grams) all-purpose flour

¾ cup (100 grams) cornstarch

¾ cup (150 grams) packed light brown sugar

½ teaspoon fine sea salt

1 stick plus 2½ tablespoons (10½ tablespoons; 5¼ ounces; 150 grams) cold unsalted butter, cut into 20 pieces

2 cold large egg yolks, lightly beaten

1 teaspoon sanding sugar, for sprinkling

½ teaspoon fleur de sel, for sprinkling

STORING

The crack-ups will keep in a covered container at room temperature for at least 1 week. Pack them airtight, and they'll be good for up to 2 months in the freezer.

More crumble than cookie, this is as seductive for its texture as it is for its nut-and–brown sugar flavor. In fact, it began life in my mind as a kind of sablé. But when I looked in the bowl and saw all the curds and crumbs, I decided to stop the blending and let the dough's inner streuselness shine.

These are baked in a 9-x-13-inch pan (I use what's called a quarter sheet pan, but a brownie pan is good too) and, once turned out, are meant to be broken into cookie-size bits (crack-ups), either in the kitchen or at the table. The fun of breaking the cookie apart and grabbing what you want makes these terrific for parties.

Makes about 20 crack-ups

Center a rack in the oven and preheat it to 350 degrees F. Line a 9-x-13-inch quarter sheet pan or baking pan with parchment paper.

Put the pecans, flour, cornstarch, brown sugar and salt in a food processor and pulse to blend. Scatter over the pieces of butter and process in long pulses until the mix looks grainy and moist. Pour in a little of the egg yolk, pulse a couple of times, then pour in more and pulse, continuing until all the yolk is in and the dough forms chunky clumps, crumbs and curds. It will look like streusel and pieces pressed between your fingers will hold together.

Turn the dough out into the pan and distribute it so that it evenly covers the bottom of the pan, then, using your fingertips and a very gentle touch, tap the dough down. Sprinkle the top of the dough with the sugar and salt.

Bake for 28 to 31 minutes, rotating the pan after 15 minutes, or until the cookie is golden brown and set. Transfer the pan to a rack and let rest for 5 minutes, then run a table knife between the cookie and the sides of the pan. Turn the cookie out onto the rack and peel away the parchment, then invert the cookie onto another rack and allow it to cool completely.

Crack the cookie into bite-size pieces, or let your guests have at it.

BREAKFAST BISCOTTI

2 cups (272 grams) all-purpose flour

1 teaspoon baking powder

½ teaspoon ground cinnamon (optional)

¼ teaspoon baking soda

1 stick (8 tablespoons; 4 ounces; 113 grams) unsalted butter, cut into chunks, at room temperature

¾ cup (150 grams) sugar

¾ teaspoon fine sea salt

Finely grated zest of 1 orange or tangerine (optional)

2 large eggs, at room temperature

⅓ cup (27 grams) old-fashioned rolled oats (not quick-cooking)

1 cup (110 grams) granola (see headnote)

¼ cup (about 35 grams) almonds (whole or slivered, blanched or unblanched), coarsely chopped

¼ cup (30 grams) plump, moist dried cranberries, coarsely chopped

I can't really encourage you to have these cookies for breakfast. Yes, they have granola and oats, dried fruit and nutritious almonds, but even I, who adore sweets, can't get behind cookies for breakfast. But minutes after breakfast — now that's a different story. I'm all for taking these to morning meetings, packing them in lunch boxes, stowing them in picnic baskets or making them a coffee-break staple.

They have a grainy, wholesome flavor and a crunch that makes them addictive. I like them with chopped almonds and dried cranberries, but almost any nut and dried fruit will work (as long as the pieces are not too large — chop them if they are). Think pistachios and cherries, or walnuts and raisins, for instance. Since the biscotti get most of their flavor from the granola, find a cereal that you like enough to eat out of hand. You can be flexible with it too — the only caveat is to beware hard, shriveled fruit. If you find granola without fruit, use it. If not, check the fruit, and if it's not moist (and most of the time it's not), pick out and discard the culprits, knowing that they won't get any softer, moister or tastier once baked.

Makes about 40 cookies

Center a rack in the oven and preheat it to 350 degrees F. Line a baking sheet with parchment paper or a silicone baking mat.

Whisk the flour, baking powder, cinnamon (if you're using it) and baking soda together.

Working in a stand mixer fitted with the paddle attachment, or in a large bowl with a hand mixer, beat the butter, sugar, salt and citrus zest, if you're using it, on medium speed until smooth and creamy, about 2 minutes. Scrape down the sides and bottom of the bowl. Add the eggs one at a time, beating for 1 minute after each one goes in. (Don't be discouraged if the mixture curdles at this point.) Beat in the oats and scrape the bowl again. With the mixer off, add the dry ingredients all at once. Pulse the mixer a couple of times and then beat on low speed until the flour is almost incorporated. Scrape down the bowl, add

Working with a stand mixer fitted with the paddle attachment, or in a large bowl with a hand mixer, beat the butter, both sugars and the salt together on medium speed until smooth, about 2 minutes. Scrape down the sides and bottom of the bowl, then add the eggs one at a time, beating for 1 minute after each one goes in. Beat in the oats, kasha and flax and scrape down the bowl again. With the mixer off, add the dry ingredients all at once, pulse the mixer a couple of times and then beat on low speed until the flour mixture is almost incorporated. Scrape down the bowl, add the dried fruit and beat on low only until there are no traces of flour and the fruit is blended into the dough.

Turn the dough out onto the counter or a piece of parchment paper and divide it in half. Shape each piece into a log that's 10 to 11 inches long. Place the logs on the lined baking sheet, each one a few inches away from one of the long sides; leave room between them, because they'll expand in the oven. Use your fingers to gently press the logs until they are about 1½ inches wide.

Bake the logs for 25 minutes, rotating the baking sheet after about 15 minutes; the logs will be cracked and lightly browned but still squeezable. Transfer the baking sheet to a rack and let the logs rest for 20 minutes. Reduce the oven temperature to 325 degrees F.

Using a wide metal spatula, transfer the logs to a cutting board and, with a long serrated knife and a gentle sawing motion, cut them into ½-inch-thick slices. Try to hold the sides of the log as you cut to reduce breakage, but the edges will probably break off despite your best efforts. Return the slices to the baking sheet, placing them cut side down, and bake for another 20 minutes, rotating the sheet at the midway mark.

Pull the sheet from the oven, flip over the biscotti and bake for about 10 minutes more. The cookies should be golden brown and almost firm to the touch — they'll get harder as they cool. Transfer them to racks to cool to room temperature.

CHOCOLATE CHIP NOT-QUITE MANDELBROT

3 cups plus 2 tablespoons (423 grams) all-purpose flour

1 teaspoon baking powder

½ teaspoon fine sea salt

3 large eggs, at room temperature

1 cup (200 grams) sugar

1 cup (240 ml) flavorless oil, such as canola

1 teaspoon pure vanilla extract

1 cup (208 grams) mini semisweet chocolate chips

2 tablespoons sugar, for sprinkling

½ teaspoon ground cinnamon, for sprinkling

Just when I thought I had completed this collection, a package arrived containing four neatly wrapped and beribboned boxes of cookies accompanied by a message and a recipe. The message was from Nancy Schnoll, a woman I'd met at my former cookie boutique, Beurre & Sel. That day, we'd begun by talking about cookies — of course — and we ended by talking about mothers. And then the package came. By the looks of the cookies, you'd have thought that they were biscotti and, technically, I guess they were. But I knew what they really were even before reading the recipe: Nancy's Mom's mandelbrot. Nancy had talked about them, and I remembered because they sounded so good and because she was so attached to them. Now I know why: They're fabulous!

The literal translation of mandelbrot is "almond bread," a name that gives you no hint that it defines a twice-baked cookie. Popular among Ashkenazi Jews, the cookie has all the characteristics of a biscotti — it's baked in a log, sliced and baked again. In fact, there are some people who think that the sweet may have originated among Jewish people who lived in the Piedmont area of Italy, where biscotti are common.

That these mandelbrot are without made with *mandel*, or almonds, is a technicality to be glossed over. The important thing about them is that, even after two bakes, they're cakey, not hard or dry; they're speckled with chocolate chips, flecked with cinnamon and reminiscent of the best chocolate chip cookies; and their ingredients are simple kitchen staples, so you can bake a batch on the spur of the moment.

A word on the chocolate chips: Nancy's note said that while she, like I, loves chopped chocolate in her cookies, she always uses miniature chips in her mandelbrot. She likes that they stay where they're put.

A word on mixing: Nancy and her mom make the mandelbrot by hand and so I am continuing the tradition. If you'd rather use a machine, use a stand mixer fitted with the paddle attachment and work on low speed.

Makes about 60 cookies

Center a rack in the oven and preheat it to 350 degrees F. Line a baking sheet with parchment paper or a silicone baking mat and have another lined sheet at hand for the second bake.

Whisk the flour, baking powder and salt together.

Working with a large bowl and a whisk, beat the eggs and sugar together until smooth. Add the oil and vanilla and continue to whisk until you have a smooth, glossy mixture that's slightly thickened. Switch to a sturdy flexible spatula, add half of the dry ingredients and stir until the flour disappears into the mixture. Add the rest and stir — you'll need to put a bit of muscle into this — until it's almost incorporated. Add the chips and continue mixing until you've got a thick, sticky dough.

Use the spatula to help you make 3 logs from the dough: Starting close to one long side of the baking sheet, drop, spread and cajole one third of the dough into a log about 3 inches wide and 12 inches long. (Get the width, and whatever the length is will be fine.) It's not a neat job and your logs won't be pretty, but it won't matter. Make another log in the center of the baking sheet and the last one close to the other long side of the sheet.

Stir the sugar and cinnamon together and sprinkle some over the logs. Save some for the second bake. (You'll have more than you need, so be generous.)

Bake the logs for 35 to 40 minutes, rotating the sheet after 20 minutes, or until the logs are golden brown on top and deeply golden brown on bottom; they'll crack a little, and that's okay. Transfer the sheet to a rack.

Using a heavy knife, cut the logs on the diagonal into ½-inch-wide slices (see page 101). Transfer the slices to the clean lined baking sheet, laying them cut side down. Sprinkle the cookies with cinnamon-sugar and bake for 10 more minutes. Place the baking sheet on a rack and let the cookies cool completely.

cookies for
every day,
any day

THEY-MIGHT-BE-BREAKFAST COOKIES

1 cup (100 grams) plump, moist dried apple slices, snipped or coarsely chopped

1 cup plump, moist raisins (160 grams) or dried cranberries (120 grams)

1¼ cups (100 grams) old-fashioned rolled oats (not quick-cooking)

1 cup (136 grams) all-purpose flour

½ cup (68 grams) whole wheat flour

¼ cup (20 grams) wheat germ

½ teaspoon ground cinnamon

¼ teaspoon baking powder

¼ teaspoon baking soda

½ cup (100 grams) sugar

Finely grated zest of 1 orange or 2 tangerines

1 stick (8 tablespoons; 4 ounces; 113 grams) unsalted butter, cut into chunks, at room temperature

½ teaspoon fine sea salt

2 large eggs, at room temperature

¼ cup (60 ml) honey

2 teaspoons pure vanilla extract

1 cup coconut, either sweetened flakes (120 grams) or shredded unsweetened (80 grams)

While these started life as a riff on the classic chocolate-chipper, somewhere along the way they morphed into a soft, not very sweet, comfort cookie with all the makings of a morning meal: wheat germ and oats, fruit, citrus (albeit just the zest), eggs, honey and coconut. They could go into a lunch box, or they could be an after-school snack, a treat with tea or even an ice-cream sandwicher, but I find myself grabbing them with my first coffee of the day.

When cookies have as many add-ins as these do, another one or two aren't a problem. Add some nuts or go for the chips that I never got around to, if you want, or swap the fruits for those you like more or happen to have in the cupboard. You could even keep my fruits and add another. This is a more-the-merrier cookie.

Makes about 38 cookies

Position the racks to divide the oven into thirds and preheat it to 350 degrees F. Line two baking sheets with parchment paper or silicone baking mats.

Even if your fruit is moist and plump, it will add to the flavor of these cookies if you give it a quick soak: Toss the fruit into a large bowl, cover with very hot tap water and let sit for at least 5 minutes. Drain and pat dry.

In another large bowl, whisk together the oats, both flours, the wheat germ, cinnamon, baking powder and baking soda.

Put the sugar in the bowl of a stand mixer, or a large bowl in which you can use a hand mixer, and add the citrus zest. Using your fingers, rub the ingredients together until the sugar is moist and fragrant. If using a stand mixer, fit it with the paddle attachment. Add the butter and salt to the bowl and mix on medium speed until soft and creamy, about 2 minutes. One by one, add the eggs, beating for 1 minute after each one goes in. If the mixture looks curdled, keep going — it will even out soon. Beat in the honey and vanilla, again ignoring any curdling. Scrape down the sides and bottom of the bowl, turn the mixer off and add the flour mixture all at once. Working on low speed, mix only until the dry

The dough can be made up to 2 days ahead, wrapped well and refrigerated. Or, you can scoop the dough and freeze the mounds, then pack them when they're solid and freeze for up to 2 months. Let them stand at room temperature while you preheat the oven. The baked cookies will keep in a covered container for up to 3 days at room temperature; they can be wrapped airtight and frozen for up to 2 months.

ingredients are partially incorporated, then mix in the coconut and dried fruit. Don't overdo the mixing; get the ingredients mostly blended, then give the dough a few turns by hand with a spatula.

Using a medium cookie scoop, scoop out level portions of the dough, or use a tablespoon to get rounded spoonfuls, and put on the baking sheets, leaving about 2 inches between the mounds. Press each mound down lightly with your fingers.

Bake for 17 to 19 minutes, rotating the pans top to bottom and front to back after 10 minutes, or until the cookies are golden brown and feel set when squeezed gently. Allow the cookies to rest on the baking sheets for 5 minutes, then transfer to a rack to cool completely.

SNOWY-TOPPED BROWNIE DROPS

If you're lucky, cookies like these turn up at your Christmas-cookie swap; if you're *really* lucky, you make these year-round and enjoy — and share — them no matter the season. At heart, they're a brownie. In fact, the recipe is a variation of my Classic Brownie (page 33), which I've been making almost forever. By adding a little more flour to the dough and baking it in a different way, you get a cookie that's only just set on the outside and moist in the center. The transformation is fascinating. To get the crackled top — the dark valleys and the white plateaus — you need to roll each ball of dough in confectioners' sugar.

Even after it's chilled, the dough is soft, so the best and easiest way to work with it and to get even cookies is to portion out the dough using a cookie scoop and to drop the scoops directly into the bowl of sugar. If you don't have a scoop, use two spoons: one to portion the dough (use a rounded spoonful) and the other to scrape the dough off the spoon and into the sugar.

These make great ice-cream sandwiches!

Makes about 20 cookies

Fit a heatproof bowl over a pan of gently simmering water, making certain the water doesn't touch the bottom of the bowl, and put the butter in the bowl. Coarsely chop 6 ounces (170 grams) of the chocolate and scatter it over the butter. Finely chop the remaining 2 ounces (57 grams) chocolate and set it aside. Leave the bowl over the simmering water, stirring occasionally, until the ingredients are just melted, taking care that they don't get so hot that they separate. Remove the bowl from the pan.

Using a whisk or a heatproof spatula, stir in the sugar. The mixture will turn grainy, but that's okay. One by one, add the eggs, whisking energetically after each one goes in and then for a minute or two more. The dough will become smoother, shinier and thicker. Whisk in the vanilla and the salt and then, less vigorously, the flour. Stir in the finely chopped chocolate. Transfer the dough to a bowl, cover and refrigerate for at least 3 hours.

5 tablespoons (2½ ounces; 71 grams) unsalted butter, cut into about 10 pieces

8 ounces (226 grams) semisweet or bittersweet chocolate

¾ cup (150 grams) sugar

2 cold large eggs

1 teaspoon pure vanilla extract

½ teaspoon fine sea salt

¾ cup (102 grams) all-purpose flour

Confectioners' sugar, for dredging

Although the cookies are best shortly after they're made, they will be good for about 3 days in a sealed container at room temperature. They will get a little firmer and a little crisper as the days go by, making them different but still delicious. If you'd like, you can wrap the cookies airtight and freeze them for up to 2 months; defrost in the packaging. If frozen and defrosted, the cookies will lose their snowy tops; you can dust them with confectioners' sugar before serving. (No, it's not the same, but a good cookie's a good cookie even when its sugar coating isn't just so.)

GETTING READY TO BAKE: Center a rack in the oven and preheat it to 350 degrees F. Line two baking sheets with parchment paper or silicone baking mats.

Put some confectioners' sugar in a small bowl. (If your sugar is very lumpy, you can sift it, but even lumpy sugar seems to be fine for these cookies.)

Using a medium cookie scoop, scoop out level portions of dough or use a tablespoon to get rounded spoonfuls. Roll each into a ball and drop it into the bowl of sugar. Gently toss the dough around in the sugar until it's generously coated, then place the ball on one of the baking sheets and repeat, giving the balls about 2 inches of spread-space.

Slide the sheet into the oven and bake the cookies for about 12 minutes, rotating the baking sheet after 6 minutes. The cookies will have spread and cracked, their sides should feel set and their centers should still be a little soft. Put the baking sheet on a rack and wait 2 minutes, then carefully transfer the cookies to the rack using a broad spatula and let cool until they are just warm or have reached room temperature.

Repeat with the second baking sheet and the remaining dough.

COFFEE MALTEDS

1½ cups (204 grams) all-purpose flour

¼ cup (40 grams) unflavored malted milk powder

½ teaspoon baking powder

1 stick (8 tablespoons; 4 ounces; 113 grams) unsalted butter, cut into chunks, at room temperature

½ cup (100 grams) sugar

¼ cup (50 grams) packed light brown sugar

1 tablespoon ground coffee, preferably from espresso beans (or use instant or powdered coffee or espresso)

½ teaspoon fine sea salt

1 large egg, at room temperature

1 large egg yolk, at room temperature

1 teaspoon pure vanilla extract

Coffee was the fragrance of my childhood, but it was for grown-ups, and I wasn't allowed even a sip. Oddly, I was treated regularly to coffee malteds, which were made with Coffee Time syrup and malted milk powder.

These cookies bring back the memory of those malteds. Instead of syrup, I use freshly ground espresso beans (although instant espresso or coffee works) and unflavored malt powder — you can find it in supermarkets — which gives the cookies a warm, mildly vanilla taste. These are chewy and their look is humble. Don't be tempted to bake them until set; they set outside the oven. Overbake these cookies, and they'll still taste good, but you'll lose their moist chewiness.

These are so good with a swipe of dulce de leche (page 486).

Makes about 36 cookies

Position the racks to divide the oven into thirds and preheat it to 350 degrees F. Line two baking sheets with parchment paper or silicone baking mats.

Whisk the flour, malt powder and baking powder together.

Working with a stand mixer fitted with the paddle attachment, or in a bowl with a hand mixer, beat the butter, both sugars, espresso and salt together on medium speed until well blended, about 3 minutes. Scrape down the bowl, return to medium speed and, one by one, beat in the egg, yolk and vanilla, beating for 1 minute after each goes in. Turn off the mixer, add the dry ingredients all at once and pulse, just to begin incorporating the flour and malt powder. When the risk of flying flour is passed, mix on low speed only until the dry ingredients disappear into the dough. You'll have a rather crumbly dough, but that's fine. Give the dough a few last turns with a sturdy flexible spatula and then reach in, knead if necessary and gather the dough into a ball.

Using a small cookie scoop, scoop out level portions of dough, or use a teaspoon to get rounded spoonfuls. Roll the dough into balls and place them an inch apart on the lined baking sheets.

STORING

Packed in a tightly covered container, the cookies will keep for up to 3 days (after that, they get firmer and are perfect for dunking . . . in coffee, of course). Wrapped airtight, they can be frozen for up to 2 months.

Bake the cookies for 14 minutes, rotating the baking sheets top to bottom and front to back after 8 minutes. The cookies will be soft and golden only around the edges; they won't look done, and they're not — they'll firm as they cool. Transfer the sheets to racks and then, after about 10 minutes, carefully lift the cookies onto the racks to cool completely.

TWO-BITE ONE-CHIP COOKIES

These are just what you'd imagine given their name: cookies as tiny as your thumbprint. They are adorable (and they can be made even smaller and more adorable; see Playing Around). And they're delicious. They're based on My Newest Chocolate Chip Cookie (page 125), but they have more flour, so that they bake to dainty domes.

You make these cookies by molding a little dough around a chocolate chip. I use dark chocolate chips, but you can use whatever you'd like. You could even go for butterscotch or peanut butter chips. The cookie's flavor is an easygoing one; it'll change partners happily.

I love these cookies for parties. They're especially good after a big meal, and they're excellent playing sidekick to ice cream. Think of them as snacks, and pile them into a bowl.

Makes about 60 cookies

1¼ cups (170 grams) all-purpose flour

⅓ cup (45 grams) whole wheat flour

⅛ teaspoon ground cinnamon (optional)

1 stick (8 tablespoons; 4 ounces; 113 grams) unsalted butter, cut into chunks, at room temperature

½ cup (100 grams) sugar

⅓ cup plus 1 tablespoon (80 grams) packed light brown sugar

½ teaspoon fine sea salt

1 large egg, at room temperature

1 teaspoon pure vanilla extract

About 60 (¼ cup; 33 grams) chocolate (or other) chips

Whisk together both flours and the cinnamon, if you're using it.

Working with a stand mixer fitted with the paddle attachment, or in a large bowl with a hand mixer, beat the butter, both sugars and the salt together on medium speed until smooth, about 3 minutes. Add the egg and beat for a minute, then blend in the vanilla. Turn the mixer off, add the dry ingredients all at once and pulse to begin the blending. Then mix on low speed until the dough comes together and the flour has disappeared. You can use the dough now, but it's easier to work with if you wrap it and refrigerate it for at least 2 hours.

GETTING READY TO BAKE: Center a rack in the oven and preheat it to 400 degrees F. Line two baking sheets with parchment paper or silicone baking mats.

For each cookie, scoop out a level teaspoon of dough, roll it between your palms into a ball, press one chip into the dough and then roll again to hide the chip and reshape the ball. Place the balls an inch apart on the baking sheets.

Slide one sheet into the oven and bake for 6 to 7 minutes (there's no need

STORING

The cookies will keep for about 1 week in a covered container at room temperature. Wrapped airtight, they'll be good for up to 2 months in the freezer. You can refrigerate the dough for up to 3 days. If you'd like, you can freeze the chip-filled dough balls on a lined baking sheet and then pack them airtight when they're solid. Let them stand at room temperature while you preheat the oven.

to rotate the baking sheet unless your oven has serious hot spots), or until the cookies are a pale golden brown. Prod them gently, and they'll still be soft. Transfer the sheet to a rack and let the cookies rest for about 5 minutes before lifting them onto the rack to cool to just warm or room temperature.

Bake the second sheet of cookies.

PLAYING AROUND

Micro Chips. Use just ½ to a scant 1 teaspoon dough for each cookie. Bury the chocolate chip as in the main recipe and bake for 5 to 6 minutes. You'll get 120 cookies, which Mary, my recipe tester, says is an appropriate batch, since you eat them by the handful.

KERRIN'S MULTIGRAIN CHOCOLATE CHIP COOKIES

½ cup (68 grams) all-purpose flour

½ cup (68 grams) whole wheat flour

½ cup (60 grams) buckwheat flour

½ teaspoon baking powder

½ teaspoon baking soda

7 tablespoons (3½ ounces; 99 grams) unsalted butter, cut into chunks, at room temperature

⅔ cup (134 grams) packed light brown sugar

½ cup (100 grams) sugar

⅛ teaspoon fine sea salt

1 large egg, at room temperature

1 large egg yolk, at room temperature

¼ cup (45 grams) kasha, preferably Wolff's medium granulation (see headnote), or toasted nuts, finely chopped

6 ounces (170 grams) bittersweet chocolate, coarsely chopped

Maldon or other flake sea salt, for sprinkling

My friend Kerrin Rousset has a wonderful, quirky way with food, mixing ingredients that you wouldn't expect to be culinary classmates and always sneaking a smidgen of healthfulness into every tasty thing she makes. Here she found a way to use whole wheat and buckwheat flours, and I found a way to use kasha.

An American, Kerrin lives in Switzerland, and this recipe originally called for rye grits, which she buys in a local market where shopkeepers happily grind it to measure. When I couldn't find rye grits (sometimes called cracked rye), I hit on the idea of using buckwheat groats, aka kasha. Be sure to use Wolff's granulated kasha (100 percent buckwheat), which is readily available. (Medium-grain buckwheat from Bob's Red Mill or the bins in your natural food market can't be used for cookies; it's too large and hard.) Wolff's bakes into the cookies just as nuts would (and you can substitute nuts if you'd like). You get toastiness, full-grain flavor and crunch. And hold on to the leftover kasha to use in the Double-Buckwheat Double-Chocolate Cookies (page 203) or Fruit and Four-Grain Biscotti (page 101).

A word on color and spreadability: Depending on your buckwheat, your cookies might be golden or mocha colored — however, they'll always be good. And depending on how cold your dough is, your cookies might spread and be like saucers, or they might bake to be like pucks. Again, both are delicious.

Makes 25 cookies

Whisk together the three flours, the baking powder and baking soda.

Working with a stand mixer fitted with the paddle attachment, or in a large bowl with a hand mixer, beat together the butter, both sugars and the salt on medium speed for 5 minutes, scraping down the sides and bottom of the bowl

The dough can be refrigerated
for up to 2 days. If you'd like, you
can freeze scooped-out balls of
dough. Let them stand at room
temperature while you preheat
the oven; frozen dough may
not spread as much. The baked
cookies can be packed airtight
and frozen for up to 2 months.

a couple of times. Add the egg and beat for about 1 minute, then add the yolk and beat for 1 minute more. Turn the mixer off, add the dry ingredients all at once and pulse the mixer a few times to start blending them in. Working on low speed, mix only until most but not all of the dry ingredients are incorporated — you should still see streaks of flour. Add the kasha, and pulse a couple of times. Add the chocolate, pulse and then, if necessary, mix on low just until everything is blended. Or do this last bit of mixing by hand, with a sturdy flexible spatula. Scrape the dough out of the bowl, form it into a ball, wrap in plastic and refrigerate for 1 hour. (You can refrigerate the dough longer; your cookies will not spread as much.)

GETTING READY TO BAKE: Center a rack in the oven and preheat it to 375 degrees F. Line a baking sheet with parchment paper or a silicone baking mat.

Remove the dough from the fridge. Using a medium cookie scoop, scoop out level portions of dough, or use a tablespoon to get rounded spoonfuls. Place the mounds of dough about 2 inches apart on the baking sheet. Sprinkle each mound with flake salt, making sure, as Kerrin advises, not to concentrate it only on the very center of the cookie.

Bake for 8 to 10 minutes, rotating the sheet at the midway mark, or just until the edges of the cookies start to brown. The cookies will be underbaked, and that's the way they should be. Transfer the baking sheet to a rack and let the cookies rest for about 2 minutes, then, working very carefully with a wide metal spatula, transfer the cookies to a rack to cool until they are just warm (delicious) or they reach room temperature. The cookies will firm as they cool.

Repeat with the remaining dough, making certain that you always use a cool baking sheet.

MY NEWEST CHOCOLATE CHIP COOKIES

My Classic Best Chocolate Chip Cookies (see Playing Around) have been my favorites for close to twenty years. I still love them, but when it comes to chocolate chip cookies, it's hard to be constant. Recipes for chocolate chip cookies are like scarves — you're always happy to have a new one. And so, here's my new cookie. Not radically different from the old one . . . but different enough that you'll want to make both.

This cookie, with its combination of all-purpose and whole wheat flours and a different mix of white and brown sugars, bakes to a chewier cookie than my classic. I added nutmeg and coriander to the dough, and it's up to you if you'd like to use them or not — or if you'd like to use even more. Or maybe you want to flavor the dough with a little instant espresso (½ to ¾ teaspoon) with or without ground cinnamon (¼ teaspoon), or even a little (¼ to ½ teaspoon) Chinese five-spice powder.

A word on timing: You can use the dough soon after it's made, but it improves with more chill time. If you can wait a day to bake the cookies, do.

Makes about 50 cookies

Whisk both flours, the baking soda, nutmeg and coriander together.

Working with a stand mixer fitted with the paddle attachment, or in a large bowl with a hand mixer, beat the butter, both sugars and the salt together on medium speed until smooth, about 3 minutes. One by one, add the eggs and beat for 1 minute after each goes in. Beat in the vanilla. Turn the mixer off, add the dry ingredients all at once and pulse to begin the blending, then mix on low speed until the dough comes together and the flour has disappeared. Add the chocolate and incorporate on low speed or mix in by hand with a sturdy flexible spatula. Wrap the dough in plastic and refrigerate it for at least 1 hour.

GETTING READY TO BAKE: Position the racks to divide the oven into thirds and preheat it to 375 degrees F. Line two baking sheets with parchment paper or silicone baking mats.

Using a tablespoon, scoop out level portions of dough. Roll each tablespoon

---

1¾ cups (238 grams) all-purpose flour

⅔ cup (91 grams) whole wheat flour

¾ teaspoon baking soda

¼ teaspoon freshly grated nutmeg

¼ teaspoon ground coriander

2 sticks (8 ounces; 226 grams) unsalted butter, cut into chunks, at room temperature

1 cup (200 grams) sugar

¾ cup (150 grams) packed light brown sugar

1¼ teaspoons fine sea salt

2 large eggs, at room temperature

2 teaspoons pure vanilla extract

10 ounces (283 grams) semisweet or bittersweet chocolate, coarsely chopped (or 1⅔ cups chocolate chips)

STORING

You can refrigerate the dough for up to 3 days. If you'd like, you can shape the dough into balls, place them on baking sheets, slide them into the freezer and then, when they're solid, pack them airtight. Let them stand at room temperature while you preheat the oven. You can keep the baked cookies covered at room temperature for at least 5 days, or wrap airtight and freeze for up to 2 months.

of dough between your palms to make a ball and place the balls at least 2 inches apart on the lined baking sheets.

Bake for 9 to 11 minutes, rotating the pans top to bottom and front to back after 6 minutes, or until the cookies have spread, puffed a little, turned a light golden brown and feel only just set around the edges. Transfer the baking sheets to racks and let the cookies rest on the sheets for at least 5 minutes before lifting them onto the racks to cool to just warm or room temperature.

Repeat with the remaining dough, being certain to use cool baking sheets.

PLAYING AROUND

My Classic Best Chocolate Chip Cookies. While very similar to my newest cookies, these are a thinner cookie with less chew. They also don't have the new spice combination. (Of course, if you like the idea of nutmeg and coriander in your chippers, you can add them to this recipe.) The mixing method is the same. Here are the ingredients: 2 cups all-purpose flour, 1 teaspoon fine sea salt, ¾ teaspoon baking soda, 1 cup sugar, ⅔ cup packed light brown sugar, 2 teaspoons pure vanilla extract, 2 large eggs, 12 ounces bittersweet chocolate, finely chopped (or use chocolate chips), and 1 cup finely chopped walnuts or pecans. I use a slightly rounded tablespoon of dough for each cookie and bake them in a 375-degree-F oven for 10 to 12 minutes.

PEANUT BROWNIE SABLÉS

FOR THE SABLÉ DOUGH

1 cup (136 grams) all-purpose flour

½ teaspoon baking powder

7 tablespoons (3½ ounces; 99 grams) unsalted butter, at room temperature

2 tablespoons natural (peanuts-only) peanut butter, smooth or crunchy

½ cup (100 grams) sugar

¼ teaspoon fleur de sel or a pinch of fine sea salt

2 large egg yolks, at room temperature

¾ cup (110 grams) salted peanuts, toasted and coarsely chopped

FOR THE BROWNIE BATTER

⅔ cup (91 grams) all-purpose flour

¼ cup (21 grams) unsweetened cocoa powder

¼ teaspoon fleur de sel or a pinch of fine sea salt

½ cup (100 grams) packed light brown sugar

½ stick (4 tablespoons; 2 ounces; 56 grams) cold unsalted butter, cut into 16 pieces

1 large egg, lightly beaten

6 ounces (170 grams) semisweet or bittersweet chocolate, finely chopped

The inspiration for this cookie came from a recipe by France's long-reigning culinary genius Alain Ducasse. It's a combination of the iconic French shortbread, *le sablé*, and the beloved American brownie, which means that the texture is a little sandy here and a little fudgy there, slightly crisp around the edges and moist and a touch chewy in the center. In this truly unusual recipe, you make an almost classic sablé dough studded with nuts and a cocoa–brown-sugar brownie batter studded with chopped chocolate, and then you mix the two together, scoop and bake.

Feeling patriotic, I tipped the balance on these and made them more American (or perhaps less French) by adding a dab of peanut butter to the sablé dough and choosing salted peanuts for the crunch. The result is a sophisticated cookie that begs to be eaten with gusto.

Merci, Hélène Samuel, for introducing me to this treat.

Makes about 36 cookies

Center a rack in the oven and preheat it to 350 degrees F. Line two baking sheets with parchment paper or silicone baking mats. Cover the bottom of a jar or glass in plastic wrap.

TO MAKE THE SABLÉ DOUGH: Whisk together the flour and baking powder.

Working with a stand mixer fitted with the paddle attachment, or in a large bowl with a hand mixer, beat the butter and peanut butter together on low speed until smooth and creamy, about 2 minutes. Add the sugar and salt and beat for 2 minutes. Add the yolks one at a time, scraping down the sides of the bowl as needed and beating for a minute after each goes in. Turn off the mixer, add the flour all at once and pulse the mixer a couple of times to start blending in the dry ingredients. Turn the mixer to low and beat only until the flour is almost incorporated. Add the peanuts and mix just until the dry ingredients disappear and the nuts are evenly distributed. Transfer the dough to another bowl or a piece of parchment and set aside. There's no need to wash the mixer bowl.

TO MAKE THE BROWNIE BATTER: Put the flour, cocoa and salt into the mixer bowl (or large bowl) and pulse just to combine. Add the brown sugar and pulse

The cookies will be fine kept in a covered container at room temperature for about 3 days. If they get a little dry, they tilt toward sablés; if humidity makes them a little moist, their brownie-ness comes to the fore. Packed airtight, the cookies will keep in the freezer for up to 2 months.

again. Toss in the cold bits of butter and mix on low speed until the ingredients are fully blended, about 2 minutes. You'll have crumbs and clumps here and there, and that's fine. Pour in the beaten egg and continue to mix on low speed until you have a batter that resembles fudge frosting. Add the chopped chocolate and pulse to mix it in.

Scrape the sablé dough into the bowl with the brownie batter and mix on low speed until homogenous.

Using a medium cookie scoop, scoop out level portions of dough or use a tablespoon to get rounded spoonfuls, leaving 2 inches of space between the mounds. Press each cookie down very gently with the jar or glass.

Slide one sheet into the oven and bake for about 10 minutes (unless your oven has serious hot spots, you don't need to rotate the baking sheet). The cookies should be set at the edges, soft in the center when lightly prodded and uniformly dull; they'll firm as they cool. Transfer the baking sheet to a rack and allow the cookies to cool completely before carefully lifting them off with a wide spatula.

Repeat with the second batch.

COCOA-TAHINI COOKIES WITH SESAME CRUNCH

When I was very young, rummaging through my grandmother's handbag was a treat, because I always knew what I would find: candy! There were always sour balls, raspberry sucking candies and, my favorite, "birdseed" (which may or may not have been the true name): sesame seeds transformed by magic into rectangles of sweet, crackly candy. I don't know if these candies still exist, but their flavor is an indelible childhood memory, one that came back to me when I made the crunch for these cookies.

My sesame crunch has all the caramel and nut flavor my grandma's had and, when chopped, as it is here, adds just the right amount of intermittent crispiness to these cookies, which are as surprising as the crunch that speckles them. The unexpected ingredient is tahini, the sesame paste best known for its role in hummus. Here it's used as you would peanut butter, to add a little more fat, another flavor and a slightly sandy texture to a cookie that is crisp on the edges and chewy at the center. While the idea of adding tahini to cookies might be new to you, and the idea of pairing tahini and chocolate even newer, I'm betting that you'll have a love-at-first-bite moment. Everything about these cookies is new except the old-timey, raiding-the-cookie-jar pleasure they deliver.

Makes about 24 cookies

TO MAKE THE CRUNCH: Put a silicone baking mat on the counter near your stove, or lightly butter the underside of a baking sheet. Sprinkle the sugar evenly over the bottom of a small heavy skillet, drizzle over the water and place the pan over medium-high heat. The sugar will boil and then, after 3 to 5 minutes, will start to change color. If during this time the sugar bubbles up the sides of the pan, wash the sides down with a brush (silicone is great here) dipped in cold water. When about one quarter of the sugar has changed color, gently stir it with a silicone spatula or wooden spoon until you've got a fairly even pale amber color (the color of beer) — a matter of seconds, not minutes. Pour in the sesame

FOR THE SESAME CRUNCH

2 tablespoons sugar

2 teaspoons water

¼ cup (40 grams) hulled white sesame seeds

FOR THE COOKIES

¾ cup (102 grams) all-purpose flour

⅓ cup (28 grams) unsweetened cocoa powder

¼ teaspoon baking soda

¾ stick (6 tablespoons; 3 ounces; 85 grams) unsalted butter, cut into chunks, at room temperature

¼ cup (63 grams) tahini (stir very well before measuring)

¾ cup (150 grams) sugar

⅓ cup (67 grams) packed light brown sugar

½ teaspoon fine sea salt

1 large egg, at room temperature

6 ounces (170 grams) semisweet or bittersweet chocolate, finely chopped, or 1 cup (170 grams) dark chocolate chips

seeds and stir to coat them evenly with caramel. Don't worry if you see a little smoke rising from the mixture, just keep stirring until the seeds are coated. Turn the caramelized seeds out onto the silicone mat (or baking sheet), spread them as thin as possible and allow to cool. Finely chop the caramelized seeds (you'll have a scant ½ cup of crunch). To clean your skillet, fill it with water and bring the water to a boil — the caramel will melt.

TO MAKE THE COOKIES: Position the racks to divide the oven into thirds and preheat it to 350 degrees F. Line two baking sheets with parchment paper or silicone baking mats.

Whisk together the flour, cocoa and baking soda.

Working with a stand mixer fitted with the paddle attachment, or in a large bowl with a hand mixer, beat the butter, tahini, both sugars and the salt together on medium speed until smooth, about 2 minutes. Add the egg and beat for a minute or so, then use a sturdy spatula to scrape down the sides and bottom of the bowl. With the mixer off, add the flour mixture all at once and beat on low speed until the dry ingredients are almost but not completely incorporated. Pour in the chopped chocolate and sesame crunch and mix until the dry ingredients have disappeared. Give the dough, which will look like frosting, a few finishing turns with the spatula.

Using a medium cookie scoop, scoop out level portions of dough or use a tablespoon to get rounded spoonfuls, placing the mounds of dough at least 2 inches apart on the baking sheet — these are spreaders.

Bake the cookies for 13 to 15 minutes, rotating the pans top to bottom and front to back after 7 minutes. At 13 minutes, the cookies will look unset; at 15, only the edges will be set. They'll both be fine, one just a little firmer than the other — it's your choice. Place the baking sheets on racks and let the cookies rest for 5 minutes before carefully transferring them to the racks to firm and cool.

STORING

The dough can be refrigerated, well wrapped, for up to 3 days. The cookies will keep in a container at room temperature for about 4 days. They'll get a little firmer and a bit sandier, but their flavor and appeal won't diminish. Wrapped airtight, they can be frozen for up to 2 months.

DOUBLE-GINGER MOLASSES COOKIES

2¼ cups (306 grams) all-purpose flour

2 tablespoons unsweetened cocoa powder

1 to 2 teaspoons instant espresso, to taste (optional)

1½ teaspoons ground ginger

1 teaspoon ground cinnamon

¼ teaspoon ground cloves

½ teaspoon baking soda

½ teaspoon fine sea salt

1½ sticks (12 tablespoons; 6 ounces; 170 grams) unsalted butter, cut into chunks, at room temperature

⅓ cup (67 grams) sugar

⅓ cup (67 grams) packed light brown sugar

1 large egg yolk, at room temperature

½ cup (120 ml) unsulfured molasses

1½ teaspoons pure vanilla extract

⅓ cup (55 grams) chopped crystallized ginger or 2 tablespoons minced fresh ginger mixed with 2 teaspoons sugar (see headnote)

7 ounces (200 grams) semisweet or bittersweet chocolate, chopped chip-size

Sugar, for rolling

I have my friend Christine Beck, who is, like me, a Paris part-timer, to thank for this recipe. The cookies belong to the chewy-molasses-cookie family, but they have so much flavor and so many surprises that they transcend the familiar. For starters, there's both crystallized ginger and powdered ginger, lots of chopped dark chocolate and an optional bit of instant espresso too, which I tacked onto the recipe because I'm an incorrigible tinkerer.

I also tinkered with the way these are baked. Classic molasses cookies are scooped, molded into balls, rolled in sugar and then pressed with a fork before baking, and you can make these cookies that way. Or you can do what I do: Mold them in muffin tins, which turn out more uniformly shaped cookies that teeter on the brink of becoming gingerbread cakes.

A word on crystallized ginger: Crystallized, or candied, ginger is sliced fresh ginger that is cooked in syrup, dredged in sugar and dried. You can usually find it in the supermarket alongside other dried fruits or in the spice section. If the ginger isn't moist and pliable, steam it before using: Put it in a strainer over a saucepan of simmering water, cover and let warm and soften for about 5 minutes; pat dry, chop and use. If you can't find crystallized ginger, you can omit it or mix 2 tablespoons minced fresh ginger with 2 teaspoons sugar and let stand for about 10 minutes, until the ginger is syrupy.

Makes about 36 cookies

Whisk the flour, cocoa, espresso (if using), spices, baking soda and salt together.

Working with a stand mixer fitted with the paddle attachment, or in a large bowl with a hand mixer, beat the butter and both sugars together on medium-low speed for about 3 minutes, scraping the bowl as needed, until fully blended. Add the yolk and beat for 1 minute, then add the molasses and vanilla, beating until smooth. Turn off the mixer, add the dry ingredients all at once and pulse the mixer until the risk of flying flour passes. Working on low speed,

Ginger-Chocolate Ganache. To make a ganache that you can use to finish the cookies, bring ⅔ cup heavy cream and four ¼-inch-thick slices of fresh ginger to a boil in a small saucepan. Turn off the heat, cover the pan and allow the cream to infuse for 20 minutes. Return the cream to the boil, then remove the ginger and pour half of the cream over 6 ounces finely chopped bittersweet chocolate. Wait for 30 seconds, stir gently and then stir in the remainder of the cream. Dip the top or one side of each cookie in the chocolate and place on a parchment-lined baking sheet. Chill for 20 minutes to set the chocolate. Bring the cookies to room temperature before serving.

STORING

You can refrigerate the dough for up to 3 days. You can also scoop out the dough, shape into balls and freeze the balls on baking sheets; when they're firm, pack them airtight and keep frozen for up to 2 months. Remove the dough from the freezer and let the balls sit at room temperature for at least 15 minutes, then roll in sugar and bake. The baked cookies can be kept in a sealed container at room temperature for up to 4 days. They'll get a little drier and a little less chewy, but that will make them even better for dunking.

mix the dough until the flour is almost but not completely incorporated. Add the crystallized ginger (or the sugared fresh ginger) and chocolate and mix until the dry ingredients disappear into the dough and the ginger and chocolate are evenly distributed. If you've got bits of dry ingredients on the bottom of the bowl, mix them in with a flexible spatula.

Gather the dough into a ball, flatten it and wrap it in plastic. Refrigerate for at least 2 hours.

GETTING READY TO BAKE: Position the racks to divide the oven into thirds and preheat it to 350 degrees F. Butter or spray regular muffin tins or, if making free-form cookies, line two baking sheets with parchment paper or silicone baking mats.

Have a medium cookie scoop at hand. Alternatively, you can use a rounded tablespoonful of dough for each cookie. If you're using tins, find a jar or glass that fits into them and can be used to flatten the dough; cover the bottom in plastic wrap. Spoon some sugar into a wide shallow bowl.

For each cookie, mold a scoop or spoonful of dough into a ball between your palms, then turn it in the sugar to coat and put in a muffin cup or on a baking sheet, leaving 2 inches between each ball of dough. If using tins, use the jar or glass to flatten each ball until it almost reaches the sides of the cup. If it's free-form, press to flatten to about ½ inch thick.

Bake the cookies for about 13 minutes, rotating the tins or sheets top to bottom and front to back after 7 minutes. The cookies should be lightly set around the edges and softer in the center. Transfer the tins or sheets to racks and let the cookies rest for 15 minutes before unmolding them and/or placing them on racks to cool completely.

If you're baking in batches, make certain to start with cool tins or baking sheets.

CHOCOLATE-CRANBERRY AND ALMOND COOKIES

Nothing makes me happier than packing cookies with extra flavor, a couple of different textures and a surprise. And so I added dried cranberries to the Do-Almost-Anything Chocolate Cookie Dough and then topped the cookies with a surprise: a sweet almond meringue crunch. I plump the cranberries in hot water so that they'll stay soft during their time in the oven, but there's nothing that says you couldn't use cranberry, pomegranate or orange juice, hibiscus tea or Grand Marnier instead of water. These are sophisticated cookies that can be made even more glam on a whim.

A word on batch size: This recipe uses one quarter of the Do-Almost-Anything Chocolate Cookie Dough. Make the full recipe of the dough and then, if you'd like, you can double, triple or quadruple this cookie recipe or use the extra chocolate dough to make other cookies (see pages 180, 200 and 245 for options).

Makes about 20 cookies

FOR THE COOKIES
1/3 cup (40 grams) plump, moist dried cranberries, chopped
1/4 recipe Do-Almost-Anything Chocolate Cookie Dough (page 494), just made and still soft (see headnote)

FOR THE TOPPING
2/3 cup (80 grams) confectioners' sugar
2 large egg whites
1 cup (100 grams) sliced almonds (blanched or unblanched)

TO MAKE THE COOKIES: Put the cranberries in a bowl, cover them with very hot tap water and steep for at least 10 minutes. Drain and pat dry between paper towels. Use a sturdy flexible spatula to blend the cranberries evenly into the dough.

Gather the dough into a ball, then pat it into a disk. Place it between two pieces of parchment paper and roll it to a thickness of 1/4 inch. Slide the dough, still between the paper, onto a baking sheet and freeze for at least 1 hour, or refrigerate for at least 3 hours.

GETTING READY TO BAKE: Center a rack in the oven and preheat it to 350 degrees F. Line a baking sheet with parchment paper or a silicone baking mat.

TO MAKE THE TOPPING: Put the confectioners' sugar in a wide bowl and pour the egg whites over it. Using your fingers or a fork, gently mix the ingredients, ignoring the lumps that form. Add the almonds and turn them around in the bowl until they are thoroughly coated.

Peel away the pieces of paper from both sides of the dough and return the dough to one piece of paper. Using a 2-inch-diameter cutter, cut out as many cookies as you can. Place them on the lined baking sheet about 1½ inches apart. Gather together the scraps, re-roll them between paper and chill.

Give the topping a stir, then spoon a little of it on each cookie, leaving as much of the liquid as you can in the bowl, and spread it across the top with a small icing spatula.

Bake for 20 to 22 minutes, rotating the sheet after 10 minutes, or until the almonds are golden brown and the cookies feel firm to the touch. Transfer the sheet to a rack and leave for 5 minutes before lifting the cookies onto the rack to cool completely.

Repeat with the rest of the dough, making sure the baking sheet is cool.

COCOA-ALMOND UGLIES

1 cup (120 grams) confectioners' sugar

2/3 cup (66 grams) almond flour

1 tablespoon unsweetened cocoa powder

1/2 teaspoon ground cinnamon

1/4 teaspoon fine sea salt

2 large egg whites

1 teaspoon pure vanilla extract

1 cup (120 grams) slivered almonds, lightly toasted and chopped (not too fine)

2 ounces (57 grams) bittersweet or semisweet chocolate, finely chopped

After tasting cookies like these in French and Italian bakeries, I spent a lot of time trying to make them at home — time well spent. Whether you call them *rochers* ("rocks"), as the French do, follow the Italian tradition and dub them *brutti ma buoni* ("ugly but good") or make up a name for them, as I did; whether you use almonds (my choice) or hazelnuts (as many Italians do) or walnuts, you get quick-to-make cookies that are crisp on the outside and chewy on the inside. The primary ingredients are few (and gluten-free) — nuts, confectioners' sugar and egg whites. To bolster their flavor and make their taste as interesting as their texture, I added cocoa, cinnamon and chopped chocolate. Make them once, and then make them any way you want — try adding ground ginger and chopped crystallized ginger to the dough instead of the cinnamon and chopped chocolate, or even along with them. Or ditch the cocoa and go for a pinch of ground coffee (or instant espresso).

A word on baking: In order not to burn the bottoms before the insides are done, the cookies are baked on an insulated baking sheet or on two baking sheets, one stacked on the other.

Makes about 20 cookies

Center a rack in the oven and preheat it to 350 degrees F. Pull out an insulated baking sheet or stack two regular baking sheets. Line the (top) sheet with parchment paper or a silicone baking mat.

Press the confectioners' sugar, almond flour, cocoa, cinnamon and salt through a fine strainer onto a piece of parchment or wax paper. (You'll use the paper as a funnel when you add these ingredients.)

Put the egg whites in a large bowl and, using a fork or a whisk, beat until frothy. No need for peaks, you just want to break up and lighten them. Whisk in the vanilla. Add the strained ingredients and chopped almonds and, with a flexible spatula, stir everything together until evenly moistened. If it takes a bit of mashing to get the dough to come together, mash away — there's no need to be gentle. Stir in the chopped chocolate.

The cookies should be kept in a covered container at room temperature. If you store them in a plastic bag, they will get too chewy, and they'll get sticky if you refrigerate or freeze them. After 3 or 4 days, the cookies will live up the meaning of to their French name, "rocks," at which point they're still delicious but best crushed and mixed into ice cream.

Use a tablespoon to scoop the dough — scrape the spoon against the side of the bowl to get level portions for each cookie, then push the dough out of the spoon onto the lined baking sheet, leaving 1½ to 2 inches between the mounds.

Bake for 20 to 22 minutes, rotating the sheet after 11 minutes, or until the cookies are dry, dull and cracked. They'll be set around the edges but have some give everywhere else. Transfer the baking sheet to a rack and allow the cookies to cool completely on the sheet. When you're ready for them, gently peel the paper or silicone mat away from the bottoms.

PINK PEPPERCORN THUMBPRINTS

No matter where I am, I always have a notebook at hand, and I'm pretty good about scribbling down ideas as they come to me. What I'm not good at is going back to the books and doing anything with the ideas. When I pick up an old notebook, it's always a revelation. And so you can imagine how I felt when I found "pink peppercorns + strawberries" in one notebook and "pink peppercorns + white chocolate" in two others. Clearly, this was a persistent idea, but not one I had ever followed through on . . . until now.

I knew the combo would be good, but I just couldn't figure out how I was going to put it together. And then I thought about thumbprints and all was revealed. The pink peppercorns — which are really not peppercorns at all, but the dried berries of a shrub related to the cashew tree — are ground with the cookies' sugar in a food processor and then the white chocolate is added with the flour and pulverized. The strawberry comes in as the jam that fills the thumbprints.

If you'd like to push this combination just a little further, after you warm the jam, add a few drops of pure rose extract or rose water.

Makes about 34 cookies

⅓ cup (67 grams) sugar

1 teaspoon pink peppercorns

¼ teaspoon fine sea salt

1½ cups (204 grams) all-purpose flour

⅓ cup (56 grams) finely chopped best-quality white chocolate

1 stick (8 tablespoons; 4 ounces; 113 grams) cold unsalted butter, cut into 16 pieces

1 large egg, lightly beaten

⅓ cup (108 grams) strawberry jam

¼ teaspoon pure rose extract or rose water (optional)

Confectioners' sugar, for dusting (optional)

Center a rack in the oven and preheat it to 350 degrees F. Line two baking sheets with parchment paper or silicone baking mats.

Put the sugar, peppercorns and salt in a food processor and pulse until the peppercorns are pulverized. Add the flour and white chocolate and pulse until the chocolate is pretty much ground. Scatter the cold butter over the dry ingredients and pulse about a dozen times, until the mixture forms large crumbs. Add the beaten egg a little at a time, pulsing after each bit goes in. You'll have a moist dough that holds together easily. Scrape the dough out onto a piece of parchment.

Using a small cookie scoop, scoop out level portions of dough or use a tea-spoon to get rounded spoonfuls. Roll each piece between your palms to make a ball. Place the balls on the baking sheets, leaving about 2 inches between

The cookie dough can be refrigerated for up to 2 days or, wrapped airtight, frozen for up to 2 months. The baked and filled cookies will keep at room temperature for up to 2 days. They'll get softer but will still be nice. Store them in a tin with parchment or wax paper between the layers.

them. Using the knuckle of your index finger, your thumb or the end of a silicone or wooden spoon, and your other hand to hold the dough steady, make a deep indentation in the center of each cookie.

Slide one sheet into the oven and bake for 8 minutes. Pull out the sheet and, with the base of a wooden spoon, poke down the center of each cookie. Return the sheet to the oven and bake for another 8 to 10 minutes, or until the bottoms are browned and the cookies feel firm; they will still be pale. Carefully transfer the cookies to a rack, and bake the second sheet.

Put the jam in a microwave-safe container, add a splash of water, stir and cover. Heat the jam in the microwave for about 45 seconds, or until it boils. If you're using the rose extract or rose water, stir it in. (You can do this on the stovetop instead.)

Dust the cookies with confectioners' sugar (it's okay if they're still warm) and, using a small spoon, fill each hollow with jam. Allow the jam to cool and set.

PRINCETON GINGERSNAPS

2 tablespoons finely chopped peeled
    fresh ginger

1 tablespoon finely chopped moist, pliable
    crystallized ginger

1 teaspoon plus 1 cup (200 grams) sugar

2 cups (272 grams) all-purpose flour

2 teaspoons baking soda

1 teaspoon ground cinnamon

1 teaspoon ground cloves

1 teaspoon ground ginger

¾ teaspoon fine sea salt

1½ sticks (12 tablespoons; 6 ounces;
    170 grams) unsalted butter, cut into
    chunks, at room temperature

¼ cup (60 ml) unsulfured molasses

1 large egg, lightly beaten, at room
    temperature

1 teaspoon pure vanilla extract

Sugar, for dredging

Melanie Clarke served these fabulous cookies at a dinner she hosted in support of the Princeton Public Library (hence the name), and I fell in love with them even before the first course was served: Knowing I was a baker, Melanie sneaked me into the kitchen early for a nibble. I left that evening with a bag of gingersnaps for the ride home and the conviction that these deserved a place in the pantheon of great all-American cookies. Absolutely packed with ginger — there's crystallized, fresh and ground in the mix — flavored with molasses, cinnamon and more cloves than you might think wise (surprise! the teaspoonful is the perfect amount) and baked until they are both crisp and chewy, they will win you over instantly. Make them once and you, like me, will thank Melanie for sharing the recipe.

Because Melanie told me that she and her sisters had made small adjustments to the recipe, which they'd gotten from their mother, I thought it would be okay if I did too, and so I mixed the fresh and crystallized ginger with a little sugar to soften it and create a small amount of syrup that makes it easier for the ginger flavors to blend throughout the dough.

A word on crystallized ginger: Crystallized, or candied, ginger is sliced fresh ginger that is cooked in syrup, dredged in sugar and dried. You can usually find it in the supermarket alongside other dried fruits or in the spice section. If the ginger isn't moist and pliable, steam it before using: Put it in a strainer set over a saucepan of simmering water, cover and let warm and soften for about 5 minutes, then pat dry and chop. If you can't find crystallized ginger, you can omit it or mix 2 tablespoons finely chopped fresh ginger with 2 teaspoons sugar and let stand for about 10 minutes, until the ginger is syrupy.

Makes about 60 cookies

Put the fresh and crystallized ginger in a small bowl. Sprinkle over the 1 teaspoon sugar, stir and let stand for about 10 minutes.

Whisk together the flour, baking soda, cinnamon, cloves, ground ginger and salt.

Toss the butter into a food processor, add the remaining 1 cup (200 grams) sugar and the molasses and whir until fully blended. Add the sugared ginger and pulse to incorporate. With the machine running, add the egg and vanilla, then continue to process until blended. Scrape down the sides and bottom of the bowl, add the dry ingredients and pulse to incorporate the flour mixture; scrape the bowl as needed. When the flour is no longer visible, you're done.

Scrape the dough out onto a work surface, pull it together into a ball and wrap well in plastic. Refrigerate for at least 2 hours.

GETTING READY TO BAKE: Position the racks to divide the oven into thirds and preheat it to 350 degrees F. Line two baking sheets with parchment paper or silicone baking mats. Pour some sugar into a small bowl.

Cut off a hunk of dough — leave the rest in the refrigerator until needed. Using a small cookie scoop, scoop out level portions of dough or use a teaspoon to get rounded spoonfuls. Roll each between your palms to form a ball. One by one, drop the balls into the sugar bowl, roll them around to coat and then place at least 2 inches apart on the baking sheets — these are spreaders. (Don't press them down.)

Bake the cookies for 14 to 19 minutes, rotating the baking sheets top to bottom and front to back after 8 minutes. Baking time depends on whether you'd like the cookies mostly soft and chewy (14 to 15 minutes), slightly more chewy than crisp (16 to 17 minutes) or chewy just at the center (18 to 19 minutes). Allow the cookies to cool for a minute or two on the baking sheets and then transfer them to cooling racks to cool completely (or not — these are awfully good still warm). The cookies will firm as they cool.

Continue baking cookies, making certain that your baking sheets are cool before using.

DOUBLE-GINGER CRUMB COOKIES

At heart, this is a plain shortbreadish snap made from Do-Almost-Anything Vanilla Cookie Dough, but the addition of fresh ginger to the dough and a simple crumb topping spiked with some ground ginger changes everything. The look says "demure," but the double layer of differing textures and the double punch of ginger say "heads up."

The trick to getting the maximum amount of flavor from the fresh ginger is to mix it with a little sugar and wait for a syrup to develop, a matter of minutes. Although there's just a bit of syrup, it's concentrated and, along with the minced ginger, spreads flavor.

A word on batch size: This recipe uses one quarter of the Do-Almost-Anything Vanilla Dough. Make the full recipe of the dough then, if you'd like, you can double, triple or quadruple this cookie recipe or use the vanilla dough to make other cookies (see pages 178, 185 and 236).

Makes about 20 cookies

TO MAKE THE COOKIES: Stir the minced ginger and sugar together in a small bowl. Leave on the counter, stirring occasionally, for 5 to 10 minutes, or until there's syrup in the bowl.

Use a sturdy flexible spatula to blend the ginger and syrup evenly into the soft dough. Gather the dough together and shape it into a disk. Place the dough between two pieces of parchment paper and roll to a thickness of ¼ inch. Slide the dough, still between the paper, onto a baking sheet and freeze for at least 1 hour, or refrigerate for at least 3 hours.

MEANWHILE, MAKE THE TOPPING: Put the dry ingredients in a bowl and whisk to blend. Drop in the pieces of cold butter and, using your fingertips, blend until you have a bowlful of crumbs, some large and some small. When you squeeze a little of the mix, it should hold together. Cover and chill the crumbs for at least 1 hour.

FOR THE COOKIES
1¼ teaspoons minced fresh ginger
1 teaspoon sugar
¼ recipe Do-Almost-Anything Vanilla Cookie Dough (page 492), just made and still soft (see headnote)

FOR THE TOPPING
¾ cup (102 grams) all-purpose flour
⅓ cup (67 grams) sugar
½ teaspoon ground ginger
¼ teaspoon fine sea salt
¾ stick (6 tablespoons; 3 ounces; 85 grams) cold unsalted butter, cut into small pieces

GETTING READY TO BAKE: Center a rack in the oven and preheat it to 350 degrees F. Line a baking sheet with parchment paper or a silicone baking mat.

Peel away the pieces of paper on both sides of the dough and return the dough to one piece of paper. Using a 2-inch-diameter cutter, cut out as many cookies as you can. Place them on the lined baking sheet about 1½ inches apart. Gather the scraps together, re-roll them between paper and chill. Sprinkle some crumb topping over the cookies.

Bake for 21 to 23 minutes, rotating the baking sheet after 12 minutes, or until both the cookies and the crumb topping are golden. Transfer the baking sheet to a rack and allow the cookies to rest for 5 minutes before lifting them onto the rack to cool completely.

Repeat with the rest of the dough, making sure the baking sheet is cool.

STORING

You can refrigerate the rolled-out dough for up to 2 days. The topping can be made up to a week ahead and kept covered in the refrigerator. The cookies will keep covered at room temperature for about 4 days, or, wrapped airtight, they can be frozen for up to 2 months.

PEANUT BUTTER CHANGE-UPS

2 cups (272 grams) all-purpose flour

¼ teaspoon baking powder

⅛ to ¼ teaspoon freshly grated nutmeg (to taste)

1½ cups (384 grams) peanut butter, at room temperature (see headnote)

2 sticks (8 ounces; 226 grams) unsalted butter, cut into chunks, at room temperature

¾ teaspoon fine sea salt

1 cup (200 grams) sugar

⅔ cup (134 grams) packed light brown sugar

2 large eggs, at room temperature

1 cup (146 grams) lightly salted peanuts, finely chopped

Sugar, for sprinkling

STORING

You can freeze the scooped-out balls of dough for up to 2 months. Let them stand at room temperature while you preheat the oven. The cookies are good keepers because even if they get a little dry — the centers will have a texture similar to the edges — they're still tasty. Keep the baked cookies in a covered container at room temperature for up to 5 days.

You'd think that once I'd had a favorite peanut butter cookie, I'd move on. But I'm a tinkerer and love that small changes make big differences in baking. Here, the change is in the texture. Instead of flattening the dough with the back of a fork to make the traditional crisscross pattern, I scoop it and get cookies with classic shortbread sandiness at the edges and centers that are softer, cakier, fuller and inexplicably more flavorful than the classics.

You can use either smooth or chunky peanut butter for these cookies (I go chunky), but you should choose a peanut butter that doesn't separate (you don't want to see a layer of oil at the top of the jar). There are many natural peanut butters that don't separate but many more that do, so be careful when you shop. Having grown up with Skippy, that's the brand I use for cookies.

By the way, I haven't abandoned my classic peanut butter cookie; see Playing Around.

Makes about 54 cookies

Position the racks to divide the oven into thirds and preheat it to 350 degrees F. Line two baking sheets with parchment paper or silicone baking mats.

Whisk together the flour, baking powder and nutmeg.

Working with a stand mixer fitted with the paddle attachment, or in a large bowl with a hand mixer, beat the peanut butter, butter and salt together on medium speed until very smooth, about 3 minutes. Add both sugars and beat for another 2 minutes. One by one, add the eggs, beating for a minute after each one goes in. Turn off the mixer, add all of the dry ingredients and pulse the machine a few times to start the blending. When the risk of flying flour has passed, mix on low speed until the flour has almost disappeared into the dough. Add the chopped peanuts and mix to incorporate, then give the dough a couple of turns with a flexible spatula to make certain that all of the dry ingredients are in.

Using a medium cookie scoop, scoop out level portions of dough. Drop the

Classic Peanut Butter Crisscross Cookies. The ingredients for the dough are: 2½ cups all-purpose flour, 1 teaspoon baking soda, ½ teaspoon baking powder, ¼ teaspoon fine sea salt, pinch of freshly grated nutmeg, 2 sticks unsalted butter, 1 cup peanut butter, 1 cup packed light brown sugar, ¾ cup sugar, 2 large eggs and 1½ cups chopped peanuts. Make the dough the same way as for the Change-Ups, but for each cookie, scoop out a level tablespoon of dough, roll it between your palms into a ball and dredge in sugar; place the cookies 2 inches apart on the baking sheets. Dip the tines of a fork in sugar and press against each cookie, first in one direction and then in a perpendicular direction, to make the crisscross pattern. Bake the cookies for about 12 minutes, until they're lightly colored but still soft.

mounds of dough about 1½ inches apart on the baking sheets. (Alternatively, you can spoon out rounded tablespoonfuls of dough and shape them into balls, but the dough is very soft and not easy to work with.) Sprinkle the tops of the mounds with sugar.

Bake for 17 to 19 minutes, rotating the pans top to bottom and front to back after 10 minutes, or until the cookies are golden brown. They'll feel set around the edges but squeezable everywhere else and that's fine — they firm as they cool. Transfer the baking sheets to racks and wait for 2 minutes, then lift the cookies onto the racks to cool completely.

Scoop and bake the rest of the cookies, being certain that the baking sheets are cool before using.

MOROCCAN SEMOLINA AND ALMOND COOKIES

It was a picture in a French magazine that won my heart and set me to dreaming about what these cookies would be like. In the picture, the sugar-coated cookies were cracked — I later learned that in Morocco the cracks are often called smiles — and you could see the slightly rough crumb in the crevices. I couldn't tell if the cookies, sometimes called *ghrieba*, sometimes *ghoriba*, would be airy or substantial, but I was betting on a shortbread-like texture, and I was right. I was also betting on a certain very agreeable graininess because of the semolina. Semolina falls somewhere on the texture continuum between whole wheat flour and cornmeal; it's golden and it's high-gluten, which is why it's the flour of choice for pasta. In a cookie, it provides a bit of bite and a slight grit, the kind of presence the French would call *sablé*, or "sandy." And then there's the almond flour, for flavor, of course, but it also adds another mysterious layer to the cookie's surprising elegance.

In Morocco, these are enjoyed with mint tea. I love them with tea of any kind, and because the cookies are not very sweet, I think they're also very good with wine, either red or white.

Makes about 38 cookies

1¾ cups plus 2 tablespoons (294 grams) semolina flour

2 cups (200 grams) almond flour

1½ teaspoons baking powder

¼ teaspoon fine sea salt

¾ cup (150 grams) sugar

1 lemon (you'll use just the zest)

2 large eggs, at room temperature

¼ cup (60 ml) flavorless oil, such as canola

1 teaspoon pure vanilla extract

1 teaspoon orange flower water (optional)

Confectioners' sugar, for dredging

Position the racks to divide the oven into thirds and preheat it to 350 degrees F. Line two baking sheets with parchment paper or silicone baking mats.

Whisk together the semolina, almond flour, baking powder and salt.

Put the sugar in the bowl of a stand mixer, or in a large bowl in which you can use a hand mixer. Finely grate the lemon zest over the sugar, then reach into the bowl and rub the ingredients together with your fingertips until the sugar is moist and fragrant. If you're using a stand mixer, fit it with the paddle attachment. Add the eggs to the sugar and beat on medium speed for 3 minutes. With the mixer running, pour in the oil down the side of the bowl and beat for another 3 minutes. Beat in the vanilla and the orange flower water, if you're

The cookies will keep for about
4 days in a covered container at
room temperature. (Dust them
with more confectioners' sugar if
the sugar seeps into the cookies.)
Because of the sugar coating,
these are not good candidates
for freezing.

using it. Turn off the mixer, add half of the dry ingredients and mix them in on
low speed, then repeat with the remaining dry ingredients, mixing only until they
disappear into the dough, which will be thick.

Sift some confectioners' sugar into a small bowl. For each cookie, spoon out a
level tablespoon of dough, roll it between your palms to form a ball and dredge in
sugar. Place the balls of dough 2 inches apart on the lined baking sheets, then use
your thumb to press down on the center of each cookie, pressing firmly enough to
make an indentation and to cause the edges to crack.

Bake for 14 to 16 minutes, rotating the pans top to bottom and front to back
after 8 minutes, or until the cookies are ever so lightly colored — they'll be golden
on the bottom — puffed, dramatically cracked and just firm to the touch. Carefully
lift the cookies off the sheets and onto racks.

ANZAC BISCUITS

There seem to be a hundred stories about Anzac Biscuits but essentially only one recipe. "Anzac" is an acronym for the Australia and New Zealand Army Corps, which was created during World War I, and because of its antipodal origins, it's known as a biscuit rather than a cookie. It's thought that these might have been the cookies most often sent to troops at the front or, quite the opposite, the ones served at fancy galas and parades and sold to raise funds for the war effort. Whatever the story, what seems to be constant is the simplicity of the ingredients — everything is basic and there are no eggs, because these were hard to come by during the war — and the sturdiness of the cookies, which were built to last and to travel. They're wonderfully good — they have the look, taste and partly crispy/partly chewy texture of great oatmeal cookies.

Two of my Australian friends, cookbook author Jennifer McLagan and food blogger Mardi Michels, sent me recipes, and yes, they were the same. Almost. One recipe called for 2 tablespoons of boiling water, the other for 1. And both had a typical British ingredient: golden syrup, a cane syrup from England commonly sold under the brand name Lyle's. If you can't find golden syrup, Mardi suggests using sweet brown rice syrup.

For me, the cookies were too sweet, especially since I opted to use sweetened shredded coconut for its easy availability and appealingly chewy texture. Because of this, I cut the amount of sugar in half.

Makes about 20 cookies

Position the racks to divide the oven into thirds and preheat it to 325 degrees F. Line two baking sheets with parchment paper or silicone baking mats.

Put the butter and golden syrup in a small saucepan and warm until the butter is melted; remove from the heat. Stir the water into the baking soda (it won't dissolve completely, but it'll come close) and then stir this into the melted butter and syrup.

Put the remaining ingredients in a large bowl and stir together, then pour

1 stick (8 tablespoons; 4 ounces; 113 grams) unsalted butter, cut into chunks

2 tablespoons Lyle's Golden Syrup (see headnote)

1 tablespoon boiling water or very hot tap water

½ teaspoon baking soda

1 cup (136 grams) all-purpose flour

1 cup (80 grams) old-fashioned rolled oats (not quick-cooking)

¾ cup (90 grams) shredded sweetened coconut

½ cup (100 grams) sugar

½ teaspoon fine sea salt

The cookies can be packed into
a tin, where they'll keep for at
least 1 week at room temperature.
Wrapped well and frozen, they
will be good for up to 2 months.

over the hot liquid. Stir with a wooden spoon or sturdy flexible spatula until well blended. You'll have a soft dough that might be a tad crumbly.

Using a medium cookie scoop, scoop out walnut-size nuggets of dough or use a tablespoon. Compress each piece of dough between your palms to form a ball that holds together and place the balls about 2 inches apart on the baking sheets — these are spreaders. Lightly press down on the balls with your fingers to make little pucks.

Bake for 17 to 19 minutes, rotating the sheets front to back and top to bottom at the midway mark, or until the cookies are golden (they'll almost be the color of carrot cookies — that's the golden syrup at work) and only just set around the edges. If you touch the cookies, they'll collapse, so you'll have to take it on faith — and color — that they're done. Transfer the sheets to racks and let the cookies rest for about 10 minutes before lifting them off the sheets and onto the racks to cool completely. If you can hold off eating the cookies, wait about 1 hour — these have a lot of butter and it takes time for it to settle back into the cookies.

GOOD, BETTER, BEST COOKIES

This cookie is proof that sometimes as good as good can be, more can be better and even more can be best. The "good" cookie is a thin toasted-almond-and-cinnamon sweet that has an unexpected (and unexplainable, at least to me) wholesome, wheaty flavor. I probably would have left the cookie there if an open jar of Biscoff Cookie Spread hadn't been sitting on the counter. (Biscoff is made with speculoos cookies, and if you don't know it, you should — it's delicious!) A swish of the spiced spread proved luscious, and so I set to work making a Biscoff filling and using it to sandwich the cookies — and they were even better. I might have even left better alone if the sandwiches didn't look as though they needed something more. When I dipped the edges in dark chocolate, I knew I'd made the right choice: They became the best they could be.

A word on quantity: If you're going to sandwich the cookies, you will get only about a dozen. Should you want more, just double the cookie and filling recipes. Want to dip them? Double the chocolate too.

Makes about 24 cookies or 12 sandwiches

TO MAKE THE COOKIES: Put the flour, almonds, sugar, cinnamon and salt in a food processor and pulse until the almonds are ground. It's okay if there are some larger pieces of almond here and there — it's better to have an uneven mix than a wet one. Scatter the pieces of cold butter over the dry ingredients and pulse until the butter is worked in and the mixture looks like moist crumbs. Lightly beat the cold water into the egg yolk and, pulsing the machine, add the yolk in 3 additions. Using long pulses, process until the dough forms clumps and curds.

Turn the dough out onto the counter, divide it in half, gather each piece into a ball and shape into a disk.

Working with one piece of dough at a time, roll the dough between pieces of parchment paper to a thickness of ⅛ inch. Slide the parchment-sandwiched dough onto a baking sheet — you can stack the slabs — and freeze for at least 1 hour, or refrigerate for at least 2 hours.

FOR THE COOKIES

1 cup (136 grams) all-purpose flour

1 cup (120 grams) sliced or slivered blanched almonds, lightly toasted

6 tablespoons (75 grams) sugar

1½ teaspoons ground cinnamon

½ teaspoon fine sea salt

¾ stick (6 tablespoons; 3 ounces; 85 grams) cold unsalted butter, cut into 12 pieces

1 tablespoon cold water

1 cold large egg yolk

FOR THE FILLING (OPTIONAL)

½ cup (140 grams) Biscoff Spread (see headnote)

¾ stick (6 tablespoons; 3 ounces; 85 grams) unsalted butter, cut into chunks, at room temperature

½ teaspoon fine sea salt

1¼ cups (150 grams) confectioners' sugar

1 tablespoon milk, or more if needed

FOR THE DIP (OPTIONAL)

4 ounces (113 grams) bittersweet or semisweet chocolate, very finely chopped

½ cup (120 ml) heavy cream

1 tablespoon (14 grams) unsalted butter, very soft

GETTING READY TO BAKE: Center a rack in the oven and preheat it to 350 degrees F. Line a baking sheet with parchment paper or a silicone baking mat. Have a 2-inch-diameter cookie cutter at hand.

Peel away both pieces of parchment paper from one sheet of dough and put the dough back on one piece of parchment paper. Cut the dough and place the circles a couple of inches apart on the lined baking sheet. Save the scraps, combine them with the scraps from the second piece of dough, re-roll, chill, cut and bake.

Bake the cookies for 11 to 13 minutes, or until they are lightly browned on both the bottoms and tops. The cookies won't get very brown; rather, they'll turn the color of roasted cashews. Transfer the baking sheet to a rack and allow the cookies to rest for at least 20 minutes before transferring them to the rack to cool completely.

Continue with the remainder of the dough, always using a cool baking sheet.

TO MAKE THE FILLING AND SANDWICH THE COOKIES (OPTIONAL): Working with a stand mixer fitted with the paddle attachment, or in a medium bowl with a hand mixer, beat the Biscoff, butter and salt together on medium speed until smooth, about 2 minutes. Reduce the speed to low and gradually add the confectioners' sugar. Return the mixer speed to medium and beat until you have a smooth mixture. Add the milk, and if the consistency looks too thick to spread, add a little more by droplets. (The filling can be covered tightly and kept at room temperature overnight; stir before using.)

Turn half of the cookies over, flat side up, and place a dollop of filling in the center of each. Be generous — you've got plenty of filling (you might even have some left over) and the cookies are good with plump middles. Spread the filling evenly over each cookie with a small icing spatula (or table knife), top with a second cookie, right side up, and swivel the cookies gently in opposite directions to "glue" them to the filling. The cookies are ready to be eaten or dipped into chocolate.

TO MAKE THE OPTIONAL DIP AND COAT THE COOKIES: Line a baking sheet with parchment paper.

Melt the chocolate in a heatproof bowl set over a pan of simmering water, or do this in the microwave. Bring the heavy cream just to a boil. Pour the cream over the chocolate, wait 30 seconds and then, using a whisk or flexible spatula and starting in the center of the bowl, stir in a small circle. When the mixture

thickens, darkens and turns glossy in the center, stir in widening circles until the ingredients are blended and the ganache is satiny. Gently stir in the butter. If necessary, transfer the chocolate to a bowl or container that's wide enough to dip the cookies ⅓ inch deep into the chocolate.

One by one, dip each sandwich into the chocolate and then lift it up, letting the excess ganache drip back into the bowl. Run the bottom edge of the sandwich against the rim of the bowl to clean away any extra chocolate and place on the lined baking sheet. When all of the cookies are dipped, slide the baking sheet into the refrigerator and chill for about 20 minutes, or until the chocolate is set. You can serve the cookies straight from the fridge, but I think their flavor is best at room temperature.

FRENCH SNACKLETTES

It must have been about twenty years ago that Arnaud Larher, then and now a Paris pastry star, gave me one of his TV Snacks to taste. It was a small nugget of a cookie — he sold them in little cellophane bags tied with ribbons — and it looked like any cookie a home baker in a hurry might make: The cookies were all different shapes, none were the same size and they were bare, not a bit of pâtisserie polish to be seen. But everything in that first bite was wonderful — the light crumbliness, the almond flavor (the dough is made with a mix of flour and nuts), the butteriness and the salt that made them snack food. Two decades ago, salt in sweets was bold. Today, while salt is no longer a surprise, the cookie hasn't lost a grain of its attraction or a speck of its snackability.

That first taste was followed by Arnaud giving me the recipe. This is my chocolate version and the one I like most. I make it in the food processor because I like to start with almonds, rather than almond flour — the nuts grind imperfectly, making the cookies' texture more interesting. (If you'd prefer to use almond flour, see Playing Around.) A smidgen of cinnamon and some chocolate chips or chopped chocolate up the cookies' appeal. See Playing Around for Vanilla French Snacklettes.

Makes about 60 cookies

Position the racks to divide the oven into thirds and preheat it to 325 degrees F. Line two baking sheets with parchment paper or silicone baking mats.

Put the almonds and sugar in a food processor and pulse and process until the nuts are mostly ground; scrape the bowl occasionally to make sure you don't have a thick layer on the bottom. Add the flour, cocoa, salt and cinnamon and pulse to incorporate. Scatter over the bits of cold butter and, working in long pulses, process until you have moist curds and crumbs. This might take a couple of minutes. Scrape the bowl as needed and check the dough often — it's ready when you can pinch a piece and have it stay together. Add the chocolate and work it in with just a couple of pulses. Turn the dough out and gather it into a ball.

1 cup (100 grams) sliced, slivered or whole almonds (blanched or unblanched)

½ cup (100 grams) sugar

¾ cup (102 grams) all-purpose flour

⅓ cup (28 grams) unsweetened cocoa powder

½ teaspoon fine sea salt or ¾ teaspoon fleur de sel

¼ teaspoon ground cinnamon

7 tablespoons (3½ ounces; 99 grams) cold unsalted butter, cut into small pieces

½ cup (85 grams) mini chocolate chips or very finely chopped semisweet or bittersweet chocolate

STORING

The dough can be refrigerated for up to 2 days; let it rest on the counter while you preheat the oven so that it will be soft enough to shape. If you'd like, you can freeze unbaked snacklettes for up to 2 months and bake them directly from the freezer, adding a minute or two to the baking time. Kept in a covered container, the cookies will be good for about 1 week. They can be packed airtight and frozen for up to 2 months.

French Snacklettes with Almond Flour.
Use 1 cup almond flour in place of the
almonds and room-temperature butter.
Whisk the almond flour, flour, cocoa and
cinnamon together. With a mixer or by
hand, beat the butter, sugar and salt
together until smooth, then add the dry
ingredients and blend until the dough
comes together. Stir in the chocolate
chips.

Vanilla French Snacklettes. Omit the
cocoa and cinnamon, but if you'd like to
keep the chocolate chips, do so. Increase
the all-purpose flour to 1 cup and, when
you add the butter, add 1 teaspoon pure
vanilla extract as well.

For each cookie, spoon out about a teaspoonful of dough and squeeze it
between your hands to form a nugget. You can press the nuggets into pyramid
shapes, if you'd like, but I often go for a haphazard look. Place them on the lined
baking sheets, leaving just a little space between them; they don't spread much.

Bake for 15 minutes, rotating the sheets top to bottom and front to back after
8 minutes. The cookies will be very soft, and that's fine — they firm as they cool.
Transfer the baking sheets to racks and let the cookies rest for 5 minutes, then
gently transfer them to the racks to cool completely.

If you have more dough, repeat, making certain your baking sheets are cool.

MOCHA-RICOTTA PUFFS

2 cups (272 grams) all-purpose flour

⅓ cup (28 grams) unsweetened cocoa powder

1 teaspoon baking soda

¾ teaspoon ground cinnamon

1 stick (8 tablespoons; 4 ounces; 113 grams) unsalted butter, cut into chunks, at room temperature

1¼ cups (250 grams) sugar

¾ teaspoon fine sea salt

2 teaspoons instant espresso or 1 tablespoon instant coffee

1 large egg, at room temperature

1 teaspoon pure vanilla extract

¾ cup (188 grams) packed whole-milk or low-fat ricotta, drained if necessary (see headnote)

A thousand things make cookies beguiling, and one of them is their ability to surprise. So often a cookie's looks are no indication of its texture or taste. These, which are adorable as puffs, don't give you even a hint that they're crisp around the edges and soft and much like a beloved devil's food cake in the center. You've got no way of knowing that there's coffee in the mix, and you probably won't be able to pick up the ricotta even after you've had a few of them, but it's what gives the puffs their noteworthy texture.

A word on the ricotta: I like to use whole-milk ricotta for these, but you can go with low-fat; just check that it isn't watery. (Skim-milk ricotta has more of a tendency to have excess water than full-fat.) You might want to line a strainer with a double thickness of dampened cheesecloth (or paper towels) and let the ricotta drain for an hour or so before using it.

Makes about 32 cookies

Position the racks to divide the oven into thirds and preheat it to 325 degrees F. Line two baking sheets with parchment paper or silicone baking mats.

Whisk the flour, cocoa, baking soda and cinnamon together.

Working with a stand mixer fitted with the paddle attachment, or in a large bowl with a hand mixer, beat the butter at medium speed until it's soft and creamy, about 2 minutes. Add the sugar and salt and beat for another 2 minutes. If the mixture has balled up around the beater, scrape it down. Beat in the instant espresso or coffee. Add the egg, followed by the vanilla, and beat for another minute or so. With the mixer at low-medium, add the ricotta and beat for about 2 minutes. The dough may look slightly curdled, but it will even out when the flour goes in. Turn off the mixer, add half of the dry ingredients and pulse to begin incorporating them, then beat on low until they're blended in. Repeat with the remainder of the dry ingredients, stopping to scrape down the beater(s) and bowl as needed. The dough will be soft, sticky, heavy and reminiscent of fudge frosting.

Using a medium cookie scoop, scoop out level portions of dough or use a tablespoon to get rounded spoonfuls. Drop mounds of dough about 2 inches apart onto the baking sheets.

Bake the cookies for 26 to 29 minutes, rotating the baking sheets from top to bottom and front to back after 15 minutes. They'll puff and spread as they bake; you'll know they're fully baked when they're firm around the edges and give slightly when gently pressed on top. Transfer the baking sheets to racks and let the cookies cool completely before carefully lifting them off the sheets with a wide spatula. Be gentle — they're soft on the bottom.

LEMON SUGAR COOKIES

I was just finishing a book signing in Chicago when Katje Sabin, a woman I'd met eight years earlier at another signing, handed me a folded piece of paper. When I returned to my hotel and opened it, I discovered that it was the best kind of present: a recipe. The handwritten note said, "This is currently my favorite cookie — thought you might enjoy!" And I did. Lots. The cookies get their strong, bright lemon flavor from zest and freshly squeezed juice, and their homey good looks from the cracks and ridges that develop as they bake. The recipe that Katje gave me turned out a very pale, chewy cookie, but I discovered that by keeping them in the oven a little longer, I could get a cookie that was both crispy and chewy. Play around and see what you like best.

Makes about 60 cookies

Position the racks to divide the oven into thirds and preheat it to 350 degrees F. Line two baking sheets with parchment paper or silicone baking mats.

Whisk the flour, baking soda and baking powder together. Finely grate the zest of 1 lemon and squeeze the juice. If you don't have ¼ cup, squeeze the juice from the second lemon.

Put the sugar and lemon zest in the bowl of a stand mixer, or in a large bowl in which you can use a hand mixer. Using your fingertips, mash and rub the ingredients together until the sugar is moist and fragrant. If you're working with a stand mixer, fit it with the paddle attachment. Add the butter and salt to the bowl and beat on medium speed until the mixture is smooth, about 2 minutes. Beat in the egg, followed by the vanilla and lemon juice. Turn off the mixer, add half of the dry ingredients and mix on low speed until they're almost incorporated. Scrape down the sides and bottom of the bowl, add the rest of the flour and beat on low speed until the dough comes away from the sides of the bowl.

Pour some sugar into a bowl. Using a small cookie scoop, scoop out level portions of dough or use a teaspoon to get rounded spoonfuls. Roll each portion into a ball between your palms, drop into the sugar, roll it around to coat

2¾ cups (374 grams) all-purpose flour

1 teaspoon baking soda

½ teaspoon baking powder

1 or 2 lemons

1½ cups (300 grams) sugar

2 sticks (8 ounces; 226 grams) unsalted butter, at room temperature, cut into chunks

½ teaspoon fine sea salt

1 large egg, at room temperature

1 teaspoon pure vanilla extract

Sugar, for dredging

and place on the baking sheets. These cookies spread dramatically, so make sure to leave about 2 inches between them.

Bake the cookies for 8 to 14 minutes, rotating the baking sheets top to bottom and front to back at the midway mark. If you bake them for 8 to 10 minutes, you'll get pale cookies that will be chewy; bake them for 12 to 14 minutes, until they're barely golden around the edges (the bottoms will be lightly browned), and you'll get cookies that are chewy in the center and crisp around the edges. The cookies will be crackle-topped and too soft to lift from the baking sheets. Transfer the baking sheets to racks and let the cookies cool completely before you move them.

Repeat with the remaining dough, always using cool baking sheets.

CHOCOLATE-CORNFLAKE HAYSTACKS

2 large eggs

½ cup (120 ml) agave nectar

¾ teaspoon fine sea salt

1 cup (120 grams) shredded sweetened
    coconut

1 cup (120 grams) pecans or other nuts,
    coarsely chopped

1 cup (160 grams) plump, moist raisins

3 cups (84 grams) cornflakes

6 ounces (170 grams) best-quality milk
    chocolate, melted

STORING

You can keep the cookies for about 3 days in a covered container, but they'll soften. I prefer to put them on a plate and leave them out. That's a good option only if the air is dry, though, not when it's humid.

If, like me, you find yourself unable to resist the allure of the no-bake corn-flake treats sometimes known in America as haystacks and called desert roses in France, then brace yourself for this baked version. Like the old-fashioned haystacks, these don't have many ingredients — it's the baking and the addition of eggs and agave nectar that make them different — but they end up being more satisfying than you'd expect. My go-to combination for these is sweetened coconut, chopped nuts, plumped raisins and high-quality milk chocolate, but this recipe is a DIYer's dream. You can change the nuts, the dried fruit and even the chocolate. Actually, you can even swap the namesake cornflakes for another kind of flaky cereal. What you don't want to leave out is the salt — it's the perker-upper here.

Makes about 35 cookies

Position the racks to divide the oven into thirds and preheat it to 300 degrees F. Line two baking sheets with parchment paper or silicone baking mats.

Working in a large bowl, whisk together the eggs, agave and salt until smooth, about 1 minute. Switch to a flexible spatula and add the remaining ingredients one at a time, mixing well after each goes in. (Adding the cornflakes close to the end increases their chances of surviving the mixing mostly intact.)

You can scoop the haystacks with a medium cookie scoop or with a tablespoon. Either way, as you portion out the mixture, try to press it a little so that it kind of, sort of, stays together, and then leave an inch or so between the raggedy mounds.

Bake the cookies for 30 to 35 minutes, rotating the pans top to bottom and front to back after 15 minutes, or until they're deeply golden brown and shiny. Transfer the baking sheets to racks and let the cookies cool completely on the sheets; they'll crisp as they cool but remain slightly chewy in the center.

ALMOND CRACKLE COOKIES

6 tablespoons (75 grams) sugar

1 large egg

1¼ cups (125 grams) sliced almonds,
blanched or unblanched

These have just three ingredients — sugar, sliced almonds and an egg — and no reason, other than a baker's faith, to turn into anything delicious. When a Parisian friend, Martine Collet, gave me the recipe, I kept asking if she'd forgotten anything. Maybe a little flour? Maybe a dab of butter? Nope. 1–2–3, and that's it. What you get are crisp, flavorful caramel-almond wafers.

Cookies with as much snap as these should be made only on dry days. But, should the weather shift, you can recrisp them in the oven.

Makes 20 cookies

Position the racks to divide the oven into thirds and preheat it to 325 degrees F.

Depending on how you want to make these, generously spray two regular muffin tins (make sure you're using baker's spray) or line two baking sheets with parchment paper or silicone baking mats. Have a small cookie scoop or a teaspoon at hand.

Whisk the sugar and egg together in a bowl for a minute or so, until well blended and just a bit thick. Add the almonds and whisk until evenly coated with the mixture. You need to use the batter right away — it separates as it stands. In fact, it's good to give the batter a stir or two as you're spooning it out.

Each cookie needs 2 teaspoons of batter. For muffin tins, use your fingers to spread the batter evenly over the base. For free-form cookies, scoop the batter onto the baking sheets, leaving at least 2 inches of space between the mounds of batter, and flatten each mound with the back of a fork.

Bake the muffin-tin cookies for about 17 minutes and the baking-sheet cookies for about 20 minutes, rotating the pans midway through baking. The cookies should be toasted-almond beige, and dry and crackled on top. Transfer the baking sheets or tins to racks and let the cookies cool for about 10 minutes.

To remove the cookies from the muffin tins, work a blunt knife around each cookie, then slip the knife under, tilt it and pop the cookie free. Or carefully lift the free-form cookies with a wide spatula.

STORING

If your kitchen is cool and dry, you can keep these in a tin or paper bag overnight. Keep them longer, and they might soften, a condition easily reversed: Place the cookies on a lined baking sheet and warm them in a 350-degree-F oven for about 6 minutes; cool on the sheet.

VANILLA POLKA DOTS

About ½ cup (96 grams) pearl sugar (sometimes called Swedish sugar)

¼ recipe Do-Almost-Anything Vanilla Cookie Dough (page 492), just made and still soft (see headnote)

There's a lot to be said for simplicity, and these cookies say it elegantly. They are made from the Do-Almost-Anything Vanilla Cookie Dough, rolled into balls, coated with crunchy pearl or Swedish sugar, flattened a bit and baked. There! That's the recipe. It makes a lovely cookie, one that's pretty in a tea-in-the-English-countryside kind of way and delicious in a way best described as snackable.

A word on batch size: This recipe uses one quarter of the Do-Almost-Anything Vanilla Dough. Make the full recipe of the dough then, if you'd like, you can double, triple or quadruple this cookie recipe or use the vanilla dough to make other cookies (see pages 149, 185 and 236).

Makes about 20 cookies

Center a rack in the oven and preheat it to 350 degrees F. Line a baking sheet with parchment paper or a silicone baking mat. Wrap the base of a jam or other flat-bottomed jar in plastic wrap. Put the pearl sugar in a small bowl.

Using a small cookie scoop, scoop out level portions of dough, or use a teaspoon to get rounded spoonfuls. Shape each portion into a ball between your palms. Roll the balls in the sugar to coat and place them on the lined baking sheet about 2 inches apart. Gently press each cookie down with the plastic-wrapped jar to slightly flatten.

Bake for 20 to 22 minutes, rotating the sheet after 11 minutes, or until the cookies are golden brown around the edges and on the bottom. Transfer the sheet to a rack and allow the cookies to rest for 5 minutes before lifting them onto the rack to cool completely.

STORING

The cookies can be kept in a covered container at room temperature for up to 1 week or wrapped airtight and frozen for up to 2 months.

CHOCOLATE-RASPBERRY THUMBPRINTS

¼ recipe Do-Almost-Anything Chocolate Cookie Dough (page 494), chilled (see headnote)

About ½ cup (160 grams) thick raspberry jam, stirred to loosen

⅓ cup (57 grams) semisweet or milk chocolate chips (optional)

This is a classic thumbprint with an optional squiggle of melted chocolate over the jam center. (I use chocolate chips here because they set well.) Since the dough is so easy to work with, this is a great cookie to make with kids. You can use any jam instead of raspberry, if you like.

A word on batch size: This recipe uses one quarter of the Do-Almost-Anything Chocolate Dough. Make the full recipe of the dough then, if you'd like, you can double, triple or quadruple this cookie recipe or use the chocolate dough to make other cookies (see pages 137, 200 and 245).

Makes about 20 cookies

Center a rack in the oven and preheat it to 350 degrees F. Line a baking sheet with parchment paper or a silicone baking mat.

Using a small cookie scoop, scoop out level portions of dough or use a teaspoon to get rounded spoonfuls. Roll each portion of dough between your palms to form smooth balls. Return to the baking sheet. Using the knuckle of your index finger, your thumb or the end of a silicone or wooden spoon, make an indentation in the center of each ball. It's easiest to do this if you steady the ball of dough with the thumb and index fingers of one hand and make the indent with the other. The dough is bound to crack around the edges, and that's fine. Fill each indentation to the top with jam.

Bake for 16 to 18 minutes, rotating the sheet after 9 minutes, or until the cookies feel firm to the touch and the jam is bubbling. Transfer the sheet to a rack and allow the cookies to cool for 5 minutes before lifting them onto the rack to cool completely.

If you want to drizzle the cookies with chocolate, melt the chips — you can do this in the microwave or in a bowl set over a pan of simmering water — stirring occasionally until completely melted and smooth. Drizzle the chocolate over the cookies. Refrigerate to set the chocolate, about 30 minutes, then return to room temperature to serve.

STORING

The cookies will keep in a covered container at room temperature for about 4 days, although they will get softer (not a bad thing). Wrapped airtight, they can be frozen for up to 2 months.

PAIN DE GÊNES BUTTONS

Sliced almonds, for the pan (optional)

2 tablespoons all-purpose flour

1 tablespoon cornstarch

Pinch of fine sea salt

7 ounces (200 grams) soft, pliable almond paste (such as Solo or Odense)

2 large eggs, at room temperature

½ stick (4 tablespoons; 2 ounces; 57 grams) unsalted butter, melted and cooled

1 tablespoon kirsch, dark rum or Grand Marnier or 2 teaspoons pure vanilla extract

See the words *pain de Gênes*, and know that almonds will abound. The cake — never mind that *pain* means "bread" in French — as glorious as it is, commemorates a moment of strife, the 1800 siege of Gênes, or Genoa, when people had to survive on almonds. Eventually the French, under Napoleon's troops, took Genoa from the Austrians, and while neither situation was probably great for the Italians, we've got this recipe, which is usually turned into a round cake or a loaf. Here the batter, baked in mini-muffin tins, makes buttons, small and cute and full of flavor. These are soft, chewy cookies with a texture that's a cross between a sponge and a pound cake. And there's a burst of almond flavor in each bite.

The cookies require a lot of mixing but, if you stop short, you won't get the right texture. Also, check your almond paste before you start. It should be soft and malleable with a texture that tempts you to play with it.

The traditional flavoring for a pain de Gênes is kirsch, but you can use rum, Grand Marnier or vanilla extract. I like to scatter some sliced almonds in the bottom of the muffin tin and then serve the buttons almond side up — optional but nice. As plain as these are, they're quite powerful — don't underestimate them.

Makes 24 cookies

Center a rack in the oven and preheat it to 350 degrees F. Butter or spray two 12-cup or one 24-cup mini-muffin tin(s). If you'd like, scatter a few sliced almonds in the base of each little cup.

Whisk together the flour, cornstarch and salt.

Working with a stand mixer fitted with the paddle attachment, or in a bowl with a hand mixer, beat the almond paste and one of the eggs together on medium speed for 5 minutes. Scrape down the bowl. If you're working with a stand mixer, replace the paddle with the whisk attachment. Turn the mixer to medium speed, add the second egg and beat until incorporated. Turn the mixer up to high and beat for 5 minutes more, scraping down the bowl as needed. You'll have a creamy mixture, rather like mayonnaise. Stir a few spoonfuls of the

STORING

The buttons will keep in a covered container at room temperature for up to 3 days, but their texture is best the day they are made. Packed airtight, they can be frozen for up to 2 months.

batter into the cooled butter (this will make it easier to incorporate the butter when needed).

Working on low speed, beat in the kirsch, other alcohol or vanilla, followed by the dry ingredients. Stop as soon as the flour disappears into the batter. Switch to a flexible spatula and fold in the butter mixture. Divide the batter evenly among the mini-muffin tins.

Bake the buttons for 11 to 13 minutes, or until the cookies are puffed, lightly golden and spring back when gently pressed. A tester inserted into the center of a button should come out clean. Unmold the cookies — if there are a few stragglers, rap the muffin tin against the counter and they'll tumble out — and place them almond side up on racks to cool until just warm or room temperature.

WHITE CHOCOLATE AND POPPY SEED COOKIES

It's surprising how much flavor poppy seeds have. If you're not familiar with them, you might think that they're just tossed into a pastry for a little crunch. But they actually have a rich flavor that builds with each bite. Here the seeds are in both the cookie and on top. There is vanilla, one of poppy seeds' best friends, in the dough, as well as in the white chocolate that, like the seeds, is both in and on the cookies. It's a wonderful combination.

I have loved poppy seeds ever since I was a little girl, when my grandmother brought me sugar cookies sprinkled with them. She was able to go to the market and have them freshly ground for her (which she did when she was making strudel). These days, poppy seeds aren't as popular, and because of that, freshness is often a question. If you can buy your seeds in bulk from a spice store rather than from the supermarket, where they're stocked in (often dusty) jars, so much the better. Poppy seeds are rich in oil and that oil can go rancid, so store the seeds in a sealed container in the freezer and always taste a few before using them.

A word on batch size: This recipe uses one quarter of the Do-Almost-Anything Vanilla Dough. Make the full recipe of the dough then, if you'd like, you can double, triple or quadruple this cookie recipe or use the vanilla dough to make other cookies (see pages 149, 178 and 236).

Makes about 20 cookies

TO MAKE THE COOKIES: Use a sturdy flexible spatula to blend the white chocolate and poppy seeds into the dough.

Gather the dough together and shape it into a disk. Working between pieces of parchment paper, roll the dough to a thickness of ¼ inch. Slide the dough, still between the paper, onto a baking sheet and freeze for at least 1 hour, or refrigerate for at least 3 hours.

GETTING READY TO BAKE: Center a rack in the oven and preheat it to 350 degrees F. Line a baking sheet with parchment paper or a silicone baking mat.

FOR THE COOKIES
⅓ cup (56 grams) finely chopped white chocolate (bar or chips)
1 tablespoon poppy seeds
¼ recipe Do-Almost-Anything Vanilla Cookie Dough (page 492), just made and still soft (see headnote)

FOR THE TOPPING
⅓ cup (56 grams) white chocolate chips
Poppy seeds, for sprinkling

Peel away the paper on both sides of the dough and return the dough to one sheet. Using a 2-inch-diameter cutter, cut out as many cookies as you can. Place them on the lined baking sheet about 1½ inches apart. Gather the scraps together, re-roll them between paper and chill.

Bake for 19 to 21 minutes, rotating the baking sheet after 10 minutes, or until the cookies are golden around the edges and on the bottom. Transfer the sheet to a rack and let the cookies rest for 5 minutes before lifting them onto the rack to cool completely.

Repeat with the rest of the dough, making sure your baking sheet is cool.

TO TOP THE COOKIES: Melt the chocolate in the microwave — be extremely careful, because white chocolate burns quickly — or in a bowl over a pan of gently simmering water. Using a small icing spatula, coat the tops of the cookies with the warm melted chocolate, then sprinkle with poppy seeds. Refrigerate just to set the chocolate, about 30 minutes.

STORING

The cookies will keep in a covered container at room temperature for up to 4 days. They can be packed airtight and frozen for up to 2 months.

EVERY-WAY SHORTBREAD FANS: THE LEMON–POPPY SEED VERSION

There are so many reasons to love shortbread as much as I do and among them are its almost universal appeal and almost infinite variability. Oh, and the ingredients are ones you've almost always got on hand. The cookies are quick to put together — you can have them in the oven in about 15 minutes. And they're easy.

The shortbread clan is a big one, and each branch of the family is different. Some shortbreads are made with eggs (like the French Vanilla Sablés, page 332); some are made without (like these and the Fennel-Orange Shortbread Wedges, page 415); some are made with rice flour (like the Rose-Hibiscus Shortbread Fans, page 191); some are rolled and cut; and some are pressed into a pan, pricked, baked and sliced into wedges. These are of the press-and-prick variety and they're beautiful; even more beautiful with a little icing.

I'm giving you a recipe for lemon–poppy seed shortbread, but take a look at Playing Around for a few other ideas, and forage in your pantry. Next time, you might want to use cinnamon or cardamom, sesame seeds or chopped walnuts, chocolate chips or espresso, butterscotch bits or candied orange zest.

Makes 12 cookies

TO MAKE THE SHORTBREAD: Center a rack in the oven and preheat it to 350 degrees F. Butter an 8-inch round cake pan, dust the interior with flour and tap out the excess. Or lightly butter a 9-inch glass pan or pie plate, line it with a parchment paper circle and dust with flour.

Toss the sugar and salt into the bowl of a stand mixer, or in a large bowl in which you can use a hand mixer. Add the lemon zest and rub the ingredients together with your fingertips until the sugar is moist and fragrant. If using a stand mixer, fit it with the paddle attachment. Add the butter to the bowl and beat on medium speed until the mixture is smooth, about 2 minutes. Beat in the

FOR THE SHORTBREAD

⅓ cup (67 grams) sugar

¼ teaspoon fine sea salt

Finely grated zest of 1 lemon

1 stick (8 tablespoons; 4 ounces; 113 grams) unsalted butter, cut into chunks, at room temperature

1 teaspoon pure vanilla extract

¼ teaspoon pure lemon oil or extract

1 cup plus 2 tablespoons (151 grams) all-purpose flour

1 tablespoon poppy seeds

FOR THE ICING (OPTIONAL)

½ cup (60 grams) confectioners' sugar, sifted

1 to 2 tablespoons milk or freshly squeezed lemon juice

Poppy seeds or sanding sugar, for sprinkling (optional)

STORING

Packed in a tightly covered container, the shortbread will keep for at least 1 week. If you didn't ice the cookies, they can be wrapped airtight and frozen for up to 2 months.

Vanilla Shortbread. Omit the lemon zest, oil or extract and poppy seeds and increase the vanilla extract to 2 teaspoons. Ice as directed, if you'd like, but use sanding sugar, not poppy seeds.

Espresso Shortbread. Omit the lemon zest, oil or extract and poppy seeds and beat 1½ teaspoons ground espresso into the butter-sugar mixture. When the shortbread is cool, dust with a combination of cocoa and confectioners' sugar.

Orange Shortbread. Omit the lemon zest and oil or extract and add the zest of 1 orange or 2 tangerines or clementines and ¼ teaspoon orange oil or extract. Keep the poppy seeds, if you'd like — they're nice with orange — or add some very finely chopped candied orange peel (page 474).

Shortbread with Nuts or Chips. Flavor the dough as you'd like and then add ½ cup toasted chopped nuts and/or ½ cup chopped chocolate or mini chocolate chips. Or, if you use an add-in like toffee bits, chop them first — the shortbread isn't really thick enough to handle chunks.

vanilla and lemon oil or extract. Turn off the mixer, add the flour all at once and mix on low speed. When the flour is incorporated, add the poppy seeds and continue to mix on low until you've got a bowl of soft, moist curds and crumbs, about 2 minutes. Squeeze a few curds, and if they hold together, you're there. (You don't want to mix the dough until it comes together uniformly).

Turn the crumbs out into the pan and pat them down evenly. To smooth the top, "roll" the crumbs using a spice bottle as a rolling pin. (You can also tamp down the crumbs with the bottom of a small measuring cup.) There's no need to be overly forceful; the point is to knit the crumbs together and compress them. Using the tines of a dinner fork and pressing straight down so that you hear the metal tap against the pan, prick lines of holes in the dough to create a dozen wedges. Finish by pressing the bottom of the tines horizontally around the edges of the dough, as though you were crimping a piecrust, to create a decorative edge. Alternatively, you can make shortbread fingers by pricking a cross in the dough to divide it into quarters and then, working from the top down, pricking vertical lines — the edge pieces will be odd-shaped, but that's just fine. Or you can make squares or diamonds; again you'll have a few odd pieces.

Bake the shortbread for about 25 minutes, rotating the pan after 12 minutes, or until the top feels firm to the touch and the edges have a tinge of color; the center should remain fairly pale. Transfer the pan to a rack and allow it to rest for 3 minutes. If the holes that defined the wedges or other shape have closed, re-prick them. Carefully run a table knife between the sides of the pan and the shortbread and even more carefully turn the shortbread over onto the rack; peel away the paper, if you used it. Then invert onto a cutting board and, using a long sturdy knife or a bench scraper, cut the shortbread along the pricked lines; lift the pieces back onto the rack and allow them to cool before icing or serving.

TO MAKE THE ICING AND FINISH THE COOKIES (OPTIONAL): Put the confectioners' sugar in a small bowl, add 1 tablespoon milk or lemon juice and stir to blend. If the icing is too thick to brush, spread or drizzle smoothly and easily, add more milk or juice drop by drop. You can just drizzle the icing over each wedge or, using a pastry brush or a small icing spatula, you can ice each wedge, covering it entirely or leaving the borders bare. Sprinkle a few poppy seeds or grains of sugar on each fan, if you'd like, and let the icing set.

ROSE-HIBISCUS SHORTBREAD FANS

Thanks to my friendship with Pierre Hermé, the fabulous French pastry chef, I fell in love with the flavor of rose in pastry. It was Pierre who began using rose in his desserts about twenty years ago, and now you find it everywhere in France and in everything from granola and yogurt to the fanciest cakes. It's a haunting flavor and one that blends beautifully with red berries and another red flower, hibiscus. There's just one caveat: A flavor as strong and aromatic as rose (particularly when it's an extract) must whisper — never proclaim — its presence. Too much rose is really too much. Actually, too much hibiscus is not a good thing either. Go easy on both flavorings, though, and you'll have an elegant cookie.

The key to the delightfully crumbly texture, the kind you get with Scottish shortbread, is rice flour, which has little gluten and no distinguishable flavor; it's there just for the sandiness it imparts.

I like to press the dough into a round cake pan, then cut the baked cookies into wedges, ice them and sprinkle each shortbread fan with a few grains of rose-colored sanding sugar. It's a girly look, but it's so pretty and particularly welcome on a chilly day when you're yearning for spring.

A word on special ingredients: My favorite rose extract is made by Star Kay White. If you can't find it, you can substitute an equal amount of rose water (Nielsen-Massey sells a lovely one). If you can't find a pure hibiscus tea (I use one from the Wild Hibiscus Flower Co.), you can use Celestial Seasonings Red Zinger. Finally, the rice flour should be white rice flour, not sweet or sticky rice flour; Bob's Red Mill sells it. If you'd prefer a recipe that uses only all-purpose flour, see Playing Around.

Makes 12 cookies

TO MAKE THE SHORTBREAD: Center a rack in the oven and preheat it to 350 degrees F. Butter an 8-inch round cake pan, dust with flour and tap out the excess.

FOR THE SHORTBREAD

¾ cup (102 grams) all-purpose flour

½ cup (85 grams) white rice flour (see headnote)

⅓ cup (67 grams) sugar

2 teaspoons hibiscus tea leaves

1 stick (8 tablespoons; 4 ounces; 113 grams) unsalted butter, cut into chunks, at room temperature

¼ teaspoon fine sea salt

½ teaspoon pure vanilla extract

¼ teaspoon pure rose extract (see headnote)

FOR THE ICING (OPTIONAL)

½ cup (60 grams) confectioners' sugar, sifted

1 to 2 tablespoons milk

Rose-colored sanding sugar, for dusting

STORING

The shortbread will keep for at least 1 week in a tightly covered container at room temperature. If you omit the icing, you can freeze the shortbread for up to 2 months.

All-Purpose Shortbread. Omit the rice flour and use 1 cup plus 2 tablespoons all-purpose flour.

Whisk both flours together.

Toss the sugar and tea into a stand mixer, or into a large bowl in which you can use a hand mixer. Rub the ingredients together with your fingertips until fragrant. If using a stand mixer, fit it with the paddle attachment. Add the butter and salt to the bowl and beat on medium speed until the mixture is smooth, about 2 minutes. Beat in the vanilla and rose extracts. Turn off the mixer, add the flour all at once and mix on low speed. After 3 to 4 minutes, you'll have a bowl of soft, moist curds and crumbs. Squeeze a few curds, and if they hold together, you're good to go. (You don't want to mix the dough until it comes together uniformly.)

Turn the crumbs into the pan and pat them down evenly. If you'd like to smooth the top, "roll" the crumbs using a spice bottle as a rolling pin. (You can also tap down the crumbs with the bottom of a small measuring cup.) Be firm but not forceful; the point is to knit the crumbs together and just lightly compress them. Using the tines of a dinner fork and pressing down so that you hear the metal tap against the pan, prick lines of holes in the dough to create a dozen wedges. Finish by pressing the bottom of the tines horizontally around the edges of the dough, as though you were crimping a piecrust.

Bake the shortbread for 25 to 27 minutes, rotating the pan after 15 minutes, or until the top feels firm to the touch and the edges have a tinge of color; the center should remain fairly pale. Transfer the pan to a rack and allow to rest for 5 minutes. Prick the holes you made again, then carefully run a table knife between the pan and the shortbread and even more carefully turn the shortbread over onto the rack. Then invert it onto a cutting board and use a long sturdy knife or a bench scraper to cut the shortbread along the pricked lines. Lift the pieces back onto the rack and allow the fans to cool before icing or serving.

TO MAKE THE ICING AND FINISH THE COOKIES (OPTIONAL): Put the confectioners' sugar in a small bowl, add 1 tablespoon milk and stir to blend. If the icing is too thick to brush or spread smoothly and easily, add more milk drop by drop. Using a pastry brush or a small icing spatula, ice each shortbread wedge. You can ice the whole wedge or leave a thin border, my preference. Or just swipe one long side of each fan with icing. Sprinkle a few grains of sanding sugar on each fan and let the icing set.

PECAN-BUTTERSCOTCH SHORTBREADS

1¾ cups (238 grams) all-purpose flour

¼ cup (32 grams) cornstarch

2 sticks (8 ounces; 226 grams) unsalted butter, cut into chunks, at room temperature

½ cup (100 grams) packed light brown sugar

¼ cup (30 grams) confectioners' sugar

½ teaspoon fine sea salt

2 tablespoons Scotch whisky

2 teaspoons pure vanilla extract

⅔ cup (80 grams) chopped pecans, toasted and cooled

3 ounces (85 grams) best-quality milk or white chocolate, finely chopped

---

STORING

The dough can be kept, covered, in the refrigerator for up to 2 days or wrapped airtight and frozen for up to 2 months. The baked cookies will keep in a covered container at room temperature for up to 4 days.

There are certain ingredients that can only be described as warm. For me, brown sugar and vanilla are warm flavors; butter is too; and nuts, if they're toasted, can be as well. All of these ingredients, along with Scotch whisky and best-quality milk or white chocolate, are in these cookies, and they're what make these tender, just a bit chewy shortbreads so different from others. I specify best-quality for the chocolate because unless you use a milk chocolate that has at least 30 percent cacao or a white chocolate that has pure cocoa butter, you won't get the warmth that's the hallmark here. If you can find a chocolate like Valrhona's Caramelia or Dulcey, with rich caramel flavors blended into them, so much the better.

Makes about 40 cookies

Sift the flour and cornstarch together.

Working with a stand mixer fitted with the paddle attachment, or in a large bowl with a hand mixer, beat the butter, brown sugar, confectioners' sugar and salt together on medium-low speed until smooth, about 4 minutes; scrape the sides and bottom of the bowl as needed. Add the Scotch and vanilla and beat for 1 minute more. Stop the mixer, add the dry ingredients all at once and pulse until the risk of flying flour has passed. Working on low speed, mix the dough until the flour and cornstarch are almost incorporated. Add the pecans and chocolate and mix in. The dough will be soft and it may have balled up around the beater(s). If there are spots of dry ingredients in the bottom of the bowl, scrape them up and stir them into the dough with a flexible spatula.

Turn the dough out and gather it together. Divide in half and shape each half into a disk.

Working with one piece of dough at a time, roll the dough between pieces of parchment paper to a thickness of ¼ inch. Slide the parchment-sandwiched dough onto a baking sheet — you can stack the slabs — and freeze for at least 1 hour, or refrigerate for at least 2 hours.

PLAYING AROUND

The cookies have a natural affinity for chocolate, milk or dark, but it's dulce de leche (page 486) that really brings out their flavors. You can put a bowl of it on the table and let everyone either dip or spread some on the cookies, or you can use it to dress up the cookies in the kitchen. Sandwich the cookies with the caramel and chill them for 30 minutes before serving.

GETTING READY TO BAKE: Center a rack in the oven and preheat it to 350 degrees F. Butter or spray two regular muffin tins and have a 2-inch-diameter cookie cutter at hand.

Working with one sheet of dough at a time, peel away both pieces of parchment paper and put the dough back on one piece of paper. Cut the dough and drop the rounds into the tins. The dough won't fill the molds now, but it will once baked. Save the scraps.

Bake for 10 to 12 minutes, or until the cookies are toasty brown and set around the edges. Transfer the tins to a cooling rack and allow the cookies to rest for at least 20 minutes, or until they reach room temperature, before unmolding.

Continue with the remainder of the dough, making certain that the muffin tins are cool. Gather the scraps together, re-roll, chill, cut and bake.

CHOCOLATE-OATMEAL BISCOFF COOKIES

A radio host once asked me if I ever take shortcuts or use ready-made ingredients when I bake. "Well," I said, "I always keep Biscoff Cookie Spread on hand." His response: "That's not a ready-made — that's a necessity for life!"

Biscoff, which is made with speculoos cookies, has just the right amount of spice to keep you dipping into the jar for more and just the right texture for swirling on toast or grilled cake or sandwiching cookies. You can use it the way you would peanut butter or Nutella, its international cousins. (In fact, if you'd like, you can use either peanut butter or Nutella in place of the Biscoff.)

In these cookies, which have oatmeal, cocoa and chocolate chips, the Biscoff isn't obvious, but it is necessary. It's part of what gives these small sweets their great texture — crispy around the edges, a little less crisp in the middle — and their delightfully off-balance flavor. You think it's all about the chocolate and then there's the spice and then it's just too good to spend time pondering.

A word on Biscoff: As good as my homemade cookie spread is (page 484), these cookies should only be made with Biscoff or another commercial brand.

A word on size: I like to make these small — they bake to about 2 inches in diameter — but you can make them smaller (use 1 teaspoon of dough for each cookie) or larger (use a medium cookie scoop, with a capacity of 1½ tablespoons). Lessen or increase the baking time by a couple of minutes.

Makes about 50 cookies

Whisk the oats, flour, cocoa and baking soda together.

Working with a stand mixer fitted with the paddle attachment, or in a large bowl with a hand mixer, beat the butter, Biscoff, both sugars and the salt together on medium speed until smooth, about 4 minutes. Beat in the egg

1½ cups (120 grams) old-fashioned rolled oats (not quick-cooking)

½ cup (68 grams) all-purpose flour

¼ cup (21 grams) unsweetened cocoa powder

½ teaspoon baking soda

1 stick (8 tablespoons; 4 ounces; 113 grams) unsalted butter, cut into chunks, at room temperature

½ cup (120 grams) Biscoff Cookie Spread

½ cup (100 grams) sugar

½ cup (100 grams) packed light brown sugar

¼ teaspoon fine sea salt

1 large egg, at room temperature

½ cup (85 grams) chopped semisweet or bittersweet chocolate, or chocolate chips

and then beat for a minute. Turn the mixer off, add the dry ingredients all at once, pulse the mixer a few times to start the blending and then mix on low speed only until they almost disappear into the dough. Add the chocolate and mix.

Wrap the dough well and refrigerate it for at least 2 hours.

GETTING READY TO BAKE: Position the racks to divide the oven into thirds and preheat it to 350 degrees F. Line two baking sheets with parchment paper or silicone baking mats. Wrap the base of a jam or other flat-bottomed jar in plastic wrap.

Using a small cookie scoop, scoop out level portions of dough or use a teaspoon to get rounded spoonfuls. Roll each piece of dough into a ball between your palms and place on the sheets, leaving an inch or so between the balls. Gently press each cookie into a round with the jar.

Bake the cookies for 11 to 12 minutes, rotating the sheets top to bottom and front to back after 6 minutes, or until they are just barely firm around the edges; the centers will seem unbaked. Transfer the sheets to racks and allow the cookies to rest for 3 minutes before carefully lifting them onto the racks to cool completely; they'll firm as they cool.

Repeat with the remaining dough, always starting with cool baking sheets.

STORING

The dough can be wrapped airtight and refrigerated for up to 2 days or frozen for up to 2 months. Tightly covered, the cookies will keep for about 5 days at room temperature; they will become crisper, but that's fine. The cookies can be wrapped airtight and frozen for up to 2 months.

CHOCOLATE-PECAN COOKIES

FOR THE COOKIES

⅓ cup (40 grams) finely chopped pecans, preferably toasted

¼ recipe Do-Almost-Anything Chocolate Cookie Dough (page 494), just made and still soft (see headnote)

FOR THE TOPPING

¾ cup (90 grams) coarsely chopped pecans

4 teaspoons sugar

2 to 3 teaspoons egg white (from 1 egg — stir to break it up before measuring)

The simple trick of mixing nuts with sugar and egg whites to create a no-fuss meringue topping makes plain (but thoroughly delicious) chocolate cookies party-plate worthy, cookie-swap worthy and Christmas-worthy too. The cookie is built on my Do-Almost-Anything Chocolate Cookie Dough.

A word on batch size: This recipe uses one quarter of the Do-Almost-Anything Chocolate Dough. Make the full recipe of the dough then, if you'd like, you can double, triple or quadruple this cookie recipe or use the chocolate dough to make other cookies (see pages 137, 180 and 245).

Makes about 20 cookies

TO MAKE THE COOKIES: Use a sturdy flexible spatula to blend the chopped pecans evenly into the dough.

Gather the dough together and shape into a disk. Place the dough between pieces of parchment paper and roll it to a thickness of ¼ inch. Slide the dough, still between the paper, onto a baking sheet and freeze for at least 1 hour, or refrigerate for at least 3 hours.

GETTING READY TO BAKE: Center a rack in the oven and preheat it to 350 degrees F. Line a baking sheet with parchment paper or a silicone baking mat.

TO MAKE THE TOPPING: Mix the pecans and sugar together in a small bowl. Add 2 teaspoons of the egg white and mix with a fork or your fingers (my choice) until blended; add more of the white only if some of the nuts are still dry. You want each nut to glisten with egg white and sugar. It's not a tragedy if you have too much white, but the cookies are prettier when there isn't excess.

TO FINISH THE COOKIES: Peel away the paper on both sides of the dough and return the dough to one piece of paper. Using a 2-inch-diameter cutter, cut out as many cookies as you can. Place them on the lined baking sheet about 1½ inches apart. Gather the scraps together, re-roll them between paper and chill.

Spoon some topping onto each cookie and use the back of the spoon or a small offset spatula to spread it, leaving a narrow border. If you'd like, instead of spreading the topping, you can mound it. A pouf of nuts makes this cookie look dramatic.

Bake for 18 to 20 minutes, rotating the sheet after 10 minutes, or until the cookies feel firm to the touch. Transfer the sheet to a rack and let the cookies rest for 5 minutes before lifting them onto the rack to cool completely.

Repeat with the rest of the dough, making sure your baking sheet is cool.

DOUBLE-BUCKWHEAT
DOUBLE-CHOCOLATE COOKIES

I doubled up on the two most important ingredients in these cookies, and I even doubled up on how you craft them. There are two kinds of buckwheat in the cookies, buckwheat flour and kasha (buckwheat groats), and two kinds of chocolate, cocoa powder and dark chocolate. There are two different ways to make them: slice-and-bake or arts-and-crafts free-form.

The buckwheat is the charmer here. The flour makes the cookies tender and gives them a subtle nuttiness that only buckwheat habitués will identify. No one will guess there's kasha in them, but it gives the cookies crunch and a fuller flavor than you'd think you'd get from such tiny nuggets. The kasha's got a fabulous texture too. It's a crunch-lover's dream. (But you must use granulated kasha, such as Wolff's, in this recipe; whole or cracked kasha is tooth-breakingly hard.)

If you roll the dough into logs, chill and slice and bake them, you'll get cookies that are firm around the very edges and cakey, soft and almost melty everywhere else. If you roll the dough out free-form, bake it and cut it any which way the instant it comes out of the oven, your cookies will be tender through and through. (Only the thinner edges of the free-form shape crisp.) Whatever you choose, these taste better and look prettier with a last-minute sprinkle of sanding sugar and flake salt.

Makes about 80 free-form or 60 round cookies

If you're going to make free-form cookies, position the racks to divide the oven into thirds and preheat it to 350 degrees F. (If you'll be making slice-and-bake cookies, preheat the oven after the logs have chilled.)

Whisk both flours and the cocoa powder together. (If the cocoa is lumpy, sift the dry ingredients, then whisk to blend.)

Working with a stand mixer fitted with the paddle attachment, or in a large bowl with a hand mixer, beat the butter, both sugars and the salt together on medium speed until smooth, about 3 minutes. Drop in the yolks and beat for

1²/₃ cups (227 grams) all-purpose flour

1 cup (120 grams) buckwheat flour

¼ cup (21 grams) unsweetened cocoa powder

2 sticks (8 ounces; 226 grams) unsalted butter, cut into chunks, at room temperature

½ cup (100 grams) sugar

¼ cup (50 grams) packed light brown sugar

1 teaspoon fine sea salt

2 large egg yolks, at room temperature

1 teaspoon pure vanilla extract

¼ cup (45 grams) kasha, preferably Wolff's medium granulation (see headnote)

4 ounces (113 grams) bittersweet chocolate, finely chopped

2 teaspoons sanding sugar, mixed with 1 teaspoon flake sea salt, such as Maldon, for sprinkling

If you'd like, you can freeze
the dough, either rolled out
or shaped into logs, for up to
2 months; be certain to wrap
it well. The logs can also be
refrigerated for up to 3 days.
The cookies can be baked (or
sliced and baked) straight from
the freezer; add a minute or two
to the baking time. The cookies
will keep covered at room
temperature for about 4 days;
they can be frozen, well wrapped,
for up to 2 months.

another minute, scraping the bowl as needed, then add the vanilla. Turn the mixer off, add the dry ingredients all at once and mix on low speed until they are almost incorporated. This takes a minute more than you might think it should; at first the dough looks crumbly and then it starts to darken, moisten and come together. Mix in the kasha and chopped chocolate. Use a large flexible spatula to give the dough another few turns and mix in any loose ingredients.

Turn the dough out and divide in half.

TO MAKE FREE-FORM COOKIES: Shape each piece of dough into a disk. One at a time, place between pieces of parchment paper and roll out to a thickness of ¼ inch. It's the thickness, not the shape, that matters. (I usually go for a rough oval or round.) Peel away both pieces of paper from one piece of dough, then return the dough to one piece of paper and slide it onto a baking sheet (if you don't loosen the bottom paper, the dough will curl during baking). Repeat with the second piece of dough. Sprinkle the dough with the sugar-salt mixture.

Bake for 14 to 15 minutes, rotating the sheets top to bottom and front to back at the midway mark, or until the cookies are set — the edges will be more set than the center, which might still have a bit of give when gently prodded. Slide each cookie slab, still on the parchment, onto the counter. Using a pizza wheel or a knife, cut the big cookie into as many cookies of whatever shape you like. I cut it into strips about 1 inch wide and then cut these diagonally so that I end up with diamond-shaped cookies. Slide the cookies, still on the paper, onto a rack to cool to room temperature.

TO MAKE SLICE-AND-BAKE COOKIES: Roll each piece of dough into a log that's 12 inches long (see page 12 for tips on log-rolling). Wrap well and freeze for at least 1 hour, or refrigerate for at least 2 hours.

When you're ready to bake, preheat the oven as on page 203. Slice each log ⅓ inch thick and place the cookies about an inch apart on two baking sheets lined with parchment paper or silicone mats. Sprinkle with the sugar-salt mixture.

Bake for 11 to 12 minutes, rotating the sheets top to bottom and front to back at the midway mark, until the cookies are firm around the edges and give slightly when pressed in the center. Transfer the cookies to racks to cool completely.

MELODY COOKIES

2¼ cups (306 grams) all-purpose flour

⅓ cup (28 grams) unsweetened cocoa powder (see headnote)

¼ teaspoon baking soda

2 sticks (8 ounces; 226 grams) unsalted butter, cut into chunks, at room temperature

¾ cup (150 grams) sugar

¾ teaspoon fine sea salt

1 teaspoon pure vanilla extract

1 large egg white

Sanding or granulated sugar, for sprinkling

STORING

The best way to freeze Melodies is unbaked: Cut out the cookies, wrap them airtight, freeze for up to 2 months and bake them straight from the freezer, adding a minute or so to the baking time if needed. The baked cookies will be good for a week or more kept at room temperature. They can be wrapped airtight and frozen for up to 2 months, but the sugar topping might melt.

Once upon a time, the Nabisco company made a cookie called Melody. They were large and round — I'm told by a cookie-dunker that they were just the right size to fit into a glass of milk — had scalloped edges and were topped with sparkly sugar. They were thin, crunchy and more cocoa-flavored than chocolatey. They were beloved. But evidently not enough, because sometime in the 1970s, production ceased. Search — I did — and you'll find eulogies to the Melody, but no recipe. Until now.

After I'd made many cookies using the Do-Almost-Anything Chocolate Cookie Dough, my husband said, "There's something about these that reminds me of Melody cookies. The flavor is so similar, but the texture is off. If they had some snap, maybe, . . . " Turns out, he was right: Crunch was the missing note!

Are they just the same as the Melodies of childhood? I don't know. However, these deliver the childish delight of a Melody and the possibility of more grown-up pleasures. My smaller cookies are still a good size for dunking into milk, but they're also right for dipping into a shot of espresso. And if you love cookies and ice cream (and of course you do), you might want to use these to make ice cream sandwiches. They not only make good sandwiches, they make pretty ones.

A word on the cocoa: I've found that cookies made with dark cocoa, such as Valrhona, come closest to tasting like the Melody of memory.

Makes about 55 cookies

Sift the flour, cocoa and baking soda together.

Working with a stand mixer fitted with the paddle attachment, or in a large bowl with a hand mixer, beat the butter, sugar and salt together on medium speed until smooth and creamy, about 3 minutes; scrape down the bowl as needed. Reduce the mixer speed to low and blend in the vanilla, followed by the egg white, and beat for 1 to 2 minutes. The white might curdle the dough and make it slippery — keep going; it will smooth out when the flour goes in. Turn

Peppermint Melody Cookies. Chocolate and crunch are peppermint's pals, so you might want to add a drop (or two, at most) of pure peppermint oil or extract to the dough when you add the vanilla.

the mixer off, add half the flour-cocoa mixture and pulse the machine to get the blending going, then mix on low only until the dry ingredients are almost incorporated. Scrape down the bowl and repeat with the remaining flour-cocoa mixture, this time beating just until the dry ingredients disappear and the dough comes together.

Scrape the dough onto a work surface, divide it in half and shape each half into a disk. Working with one piece of dough at a time, sandwich the dough between pieces of parchment paper and roll out to a thickness of ⅛ inch. Slide the dough onto a baking sheet — you can stack the slabs — and freeze for at least 1 hour, or refrigerate for at least 2 hours.

GETTING READY TO BAKE: Position the racks to divide the oven into thirds and preheat it to 350 degrees F. Line two baking sheets with parchment paper or silicone baking mats. I use a 2-inch-diameter scalloped cookie cutter, but you can make the cookies smaller or larger if you'd like; the baking times will be almost the same, though the yield, of course, will change.

Working with one piece of dough at a time, peel away both pieces of paper and return the dough to one piece of paper. Cut out as many cookies as you can. Place them on the lined baking sheets, leaving a generous inch between rounds; reserve the scraps. Sprinkle the cookies with sanding or granulated sugar.

Gather together the scraps from both pieces of dough, re-roll them between paper until ⅛ inch thick and chill thoroughly.

Bake the cookies for 15 to 17 minutes, rotating the pans front to back and top to bottom at the midway mark. The cookies are done when they feel firm to the touch around the edges and give only the least little bit when poked in the center. Remove the baking sheets from the oven and let the cookies rest on the sheets for about 2 minutes before transferring them to cooling racks with a wide spatula. Let cool completely.

Cut out and bake the remaining dough, always using cool sheets.

GRAHAM CRACKER COOKIES

It only takes a tiny nibble to know that these are very special graham cookies. They're not exactly like the packaged cookies (they're decidedly better), but they have that particular graham cracker texture — both crisp and crumbly. They're pleasantly brittle (the effect of the baking soda), yet meltable when dunked in milk or tea. They've got that distinctive graham flavor — it comes from whole wheat flour, which in earlier times was referred to as graham. I don't understand why I get such a kick out of creating homemade versions of boxed cookies, but I do, and I think you will too. Just be sure to keep the dough thin. These have a tendency to rise and puff in the oven, and if they start out thick, they'll end up too thick. Part of the pleasure of the texture comes from their being slim.

I have purposely kept these on the lower end of sweet. With less sugar than the store-boughts, you get the full flavor of the wheat and honey. It also gives you the chance to pair these with savories like cheese and red wine. If you want to go full-out savory, try the Garam Grahams (page 391).

Makes about 48 cookies

Stir the milk, honey and vanilla together in a measuring cup with a spout.

Put both flours, the baking soda, cinnamon and salt in a food processor and pulse a few times to mix. Add the brown sugar and pulse to incorporate. Scatter the cold butter cubes over the dry ingredients and pulse in long spurts just until the butter is cut in and the mixture resembles coarse meal. (If you overmix and a few clumps form, it's fine.) Pour the liquid ingredients into the bowl while pulsing in long spurts. Keep pulsing until the dough comes together and starts to pull away from the sides of the bowl; it will almost form a ball on the blade. Lift off the lid, remove the blade and, using a flexible spatula, stir in any ingredients that might have escaped blending.

Have four large pieces of parchment paper and some flour for dusting at hand.

Sprinkle some flour over one piece of the paper. Divide the dough — which will be very soft and sticky — in half and place one piece on the paper. Shape

1/3 cup (80 ml) whole milk, at room temperature

1/4 cup (60 ml) honey

1 teaspoon pure vanilla extract

1 3/4 cups (238 grams) all-purpose flour, plus extra for dusting

3/4 cup (102 grams) whole wheat flour

1 teaspoon baking soda

3/4 teaspoon ground cinnamon

1/2 teaspoon fine sea salt

3/4 cup (150 grams) packed light brown sugar

7 tablespoons (3 1/2 ounces; 99 grams) cold unsalted butter, cut into 14 pieces

FOR SPRINKLING (OPTIONAL)

1/4 cup (50 grams) sugar

2 teaspoons ground cinnamon

The rolled-out dough can be refrigerated for up to 3 days or, wrapped airtight, frozen for up to 2 months. The baked cookies can be kept in a plastic bag or tightly covered container for at least 2 weeks or frozen for up to 2 months. If the cookies get soggy — they're sensitive to humidity — pop them into a 350-degree-F oven for 3 minutes; cool them on the baking sheet.

it into a rough rectangle, sprinkle the top with flour, cover with another piece of paper and roll the dough out until it's roughly 12 x 8 inches and ⅛ inch thick. (The thickness is more important than the size here.) Repeat with the second piece of dough. Stack the dough, still between paper, on a baking sheet and freeze for at least 3 hours. Because the dough is very sticky, it needs a very good chill before you can work with it.

GETTING READY TO BAKE: Position the racks to divide the oven into thirds and preheat it to 350 degrees F. Set out a ruler, a pizza wheel (or knife) and a table fork.

Remove one piece of dough — leave the other piece in the freezer — peel off both pieces of paper and return the dough to one piece. Trim the edges of the dough so that they're as straight as you can get them (or if you don't care about symmetry and just want a bunch of tasty cookies, leave the ragged edges). Using the pizza wheel or knife, cut into 2-inch-wide strips. Don't remove the strips; leave them on the paper. Now cut the strips into squares, again leaving them on the paper. (I like the 2-x-2-inch size, but you can cut whatever size or shape you want.) Prick the dough all over with the fork. If you trimmed the edges, gather the scraps of dough and reserve. Slide the dough, still on paper, onto a baking sheet and freeze (or refrigerate) while you work on the second piece of dough. (If you have dough scraps, combine them, re-roll, chill, cut and then bake them.) Stir the optional sugar and cinnamon together and lightly sprinkle the dough with the mix.

Bake for 18 to 20 minutes, rotating the pans top to bottom and front to back after about 10 minutes. The cookies should be deeply golden brown, lightly puffed — the lines you cut will have baked together — and only a little springy to the touch. Transfer the baking sheets to a rack and cut along the original lines (taking care not to mar your baking sheet). When the cookies have reached room temperature, break them apart.

SALT-AND-PEPPER
SUGAR-AND-SPICE GALETTES

These are definitely winter cookies, but not traditional Christmas cookies, despite the spices. First you taste the cinnamon, the hint of ginger
and cloves, and you think you know what's in store. But then comes the
salt — enough to make it unmissable — and the coarsely ground black
pepper. I love the effect these have on the unsuspecting: puzzlement followed by pleasure. I also love that they're substantial: They're thick cookies, which is why they're called *galettes*, French for "pucks."

I make these with a combination of all-purpose and almond flours — the
latter brings a welcome crumbliness — but you can omit the almond flour,
if you'd like, and increase the all-purpose flour to 2¼ cups (306 grams).

Makes about 36 cookies

Whisk the flour, cinnamon, salt, pepper, ginger and cloves together.

Working with a stand mixer fitted with the paddle attachment, or in a large
bowl with a hand mixer, beat the butter and sugar together on medium-low
speed until smooth, about 3 minutes. Add the egg and beat until well incorporated, about 2 minutes. Beat in the vanilla. Reduce the mixer speed to low, add
the almond flour and mix just until it is almost incorporated. Stop the mixer,
add the flour-and-spice mixture all at once and pulse until the risk of flying flour
has passed. Working on low speed, mix only until the dry ingredients are fully
blended into the dough.

Turn the dough out onto a work surface and gather it together. Divide it in
half and shape each piece into a disk.

Working with one piece of dough at a time, roll the dough between pieces
of parchment paper to a thickness of ¼ inch. Slide the parchment-sandwiched
dough onto a baking sheet — you can stack the slabs — and freeze for at least
1 hour, or refrigerate for at least 2 hours.

GETTING READY TO BAKE: Center a rack in the oven and preheat it to
350 degrees F. Have two regular muffin tins and a 2-inch-diameter cookie
cutter at hand.

1¾ cups (238 grams) all-purpose flour

1 teaspoon ground cinnamon

½ teaspoon fine sea salt

¼ teaspoon coarsely ground black pepper

Pinch of ground ginger

Pinch of ground cloves

2 sticks (8 ounces; 226 grams) unsalted
    butter, cut into chunks, at room
    temperature

½ cup (100 grams) sugar

1 large egg, at room temperature

¼ teaspoon pure vanilla extract

⅔ cup (66 grams) almond flour

Fleur de sel and/or sugar, for dusting
    (optional)

Working with one piece of dough at a time, peel away both pieces of parchment and return the dough to one piece of paper. Cut the dough with the cookie cutter and place the rounds in the tins. The dough won't fill the muffin cups now, but it will once it's baked. Save the scraps. If you'd like, dust the tops of the cookies with salt, sugar or a combination of the two.

Bake the cookies for 14 to 17 minutes, or until their tops are toasty brown. Transfer the tins to a rack and allow the cookies to cool for at least 20 minutes, or until they reach room temperature, before unmolding.

Continue with the other piece of dough, making certain that the tins are cool. Gather the scraps together, re-roll, chill, cut and bake.

Maureen Dudgeon won the Fonseca Bin 27 Cookie Rumble Contest with this recipe, and one of her prizes was a day in the kitchen with me. We've been friends ever since — baking together will do that. The cookie is reminiscent of the World Peace Cookie (page 335), but it's got extras that take it in a very different direction.

The idea of the Rumble was to come up with cookies to savor with port (Bin 27 is a ruby port) and, not surprisingly, many of the entries were chocolate, one of port's coziest companions. Maureen's cookie is deeply, darkly and definitely chocolate and it's got something else too — port and figs. Before adding them to the dough, Maureen simmers snipped figs (I think Black Mission are best here) in port; I cook them until the fruit has absorbed all of it. The boozy figs flavor the dough the instant they're mixed in, but they do most of their work while the dough is chilling and setting. If you make the dough at least a day in advance, you'll get the fullest flavor. Adding port, figs and toasted walnuts to a chocolate cookie changes much about it, including the way you'll want to eat it, which is slowly, in small bites. And, yes, with a glass of port.

A word on timing: Fourteen minutes baking time is best for this cookie — if your oven heat varies, the cookies will still be fine.

Makes about 48 cookies

Center a rack in the oven and preheat it to 350 degrees F. Line a baking sheet with parchment paper or a silicone baking mat.

Scatter the walnuts across the sheet. Bake for about 10 minutes, stirring a few times, until the nuts are lightly browned. Turn the nuts into a bowl, stir in ¼ teaspoon of the salt and set aside (turn off the oven).

Stir the figs and port together in a small saucepan over medium heat and bring to a boil, then lower the heat and simmer, stirring, until the liquid is absorbed, 1 to 2 minutes. Spoon the mixture into a bowl and let cool while you start to make the dough.

Sift the flour, cocoa and baking soda together.

1 cup (120 grams) walnuts, finely chopped

¾ teaspoon fine sea salt

4 ounces (113 grams; about 15) dried figs, preferably Black Mission, stems trimmed, snipped into small pieces

¼ cup (60 ml) ruby port

1¾ cups (238 grams) all-purpose flour

½ cup (43 grams) unsweetened cocoa powder

¾ teaspoon baking soda

2 sticks (8 ounces; 226 grams) unsalted butter, cut into chunks, at room temperature

1 cup (200 grams) packed light brown sugar

⅓ cup (67 grams) sugar

1½ teaspoons pure vanilla extract

Working with a stand mixer fitted with the paddle attachment, or in a large bowl with a hand mixer, beat the butter, both sugars and the remaining $\frac{1}{2}$ teaspoon salt together on medium speed until creamy, about 2 minutes. Beat in the vanilla, then scrape down the sides and bottom of the bowl. With the mixer off, add the dry ingredients all at once and then pulse until the risk of flying flour has passed. Mix on low speed until you have a bowl of moist curds and crumbles that hold together when pressed, 1 to 2 minutes. Add the figs and walnuts and pulse to incorporate.

Turn the dough out onto the counter, gather it into a ball and divide it in half.

Working with one half at a time, roll the dough into logs that are 12 inches long. Don't worry about the diameter — get the length right, and all will be fine. (If you get a hollow in the logs — it happens — just start over; see page 12 for log-rolling tips.) Wrap the logs in plastic wrap and freeze them (my preference; this dough works best frozen) for at least 2 hours, or refrigerate them for at least 3 hours. If you can freeze the dough overnight, do it — the increased rest time will increase the flavor. If you freeze the dough, you don't need to defrost it before baking — just slice the logs into cookies and bake the cookies for a minute longer.

GETTING READY TO BAKE: Center a rack in the oven and preheat it to 325 degrees F. Line two baking sheets with parchment paper or silicone baking mats.

Using a long sharp knife, slice the logs into rounds that are $\frac{1}{2}$ inch thick; the rounds might crack as you're cutting them — just squeeze the bits back into each cookie. Arrange the rounds on the baking sheets, leaving about 2 inches between them.

Bake the cookies one sheet at a time for 14 minutes, without opening the oven. The cookies won't look done and they'll still be soft, but that's fine — they firm as they cool. Transfer the baking sheet to a rack and let the cookies cool completely.

STORING

Well wrapped, the logs of dough can be frozen for up to 2 months. Packed in a container, the cookies will keep at room temperature for up to 3 days. They can be frozen, well wrapped, for up to 2 months.

ALMOND CRESCENTS

2 sticks (8 ounces; 226 grams) unsalted
    butter, cut into chunks, at room
    temperature

½ cup (100 grams) sugar

½ teaspoon fine sea salt

1½ teaspoons pure vanilla extract

¼ to ½ teaspoon pure almond extract,
    to taste (optional)

1¾ cups (238 grams) all-purpose flour

1⅓ cups (133 grams) almond flour

Granulated or confectioners' sugar,
    for coating

Made with almond flour and flavored with vanilla — although many people think that almond extract should be the up-front taste, and I've given you that option — these molded crescent cookies can be covered with a heavy layer of powdered or granulated sugar right after they come from the oven. Snowy, they are a Christmas cookie; dredged in granulated sugar, they're made for every other day of the year.

One bite, and I'm a kid happy that I was at the door when my mother came home from the bakery. She shopped there every day, always for bread, often for cakes and at least once a week for cookies that came in a white box lined with tissue paper. Crescents, made in a much smaller size than these, were always a part of the weekly assortment and always a favorite. I don't think I remembered their name until recently, but friends did — I served a plate of them and there was a chorus of "*Kipfel!* Vanilla *kipfel!*" and one lone *Butterhornchen* ("butter horns" in German). As soon as I heard "*kipfel,*" it came back to me that was what my mother and grandmother called these and that was what they were called in the Eastern European bakeries of my childhood.

A word on size: Crescents can be made in just about any size you'd like. I make these rather large, but if you'd like them smaller (and more like the ones that turn up in an assortment of bakery cookies), you'll get pretty cookies using a small scoop (2 teaspoons) and rolling the dough into a log about 2½ inches long before bending it. Bake them for about 19 minutes.

Makes about 24 cookies

Position the racks to divide the oven into thirds and preheat it to 350 degrees F. Line two baking sheets with parchment paper or silicone baking mats.

Working with a stand mixer fitted with the paddle attachment, or in a large bowl with a hand mixer, beat the butter, sugar and salt together on medium speed until smooth, about 3 minutes. Beat in the vanilla and the almond extract, if you're using it, then scrape down the sides and bottom of the bowl. With the machine off, add the all-purpose flour all at once and then pulse the mixer to

cookies for weekends, holidays and other celebrations

MERINGUE SNOWBALLS

¾ cup (150 grams) plus 1 tablespoon sugar

2 tablespoons confectioners' sugar

3 large egg whites, at room temperature

¼ teaspoon cream of tartar (or ½ teaspoon distilled white vinegar)

Pinch of fine sea salt

Never underestimate the pleasures of meringue. Simple to the point of plain, meringue delivers delight with every messy bite. As neat as you may be, it's impossible to eat a meringue without producing a pile of shards and crumbs, and that's part of the cookie's charm.

In France, you can find meringues everywhere: Pastry shops sell jumbo-size cookies in colors that rival Easter eggs; supermarkets sell small, spirally meringue kisses in boxes and bags; and even home cooks who rarely bake will make a batch of meringues to use up extra egg whites and serve with ice cream or fruit.

Because they are made of just egg whites and sugar, meringues can be flavored in as many ways as you can imagine . . . or not at all. Even a plain meringue is a treat. My favorite meringue is mint–chocolate chip (it reminds me of the mint–chocolate chip ice cream that I used to get as a child at Howard Johnson's — although they colored their ice cream green and I leave my meringues white), but I also like coffee–chocolate chip, rose, almond and lemon. See Playing Around for recipes.

A word on size: This recipe makes hefty snowball-size meringues, but the mixture lends itself to small cookies and cookies in shapes other than round. Play around and discover what you like most. And, while you're playing, try piping out the meringue; it's beautiful piped through an open star tip.

Plan Ahead! The whites must be at room temperature to get the volume that makes meringues so lovely, so leave them out, covered, for 1 hour or more before setting to work. Also, you'll need to dedicate your oven to the meringues for a minimum of 3 hours. If you'd like, you can make them in the evening and let them camp out in the oven overnight.

Makes about 10 snowballs

Tinted Snowballs. If you'd like to color the meringue, scoop some of the finished meringue into a bowl and add food coloring, drop by drop and mixing after each addition, until you have a color that's a shade or two darker than you'd like. Fold the colored meringue into the rest of meringue. You don't have to be thorough — leave the mixture streaky, and it will form beautiful patterns when baked.

Vanilla Snowballs. Add 1½ teaspoons pure vanilla extract to the meringue after the ¾ cup sugar has been incorporated.

Almond Snowballs. Add 1 teaspoon pure almond extract to the meringue after the ¾ cup sugar has been incorporated. Sprinkle the tops of the snowballs with sliced almonds before baking.

Mint-Chocolate Chip Snowballs. Add 1 teaspoon pure peppermint extract or oil to the meringue after the ¾ cup sugar has been incorporated. Just before scooping, fold in ⅓ cup finely chopped semisweet or bittersweet chocolate or mini chocolate chips.

Lemon or Orange Snowballs. Add 1 teaspoon pure lemon or orange extract or oil to the meringue after the ¾ cup sugar has been incorporated. If you'd like, just before scooping, fold in about ¼ cup finely chopped candied lemon or orange peel (see page 474 for a recipe for candied orange peel).

Green Tea and Pistachio Snowballs. Whisk 2 teaspoons matcha green tea (see page 319) into the sifted sugars. Just before scooping, fold in ⅓ cup finely chopped pistachio nuts, salted or not.

Center a rack in the oven and preheat it to 250 degrees F. Line a baking sheet with parchment paper or a silicone baking mat.

Push the 1 tablespoon granulated sugar and the confectioners' sugar through a fine-mesh sieve; set aside.

Working with a stand mixer fitted with the whisk attachment, or in a large bowl with a hand mixer (make sure your tools are impeccably clean and free of even a trace of fat, grease or yolk — egg whites' enemies), beat the whites, cream of tartar (or vinegar) and salt on medium-high speed until the whites form soft peaks, about 3 minutes. Slowly add the ¾ cup (150 grams) granulated sugar, 1 tablespoon at a time; it will take 5 minutes or even a little longer to get all the sugar into the whites, but, as persnickety as it seems, it will be worth your patience. After all the sugar is incorporated, beat for another 2 minutes or so. You'll have stiff, glossy, beautifully white peaks. Switch to a flexible spatula and fold in the reserved sugar mix.

I like to shape the snowballs with a large cookie scoop, using a heaping scoop for each meringue. Yes, you get a kind of blob, but one with a nice round top. Alternatively, you can use a tablespoon — or serving spoon — and really pile on the meringue before turning it over onto the baking sheet. No matter how you choose to shape the meringues, leave at least 2 inches between the snowballs.

Bake the meringues — don't open the oven — for 1 hour and 15 minutes. The snowballs will have puffed and cracked but not colored (though they might be pale beige here and there, and that's fine). Turn off the heat and prop the oven door open with the handle of a wooden spoon. Leave the meringues to finish baking and drying for another 2 hours, or for as long as overnight.

When you're ready to serve the meringues, peel them off the paper or mat.

Rose Snowballs. Add 1 teaspoon pure rose extract to the meringue after the ¾ cup sugar has been incorporated. If you'd like, tint the snowballs pale red or rose pink and sprinkle the tops with pink sanding sugar before you bake them. For further embellishment, you could fold in some crushed rose tea leaves just before scooping the meringue.

Coffee-Chocolate Chip Snowballs. Add 1½ teaspoons instant coffee or espresso to the meringue after the ¾ cup sugar has been incorporated. Just before scooping, fold in ⅓ cup finely chopped semisweet or bittersweet chocolate or mini chocolate chips.

SWEDISH DREAM COOKIES

This recipe came to me from my assistant, Mary Dodd, who got it from her aunt Marie Malchodi, who has been making these cookies for Christmas for more than twenty years. Neither Mary nor Marie is Swedish, but the first time I baked these, my son's Swedish friend, Bella, was visiting. I told her nothing about the cookies but just served them at brunch, and her first words after her first cookie were, "This tastes like home!"

My guess was that it was the cardamom, a beloved spice in Sweden. But Bella thought the butteriness was pretty swell, ditto the tender, crumbly texture. "Yes, it tastes like home, but at home we put jam in the center."

In Sweden, the cookie is known as *drommar*, Swedish for "dream," and as I know it, and as Marie makes it, each cookie has a whole almond pressed into it. But if you wiggle your finger into the cookie's belly and fill the thumbprint with jam, you'll make what I now think of as Bella Buttons, and they're pretty dreamy too.

A word on the brown butter: Part of the wonder of this cookie is the butter, which is melted and kept over low heat until it browns. It's then chilled until it firms, a matter of a couple of hours. If you leave it longer — and you can — be careful: The first time I made these, I refrigerated the butter overnight and then snapped a table knife in two trying to cut the butter into chunks so that I could get it out of its container. I should have waited for it to soften. Or I should have dunked the bottom of the Pyrex measuring cup into hot water so that I could unmold the butter and cut it on a board.

A word on mixing: You can make these cookies with a mixer (stand or hand) or by hand, but I think you get the best texture when you use a food processor. Whether you use a mixer or manpower, the order in which the ingredients are added remains the same.

Makes about 36 cookies

2 sticks (8 ounces; 226 grams) unsalted butter, cut into chunks

2 cups (272 grams) all-purpose flour

1 teaspoon ground cardamom

1 teaspoon baking powder

½ cup (100 grams) sugar

½ teaspoon fine sea salt

2 teaspoons pure vanilla extract

36 to 40 whole almonds, blanched or unblanched, or about ⅓ cup (108 grams) thick jam or marmalade

Place the chunks of butter in a medium saucepan over low heat and prepare to be patient: You want to melt the butter and then let it simmer away until it turns a deep golden color and there are specks of brown on the bottom of the pan, a process that, depending on your pan and your heat source, could take up to 20 minutes. When the butter is a lovely deep gold, pour it and the specks into a heatproof bowl or a heatproof measuring cup. Let it cool at room temperature for about 30 minutes, then cover and chill until it firms, about 2 hours, or for up to overnight (see page 227).

GETTING READY TO BAKE: Position the racks to divide the oven into thirds and preheat it to 350 degrees F. Line two baking sheets with parchment paper or silicone baking mats.

Whisk the flour, cardamom and baking powder together.

Put the sugar and salt in a food processor. Unmold the butter, cut it into chunks and drop it into the bowl. Pour in the vanilla, pulse and then process until the mixture is well blended and smooth. Add the dry ingredients, pulse and then process until the dough forms moist curds. Scrape the bottom of the bowl a couple of times just to be certain the dough hasn't packed down and formed a dense layer. Remove the bowl from the food processor, and remove the blade from the bowl.

Using a small cookie scoop, scoop out level portions of dough or use a teaspoon to get rounded spoonfuls. Form each scoop of dough into a ball and place on the baking sheets, leaving a generous inch between the cookies. If you're making nut cookies, stabilize each ball by holding it with one hand and press an almond into the center with the other. The dough will crack, but that's okay. For thumbprints, stabilize the balls and make an indentation in their centers using your thumb, the knuckle of your index finger or the end of a wooden spoon. Put enough jam in each indent to mound slightly over the top (about ½ teaspoon).

Bake for 16 to 19 minutes, rotating the sheets top to bottom and front to back after 9 minutes, or until the cookies are golden brown and just firm to the squeeze. These are exceedingly fragile, so transfer the baking sheets to racks and let the cookies rest for at least 10 minutes before lifting them onto the racks to cool.

If you have more dough, shape and bake it, always using cool sheets.

STORING

These cookies are wonderful the day they are made and maybe even a tiny bit more wonderful the next day, when the cardamom has had time to truly settle in. Kept in a closed container, they'll be good for at least 4 days at room temperature (the almond cookies keep better than the jam cookies); wrapped airtight, they'll hold in the freezer for up to 2 months.

CHOCOLATE SAUCISSON

12 plump, moist dried Turkish apricots, cut into small pieces

6 ounces (170 grams) Biscoff cookies, Petit Beurre or vanilla wafers

2 large organic eggs (see headnote), at room temperature

1 stick (8 tablespoons; 4 ounces; 113 grams) unsalted butter, melted and cooled

½ cup (100 grams) sugar

½ teaspoon fine sea salt

1 cup (85 grams) unsweetened cocoa powder

½ cup (70 grams) shelled pistachios (rub off any loose skins), lightly toasted and coarsely chopped

About 1 cup (120 grams) confectioners' sugar, for rolling

A cross between candy and the best chocolate cookie dough you can imagine, these unbaked cookies are popular in Italy and France, where, because of their shape, they're called *salame* or *saucisson*. But they're sometimes called mosaic, because of the beautiful pattern the add-ins make. And they're also made in Russia and Romania and Portugal and probably just about every other European country. I didn't have to travel far to get the base for this recipe: It was given to me by my friend Matt Wick, a Connecticut chef. It's a cocoa log studded with crushed cookies — usually vanilla wafers, but I couldn't resist the allure of Biscoff cookies (see page 197) — chilled until it's firm enough to slice and rolled in confectioners' sugar to suggest the bloom that gives saucisson and some salami their distinctive look. Working, as I always do, under the assumption that good can always be better, I added pistachios and bits of dried apricot. Not only did they make the log even better looking, they made it crunchier, chewier and more interesting.

Because the cookies depend almost entirely on cocoa for their flavor, I urge you to choose a cocoa with a taste that's as deep as its color (Valrhona and Guittard make great cocoa). As for the fruit and nuts, the choice is yours. That said, it's nice to toast the nuts and plump the fruit. If you'd like to add another flavor to the mix, you can soak the fruit in tea, juice or something boozy.

This makes a big, fat log that weighs in at 1½ pounds and keeps for a long time, ready to be sliced whenever you want something wonderful as a nibble-along with coffee, ice cream, pudding or fruit desserts. Of course, it's also perfect go-it-alone snack fare. If you want smaller cookies, you can make 2 logs from the recipe or cut the recipe in half.

A word on the eggs: Because the eggs are not cooked, use super-fresh organic and/or local eggs.

Makes about 20 cookies

Wrapped well, the log will keep in the refrigerator for up to 1 week and in the freezer for up to 2 months. It should be cut and served while cold, so don't defrost.

Put the apricots in a heatproof bowl and add enough very hot tap water to cover them (or see page 230 for some ideas for liquid that is tastier than water) and set aside to soak. When you're ready for the apricots, drain and pat dry between paper towels.

The Biscoff cookies need to be broken into small pieces (not crumbs). You can do this with your fingers or do what I do: Cut them into rough, uneven cubes using a serrated knife.

Working in a large bowl, whisk the eggs, butter, sugar and salt together until you have a mixture with a beautiful sheen. Switch to a sturdy flexible spatula and stir in the cocoa; it's easiest to do this in 3 or 4 additions. The dough will be thick — almost like a paste — but just keep mixing and making sure to get to the bottom of the bowl. One by one, stir in the apricots, cookie pieces and pistachios.

Lay a large piece of parchment on the counter and butter it. Reach into the bowl and gather the dough together in a ball, place it in the center of the parchment and work it into a chubby log between 10 and 12 inches long. Because this isn't baked, there's no need to be precise, but I wouldn't suggest that you make the log shorter than 10 inches. Short and squat, the salami becomes bologna and it's hard to cut and have the cookies stay intact. Check that the log is solid (feel along it to see if there are hollow spots and, if so, re-roll; see page 12 for tips on rolling logs), then wrap it tightly in the parchment. Freeze the log for at least 3 hours or refrigerate it for at least 6 hours.

When you're ready to serve, put the confectioners' sugar on a piece of parchment or wax paper, unwrap the log and roll it in the sugar until it's coated. Using a long slicing knife, cut the log into cookies that are about ½ inch thick (you can cut them thicker, but not thinner). Serve immediately. These are soft and a little messy by nature and will hold their pick-upability for about 10 minutes at room temperature, so refrigerate the uncut portion of the log or refrigerate any cookies you aren't serving.

PFEFFERNEUSSE

I know that pfefferneusse are keyed to Christmas, but if you love spice cookies as much as I do, you won't put this recipe away until it's time to pull out the beach blankets. Traditionally, pfefferneusse (the name is German for "peppernut") are made with chopped nuts, lots of spice — including the freshly ground pepper referenced in the name — and citrus. Their distinguishing characteristics are their spiciness and their solidity — some pfefferneusse are harder than nuts, built to last through the twelve days of Christmas and beyond.

My pfefferneusse have plenty of spices. The blend includes what I think of as the holiday spices — cinnamon, nutmeg and cloves — as well as cardamom, salt, pepper and some dry mustard, which has the effect of sparking all the others. Together the spices have a slow build and a long finish.

I tinkered and tinkered with the spice blend until I came to this mix and then, when I was certain it was perfect, I thought the cookie might be nice with two other ingredients that go well with the spices: espresso and chocolate. Rather than fold them into the dough, I turned them into a glaze. Dipping the cookies gives them a topknot of chocolate and a welcome touch of creaminess.

Makes about 40 cookies

Position the racks to divide the oven into thirds and preheat it to 350 degrees F. Line two baking sheets with parchment paper or silicone baking mats.

TO MAKE THE COOKIES: Whisk the flour, all the spices, the baking powder and the baking soda together.

Put the sugar and zest in the bowl of a stand mixer or in a large bowl in which you can use a hand mixer. Reach in and use your fingertips to rub and mix the ingredients together until the sugar is moist and aromatic. If using a stand mixer, fit it with the paddle attachment. Add the butter to the bowl and beat on medium speed until well blended, about 2 minutes. Add the eggs one at a time,

FOR THE COOKIES

2 cups (272 grams) all-purpose flour

1 teaspoon ground cinnamon

1/2 teaspoon fine sea salt

1/2 teaspoon freshly ground pepper (black or white)

1/2 teaspoon freshly grated nutmeg

1/2 teaspoon ground cloves

1/4 teaspoon ground cardamom

1/4 teaspoon dry mustard, such as Colman's

1/2 teaspoon baking powder

1/8 teaspoon baking soda

2/3 cup (134 grams) sugar

Finely grated zest of 2 tangerines or clementines, 1 orange or 1 lemon

3/4 stick (6 tablespoons; 3 ounces; 85 grams) unsalted butter, cut into chunks, at room temperature

2 large eggs, at room temperature

1/2 cup (60 grams) finely chopped pecans (toasted if desired)

Confectioners' sugar, for dusting, if you're not glazing the cookies

FOR THE GLAZE (OPTIONAL)

3 ounces (85 grams) semisweet or bittersweet chocolate, coarsely chopped

1/2 teaspoon ground espresso beans or 1/4 teaspoon instant espresso

1 tablespoon unsalted butter, at room temperature

Peppercorns in a grinder, for dusting (optional)

beating for 1 minute after each one goes in. The mixture might look curdled — if so, ignore it. Scrape down the sides and bottom of the bowl with a flexible spatula, turn off the mixer, add the dry ingredients all at once and pulse a few times to start the blending. Then mix on low speed until most of the flour is incorporated. Add the chopped nuts and mix only until the dry ingredients have disappeared into the dough. Give the dough a few good turns with the spatula to make certain that everything is blended.

Using a small cookie scoop, scoop out level portions of dough or use a teaspoon to get rounded spoonfuls. Shape each mound of dough into a ball between your palms and place onto the baking sheets about 1½ inches apart (these puff but don't spread much).

Bake the cookies for 20 to 22 minutes, rotating the sheets top to bottom and front to back after 10 minutes, or until the cookies are firm to a gentle squeeze, puffed, cracked, light beige on top and golden brown on the bottom. Transfer the sheets to racks. If you're going to dust the cookies with sugar, allow them to rest for 10 minutes, dust them and transfer them to the racks to cool completely. If you're going to glaze the cookies, let them cool completely on the sheets.

TO MAKE THE GLAZE AND FINISH THE COOKIES (OPTIONAL): Set a heatproof bowl over a saucepan of simmering water (the water shouldn't touch the bottom of the bowl), toss in the chocolate and espresso and heat, stirring, until the chocolate is melted and smooth. Or do this in a microwave oven. Remove the bowl from the pan, add the butter and stir to blend.

One by one, dip the tops of the cookies into the chocolate and then, if you'd like, give each a grind of pepper while the chocolate is still wet. Return the cookies to the racks and let the glaze set. Unless your room is very warm, the glaze will set in about 20 minutes. If you're impatient, you can hasten the setting by refrigerating the cookies.

STORING

The dough can be kept covered in the refrigerator for up to 3 days. Dry and firm by nature, the cookies will keep in a covered container for weeks and become even drier and firmer. If they become too dry for you to find them enjoyable, add a wedge of apple to the container, and the cookies will soften overnight. With or without glaze, the cookies can be packed airtight and frozen for up to 2 months; if you want to dust the cookies with confectioners' sugar, wait until they've defrosted to give them the dusting.

CHRISTMAS SPICE COOKIES

When you start with something really good, it doesn't take much to make it better. And that's the story of this cookie. I started with my Do-Almost-Anything Vanilla Cookie Dough, and then I added the spices that always make me think it's Christmas: cinnamon, ginger, cloves and allspice. The result is a cookie that's perfect with coffee or tea, mulled cider, mulled wine or a late-night cognac. The cookies are nice left plain or sprinkled with sanding sugar before baking, but I usually can't resist the allure of a spiral of melted white chocolate in the center or a faint brushstroke of chocolate across the top.

A word on batch size: This recipe uses one quarter of the Do-Almost-Anything Vanilla Dough. Make the full recipe of the dough then, if you'd like, you can double, triple or quadruple this cookie recipe or use the vanilla dough to make other cookies (see pages 149, 178 and 185).

Makes about 18 cookies

FOR THE COOKIES

¼ teaspoon ground cinnamon

¼ teaspoon ground ginger

Pinch of ground cloves

Pinch of ground allspice

¼ recipe Do-Almost-Anything Vanilla Cookie Dough (page 492); just made and still soft (see headnote)

FOR THE TOPPING (OPTIONAL)

Sanding sugar or ½ cup (85 grams) white chocolate chips

TO MAKE THE COOKIES: Mix the spices together in a small bowl and, using a flexible spatula, blend them evenly into the dough. Gather the dough together and shape into a disk.

Place the dough between pieces of parchment paper and roll it to a thickness of ¼ inch. Slide the dough, still between the paper, onto a baking sheet and freeze for at least 1 hour, or refrigerate for at least 3 hours.

GETTING READY TO BAKE: Center a rack in the oven and preheat it to 350 degrees F. Line a baking sheet with parchment paper or a silicone baking mat.

Peel away the paper on both sides of the dough and return it to one piece of paper. Using a 2-inch-diameter cutter, cut out as many cookies as you can. (You can use any size or shape cutter you like, just know that the yield will be different.) Place them on the lined baking sheet about 1½ inches apart. Gather the scraps together, re-roll them between paper and chill.

If you're using sanding sugar, sprinkle the tops of the cookies with it.

Bake for 19 to 21 minutes, rotating the sheet after 10 minutes, or until the

The rolled-out dough can be wrapped and refrigerated for up to 3 days or frozen for up to 2 months. The cookies will keep in a covered container at room temperature for up to 1 week. They can be wrapped airtight and frozen for up to 2 months.

cookies feel firm to the touch. Transfer the sheet to a rack and let the cookies rest for 5 minutes before lifting them onto the rack to cool to room temperature.

Repeat with the rest of the dough, making sure your baking sheet is cool.

TO MAKE THE GLAZE AND FINISH THE COOKIES (OPTIONAL): If you want to give the cookies a spiral or swipe of white chocolate, melt the chocolate in a microwave or in a bowl set over a pan of simmering water. For the spiral, use a small pastry bag fitted with a tiny decorating tip or drizzle the chocolate off the tip of a small spoon. For the swipe, use a narrow pastry brush and only a little bit of chocolate and brush it across the cookie lightly. Refrigerate the cookies for about 20 minutes just to set the decoration.

GOZINAKI

When you're baking cookies every day, word gets around. And because the world of sweets in general and cookies in particular is generous, cookie lovers will often send me a recipe they're attached to or that's especially interesting. Gozinaki is one of those interesting recipes. It was sent to me by Kim Allen, a Californian, and it came to her in the nicest way. When her daughter was a freshman in college on the East Coast, she returned home for Christmas break with her roommate, Nano Liklikadze, a young woman from Georgia (the country, not the state). During her stay, Nano made gozinaki, a cookie that was part of her holiday tradition, and Kim, bless her, took notes.

Depending on your perspective, gozinaki can be a confection or a cookie – I'm going with cookie, in part because it reminds me of something my Russian grandmother made, and she called that a cookie. It's essentially toasted walnuts held together with a honey syrup and then cut into diamond shapes. That something this simple can be this delicious is reason to rejoice. If you put in just 30 minutes or so of pleasant kitchen work, you'll have a cookie that will stay delectable through the twelve days of Christmas. And each time you make gozinaki, you can play around with it and add more flavors and textures (see Playing Around). Or not: The cookies are perfect as their own three-ingredient wonders.

Makes 28 cookies

Center a rack in the oven and preheat it to 350 degrees F. Line a baking sheet with parchment paper or a silicone baking mat.

Spread the walnuts out on the sheet and bake for about 10 minutes, stirring two or three times, until lightly toasted. Finely chop the nuts; Kim says they should be the size of lentils or gravel.

Set a glass filled with cold water next to the stovetop. Have a cutting board or a baking sheet (if it's rimmed, turn it over) dampened with cold water at the ready, as well as a rolling pin.

Pour the honey into a heavy medium saucepan and place it over medium

2½ cups (300 grams) walnuts
½ cup (120 ml) honey
½ cup (100 grams) sugar

The cookies will keep for at least 1 week in a covered container at room temperature: Line the container with parchment or wax paper and put a piece of paper between each layer of cookies. I prefer to pack them like this and then store them in the fridge, where they'll stay for about 2 weeks; take them out 15 minutes before serving. These are not made for freezing.

heat. Stand by and stir frequently with a silicone spatula. When the honey begins to boil around the edges of the pan, start adding the sugar, stirring as it goes in. Bring the honey to a boil, still stirring, and, as soon as it boils in the center — watch out, it will bubble up — start testing it: Drop a tiny bit of honey into the cold water. At first the honey will separate into strands, but very soon after, it will fall to the bottom of the glass and form a ball. This is your sign that the honey is at the right temperature. This can take as little as 3 or 4 minutes. Turn off the heat, add the walnuts and stir them around in the honey until they are glistening and coated with syrup.

Scrape the mixture out onto the dampened cutting board or baking sheet. Immediately use the spatula to spread the mixture out just so that it isn't in a clump or mound — don't worry about precision. Moisten the rolling pin and roll the gozinaki into a rectangle that's between ¼ inch and ½ inch thick. Run your hands under cold water, shake off the excess and even the sides as best as you can. (If your rectangle resembles an amoeba, it'll still be fine.) Set the gozinaki aside until it firms, about 20 minutes.

Use a chef's knife to cut the gozinaki into diamond shapes about 2 inches long and 1 inch wide. Once cut, the cookies are ready to serve.

PLAYING AROUND

Once you've made your first batch of three-ingredient gozinaki, you might want to add another flavor or texture. Here are some ideas to get you started.

Multi-Seed Gozinaki. Add 2 tablespoons each sesame, flax and sunflower seeds to the honey when you add the walnuts.

Mixed-Nut Gozinaki. Walnuts are traditional for these cookies, but they can be made with other nuts or a mix of nuts. Consider almonds, cashews, macadamias, pine nuts and/or pistachios. Whatever nuts you use, toast them first.

Orange Gozinaki. Before you get started, grate the zest of 1 or 2 oranges over the sugar and use your fingertips to blend the ingredients together until the sugar is moist and fragrant. If you'd like, when you stir the walnuts into the orange-flavored honey syrup, you can also stir in about ⅓ cup chopped candied orange peel, homemade (page 474) or store-bought.

Dried-Fruit Gozinaki. Dried fruits such as cherries, cranberries, dates, figs, apricots and/or raisins are nice in gozinaki. Aim for about ⅔ cup chopped fruit. Cut, chop or snip the fruit into small pieces, soak in very hot tap water for about 10 minutes, drain and pat thoroughly dry. Stir the fruit into the honey syrup along with the walnuts.

Chocolate Gozinaki. You can add chocolate to the gozinaki or top it with melted chocolate, or go all out and add it in and out. To add chocolate to the mix, use chocolate chips of any variety (about ½ cup) and add them after the walnuts have been stirred into the syrup. To add a chocolate topping, melt about 1 cup chips or chopped chocolate and drizzle over the surface. When the gozinaki has cooled to room temperature, cut it into diamonds and refrigerate it for 20 minutes to set the chocolate.

LITTLE RASCALS

2/3 cup (134 grams) sugar

2/3 cup (80 grams) walnuts (whole or pieces)

1/4 teaspoon fine sea salt

Pinch of ground cinnamon (optional)

A little finely grated lemon zest (optional)

1 1/4 cups (170 grams) all-purpose flour

1 stick (8 tablespoons; 4 ounces; 113 grams) cold unsalted butter, cut into small pieces

1 large egg, lightly beaten

Confectioners' sugar, for dusting

About 1/4 cup (about 80 grams) thick jam, such as raspberry, strawberry, cherry or apricot

When I discovered that the German name for these cookies, which I grew up with, translated as "Little Rascals," it made me love them even more. Not that their proper name, *Spitzbuben*, didn't also sound comical to my American ears, but Little Rascals was irresistible. Happily, the cookie is as irresistible as its name. Essentially jam-filled sandwich cookies, these are made with walnuts and very little flavoring: a pinch of cinnamon, if you'd like; a scrape of lemon zest, if that's your fancy. Mostly the flavor is butter, sugar and nuts. The texture is best described as crumbly and a little gritty (in the best way). Half the cookies, which are always made small and often made for Christmas, are baked whole and the other half are given peeka-boo cutouts. When the cookies are cool, they're sandwiched with a tiny bit of jam that pushes up alluringly through the cutout. They seem a lot like linzer cookies' simpler cousins, don't they? And wouldn't they be great for Valentine's Day if you used heart-shaped cutters?

A word on the jam filling: If you'd like, you can bring the jam to a boil (I do this in the microwave), let it cool and then spoon it onto the cookies — boiling will thicken the jam and make it less sticky. But using jam straight from the jar is fine too.

Makes about 28 sandwiches

Put the sugar, walnuts, salt, and cinnamon and zest, if you're using them, in a food processor and pulse until the nuts are ground. It's better to have a few discernible pieces of nuts than nut butter, so keep an eye on the mix as you go. Add the flour and process to incorporate. Scatter over the pieces of cold butter and pulse until the mixture forms crumbs and resembles streusel. Add the egg a little at a time, pulsing after each bit goes in. Pulse a few more times, until you have a soft dough.

Scrape the dough out onto a work surface, divide it in half and shape each into a disk.

Working with one piece of dough at a time, roll the dough 1/4 inch thick

between pieces of parchment. Slide the dough, still sandwiched between the paper, onto a baking sheet — you can stack the slabs — and freeze for at least 1 hour; longer is better. This dough remains soft even when frozen, so it's best to get it as cold as you can before cutting it.

GETTING READY TO BAKE: Center a rack in the oven and preheat it to 350 degrees F. Line two baking sheets with parchment paper or silicone baking mats. Have two cookie cutters at the ready: one 1½ inches in diameter and the other a little less than 1 inch (the cutters can be plain or scallop-edged).

Pull out one piece of dough; keep the other in the freezer. Peel away both pieces of parchment and return the dough to one piece of paper. Working quickly, cut out as many 1½-inch rounds as you can, placing them on the baking sheets a scant 2 inches apart. Use the smaller cutter to remove the centers of half of the cookies. If the dough breaks while you're cutting out the centers, patch it; if the dough is really soft and you're not having fun cutting it, slide the baking sheet into the freezer and give it a 10-minute chill. Reserve the scraps, then combine them with the scraps from the second piece of dough, shape into a disk, re-roll, freeze, cut and bake.

Bake the cookies for 14 to 16 minutes, rotating the sheet after 10 minutes, or until pale golden brown. Transfer the baking sheet to a rack and allow the cookies to cool completely.

Repeat with the remaining dough, always using a cool baking sheet.

To finish the cookies, dust the cut-out cookies with confectioners' sugar. Turn the whole cookies over, bottoms up, and place about ½ teaspoon of jam in the center of each one. Top with the cut-out cookies, pressing down lightly to push the jam toward the edges.

CHERRY-NUT CHOCOLATE PINWHEELS

These look dainty, with their swirls of plump, syrupy cherries and walnuts, but they've got a bit of heft and enough chew to satisfy cookie lovers of the monster variety. They're one of the quartet of cookies made with Do-Almost-Anything Chocolate Dough, which means that they're not just delectable, but easy — the dough is a pleasure to work with. For the holidays, I like having red fruit in the mix, but if you'd prefer dried apricots or raisins or even dried pineapple, make the change.

I sprinkle the cookies with sanding sugar before they go into the oven and then decorate them with melted white chocolate. It's completely optional — the cookies are great plain — but they're so nice with a bit more chocolate.

A word on batch size: This recipe uses one quarter of the Do-Almost-Anything Chocolate Dough. Make the full recipe of the dough then, if you'd like, you can double, triple or quadruple this cookie recipe or use the chocolate dough to make other cookies (see pages 137, 180 and 200).

Makes about 18 cookies

¼ recipe Do-Almost-Anything Chocolate Cookie Dough (page 494), just made and still soft (see headnote)

6 ounces (about 1 heaping cup; 170 grams) dried cherries, snipped or finely chopped

⅔ cup (80 grams) finely chopped walnuts

⅔ cup (160 ml) water

3 tablespoons sugar

Sanding sugar, for topping (optional)

⅓ cup (56 grams) white chocolate chips, for topping (optional)

Gather the dough together and pat it into a square. Place the dough between pieces of parchment paper and roll into a 9-inch square. Don't worry about the thickness — just get close to the size, and you'll be fine. Slide the dough, still between the paper, onto a baking sheet and freeze for at least 1 hour, or refrigerate for at least 3 hours.

Put the cherries, nuts, water and sugar in a small saucepan, stir and bring to a boil over medium heat. Lower the heat so that the liquid just simmers and cook, stirring so that nothing sticks, until the syrup reduces and the mixture is thick enough to spread, about 10 minutes. Scrape it into a bowl and let cool to room temperature.

Peel away the paper on both sides of the dough and return the dough to one piece of paper. Spread the cherry filling over the dough, leaving about 1 inch bare at the edge farthest from you and about ¼ inch bare on the other

STORING

The filling can be made up to 3 days ahead and kept tightly covered in the refrigerator. You can freeze the rolled-up dough for up to 2 months, and slice and bake the cookies straight from the freezer. You can keep the baked cookies in a covered container at room temperature for up to 4 days. Packed airtight, they can be frozen for up to 2 months.

sides. Wait a few minutes, until the dough is soft enough to roll without cracking, and then roll it from the side closest to you, trying to get as tight a roll as you can. Finish with the seam on the bottom, wrap the parchment paper around the dough and freeze for at least 1 hour.

GETTING READY TO BAKE: Center a rack in the oven and preheat it to 350 degrees F. Line a baking sheet with parchment paper or a silicone baking mat.

If the ends of the log are ragged (they usually are), trim them. Using a long sharp knife, cut ½-inch-thick cookies and place them on the lined baking sheet an inch apart. If you'd like to dust the cookies with sanding sugar, do that.

Bake for 23 to 25 minutes, rotating the sheet after 12 minutes, or until the cookies feel firm to the touch. Transfer the sheet to a rack and let rest for 5 minutes, then lift the cookies onto the rack to cool completely.

If you'd like to give the cookies the white-chocolate treatment, melt the chocolate in the microwave or in a bowl set over a pan of simmering water. When the chocolate is melted and smooth, drizzle it over the cooled cookies. Pop them into the fridge for about 20 minutes to set the chocolate.

DATE-NUT PINWHEELS

FOR THE FILLING

¾ cup (113 grams) chopped pitted dates

½ cup (60 grams) finely chopped walnuts or pecans

½ cup (120 ml) water

2 tablespoons sugar

1 teaspoon freshly squeezed lemon juice or 2 teaspoons orange juice

FOR THE DOUGH

1¾ cups (238 grams) all-purpose flour

¼ teaspoon baking powder

⅛ teaspoon baking soda

1 stick (8 tablespoons; 4 ounces; 113 grams) unsalted butter, cut into chunks, at room temperature

1 cup (200 grams) packed light brown sugar

¼ teaspoon fine sea salt

1 large egg, at room temperature

Growing up in New York City, I remember date-nut bread, date pudding, date-nut cake and cookies with a filling that might have been the date version of Fig Newtons. The dried dates used to make these sweets were an everyday ingredient, as common then as dried cranberries are now. Of course they're still available, but they and the wonderful recipes they were used in seem to have fallen out of fashion. A shame, because, as I was reminded when I made these cookies, they're great!

These cookies never went out of style for my friend Oklahoma chef John Bennett, who gave me this recipe. He makes batches to serve with tea or ice cream; for lunch, dinner, snack time or anytime; and for no reason other than that they're good.

You'll understand when you make them. The dough is sweetened with brown sugar and bakes to that much-loved combo: slightly crisp on the outside, chewy inside. And the filling, a quick-cooking mix of chopped dates, nuts, water and sugar, is thick, pleasantly sticky and scrumptious. You might think that adding sugar to already sweet dates is too much — I did, but I was wrong.

The original recipe calls for slicing the cookies ¼ inch thick. They are very good that way, but I think they're even better when you go big and slice them ½ inch thick. Cut a few thin and a few thick and decide for yourself. (If you cut the cookies ¼ inch thick, the baking time will be 11 to 13 minutes.)

A word on stickiness: Dates are sticky by nature and therefore not so easy to pit and chop. You'll find this recipe quick to make if you buy dates that are already pitted and even quicker if you buy them pitted and chopped. They're easy to find in the supermarket.

Makes about 18 cookies

You can make the filling up to 3 days ahead and keep it tightly covered in the refrigerator. The rolled-out dough can be refrigerated for up to 3 days or wrapped airtight and frozen for up to 2 months. The filled log can be refrigerated overnight or frozen for up to 2 months. The baked cookies are good keepers — pack them into a covered container, and they'll keep for 4 days or more. They are not good candidates for freezing.

TO MAKE THE FILLING: Put all of the ingredients in a small saucepan and bring to a boil over medium heat, stirring, then reduce the heat so that the mixture simmers gently. Stay at the stove, stirring regularly, until the liquid has been absorbed and the dates and nuts are soft, thick and spreadable, just a few minutes. Scrape the filling into a bowl and let cool to room temperature.

TO MAKE THE DOUGH: Whisk the flour, baking powder and baking soda together.

Working with a stand mixer fitted with the paddle attachment, or in a large bowl with a hand mixer, beat the butter, brown sugar and salt together on medium speed until smooth and creamy, about 3 minutes, scraping down the bowl as needed. Add the egg and beat for another minute or so, until it's thoroughly blended in. Turn off the mixer and add the dry ingredients all at once, then pulse the mixer a few times. When the risk of flying flour has passed, mix at low speed until it's thoroughly incorporated. You'll have a soft dough that will clean the sides of the bowl.

Turn the dough out onto a piece of parchment paper and shape it into a rectangle. Cover with another piece of paper and roll the dough until it's about 12 x 10 inches; slightly larger is better than smaller here. While you're rolling, stop to peel the pieces of paper away from the dough frequently, so that they don't get rolled into the dough and form creases. Slide the dough, still between the paper, onto a baking sheet and refrigerate for at least 2 hours, or freeze for at least 1 hour.

TO FILL AND ROLL THE DOUGH: Remove the dough from the refrigerator or freezer and leave it on the counter until it's supple enough to bend without cracking. (This doesn't take long.)

Peel away the paper on both sides of the dough and return the dough to one of the pieces of paper. Position the dough so that a long side is parallel to you. Using an icing spatula (or the back of a spoon), spread the filling over the dough, leaving about 1 inch of dough bare at the top and about ½ inch on the other sides. Starting with the long edge closest to you, and using the paper to help you, roll the dough up into a log, trying to keep it as compact as possible. The ends will be ragged, but that's fine — they'll be trimmed before baking.

Wrap the log and refrigerate it for at least 1 hour.

GETTING READY TO BAKE: Position the racks to divide the oven into thirds and preheat it to 350 degrees F. Line two baking sheets with parchment paper or silicone baking mats.

Unwrap the log, place it on a cutting board and trim away the ragged edges, cutting until you can see spirals of filling. Using a sharp thin knife, cut the log into ½-inch-thick rounds. Don't worry if there are gaps between the filling and the dough — they'll fill in as the cookies bake. Place the cookies on the baking sheets, leaving about 1½ inches between them. If you haven't used the entire log, return the remainder to the refrigerator.

Bake for 15 to 17 minutes, rotating the baking sheets top to bottom and front to back after 8 minutes. The cookies will spread and puff and brown lightly; they should still be soft if poked gently. Let the cookies rest on the baking sheets for 2 minutes, then gently transfer them to a rack to cool until they are just warm or at room temperature.

If you have more dough, slice and bake, using a cool baking sheet.

BRUNO'S NEW YEAR'S WAFFLES

My friend Bruno comes from the north of France, where the foods of the region often resemble those of its neighbor, Belgium, more than those of the motherland. In the small town that Bruno came from, every family made waffles for the New Year. On the first of January, families would visit one another, bringing with them their good wishes for the year and sharing waffles and a drink. It was like a town-wide open house. The first year that Bruno was in Paris, he made waffles for the New Year, packed them up and went visiting his new friends, only to find that they were shocked that someone would show up unannounced and wondered why they should be eating waffles. Call it a country mouse–city mouse moment.

But you can't keep a good man and his waffles down. Now that Bruno's been a Parisian for many years, he makes hundreds of waffles and takes them to his colleagues at the office, all of whom love them and love him for starting this delicious tradition.

These are made without a leavener but with lots of brown sugar and cinnamon (hallmarks of the north) and rum too. In France, they're baked in a special iron that turns out the thinnest-possible waffles. Not having that tool, I decided to use a pizzelle iron. The cookies might not be authentic, but they are beautiful. I use just a tiny bit of dough (these waffles are made with a firm dough, not a batter), place the ball of dough in the middle of the pattern and rejoice when it spreads in odd and off-center ways.

The waffles, which are especially crisp, are snackable as soon as they cool and even more tempting sandwiched with a simple buttercream. I make a filling with cinnamon and espresso. If you can find chicory, use it instead of the coffee and you'll have another flavor from northern France. And don't stop there — the wafery waffles make wonderful ice cream sandwiches (see Playing Around), and the buttercream is good on brownies.

Plan Ahead! The dough should be made at least 1 day ahead.

Makes about 120 cookies

FOR THE WAFFLES
1¾ cups (238 grams) all-purpose flour

1 teaspoon ground cinnamon

¼ teaspoon fine sea salt

1¼ cups (250 grams) packed light brown sugar

1 stick plus 1 tablespoon (9 tablespoons; 4½ ounces; 125 grams) unsalted butter, cut into chunks

1 large egg, lightly beaten, at room temperature

1 tablespoon dark rum or 2 teaspoons pure vanilla extract

FOR THE FILLING (OPTIONAL)
1 stick (8 tablespoons; 4 ounces; 113 grams) unsalted butter, cut into chunks, at room temperature

1½ cups (180 grams) confectioners' sugar

1½ teaspoons instant espresso or instant coffee

½ teaspoon ground cinnamon

Pinch of fine sea salt

Waffle Ice Cream Sandwiches. The crispy cookies make excellent caps for a puck of ice cream (vanilla, page 461; chocolate, page 466; coffee; caramel; butter pecan . . .). Because they're so fragile, the best way to make the sandwiches is to scoop the ice cream onto a piece of plastic wrap and press it into the size puck you want, then lift it onto a cookie and top with another. Freeze immediately and wrap airtight when solid.

STORING

The dough can be refrigerated for up to 3 days, as can the filling; let the filling soften to a spreadable consistency at room temperature. The dough can also be wrapped airtight and frozen for up to 2 months. The plain cookies will keep for at least a week as long as they're safe from humidity. Filled, you can keep them at room temperature for 2 days or so.

TO MAKE THE WAFFLES: Whisk the flour, cinnamon and salt together in a large bowl.

Put the brown sugar and butter in a small saucepan and warm over medium-low heat, stirring frequently, until the butter melts and the sugar dissolves. Pour the hot mixture over the flour and mix with a sturdy flexible spatula. Blend in the egg, followed by the rum. You'll have a smooth dough. Wrap the dough and refrigerate it overnight.

Heat a pizzelle maker according to the manufacturer's instructions. If you have to butter or spray it, do so for the first batch and then see if the butter in the waffles isn't sufficient to make the iron nonstick. Have a long (and broad, if possible) icing spatula and a cooling rack at hand.

I use a level ½ teaspoon of dough for each waffle, but you might want more; make a couple, and see what you like. Spoon off pieces of dough and roll them into balls between your palms. Place a ball in the center of the pizzelle iron (if your iron makes 2 pizzelles at a time, use 2 pieces of dough), close the iron and bake for 20 to 40 seconds (pizzelle irons can vary enormously — check at 20 seconds and then continue baking until you've got the color you want). The waffle(s) should be golden but not set. Use the spatula to get under the waffles and transfer as gently and as quickly as you can to the rack. The waffles will crisp in a matter of seconds. Repeat until you've used up the dough (or you've got as many as you'd like).

If you want to fill the waffles, let cool completely (ditto if you want to make ice cream sandwiches).

TO MAKE THE FILLING AND SANDWICH THE COOKIES (OPTIONAL): Working with a stand mixer fitted with a paddle attachment, or in a large bowl with a hand mixer (or a flexible spatula), beat all the ingredients together until very smooth.

The cookies are very delicate, so the best way to fill them is to put one on a flat surface, cover most of it with filling and then top with another, pressing down only just enough for it to stick to the filling.

DEVIL'S FOOD WAFFLETS WITH CHOCOLATE SAUCE

All through Europe, particularly in the north, in lands where breakfast is traditionally bread, waffles aren't morning fare, but they are beloved. Pastry shops sell soft, puffy waffles — room temperature, without syrup or powdered sugar — as an eat-out-of-hand after-school treat. And at home and in restaurants, waffles are served as dessert, often with ice cream and chocolate sauce. These wafflets can be either a snack or a dessert, but if you decide to serve them for breakfast, who am I to judge?

The batter is based on cocoa powder and buttermilk and comes deliciously close to one you'd use to make a devil's food cake. Outside of America, these would be made in a Belgian waffle iron, the kind with the deepest indentations, but I've made them in everything from a Belgian iron to a pizzelle press and they're always good, so you can use whatever type of iron you have. The wafflets are small, and because I drop batter onto the iron in various places, each one is a different size and shape.

I can't resist playing around, so I've done a very un-European thing to the waffles: I've dried them in the oven so that they're truly like a cookie, more crisp and crackery than soft and cakey. Whether you crisp the wafflets or not, you'll want to have the chocolate sauce close by so that you can dip or even double dip. You also might want to turn the wafflets into ice cream sandwiches — they're perfect for the job.

Makes about 40 wafflets

TO MAKE THE WAFFLETS: Put the butter in a 2-cup microwave-safe measuring cup, cover and melt in the microwave (or do this in a pan on the stove). Pour the buttermilk over the butter. If the milk was cool and caused the butter to congeal, pop it back into the microwave (or over the heat) for just a couple of seconds to warm it. Whisk the butter and buttermilk together and then whisk in the egg and vanilla to blend.

Whisk the flour, sugar, cocoa, baking powder, baking soda and salt together

FOR THE WAFFLETS

7 tablespoons (3½ ounces; 99 grams) unsalted butter, cut into chunks

1 cup (240 ml) buttermilk, preferably at room temperature

1 large egg, at room temperature

1 teaspoon pure vanilla extract

1 cup (136 grams) all-purpose flour

½ cup (100 grams) sugar

⅓ cup (28 grams) unsweetened cocoa powder (sifted if lumpy)

2 teaspoons baking powder

½ teaspoon baking soda

¼ teaspoon fine sea salt

FOR THE SAUCE

½ cup (120 ml) heavy cream

½ cup (120 ml) whole milk

2 teaspoons sugar

Pinch of fine sea salt

3 ounces (85 grams) semisweet or bittersweet chocolate, coarsely chopped

1 tablespoon unsalted butter

The batter is best used as soon as it's mixed. Although the cookies are best eaten soon after they're baked, or packed airtight and frozen for up to 2 months, they can be kept in a covered container at room temperature overnight. The sauce will keep in a covered jar in the refrigerator for at least 1 week; serve cold or at room temperature.

in a large bowl. Pour the liquid ingredients over the dry and whisk until you have a smooth batter.

Heat a waffle (or pizzelle) maker according to the manufacturer's instructions. If you have to grease or spray it, do so for the first batch and then see if the butter in the waffles isn't sufficient to make the iron nonstick after that. Have small tongs or a small icing spatula and a cooling rack at hand.

You need a tablespoon of batter for each wafflet. Depending on your iron, you should be able to make at least 2, and up to 4, cookies at a time. Drop the spoonfuls of batter on the iron and wait a couple of seconds for the batter to start baking, then close the iron. Bake until the iron signals the waffles are done, or until they are brown and set on both sides; they'll still be soft. (My iron has heat settings; I bake these between medium and high.) It may take you a batch to figure out the baking — the first batch is for the baker. When the wafflets are baked, use the tongs or spatula to transfer them to the rack. Repeat until you've baked all the batter. The wafflets can be served as soon as they come off the iron or when they've reached room temperature.

IF YOU'D LIKE TO CRISP THE COOKIES: Center a rack in the oven and preheat it to 200 degrees F.

Place a rack over a baking sheet and arrange the wafflets in a single layer on the rack. Alternatively, you can put the wafflets directly on the oven rack. Bake for 30 to 45 minutes, or until they are crisp and dry. Let cool to room temperature.

TO MAKE THE SAUCE: Put the cream, milk, sugar and salt in a medium saucepan and bring to a boil over medium heat, stirring until the sugar is dissolved. Lower the heat, add the chocolate and heat, stirring, until the chocolate is melted. Remove the pan from the heat and stir in the butter, then pour the sauce into a heatproof bowl or jar. Press a piece of plastic against the surface and let the sauce cool to room temperature. It will thicken a little when it cools; it will thicken a bit more if, after it comes to room temperature, you cover it tightly and refrigerate it.

Serve the wafflets with the sauce, dunking the wafflets into the sauce or spooning it over them.

THREE-WAY SUGAR-CONE PIZZELLES

1 large egg

3 tablespoons sugar

1 tablespoon packed light brown sugar

1/2 teaspoon ground cinnamon

1/4 teaspoon fine sea salt

4 1/2 tablespoons (2 1/4 ounces; 64 grams) unsalted butter, melted and cooled

1/2 teaspoon pure vanilla extract

1/4 teaspoon pure almond extract

1/2 cup (68 grams) all-purpose flour

Pizzelles are always beautiful, but often their taste doesn't live up to their looks. Taste rules with these. So does versatility. The inspiration was the classic sugar cone, but the reality became that and more. The reason is the brown sugar (which I think of as a flavoring here), vanilla, almond and cinnamon.

Make the pizzelles and, if you have a cone mold, you can shape the cookies around the mold. If you don't have a mold, you can try turning the pizzelles into ice cream cones freehand, or you can press the hot-off-the-iron cookie around the bottom of a glass, a jar or a small bowl and make an ice cream cup. Or, and this is what I do most often, you can just flip them off the iron and onto a rack, let them cool and serve them flat, sandwiching ice cream.

A word on batch size: This recipe is easily doubled or tripled.

Makes about 10 pizzelles

Working in a bowl with a whisk, energetically beat the egg, both sugars, the cinnamon and salt together. When the mixture is smooth and seems slightly thickened, gently whisk in the butter and both extracts; you'll have a shiny batter. Finish by whisking in the flour until fully incorporated. Cover the bowl and let the batter rest at room temperature for at least 15 minutes, or for up to 1 hour.

Heat a pizzelle maker according to the manufacturer's instructions. If you have to butter or spray it, do so for the first batch and then see if the butter in the pizzelles isn't sufficient to make the iron nonstick. Have a long (and broad, if possible) icing spatula and a cooling rack at hand. If you are going to shape the pizzelles over a cone mold or a bowl (see headnote), have that at hand too.

You'll have to play with the batter to see what works best for your pizzelle maker; 1 tablespoon of batter is perfect for mine. Spoon the batter onto the center of the iron. If your iron makes 2 pizzelles at a time, you can double up, but I don't when I'm going to mold the cookies. Close the iron and bake for

The batter can be refrigerated, covered, for up to 1 day. Unless you live in a wildly humid place, you should be able to pack the pizzelles airtight and keep them for at least 5 days. They can also be frozen for up to 2 months. To return them to crisp, heat them very briefly in a 350-degree-F oven and cool on a rack.

20 to 35 seconds — check at 20 seconds and continue baking if necessary until you've got the color you want. (If your pizzelle maker has a choice of settings, set it at medium and check the color after 20 seconds.) The pizzelle should be golden and still supple. If you're not going to mold the pizzelle, use the spatula to get under it and then flip it onto the rack. If you are going to mold the pizzelle, work quickly and carefully — these are very, very hot! Either mold it around the cone mold or center it on the overturned glass or bowl and press against the edges. Pizzelles set in a matter of seconds.

Serve the pizzelles as soon as they cool, or wrap them airtight — they're sensitive to humidity.

FORTUNE COOKIES

After all the things I've baked over the years, I'm still gleeful when I make something that I've always thought of as not "homemakable." And so, just as you'd imagine, I was pretty tickled when I turned out these fortune cookies. Not that there's anything difficult about them, but they are fussy and like children: Turn your back on them and they'll do whatever they want.

The batter is a mix-it-together-in-a-flash blend of egg whites, sugar, flour and very soft butter. It's a breeze. Spreading it on a baking sheet using a homemade stencil — also easy. But there's a learning curve for shaping the cookies, and it involves a few broken ones. However, once you get the hang of it, you'll be very pleased with yourself.

Have fun making these. And have fun making up the fortunes. It's your chance to rule the world. Be kind, gentle, funny and inspiring, and don't forget to do what I do: Stuff a cookie or three with orders to hug the baker. You can always say it'll bring good fortune . . . and more cookies.

A word on temperature: In order to make an easily spreadable batter — and spreadability is all-important with these — make sure your butter is soft (not oily, but easily smearable) and your egg whites are at room temperature.

A word on baking: I've made these on buttered baking sheets and on baking sheets lined with silicone baking mats — the buttered sheets are better.

Makes about 18 cookies

3½ tablespoons (1¼ ounces; 49 grams) unsalted butter, very soft
¼ cup (50 grams) sugar
Pinch of fine sea salt
¼ teaspoon pure vanilla extract
¼ teaspoon pure almond extract
2 large egg whites, beaten with a fork, at room temperature
⅓ cup (45 grams) all-purpose flour

Center a rack in the oven and preheat it to 350 degrees F. Butter two smooth baking sheets (see headnote). Have a teaspoon, two small offset icing spatulas (one for spreading — you can use the back of a spoon, but a spatula is easier — and one for removing the cookies from the baking sheet), a cooling rack, a glass measuring cup (you'll use it to bend the cookies) and a mini-muffin tin at hand.

For the arts-and-crafts part of the project, cut 18 to 20 strips of paper,

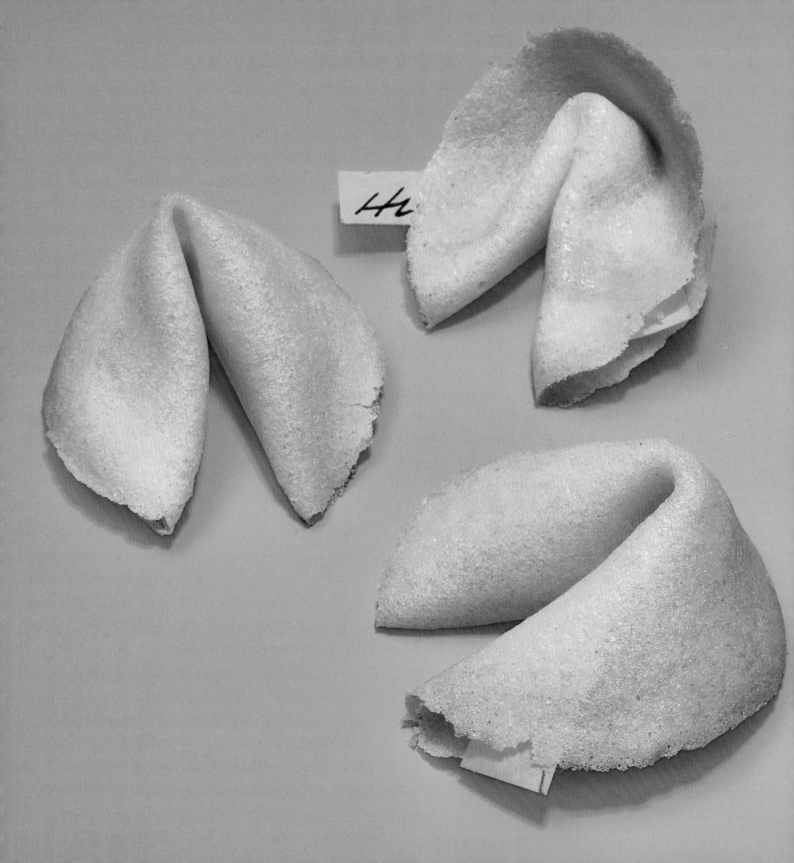

4 to 5 inches long and about ⅓ inch wide, and write your fortunes. Then use the top of a yogurt container or even a piece of the side of a waxed cardboard milk container to make a stencil: Cut out an inner circle that's 3 inches in diameter and leave yourself enough material around the opening to easily lift the stencil off the baking sheet.

Working with a mixer (stand or hand) or in a bowl with a sturdy flexible spatula, beat the butter until very creamy. Add the sugar and salt and mix until incorporated. Blend in the extracts. Little by little, work the whites into the mixture. Don't be discouraged when your batter looks like egg drop soup — it will all be fine. When you've done the best that you can with the whites, stir in the flour.

Because it takes some practice to fold and shape these, I suggest you make just one or two for the first batch. Lay the stencil flat against the baking sheet, spoon a rounded teaspoonful of batter into the center of it (more batter will make the cookies too thick; less will make them way too fragile) and use a small offset spatula (or the back of a spoon) to spread the batter evenly across the circle. The layer will be thin, and that's what will make your cookies wonderful. (Try not to make them much thicker in the center than around the edges.) Don't worry about getting batter on the stencil — it's actually a good thing (it means you've gone to the borders). Gently peel away or lift the stencil.

Bake for 6 to 7 minutes, or until the edges of the cookie(s) are just lightly browned. Now, working quickly and with the confidence that you'll really only have once you've got some experience, transfer the baking sheet to a rack on the counter and slide the offset spatula under one of the cookies. Flip the cookie over onto the counter, place a fortune just a little above the middle of it (the ends will extend beyond the cookie) and fold the cookie up over the fortune (the top edges should just about meet), then bend the straight side of the cookie over the edge of the measuring cup, curl the cookie and tuck it into the mini-muffin pan to shape it; hold it for a few seconds so that it cools in its shape.

Continue to bake and shape the cookies, always making sure the baking sheet is cool and buttered, and never baking more than 3 cookies at a time, because they'll harden too quickly for you to fold them nicely. The cookies set almost instantly, so you can serve them as soon as you like.

STORING
The least bit of humidity is enough to make these go soft, so store them in a covered container and hope that the weather stays dry; they'll be good for 1 week.

MAPLE–STAR ANISE COOKIES, SANDWICHED OR OPEN-FACED

Star anise rarely gets to take center stage. If you know it, you can pick it out even when it's used sparingly, as it almost always is. It's got a distinctive, leaning-toward-licorice taste prized in Asian cuisines, and it adds a touch of mystery to spice blends that include ginger and cinnamon, its mates in these cookies. Add maple syrup and brown sugar, and the flavors in these chubby cookies, with their light sugar crust and soft innards, conspire to create warmth and happiness.

These can easily be piled into the cookie jar as soon as they're cool, and they'll go fast. But make a gently spiced cream cheese frosting and use it to frost either the tops or bottoms of the cookies or, better yet, to fill and sandwich them, and they'll go even faster.

Makes about 48 cookies or 24 sandwiches

FOR THE COOKIES

1½ cups (204 grams) all-purpose flour

½ cup (68 grams) whole wheat flour

¾ teaspoon baking soda

1¼ teaspoons ground star anise

½ teaspoon ground ginger

¼ teaspoon ground cinnamon

2 sticks (8 ounces; 226 grams) unsalted butter, cut into chunks, at room temperature

½ cup (100 grams) packed light brown sugar

¼ cup (50 grams) sugar

Finely grated zest of 1 orange

½ teaspoon fine sea salt

1 large egg, at room temperature

2 tablespoons maple syrup

1 teaspoon pure vanilla extract

Raw or granulated sugar, for coating

FOR THE FILLING OR FROSTING (OPTIONAL)

1 recipe Cream Cheese Frosting (page 490)

2 teaspoons pure maple syrup

⅛ teaspoon ground star anise

⅛ teaspoon ground ginger

⅛ teaspoon ground cinnamon

Position the racks to divide the oven into thirds and preheat it to 350 degrees F. Line two baking sheets with parchment paper or silicone baking mats.

TO MAKE THE COOKIES: Whisk both flours, the baking soda, star anise, ginger and cinnamon together.

Working with a stand mixer fitted with the paddle attachment, or in a large bowl with a hand mixer, beat the butter, both sugars, the orange zest and salt on medium speed for 3 minutes, scraping down the bowl as needed. Add the egg, followed by the maple syrup and vanilla, and beat for another 2 minutes. Turn off the mixer, add the dry ingredients all at once and pulse until the risk of flying flour has passed. With the mixer on low, scraping the bowl when necessary, beat until the dry ingredients are fully incorporated.

Put some raw or granulated sugar in a small bowl. Using a small cookie scoop, scoop out level portions of dough or use a teaspoon to get rounded spoonfuls. Roll each cookie between your palms to make a ball, dredge in the sugar and place on the baking sheets, leaving a generous 2 inches of space between the balls — these are spreaders.

The dough can be kept covered in the refrigerator for up to 3 days (bake cold dough for 1 to 2 minutes longer) or wrapped airtight and frozen for up to 2 months. Unfilled or unfrosted, the cookies will keep in a covered container for about 4 days at room temperature or for up to 2 months, wrapped airtight, in the freezer. Sandwich cookies should be kept covered in the refrigerator (they'll keep for up to 4 days); frosted cookies can be kept for the same amount of time.

Bake for 11 to 12 minutes, rotating the sheets top to bottom and front to back after 5 minutes, or until the tops of the cookies have crusted — they'll still feel a little soft — and the edges are set. Transfer the sheets to racks and let the cookies rest for 5 minutes, then carefully lift them onto the racks and cool completely.

Repeat with the remaining dough, making certain that the baking sheets are cool.

TO MAKE THE FILLING OR FROSTING AND FINISH THE COOKIES (OPTIONAL): Put the cream cheese frosting in a bowl and, using a flexible spatula (or a mixer), beat in the remaining ingredients, beating until the mixture is smooth.

To frost the cookies, use a small offset icing spatula or a table knife to cover the tops or bottoms of the cookies. Frosted cookies can be refrigerated for 30 minutes to set the frosting or left at room temperature. If you'd like to make sandwich cookies, generously cover the bottoms of half the cookies with filling, sandwich the cookies and refrigerate; cover after about 30 minutes. Remove the cookies from the refrigerator about 15 minutes before serving.

You know those puff pastry cookies that look like hearts or butterflies and are called elephant ears or palmiers? The ones that are all golden brown because the sugar that they were rolled in caramelized in the oven? Well, these are close.

The base is the almost magical yeasted Sour Cream Puff Dough, which gets the same treatment you'd give to puff pastry, meaning you roll the dough out until it's twice as long as it is wide, fold it like a letter, turn it so it looks like a book and do it again and then again. Each time you roll the dough out on sugar, sugar becomes embedded in the dough, and then every part of the dough that touches the baking sheet becomes caramelized when baked. Because the sour cream dough is yeasted, it's lighter than traditional puff pastry. That you might want to eat these cookies the way you do popcorn is only to be expected.

A word on amounts: I'm giving you a recipe that uses half of the Sour Cream Puff Dough. If you'd like, you can double the amount of sugar here and roll and bake the full batch. Or make savory Sour Cream–Everything Seed Knots (page 444) with the other half of the dough. (The dough you don't use now can be refrigerated for up to 4 days.)

Makes about 30 cookies

Clear a large work surface and have a ruler at hand. Sprinkle the surface with some sugar, place the dough on the sugar and sprinkle some sugar over the dough. (You're going to roll and fold the dough 3 times; by the end of the third roll, you'll have used the full ½ cup sugar.) Roll the dough, lifting it from time to time to make sure it's not sticking and sprinkling the work surface with sugar as needed, until it's about 16 inches long and 8 inches wide. It's hard to be exact, but the closer you can come to these measurements and to having the dough be twice as long as it is wide, the more evenly it will puff in the oven. Fold the dough in thirds as you would a business letter (i.e., lift the bottom third of the dough, the end closest to you, over the center of the dough and then bring the top third of the dough over until the edge of that piece reaches the bottom fold). Give

½ cup (100 grams) sugar, plus extra for the last rollout

½ recipe Sour Cream Puff Dough (page 497; make the full recipe and reserve the other half — see headnote), chilled and ready to roll

All-purpose flour, for dusting, if needed

STORING

While the dough can be wrapped and refrigerated for up to 4 days, once you start rolling the dough in sugar, you must go right through and bake the cookies, stopping just to refrigerate or freeze the dough briefly between rolls and turns. The cookies are best eaten the day they are baked.

the dough a quarter turn, so that the long side that looks like the pages of a book is on your right. This is the basic technique for this dough and it's the one you'll repeat, always turning the dough in the same direction.

If your room is very hot and/or the dough is very soft and you think you'll have trouble continuing to roll it, slide it onto a parchment-lined baking sheet and pop it into the refrigerator or freezer for 15 minutes. And, if your dough gets soft and seems to tear, patch it as best you can, sprinkling the tear with flour, and give it a chill before carrying on.

If you think you need to dust the work surface and the dough with flour, do so, but be stingy. Roll, fold and turn the dough two more times, always rolling it on sugar and sprinkling sugar on top of the dough (using only as much flour as you need to keep things moving if necessary). When you have completed 3 full turns, chill the dough until you're ready to bake it, up to 2 hours.

GETTING READY TO BAKE: Position the racks to divide the oven into thirds and preheat it to 375 degrees F. Line two baking sheets with parchment paper or silicone baking mats.

Sprinkle additional sugar on the work surface and over the dough and roll the dough out once more into a 16-x-8-inch rectangle. Using a bench scraper, a pizza wheel or a knife (being careful not to mar your counter), cut the dough in half from top to bottom and then crosswise into 1-inch-wide bands. If you'd prefer smaller cookies, cut the bands crosswise in half to make nuggets. Place the cookies on the baking sheets, leaving an inch or so between them.

Bake for 14 to 16 minutes, rotating the sheets top to bottom and front to back after 8 minutes, or until the cookies are puffed and golden brown. Transfer the baking sheets to racks and allow the cookies to rest for 3 minutes or so, then carefully lift them onto the racks to cool to just warm or to room temperature.

PLAYING AROUND

Caramel-Sugar Twists. Cut the dough into bands that are ½ inch wide, twist them before placing them on the baking sheet and gently press the ends onto the sheet. Even though you press the ends, the dough might still rise so exuberantly in the oven that the twists will turn into bent bands — no matter, they'll still be good.

FRIENDSHIP COOKIES

FOR THE DOUGH

4 ounces (113 grams) cold full-fat cream
  cheese, cut into 4 pieces

1 stick (8 tablespoons; 4 ounces; 113 grams)
  cold unsalted butter, cut into 4 pieces

1 cup (136 grams) all-purpose flour

¼ teaspoon fine sea salt

FOR THE FILLING

¼ cup (40 grams) plump, moist raisins

⅔ cup (212 grams) seedless raspberry jam,
  apricot jam or marmalade

2 tablespoons sugar

½ teaspoon ground cinnamon

¼ cup (30 grams) chopped pecans,
  walnuts or almonds

4 ounces (113 grams) finely chopped
  semisweet or bittersweet chocolate
  or ⅔ cup (113 grams) mini chocolate
  chips

FOR THE GLAZE

1 large egg

1 teaspoon cold water

2 tablespoons sugar, preferably sanding
  sugar

In truth, these are rugelach, but while I've been making them for decades, I still don't know if I'm pronouncing their name correctly. I go with a short u, as in rug, but perhaps the u is long, as in rue. Recently I decided to stop worrying about this detail and just call these roll-up sweets Friendship Cookies, because no matter whom I serve these to, the recipients want to follow me home and be my best friend.

I learned to make rugelach from my mother-in-law, who made the cream cheese dough in a bowl with a wooden spoon (which is how I made it until I got a food processor). She filled her almost crescent-shaped cookies with cinnamon-sugar, currants and nuts, and I did too, for a while. Soon after those first forays, though, I succumbed to the lure of a layer of jam and the appeal of some chocolate pieces. And that's pretty much been my standard. Recently I fiddled with the dough again, adding crushed Triscuits to it, and came up with cocktail cookies I'm crazy about. When you're ready to move to the salty side, give them a try (see pages 388 and 441).

A word on the filling: I'm giving you what I consider my classic, but I mix it up lots and you should too. Try using dried cherries or bits of dried apricots in place of the raisins. And, if you'd like, soak the fruit in tea or something stronger (cherries are great in kirsch or port; apricots in rum, Grand Marnier or amaretto). Of course you can change the nuts as well as the cinnamon and jam. You could even forget the jam . . . as long as you're not making rugelach for my husband.

Makes 32 cookies

TO MAKE THE DOUGH: Let the pieces of cream cheese and butter rest on the counter for 5 minutes — you want them to be slightly softened but still cool.

Put the flour and salt in a food processor and pulse to blend. Scatter the chunks of cream cheese and butter over the dry ingredients and pulse the machine 6 to 10 times. Once you've got everything broken up, process in long

Wrapped airtight, the dough can be frozen for up to 2 months. The cookies are truly at their best soon after they're made. If you must keep them overnight, pack them in a container and then reheat them briefly in a 350-degree-F oven before serving. The baked cookies can be wrapped airtight and frozen for up to 2 months, but the best way to freeze these is unbaked; bake them directly from the freezer, adding a few extra minutes of oven time.

pulses, scraping down the sides of the bowl often, just until the dough forms large curds — don't work it so long that it forms a ball on the blade.

Turn the dough out and gather it together. Divide it in half and shape each half into a disk; work with one disk at a time. Lightly flour a piece of parchment paper, set the dough on the paper, flour the top of the dough, cover with another piece of parchment and start rolling. You're aiming for a circle that's 11 to 12 inches in diameter. Don't worry about getting it perfectly round — ragged edges are just fine. Slide the dough, still sandwiched between the paper, onto a baking sheet — you can stack the slabs — and freeze for at least 1 hour, or refrigerate for at least 2 hours.

GETTING READY TO BAKE: Position the racks to divide the oven into thirds and preheat it to 325 degrees F. Have two baking sheets and a pizza wheel (or knife) at hand. If you've got silicone baking mats, line the baking sheets with them — they make removing the roll-ups much easier. If not, use parchment paper.

TO MAKE THE FILLING AND SHAPE THE RUGELACH: Toss the raisins into a small bowl and cover with very hot tap water. Allow them to soak while you're working on the rest of the filling. Drain and pat them dry before using.

Stir the jam. If you think it will be hard to spread a layer on the dough, add a splash of water and warm it in the microwave just to thin it a bit. Let it cool — you don't want to melt the dough.

Stir the sugar and cinnamon together.

Working with one piece of dough at a time, peel away both pieces of parchment and put the dough back on one piece. With a pastry brush or an offset spatula, spread a thin layer of jam over the dough. Sprinkle over half of the cinnamon-sugar, half of the nuts, half of the raisins and half of the chopped chocolate. Cover the filling with a piece of parchment and press very gently to "glue" the filling to the dough; remove the paper. Using the pizza wheel or a knife, cut the circle into quarters and cut each quarter into 4 wedges. Test the dough: If you think you can roll it up, get to work; if the dough cracks, let it rest on the counter for a few minutes. Starting at the base of each wedge, roll the dough up. The jam will ooze out and be messy — that's just how it goes. Place the rugelach on the lined baking sheet, making sure the points are underneath, and refrigerate while you fill and shape the second batch of rugelach.

TO GLAZE AND BAKE THE RUGELACH: Beat the egg lightly with the cold water and brush a thin coat of the glaze over the tops of the rugelach. Sprinkle with the sugar.

Bake the roll-ups for 37 to 40 minutes, rotating the sheets front to back and top to bottom after 20 minutes, or until they are beautifully golden. The jam will have bubbled and burned around the edges, but the bottoms will be fine. You want to lift the rugelach off the baking sheet as soon as they come from the oven, especially if you've baked them on parchment — if you wait, the jam will glue the cookies to the paper. Transfer them to racks and cool to just warm or to room temperature before serving.

VALENTINE'S DAY SHARE-A-HEART

FOR THE COOKIES

1½ cups (204 grams) all-purpose flour

1¼ cups (150 grams) confectioners' sugar

¼ cup (21 grams) unsweetened cocoa powder

1 teaspoon fine sea salt

1 stick plus 1 tablespoon (9 tablespoons; 4½ ounces; 128 grams) cold unsalted butter, cut into 18 pieces

1 cold large egg yolk

1 tablespoon ice water

Sanding sugar, for sprinkling (optional)

FOR THE ICING (OPTIONAL)

1 cup (120 grams) confectioners' sugar

1 to 2 tablespoons water

Unsweetened cocoa powder (optional)

Sanding sugar, sprinkles or small candies, for decorating (optional)

I love the idea of a big cookie, a really big cookie, one that can be put in the center of the table, within easy reach of everyone, and picked at and broken and cracked and nibbled while the conversation keeps going. And I love this giant cookie because of its deep chocolate flavor and its fabulous texture: part flaky shortbread and part crisp snap. I originally created it for Valentine's Day, cutting the dough into two large hearts and using the scraps to make smaller cookies, and it's great for this celebration not just because it's shareable, but because it's so easy to decorate with anything from a dusting of sugar to XOXOs made from candy or a fancy filigree picked out in royal icing (page 488). It's the proverbial blank canvas. I've decorated many of these, but my favorites are the simplest designs: covering the entire cookie with cocoa icing and then piping XOXOXO across the middle in white icing; or going very old-school and putting the fanciest cake stencil I can find (you can use a doily) over the cookie, covering it with confectioners' sugar and then lifting off the stencil; or just icing the edges of the heart and trimming it with colorful sprinkles.

Of course, any cookie that's this delicious, this easy to work with and so reliable shouldn't be a once-a-year treat. Turn to this recipe whenever you want to make decorated cut-out cookies — I do.

Makes 2 large hearts plus a variable number of smaller cookies

TO MAKE THE COOKIES: Put the flour, sugar, cocoa and salt in a food processor and pulse to blend. Scatter over the chunks of cold butter and pulse until they are cut in and the mixture looks grainy. Lightly beat the yolk and water together in a small bowl and add a little at a time, pulsing after each addition. Then process in 10-second pulses until the dough forms clumps and curds. Pinch the dough, and it should hold together — if it doesn't, pulse a few more times.

Turn the dough out onto the counter, divide it in half and shape each piece into a disk.

Working with one piece of dough at a time, put it between pieces of parchment paper and roll into a circle, turning the packet over frequently and lifting

the paper often so that it doesn't roll into the dough and create creases. Try to get a circle that's about 9 inches in diameter and about ⅛ inch thick, but a little thicker is fine. Slide the rounds, still between the paper, onto a baking sheet — you can stack the slabs — and freeze for at least 1 hour, or refrigerate for at least 2 hours.

GETTING READY TO BAKE: Position the racks to divide the oven into thirds and preheat it to 350 degrees F.

Again working with one sheet of dough at a time, peel away the top and bottom pieces of paper and then replace them (if you don't loosen them, the dough may buckle during baking). Using a pencil, draw a large heart on the top paper and use a sharp knife to cut out the heart. Lift off the top paper, remove the excess dough (save the scraps) and slide the heart, still on the bottom piece of paper, onto a baking sheet. If you don't plan to decorate the cookies, you can sprinkle them with sanding sugar, if you'd like.

Bake the hearts for 19 to 22 minutes, rotating the baking sheets top to bottom and front to back after 10 minutes, or until they're dull, a little crinkled, set around the edges and almost firm at their centers. Transfer the baking sheets to racks and let the cookies rest for 5 minutes, then carefully slide them, paper and all, onto the racks to cool completely.

While the big hearts are baking, gather the scraps together, re-roll them, chill and then use small heart-shaped cutters to cut out additional cookies; bake for 16 to 18 minutes, or until done, as above.

TO MAKE THE ICING AND FINISH THE COOKIES (OPTIONAL): Mix the confectioners' sugar with 1 tablespoon water. If it's too thick to run off the tip of a spoon and form a ribbon, add more water drop by drop. If you want chocolate icing, scrape some of the white icing into a small bowl and stir in as much cocoa as you need to get the color you like. Use an offset icing spatula or a table knife to cover the cookies with icing and then decorate any way you want. If you're using sanding sugar, sprinkles or small candies, sprinkle them over the icing while it's still wet. Allow the icing to set at room temperature.

GREEK HONEY DAINTIES

You may know these fabulous cookies as the Greek specialty *meloma-karona*, but the mother of Connecticut chef Matt Wick likes to call them Honey Dainties. Whatever you call them, they're kind of remarkable: the ingredient list looks plain to the point of drab — definitely unpromising — and the dough itself doesn't look like anything special. But what happens in the oven is magical. Under heat, the cookies become sandy, with a melt-in-your-mouth texture that borders on evanescent — they melt so quickly, you almost expect to hear them go *pouf!*

Once the cookies are baked and cooled, you spoon over a honey syrup that works its way into them — but not all the way, so that you get the moist honey layer and then that lovely sandy texture. The cookies are finished with chopped walnuts.

Like Mrs. Wick, I make these fairly large, but you can go smaller, if you'd like (just watch the baking time). Unlike Mrs. Wick, I change them up a bit; see Playing Around.

Makes 18 cookies

Center a rack in the oven and preheat it to 350 degrees F. Line a baking sheet with parchment paper or a silicone baking mat.

TO MAKE THE COOKIES: Whisk the flour, baking powder and baking soda together.

Working with a stand mixer fitted with the paddle attachment, or in a large bowl with a hand mixer, beat the butter and sugar together on medium-low speed until blended, about 3 minutes. With the mixer running, slowly pour in the oil, followed by the orange juice, and beat until you have a creamy, homogenous mixture that resembles mayonnaise. Turn off the mixer, add the dry ingredients all at once and pulse just to begin the blending, then mix on low speed only until the flour is fully incorporated. You'll have a very soft dough.

You need about 2 teaspoons of dough for each cookie — I use a small cookie scoop to portion the dough, but you can use a teaspoon and scoop out rounded teaspoonfuls of dough. Gently shape each piece into a ball and then work the

FOR THE COOKIES

1¾ cups (238 grams) all-purpose flour

1 teaspoon baking powder

½ teaspoon baking soda

1 stick (8 tablespoons; 4 ounces; 113 grams) unsalted butter, cut into chunks, very soft

⅓ cup (67 grams) sugar

⅓ cup (80 ml) flavorless oil, such as canola

1 tablespoon orange juice

FOR THE SYRUP

¾ cup (150 grams) sugar

½ cup (120 ml) water

⅓ cup (80 grams) honey

About ⅓ cup (40 grams) finely chopped walnuts, for decorating

STORING

Packed between layers of parchment or wax paper, the cookies will keep in a covered container at room temperature for up to 3 days. Packed airtight, they can be frozen for up to 2 months; defrost in the wrapping.

ball into an oval: I find it easiest to rest the dough between my thumb and index finger, and then make an elongated "okay" sign, bringing the tips of my thumb and index fingers together and patting the dough in place to form the oval with my other hand. As you shape the cookies, place them on the lined baking sheet, leaving at least 2 inches between them (these expand more than you'd think they would). Pat the cookies down lightly and finish by poking a few holes in each one using a skewer or toothpick — but don't go all the way down to the baking sheet.

Bake the cookies for 15 to 17 minutes, rotating the pan after 8 minutes, or until they are very lightly golden on top; they'll be darker on the bottom. Using a wide spatula and working carefully — these are very fragile — transfer the cookies to a rack and cool completely.

MEANWHILE, MAKE THE SYRUP: Stir the sugar, water and honey together in a small saucepan, bring to a boil over medium heat, lower the heat and simmer for 5 minutes. Pour the syrup into a heatproof measuring cup or bowl and let cool to room temperature.

TO FINISH THE COOKIES: Line a baking sheet with aluminum foil and place the rack of cookies over the sheet. Spoon the syrup over the cookies, aiming to cover their surface. When you've spooned syrup over each cookie, lift the rack onto the counter and pour the syrup that's on the foil back into the cup or bowl. Return the rack to the baking sheet and, once again, spoon syrup over the cookies. If there's still syrup on the foil after this round, repeat. Sprinkle some walnuts down the center of each cookie, pressing the nuts down lightly. Let the cookies rest for about 1 hour before serving or storing.

PLAYING AROUND

Christmas-Spiced Honey Dainties. Whisk 1 teaspoon ground cinnamon, ¼ teaspoon ground ginger, ¼ teaspoon fine sea salt, a pinch of cloves and a few gratings of nutmeg into the dry ingredients. Before you put anything else in the mixer bowl, grate the zest of 1 orange over the sugar and work the two ingredients together with your fingers until the sugar is moist and aromatic. Add the butter and beat and then, when you add the oil and orange juice, add 1 teaspoon pure vanilla extract as well. Finish the dough and bake as at left. If you want to flavor the syrup — a nice touch — add a short cinnamon stick, a few strips of orange peel and 1 whole clove to the pan and boil as at left, then strain.

KAMISH

FOR THE COOKIES

3 cups (408 grams) all-purpose flour

2 teaspoons baking powder

1 teaspoon ground cinnamon

½ teaspoon fine sea salt

3 large eggs, at room temperature

1 cup (200 grams) sugar

1 cup (240 ml) flavorless oil, such as canola

1 teaspoon pure vanilla extract

2 cups (300 grams) almonds, coarsely
    chopped

½ cup (60 grams) shredded sweetened
    coconut

FOR SPRINKLING

⅓ cup (67 grams) sugar

¼ cup (30 grams) shredded sweetened
    coconut

2 teaspoons ground cinnamon

When I was very young, my grandmother, a wonderful baker, used to come to visit us with boxes of sweets. There'd be sugar cookies (some with poppy seeds); apple squares; heavy, moist honey cakes; and mandelbrot, a crunchy cookie that didn't interest me. Sadly, by the time I came to appreciate those sweets — think of them as the Eastern European version of biscotti — my grandmother was no longer alive to make them. But there are many other grandmothers, and I have tasted many of their mandelbrots, all good, but few as wonderful as this one from Toby Reichert, which she refers to as *kamish*. I first had it in Toronto, where her daughter, Adell Schneer, a food editor there, made the cookies for me. Since then, they've been the standard against which I measure all other mandelbrot.

Mandelbrot is Yiddish for "almond bread" and, indeed, while some people add chocolate chips, dried fruit or coconut, as Toby does, if it doesn't have almonds, then your cookie can't be considered a member of the mandel tribe. Toby's addition of coconut is both unusual and inspired, as is the way she sprinkles cinnamon-sugar and coconut on the cookies before they return to the oven for their second bake.

Adell added a note to the recipe, explaining that her mother sometimes leaves the cookies in the oven to dry overnight because they are best really toasty and crisp. I think they're perfection without the overnight rest, but if you think drier, crisper and toastier would be even more to your liking, turn off the oven and leave them there until morning. (Just remember they're there before you preheat the oven to bake something else.)

A word on the almonds: I prefer to chop whole unblanched almonds for the cookies, but if you've got blanched, it's fine, and if you've got slivered, that's okay too. Whatever you've got, chop them very coarse — it's good to have large chunks of almond here and there.

Makes about 60 cookies

TO MAKE THE COOKIES: Whisk together the flour, baking powder, cinnamon and salt.

Working in a large bowl, whisk the eggs and sugar together until pale in color, about 2 minutes. Beat in the oil — the mixture will thicken slightly — followed by the vanilla. Switch to a flexible spatula, add half of the flour mixture and stir it in gently; add the remaining flour and stir to blend. Fold in the almonds and coconut. Cover the bowl and refrigerate the dough for at least 30 minutes, or for up to 2 hours.

GETTING READY TO BAKE: Position the racks to divide the oven into thirds and preheat it to 350 degrees F. Line two baking sheets with parchment paper or silicone baking mats.

Mix the sprinkling ingredients together in a small bowl. Sprinkle half of the mixture on a piece of parchment or wax paper.

Working with one quarter of the dough at time, roll the dough on the sugared paper into a 12-inch-long log. Place 2 logs on each lined baking sheet, positioning them so that each log is about 2 inches from a long side of the sheet.

Bake the logs for 25 minutes, rotating the baking sheets top to bottom and front to back after 12 minutes. Transfer the baking sheets to racks and let the logs (which will have expanded and cracked) rest for 15 minutes.

Lower the oven temperature to 300 degrees F.

Working with one log at a time, use a long serrated knife to cut the logs into ½-inch-thick slices. This is a case in which perfection will be out of reach — accept it. Return the slices to the lined baking sheets, placing them cut side down. Sprinkle the cookies with half of the remaining sugar mixture.

Bake the cookies for 20 minutes, rotating the sheets after 10 minutes. Remove the baking sheets, turn the cookies over and sprinkle with the rest of the sugar mixture. Bake for 20 minutes more. Transfer the baking sheets to racks and allow the mandelbrot to cool completely.

HAMANTASCHEN

These fruit-filled cookies are named for Haman, the villain of the Book of Esther. To make a long and evil story short, Mordecai, the son of Esther, considered the Queen of the Jews in biblical times, refused to bow down to Haman, the Grand Vizier of Persia, who — and this is key — wore a tri-cornered hat. Enraged, Haman plotted to kill all the Jews. Esther and Mordecai learned of the plot, foiled it, saved the Jews and did away with Haman.

Jewish children commemorate Esther's daring feat by reenacting the story for the holiday of Purim, complete with noisemakers that are wound up every time Haman's name is mentioned. And then, to celebrate the victory, there are these cookies, made with a soft, sweet dough, filled with jammy dried fruit and nuts and shaped like Haman's triangular hat. Maybe this is what is meant by "sweet revenge."

A word on the filling: You'll have leftover filling. If you'd like, you can cut the recipe in half, but I never do. The cooked fruit makes a jam that's great on toast.

Makes about 24 cookies

TO MAKE THE DOUGH: Whisk together the flour and baking powder.

Working with a stand mixer fitted with the paddle attachment, or in a large bowl with a hand mixer, beat the sugar, oil, egg, juice, vanilla and salt on medium speed for about 2 minutes, until the mixture is smooth and shiny. Turn the mixer off, add the flour all at once and pulse to incorporate, stopping to scrape down the sides and bottom of the bowl as needed. What you'll have will look more like a batter than a dough, but that's fine. Wrap it in plastic and refrigerate it for 1 hour, the time it takes for it to remind itself that it's a dough.

Remove the dough from the refrigerator, divide it in half and form each half into a disk. Keep one piece in the refrigerator while you work on the other. Generously flour a piece of parchment paper, place the dough on it, flour the dough, cover with another piece of parchment and roll it out to a thickness of

FOR THE DOUGH

2 cups (272 grams) all-purpose flour

2 teaspoons baking powder

2/3 cup (134 grams) sugar

1/2 cup (120 ml) flavorless oil, such as canola

1 large egg, at room temperature

2 tablespoons orange juice

1 teaspoon pure vanilla extract

1/4 teaspoon fine sea salt

FOR THE FILLING

8 ounces (226 grams) plump, moist mixed dried fruit, such as apricots, prunes, figs, cherries and/or raisins, snipped or chopped into small pieces

About 3/4 cup (180 ml) orange or apple juice

1 tablespoon honey

1 tablespoon jam, such as apricot or cherry, or orange marmalade

1/4 cup (25 grams) sliced almonds or chopped walnuts

⅛ inch — not thinner and, if you can manage it, not thicker either. Roll on both sides of the dough and peel away the papers a few times so that you don't roll the paper into the dough. Flour the dough, if needed — this dough is soft and sticky. Roll out the second piece of dough, stack one piece, still between the paper, on top of the other on a baking sheet and freeze for at least 2 hours.

TO MAKE THE FILLING: While the dough is resting, put the fruit and juice in a medium saucepan and bring to a boil. Lower the heat, cover and simmer slowly, stirring occasionally, until the fruit is soft and the liquid has been absorbed, about 12 minutes. If the liquid disappears before the fruit is soft, add a little more (the additional liquid can be water). Add the honey, jam and nuts and stir over low heat for about 3 minutes. Scrape the chunky jam into a bowl and cool to room temperature.

TO FILL AND BAKE THE HAMANTASCHEN: Center a rack in the oven and preheat it to 375 degrees F. Line two baking sheets with parchment paper or silicone baking mats. Have a 2¾- to 3-inch-diameter round cookie cutter at hand.

Working with one piece of dough at a time (keep the other frozen — even after chilling, the dough will be very soft), peel away both pieces of paper and put the dough back on one piece. Cut out as many circles as you can. I find it best to transfer the rounds of dough to the lined baking sheet as they're cut. (If you find the dough too soft to work with, just pop the sheet of circles back into the freezer for about 15 minutes.) Place a heaping teaspoonful of filling in the center of each cookie. Lift two sides of the cookie and pinch together the point where they meet. Lift the remaining side and pinch together the points where it meets the other two sides of the dough; you'll have a triangle with a mound of filling peeking above the dough.

Bake the hamantaschen for 15 to 17 minutes, rotating the sheet after 8 minutes, or until the cookies are deep brown around the edges and the pinched-together points and paler in the center. (While this batch is baking, you can form the second batch — stow them in the fridge until the oven is free.) Leave the cookies on the baking sheet for a couple of minutes, then carefully transfer them to a rack to rest until they are only just warm or at room temperature.

Bake the second batch on cooled baking sheets.

MATZO MORSELS

"You don't have to be Jewish to love Levy's Real Jewish Rye," was the tag line of a brilliant advertisement. And it's the line that came to mind the first time I served these no-bake morsels. I made them for a friend for Passover, the Jewish holiday during which nothing leavened is eaten and cracker-like matzo stands in for the daily loaf. Now I make them all year long, just because they're great.

Nothing more than crumbled matzo, dried fruit and chocolate chips bound together with melted chocolate and butter, the morsels are crunchy and chewy, a bit salty and a lot chocolatey.

Makes about 40 morsels

Line a baking sheet with parchment paper or a silicone baking mat.

Put the raisins or cranberries in a heatproof bowl, add enough very hot tap water to cover them and set aside to soak. When you're ready for them, drain and pat them dry between paper towels.

Toss the chunks of butter into another heatproof bowl, cover with the chopped chocolate and place the bowl over a pan of simmering water (the water shouldn't touch the bottom of the bowl). Heat, stirring occasionally, until the ingredients are melted and smooth; don't heat so much that the butter and chocolate separate. If the bowl is large enough to hold all of the ingredients, you can continue working in it; if not, scrape the butter and chocolate into a larger bowl.

Working with a flexible spatula, stir in the salt, followed by the bits of matzo. When all the pieces of matzo are coated with chocolate, stir in the chocolate chips and dried fruit, stirring until everything is coated in chocolate.

The best way to shape these is to use a small cookie scoop, so you can neatly pack the matzo. If you don't have a scoop, use a rounded teaspoon for each cookie and cup your hand to press the mix into the spoon and shape it. However you're shaping the cookies, put them on the baking sheet as you go. When all the mix is used, slide the baking sheet into the freezer to set the chocolate, about 20 minutes. Once the chocolate is set, the cookies are ready to be served.

1 cup (about 140 grams) plump, moist raisins or dried cranberries

½ stick (4 tablespoons; 2 ounces; 56 grams) unsalted butter, cut into chunks

6 ounces (170 grams) semisweet or bittersweet chocolate, coarsely chopped

¾ teaspoon fine sea salt

4 pieces (about 115 grams) unsalted matzo, crumbled (about 2 cups)

½ cup (85 grams) chocolate chips (semi-sweet, milk, or white chocolate or butterscotch)

STORING

The cookies can be kept covered in the refrigerator for up to 4 days or packed airtight and frozen for up to 2 months. They're surprisingly good snacked on just a few minutes out of the freezer.

COCO-ALMOND THUMBPRINTS

FOR THE MACAROONS

2 cups (200 grams) sliced or slivered almonds (blanched or unblanched)

1 cup (120 grams) shredded sweetened coconut

½ cup (100 grams) sugar

2 large egg whites

FOR THE CHOCOLATE FILLING

3 ounces (85 grams) semisweet or bittersweet chocolate, coarsely chopped

3 tablespoons heavy cream

I first made these as a Passover dessert and they were just right: free of wheat and leavening, as foods for Passover must be, and familiar as a play on the popular-for-Passover coconut macaroon. And then, after Passover ended, I kept the recipe on the top of the pile to make for friends who were on gluten-free diets.

The cookies themselves, really macaroons, have just four ingredients: almonds, coconut, sugar and egg whites. Made in a food processor, they come together in 5 minutes. Roll the dough between your palms to form little balls, press an indent into their bellies and pop them into the oven, then decide what you'd like to fill them with. I almost always go for a thick chocolate ganache, but they're wonderful with jam (the traditional filler), Nutella (or Fauxtella, page 480), peanut butter, citrus curd (page 467) or, if it's summer, a fresh berry or two nestled into each cookie just before you serve them. Oh, if you fill the cookies with chocolate and they remind you of an Almond Joy, I'll understand.

A word on the almonds and egg whites: To get the best texture, start with sliced (my preference) or slivered almonds and grind them in a food processor. If you use almond flour instead, the macaroons will be heavy and their texture won't be nearly as interesting; when you use the processor, you get a somewhat uneven mix. It's nice to have a few larger pieces of nuts here and there. As for the whites, I can't give you an exact measurement for them. In all likelihood, you'll need both whites, but just before the last bit goes into the processor, pinch the dough: If it holds together and feels as though you'll have an easy time rolling balls between your palms, call it quits.

Makes about 30 cookies

Center a rack in the oven and preheat it to 350 degrees F. Use an insulated baking sheet or stack two regular baking sheets, one on top of the other. Line the (top) sheet with parchment paper or a silicone baking mat.

TO MAKE THE MACAROONS: Put the almonds, coconut and sugar in a food processor and pulse until the nuts are ground. There should still be a few larger pieces of nuts scattered throughout the mix. Pour the whites into a small bowl and stir them with a fork just to break them up. Add a bit of the whites to the processor, pulse to incorporate them, and then keep doing this until you've got a dough that holds together when you squeeze it. You'll probably use all the whites, but you might need a tad less. Keep in mind that it's better to have a moist dough than a dry one. Remove the bowl from the machine and the blade from the bowl.

Drop rounded teaspoonfuls of dough about 1½ inches apart onto the baking sheet, or use a small cookie scoop. Shape each mound of dough into a ball between your palms, pressing so that the ball is compact, then make a small indentation in each cookie, using the knuckle of your index finger, your thumb or the end of a wooden spoon — steady the cookie with one hand while you're pressing into it with the other so that it doesn't crack too much. (It will always crack — it's unavoidable — but if you stabilize the cookie, the cracks won't split the cookie in two.)

Bake the cookies for 14 to 16 minutes, rotating the pan at the midway mark, or until they are firm and golden brown on their bottoms; they won't color much elsewhere. Transfer the baking sheet to a cooling rack.

TO MAKE THE FILLING: Put the chocolate and cream in a microwave-safe bowl or measuring cup and heat them in the microwave until the chocolate melts; stir to smooth the ganache. Alternatively, you can heat the chocolate and cream together in a small bowl set over a pan of simmering water.

TO FINISH THE COOKIES: Using a small spoon, fill each macaroon with enough chocolate to come level with the top of the cookie. Allow the chocolate to set at room temperature. (The chocolate will never be hard — a good thing.) If you're in a hurry, you can pop the macaroons into the refrigerator for 10 to 20 minutes to set the ganache.

"CORKED" BRETON GALETTES

I'm never sure what to do when I offer someone a Breton galette. Should I mention that it's salty or should I let that be a surprise? I usually opt for surprise, because I remember how happy I was the first time I discovered the cookie. It's a classic from Brittany, in the west of France, the only part of the country that uses salted butter for everything from fried eggs to elegant desserts.

The cookie is always thick, like a puck; always rich with butter; and always an unexpected cross between chewy and just slightly crunchy. The texture comes from the unusual addition of baking powder and the effect that the leavening has on a cookie this chubby. The flavor comes from basic ingredients — just flour, butter, sugar and eggs — yet finishing one cookie spurs an urge to take another.

Since probably forever, galettes (sometimes called *palets*, another word for "puck" or "disk") were plain butter cookies, never decorated, never iced, never fussed over. But things change . . . even classics. One day, wandering around Paris, I came across a pastry shop that had filled galettes. The cookies themselves were traditional, but each had an indentation (like a thumbprint cookie) and was a mini container for something soft and sweet. A few inquiries, and I discovered that the indents came not from thumbs, but from neat, more symmetrical wine corks.

As soon as the galettes come from the oven, press a cork into the center of each cookie. As the cookies cool, a little crust forms on the indentation, and then it's ready to be filled with whatever pleases you. I usually go for jam, but don't let my loyalty stand in the way of your creativity. See Playing Around for some ideas.

A word on butter: Since salted butter from Brittany is so much saltier than ours, I use regular butter and add fleur de sel (or sea salt) to the dough.

Makes about 36 cookies

FOR THE COOKIES

2¼ cups (306 grams) all-purpose flour

2½ teaspoons baking powder

2 sticks (8 ounces; 226 grams) unsalted butter, cut into chunks, at room temperature

1 cup (200 grams) sugar

1¼ teaspoons fleur de sel or ¾ teaspoon fine sea salt

2 large egg yolks, at room temperature

FOR THE FILLING

About ¾ cup (240 grams) thick fruit jam or marmalade

1 tablespoon water

STORING

You can wrap the logs of dough airtight and refrigerate them for up to 3 days or freeze for up to 2 months. Unfilled cookies can be kept in a covered container for about 3 days, but filled cookies are best eaten the day the jam goes in or the next day; pack in a single layer or in layers separated by parchment or wax paper.

Other fanciful fillings and flourishes.
Think about filling the indentations with citrus curd (page 467), marmalade, finely chopped berries tossed with a little jelly (thin the jelly with water if necessary), pastry cream, chocolate ganache (page 476 or 479) or dulce de leche (page 486). For even more fun, after you've filled the cookies, top the filling with a whole berry or a slice of soft fruit, a tiny meringue or a dusting of chopped toasted or caramelized nuts, sprinkles or chopped chocolate.

TO MAKE THE COOKIES: Whisk the flour and baking powder together.

Working with a stand mixer fitted with the paddle attachment, or in a large bowl with a hand mixer, beat the butter, sugar and salt together on medium-low speed until smooth. Add the yolks one at a time, beating until each one is fully incorporated. Turn off the mixer, add the dry ingredients all at once and pulse the machine just until the risk of flying flour passes. Mix on low speed, scraping the bowl as needed, until the flour is incorporated. The dough will be thick and it will almost clean the sides of the bowl; press a bit between your fingers, and it should hold together.

Turn the dough out onto a work surface, press and gather it together and divide it in half. Shape each piece into a log about 6 inches long and a scant 2 inches in diameter (see page 12 for logging tips). Wrap the logs and freeze for at least 1 hour, or refrigerate for at least 2 hours.

GETTING READY TO BAKE: Center a rack in the oven and preheat it to 325 degrees F. Lightly butter or spray regular muffin tins or use nonstick pans. Have a wine cork at hand (you can also make the indentations with the handle of a wooden spoon).

Working with a sturdy knife, cut one log into about 18 cookies, each about ⅓ inch thick. Drop them into the muffin tins. (You can cut as much of the remaining log as will completely fill both tins now, or cut and bake it later.)

Bake the galettes for 18 to 20 minutes, turning the tins after 10 minutes, or until the edges are golden brown; the bottoms should be browned as well. Because of the baking powder, the cookies have a tendency to dip in the center as they bake. Happily, the concavity works to the cookies' advantage — it makes a nice border around the indentation.

Remove the cookies from the oven and immediately plunge the cork (or the handle of a wooden spoon) into the center of each one. Be gentle but firm, and make certain that the indent goes down almost to the base of the cookie. Cool the cookies in the tins, then pop them out when they reach room temperature.

Repeat with the remaining dough, using cool tins.

TO MAKE THE FILLING AND FINISH THE COOKIES: Put the jam in a microwave-safe bowl or a small saucepan, add the water and bring to a boil.

Spoon enough jam into each indentation for it to come level with the top of the galette. Refrigerate the cookies for about 30 minutes, just to set the jam. Bring back to room temperature before serving.

BIARRITZ COOKIES

FOR THE COOKIES

¾ cup (75 grams) almond flour

½ cup plus 1 tablespoon (75 grams) all-purpose flour

½ cup plus 2 tablespoons (75 grams) confectioners' sugar

½ stick (4 tablespoons; 2 ounces; 56 grams) unsalted butter, melted and cooled

3 tablespoons whole milk, at room temperature

3 large egg whites, at room temperature

3 tablespoons sugar

FOR THE CHOCOLATE COATING

4 ounces (113 grams) semisweet or bittersweet chocolate (not chips), coarsely chopped

3 tablespoons heavy cream

1 teaspoon light corn syrup

STORING

Packed in a covered container at room temperature, these cookies seem to keep endlessly. Without the chocolate coating, you'll polish them off well before they'll be stale; with the coating, you can count on them being snackable for more than a week.

When I was a kid, the mention of Biarritz, the French oceanside resort, conjured up visions of Hollywood glamour, Cary Grant types and women in shimmering gowns and diamond necklaces. When I went there many years later, try as I might to envision Grant and some bejeweled belle drinking champagne from coupes, I couldn't. All I could think of were the cookies that bore the town's name. They were elegantly thin cookies, their bases covered in dark chocolate, and I knew all about them because Pepperidge Farm used to make them. The Biarritz is now gone from their lineup, but not from mine.

Like the originals, my barely sweet cookies are made with a mixture of almond flour, sugar and flour. Their crispness — they're crisp enough to snap audibly with each bite — comes from beaten egg whites, and their shape is the result of piping out quarter-size mounds and then giving the baking sheet a good rap on the counter to flatten them. The finishing touch is the chocolate slick on their flat sides. If you'd like, use the chocolate to make sandwich cookies — they'll be twice as great (see Playing Around).

A word on roundness: I have never had all of my cookies come out perfectly round, but I have had better luck using silicone baking mats rather than parchment paper. In addition, the silicone cookies bake more evenly and are smoother on the bottom, making them easier to coat with chocolate.

Makes about 48 cookies

Center a rack in the oven and preheat it to 325 degrees F. Line two baking sheets with silicone baking mats (see headnote) or parchment paper.

TO MAKE THE COOKIES: Press both flours and the confectioners' sugar through a strainer into a large bowl. Mix the melted butter and milk together and stir them into the dry ingredients with a flexible spatula until smooth.

Biarritz Sandwiches. Anything with bottoms as flat as the Biarritz's seems to scream "sandwich me." If you decide to sandwich the cookies, use a more generous amount of the chocolate coating or make ganache (page 476 or 479) to use as the filling. The cookies are also good sandwiched with jam or Nutella (or Fauxtella, page 480), or both.

Working with a stand mixer fitted with the whisk attachment, or in a large bowl with a hand mixer, beat the egg whites at medium-high speed until they begin to whiten. Add the sugar in a slow, steady stream, then continue to beat until the whites form stiff, glossy peaks.

Spoon about one third of the whites over the nut-and-flour mixture and stir vigorously with the spatula to loosen and lighten the batter. Turn the rest of the whites over onto the batter and quickly fold them in, using a bit more energy than you'd normally use. The whites will deflate — which is fine — and you'll have a smooth batter.

Spoon half of the batter into a pastry bag fitted with a ½-inch plain tip (or spoon into a zipper-lock plastic bag and snip off a ½-inch piece of one corner) and, holding the bag about an inch or two above the baking sheet, pipe mounds that are the size of a quarter or a bit larger, leaving at least 2 inches of space between them. Refill the pastry bag if necessary to complete the baking sheet. (You'll pipe and bake the remaining batter when the first sheet of cookies is done.) Rap the pan against the counter twice to flatten and round the mounds.

Bake for 19 to 22 minutes, rotating the sheet after 10 minutes, or until the cookies are firm and, most important, golden brown around the rims. Transfer the baking sheet to a rack and allow the cookies to cool completely on the sheet. As soon as the first sheet comes out of the oven, pipe and bake the remaining cookies.

When you're ready to coat the cookies, carefully lift or peel them off the mats or parchment.

TO MAKE THE COATING AND FINISH THE COOKIES: Place the chocolate and cream in a microwave-safe bowl and warm in the microwave, heating in spurts and stirring frequently, until the chocolate is melted and the mixture is smooth. Don't overheat — it's better to remove the bowl from the microwave when the mixture is almost melted and let the residual heat complete the job. Alternatively, you can melt the chocolate and cream in a bowl set over — not touching — a pan of simmering water. Stir in the corn syrup.

Using a small icing spatula, spread enough coating over the bottom of each cookie to cover the surface. Transfer the cookies, chocolate side up, to the racks and let stand until the chocolate firms and is no longer wet or tacky. Figure on about 1 hour, although it could be more or less, depending on the heat and humidity in your room.

ZAN'S BIRTHDAY COOKIES

If these look like they were made for candles, so much the better. I created them for a friend's daughter, Zan, for her birthday. It was only after I tasted them that I realized I'd channeled the spirit of a German chocolate cake. The base of the cookie is a chewy cocoa brownie with chopped chocolate and sweet coconut mixed in. The filling is a light pastry cream flavored (and textured) with both toasted and untoasted coconut. And the topping is a layer of crunchy cocoa streusel. (You'll have extra streusel, which you can use to top other cookies or, if you'd like, you can bake it in a 300-degree-F oven until it's crispy and sprinkle it over ice cream or yogurt.) You get all the pleasure of a thick slice of cake in a small, elegant package.

Happily, as beautiful as these cookies are, they're not difficult, because everything for them can — and should — be made ahead. In fact, each element works best after it's spent time in the refrigerator. And the whole cookie works best — and is easier to make — if you use cookie scoops for the "cake" and cream and a teaspoon for the crumbs.

Makes about 24 cookies

TO MAKE THE COOKIE DOUGH: Put the flour in a bowl, sift the cocoa over it and whisk to blend.

Put the butter, both sugars, and the salt into the bowl of a stand mixer, or into a large bowl that you can use with a hand mixer. Working with a spatula, toss the ingredients together lightly just until the butter is coated with sugar. If using a stand mixer, fit it with the paddle attachment. Mix on medium-low speed, scraping the bowl as needed, until the mixture is smooth, about 3 minutes. Add the eggs one at a time, beating for 1 minute after each one goes in. Beat in the vanilla extract. Scrape the bowl, give the mixture one more spin and then, with the mixer off, add the dry ingredients all at once. Pulse the mixer to start incorporating the flour-cocoa, then mix on low speed only until it disappears into the dough. You'll have a dough that's thick, like a brownie dough. Toss in the chopped chocolate and coconut and pulse just to combine. Cover the dough and refrigerate until needed.

FOR THE COOKIE DOUGH

1¾ cups (238 grams) all-purpose flour

⅓ cup (28 grams) unsweetened cocoa powder

2 sticks (8 ounces; 226 grams) unsalted butter, cut into 16 pieces, at cool room temperature

1¼ cups (250 grams) packed light brown sugar

½ cup (100 grams) sugar

½ teaspoon fine sea salt

2 large eggs, at room temperature

½ teaspoon pure vanilla extract

3 ounces (85 grams) semisweet or bittersweet chocolate, finely chopped

⅓ cup (40 grams) shredded sweetened coconut

FOR THE TOASTED COCONUT PASTRY CREAM

1 cup (120 grams) shredded sweetened coconut

1 cup (240 ml) whole milk

2 large egg yolks

2 tablespoons sugar

2 tablespoons cornstarch

Pinch of fine sea salt

1 teaspoon pure vanilla extract

ingredients continue

TO MAKE THE PASTRY CREAM: Center a rack in the oven and preheat it to 350 degrees F. Line a baking sheet with parchment paper or a silicone baking mat.

Spread half of the coconut over the sheet. Bake the coconut, stirring and turning it often, until it is lightly toasted, about 8 minutes; set aside.

Bring the milk to a boil in a medium saucepan.

Meanwhile, whisk the yolks, sugar, cornstarch and salt together in a medium bowl for a minute or two, until blended. Whisking constantly, drizzle in one quarter of the hot milk. When the yolks are warm, add the liquid in a steady stream, whisking. Pour the mixture into the saucepan, put it over medium heat and, whisking vigorously, bring to a boil. Keep at a boil — never stop whisking — for 1 to 2 minutes, then press the cream through a sieve into a clean bowl. Stir in the vanilla extract and the toasted and untoasted coconut.

Press a piece of plastic wrap against the surface of the cream and refrigerate it until it's thoroughly chilled, at least 2 hours.

MEANWHILE, MAKE THE TOPPING: Put all the dry ingredients in a large bowl and, using your fingers, mix them together, making sure that there aren't any lumps of brown sugar or cocoa. Drop in the cold butter cubes and squeeze, rub or otherwise mush everything together until you have clumps and curds (or do this in a mixer with the paddle attachment). Cover and refrigerate for at least 2 hours.

GETTING READY TO BAKE: Center a rack in the oven and preheat it to 325 degrees F. Butter or spray two regular muffin tins.

Have a medium cookie scoop for the dough, a small scoop for the coconut cream and a teaspoon for the crumbs. (If you don't have scoops, use spoons to approximate the capacities.) Find a spice jar or a glass that fits into the tins and can be used to flatten the ingredients and wrap the base in plastic (or use your fingers).

Scoop or spoon 1½ tablespoons of dough into each of the muffin cups and flatten with the jar (or your fingers) just until the dough touches the sides of the cup. Next, scoop or spoon 2 teaspoons cream onto each round of dough, gently flattening it so that it reaches the sides. Finally top with crumbs, using about a teaspoon of crumbs for each cookie and scattering the crumbs over the cream.

Bake the cookies, one tin at a time, for 25 minutes. It's difficult to tell when a chocolate cookie is properly baked, so you have to take a leap of faith. The crumbs will be dry and the cream will have turned just slightly beige, but it's really the time that counts. Transfer the tin to a rack and cool the cookies to room temperature before unmolding. Use a table knife to loosen the edges and pop them out.

Repeat with the second tin.

FOR THE CRUMB TOPPING

1 cup (136 grams) all-purpose flour

⅓ cup (67 grams) packed light brown sugar

¼ cup (21 grams) unsweetened cocoa powder

2 tablespoons sugar

½ teaspoon fine sea salt

5½ tablespoons (2¾ ounces; 78 grams) cold unsalted butter, cut into small cubes

PLAYING AROUND

Ringed Birthday Cookies. If you have 2-inch baking rings (see page 25), build the cookie layers in them. Bake the dough in the rings on lined baking sheets just as you would the muffin-tin cookies. Leave the rings in place for at least 20 minutes before lifting them off, rinsing and reusing.

STORING

The cookie dough can be covered and refrigerated for up to 3 days. The pastry cream and the crumbs can be refrigerated for up to 3 days; use directly from the refrigerator. Covered, the cookies will hold at room temperature for up to 3 days.

SUNNY-SIDE-UP MERINGUES

¾ cup (150 grams) plus 1 tablespoon sugar

2 tablespoons confectioners' sugar

3 large egg whites, at room temperature

¼ teaspoon cream of tartar (or
  ½ teaspoon distilled white vinegar)

Pinch of fine sea salt

1 teaspoon pure vanilla extract or
  ¼ teaspoon pure lemon extract or oil

1 recipe Mixed Citrus Curd (page 467)
  or store-bought lemon curd

Despite their name and the fact that they look like sunny-side-up eggs, these are made to follow a good dinner. They're a cookie with style and they deserve to be "presented" (and maybe even eaten with a knife and spoon).

The cookies are pure and simple meringues, but rather than being spooned out and allowed to go ragged on the baking sheet, they are scooped neatly so that they bake into domes. Domes with a crater. After you scoop them, use your thumb to make a hollow in the centers. (Many meringues later, I discovered the trick to not having the meringue stick to your fingers: a splash of water. Wet fingers make smooth indents.) Although the meringues rise and puff, the hollows remain. And that's where the sunny-side-up part comes in: Right before you take the meringues to the table, you fill them with bright yellow Mixed Citrus Curd (page 467; or use store-bought).

Hollowing out the centers of the meringues quite literally leaves room for invention. Fill the center with fruit, and you can call the cookie a Pavlova. Fill with ice cream, serve them frozen and you can call them vacherins. Fill with whipped cream, and you can pull out your French accent and call them meringue Chantilly.

Makes 12 meringues

Center a rack in the oven and preheat it to 250 degrees F. Line a baking sheet with parchment paper or a silicone baking mat.

Push the 1 tablespoon granulated sugar and the confectioners' sugar through a fine-mesh strainer; set aside.

Working with a stand mixer fitted with the whisk attachment, or in a large bowl with a hand mixer (make sure your tools are impeccably clean and free of even a trace of fat, grease or yolk, egg whites' enemies), beat the whites, cream of tartar (or vinegar) and salt on medium-high speed until the whites form soft

STORING

Kept away from humidity the unfilled meringues will be fine for days. Store them in a box or just put them on a plate and leave them uncovered.

peaks, about 3 minutes. Add the remaining ¾ cup granulated sugar, 1 tablespoon at a time. It will take 5 minutes or even a little longer to get all the sugar into the whites, but, as persnickety as it seems, it will be worth your patience. Add the extract and beat for another 2 minutes or so. You'll have stiff, glossy, beautifully white peaks. Switch to a flexible spatula and fold in the reserved sugar mix.

To shape the meringues, I use a large cookie scoop. If you don't have a scoop like this, or an ice cream scoop (which will be larger, but which will give you the nice rounded top that's appealing here), you can use a serving spoon. If you're using the large scoop, run the base of the scoop against the side of the bowl after you scoop so that each meringue is a level scoopful; if you're spooning out the meringues, you may need to use a rounded spoonful to get domes of a size equivalent to the scoop. No matter what you're using, leave at least 2 inches between the meringues.

To create the indents, run your thumb under cold water, shake off the excess and then use it to make a thumbprint. After you've pressed it into the meringue, run your thumb around the crater, quickly and lightly smearing the meringue to smooth the interior.

Bake the meringues — undisturbed — for 1 hour and 15 minutes. They will puff and crack, but they shouldn't color (they might be pale beige here and there, and that's fine). Turn off the heat and prop the oven door open (just a crack; enough to let air out) with the handle of a wooden spoon. Leave the meringues to finish baking and drying for another 2 hours, or for as long as overnight. They're ready when you can easily peel them off the paper or mat.

When you're ready to serve, put a spoonful of curd in the center of each meringue. You don't want to do this too much in advance, because the curd softens the meringue.

ROUSQUILLES

I spotted these white-glazed ring cookies (the name *rousquilles* means "little wheels") the first day we were in Barcelona, bought some and then bought them every day thereafter. I'd find them in fine pastry shops, supermarkets and neighborhood bodegas. Sometimes they'd be tossed into a basket and you could buy them the way you might loose candy; sometimes they'd be small enough to call tea treats; sometimes they were large enough to wear as bracelets; and they always had the flavor of anise, sometimes strong, sometimes faint. You could catch the flavor of honey in the cookies and sometimes something else, the occasional addition of orange flower water. There was a lot going on with this cookie, and all of it interested me.

A little research, and I discovered that the origin of the cookie is, indeed, Catalan — I'd experienced it at its source — and that it's found in the Languedoc-Roussillon region of France as well. It's pretty much the same across the border, and pretty much an anytime-of-day cookie no matter where you find it. A French encyclopedia of pastry suggests enjoying it with Banyuls, the sweet red wine of the French Southwest, or Muscat, a floral white wine, or having it with breakfast, as an afternoon snack or after dinner with coffee.

A word on flavorings: Anise seeds and orange flower water are traditional but divisive (my husband appreciates neither), so you have my permission to omit the seeds and, if you'd like, to choose an alternative to the flower water (either milk or white wine will do).

A word on the egg white: To get the small amount of egg white needed for the glaze, put 1 egg white in a bowl, break it up with a fork and then measure it.

Makes about 30 cookies

Center a rack in the oven and preheat it to 325 degrees F. Line a baking sheet with parchment paper or a silicone baking mat. Have two round cookie cutters at hand, one 1¾ inches in diameter, the other ¾ inch.

FOR THE COOKIES

1½ cups (204 grams) all-purpose flour

½ cup (60 grams) confectioners' sugar

1½ teaspoons anise seeds (optional)

½ teaspoon baking soda

½ teaspoon fine sea salt

½ stick (4 tablespoons; 2 ounces; 56 grams) cold unsalted butter, cut into small chunks

2 cold large egg yolks (save one of the whites for the glaze)

2 tablespoons orange flower water, milk or white wine

2 teaspoons honey

Confectioners' sugar, for dusting, if you're not using glaze

FOR THE GLAZE (OPTIONAL)

¾ cup (90 grams) confectioners' sugar

3 tablespoons water

Scant 2 tablespoons egg white

Put the flour, sugar, anise seeds (if you're using them), baking soda and salt in a food processor and pulse just to blend. Drop in the pieces of cold butter and work in long pulses until you've got a grainy mixture. Stir the yolks, orange flower water (or whatever you're using) and honey together and add it in small measures, pulsing in short spurts after each bit goes in. When all the liquid is in, process, stopping to scrape the bottom of the bowl if needed, until you have a mass of moist curds.

Scrape the dough out onto the counter and knead it lightly and briefly, just to corral the curds into cohesion. Place the dough between two pieces of parchment paper and roll it to a thickness of ¼ inch.

Peel away both pieces of parchment and return the dough to one piece. Using the larger cutter, cut out as many circles as you can. Transfer them to the baking sheet (you can place them close together; they don't spread much), and remove their centers with the smaller cutter. Gather the scraps of dough together, press them into a disk, re-roll and cut again; you can gather, re-roll and cut the scraps one more time.

Bake the cookies for 18 to 20 minutes, rotating the sheet after 10 minutes, or until the cookies are golden brown and firm enough to lift off the paper or mat. Place the baking sheet on a rack. If you're not going to glaze the cookies, dust them with confectioners' sugar when they've cooled to room temperature.

MEANWHILE, MAKE THE OPTIONAL GLAZE: Put the sugar and water in a small saucepan and bring to a boil. Keep the mixture at a boil until it reaches 235 to 240 degrees F on a candy thermometer, about 4 minutes. (This is the soft-ball stage for sugar. To test it without a thermometer, drop a tiny bit of the liquid into a glass of cold water, reach in and squeeze the sugar — if it forms a soft, pliable ball between your fingertips, you're there.) Meanwhile, whisk the egg white in a small bowl (or use a hand mixer) until it forms soft peaks, 1 to 2 minutes.

Anchor the egg white bowl (I put it on a silicone pot holder, but you can use a dish towel) and, whisking all the while, pour in the sugar syrup in a slow, steady stream. The glaze is ready to use as soon as the last of the syrup goes in, at which point it should be smooth and shiny.

Using a pastry brush, brush each cookie with glaze. Allow the glaze to set — it will harden — at room temperature.

CHOCOLATE CRÈME SANDWICHES

FOR THE COOKIES

2½ cups (340 grams) all-purpose flour

½ cup (43 grams) unsweetened cocoa powder

1 stick plus 5 tablespoons (13 tablespoons; 6½ ounces; 183 grams) unsalted butter, cut into chunks, at room temperature

⅔ cup (134 grams) sugar

¾ teaspoon fine sea salt

1 large egg white, at room temperature

1 teaspoon pure vanilla extract

FOR THE FILLING

¾ stick (6 tablespoons; 3 ounces; 85 grams) unsalted butter, cut into chunks, at room temperature

1¼ cups (150 grams) confectioners' sugar

2 teaspoons pure vanilla extract

¼ teaspoon fine sea salt

These are not Oreos, but they will no doubt remind you of them. Mine are a little less brittle and a little less sweet than the originals, but they're just as snackable. Snackable, as in perfect for kids' lunch boxes and as in just right for midnight.

The dough for these cookies is a joy to work with: It doesn't budge in the oven. Whatever size and shape you choose for the dough is what the cookies will be. I usually cut these with a plain 2-inch round cutter — however, because they are so well behaved, you can use a scalloped cutter or choose to make them a different size.

The filling is just as variable. I've chosen classic vanilla, but you can flavor the crème with a small amount of peppermint, orange or lemon oil (start with a few drops and keep tasting), pure rose extract or espresso powder. You can also tint the filling. Although the filling doesn't truly set, it is thick enough to play with, and can be doubled to make chubbier sandwiches. (For a change, try filling these with Fauxtella, page 480, or Espresso Filling and Spread, page 485.)

A word on cocoa: The darker the cocoa you use for these, the darker and more like Oreos your cookies will be. I use cocoa powder made by Valrhona; it's very dark brown with hints of red. If you want an even darker color, you can use a combination of black cocoa (available online from King Arthur Flour) and Dutch-processed cocoa powder. As with all cookies, it's the taste that counts. Because cocoa has no fat, it will never have the richness of your favorite chocolate, but it will give rich flavor to whatever you're baking, so choose your cocoa as carefully as you choose your chocolate.

Makes about 22 sandwiches

TO MAKE THE COOKIES: Whisk the flour and cocoa together.

Working with a stand mixer fitted with the paddle attachment, or in a large bowl with a hand mixer, beat the butter, sugar and salt together on

The rolled-out dough can be
frozen, wrapped airtight, for up to
2 months. The dough can also be
cut into rounds, wrapped airtight
and frozen for up to 2 months; no
need to defrost before baking.
The filling can be made ahead
and kept tightly covered in the
refrigerator for up to 3 days.
Once baked and filled, the
cookies are best served that day,
but they can be wrapped well and
refrigerated for up to 2 days. The
cookies are good cold or at room
temperature.

medium speed until smooth, about 3 minutes. Add the egg white and mix for
2 to 3 minutes, scraping the bowl as needed, until the white, which will curdle the
mixture at first, is fully incorporated and the mixture is once again smooth. Mix
in the vanilla. Turn off the machine, add the flour and cocoa all at once and pulse
until the risk of flying flour has passed. Turn the mixer to medium and mix until you
have a dough that holds together and forms clumps when pinched — it shouldn't
come together in a ball.

Scrape the dough out onto a work surface and knead it until it comes together.
Divide the dough in half and flatten into disks.

Working with one piece of dough at a time, roll the dough between pieces of
parchment paper to a thickness of 1/8 inch. Slide the dough, still between paper,
onto a baking sheet — you can stack the slabs — and freeze for at least 1 hour.

GETTING READY TO BAKE: Position the racks to divide the oven into thirds and
preheat it to 350 degrees F. Line two baking sheets with parchment paper or
silicone baking mats. Have a 2-inch-diameter cookie cutter (or the cutter of your
choice) at hand.

Working with one sheet of dough at a time, peel away both pieces of parchment paper and put the dough back on one piece of paper. Cut the dough and
place the rounds on the baking sheets, leaving an inch between them. Gather
together the scraps from both pieces of dough, re-roll them and freeze until firm.

Bake for 12 to 14 minutes, rotating the pans top to bottom and front to back
after 7 minutes, or until the cookies feel firm to the touch. Transfer the sheets to
racks and allow the cookies to rest for at least 5 minutes before lifting them onto
the racks to cool to room temperature.

Cut and bake the remaining dough, using cool baking sheets.

TO MAKE THE FILLING: Working with a stand mixer fitted with the paddle
attachment, or in a large bowl with a hand mixer, beat all the ingredients together
on medium speed until smooth, about 4 minutes. The filling will look like cream
cheese.

TO FINISH THE COOKIES: Put a spoonful of filling on the bottom of half of the
cookies. Top with the remaining cookies, bottom side down, and jiggle the cookies,
twisting them in opposite directions, to spread the filling evenly. The cookies can
be eaten immediately, although the filling will be soft and squish out at first bite.
If you'd like neater cookies (with filling that will still squish, but less so), give the
filling a couple of hours to set and firm a little, or chill the cookies for 1 hour.

PUMPKIN WHOOPIE PIES WITH DULCE DE LECHE FILLING

I liked these big pumpkin-spice cookies when I first made them and thought of them as cookies. But when I sandwiched them with a marshmallow crème and dulce de leche filling, officially turning them into whoopie pies, "like" became too mild a word for how I felt about them. They passed over into love 'em territory, and they've stayed there ever since.

The cookies themselves have the soft, light texture and flavor of spice cake. In fact, they'd be exactly like spice cake if they didn't have the surprise of fresh cranberries, which, in addition to adding color and pop, have just the right the amount of pucker to make the sweet a grown-up dessert.

As for the filling, sticky, sweet fluff is a must. It's just about part of the definition of whoopie pies. For these, it's paired with store-bought or homemade dulce de leche. It's the perfect combo, but when you're ready for a swap, sandwich the cookies with a spiced cream cheese filling (page 264).

A word on size and pans: I'm Goldilocks when it comes to whoopie pies — I like them not too big and not too small. For me, baking them in muffin tins is just right. You can scoop the dough out onto lined baking sheets and bake the cookies free-form if you'd like — they'll be fine, though not perfectly round. If for you a whoopie pie isn't a whoopie pie unless it's the size of a Whopper, see Playing Around and go for it.

Makes 16 cookies

Position the racks to divide the oven into thirds and preheat it to 375 degrees F. Butter or spray two standard muffin tins (do this even if the tins are nonstick).

TO MAKE THE COOKIES: Whisk the flour, cinnamon, cardamom, baking powder and baking soda together.

Working with a stand mixer fitted with the paddle attachment, or in a large bowl with a hand mixer, beat the butter, sugar and salt together on medium

FOR THE WHOOPIE PIES

1¾ cups (238 grams) all-purpose flour

¾ teaspoon ground cinnamon

½ teaspoon ground cardamom

½ teaspoon baking powder

½ teaspoon baking soda

1 stick (8 tablespoons; 4 ounces; 113 grams) unsalted butter, cut into chunks, at room temperature

¾ cup (150 grams) sugar

½ teaspoon fine sea salt

1 large egg, at room temperature

1½ teaspoons pure vanilla extract

½ cup (113 grams) pumpkin puree (not pumpkin pie filling)

½ cup (120 ml) buttermilk, preferably at room temperature

¾ cup (about 75 grams) fresh cranberries, coarsely chopped (if frozen, don't thaw)

FOR THE FILLING

1 stick (8 tablespoons; 4 ounces; 113 grams) unsalted butter, cut into chunks, at room temperature

1 cup (96 grams) marshmallow crème (or Marshmallow Fluff)

¼ cup (30 grams) confectioners' sugar

Pinch of fine sea salt

¼ cup (75 grams) dulce de leche, homemade (page 486) or store-bought

Whopper-Size Whoopie Pies. If you use a large cookie scoop (one with a capacity of 3 tablespoons) to portion out the dough, you can make 6 really big pies (12 cookies; 6 pies). These bake best when you use an insulated baking sheet or stack two sheets one on top of the other. Line the (top) sheet with parchment paper or a silicone baking mat and bake the cookies for 15 to 17 minutes.

STORING

The unfilled cookies can be kept covered at room temperature for up to 1 day. Once filled, they can be kept covered in the refrigerator for a day or two, but they're really best the day they're made.

speed until smooth, about 2 minutes. Add the egg and beat for another 2 minutes or so, until creamy. Beat in the vanilla. Reduce the mixer speed to low, add the pumpkin puree and beat until it's fully incorporated; don't be discouraged when the mixture curdles — it will soon smooth out. Turn off the mixer, scrape down the bowl and add half of the dry ingredients. Pulse to begin the mixing and then mix on low, scraping the bowl as needed, until the flour mixture is blended in. Beat in the buttermilk. Turn off the mixer, add the remaining dry ingredients, pulse and then mix on low until you have a lovely smooth batter. Switch to a flexible spatula and fold in the cranberries. Don't be too thorough — it's better to have an uneven mix than to break the berries and turn the batter red.

Using a medium cookie scoop, scoop out level portions of dough, or use a tablespoon to get rounded spoonfuls, and fill the muffin tins. The scoops of dough will sit upright in the center of the tins, but when baked they'll melt evenly into the cups.

Bake the whoopie pies for 11 to 12 minutes, rotating the pans top to bottom and front to back after 6 minutes, or until they are puffed, golden brown and springy to the touch. Transfer the pan to a rack and let the cookies rest for 5 minutes, then turn them out on the racks and allow them to cool completely.

TO MAKE THE FILLING: Working with a stand mixer fitted with the paddle attachment, or in a medium bowl with a hand mixer, beat the butter, marshmallow crème, sugar and salt together on medium-high speed, scraping the bowl and beater(s) as needed, for about 3 minutes, until very smooth. Lower the mixer speed, add the dulce de leche and beat until thoroughly blended.

Using a spoon or a small cookie scoop, place the filling on the flat sides of half of the cookies; sandwich with the other cookies, flat sides down. The cookies can be eaten now, but the filling benefits from a 30-minute stay in the refrigerator. Just don't eat them from the fridge — you'll deprive yourself of the cookies' wonderful texture.

MACARONS

FOR THE MACARONS

2 cups (200 grams) almond flour

1²⁄₃ cups (200 grams) confectioners' sugar

²⁄₃ cup (150 ml) egg whites (about
    5 large egg whites; see headnote),
    at room temperature

Food coloring (optional)

1 cup (200 grams) sugar

¼ cup (60 ml) water

**FOR THE FILLING, CHOOSE ONE
    OR MORE**

Milk Chocolate Ganache or Dark
    Chocolate Ganache (page 476 or 479)

White Chocolate Ganache Glaze and
    Filling (page 477)

Salted Caramel Filling (page 482)

Cream Cheese Macaron Filling (page 481)

Thick jam

Nutella (or Fauxtella, page 480), Biscoff
    (or Spiced Cookie Filling and Spread,
    page 484), Dulce de Leche (page
    486), Espresso Filling and Spread
    (page 485) or other thick spread

These are the macarons — ranging from ballet-slipper pink to charcoal, the hue of licorice macs — that Parisians adore and visitors to the city's pâtisseries buy by the boxful. They are fanciful, elegant sandwich cookies, as light as the almond meringue they're made of. The tops of the cookies, called "shells," are smooth; the rim around their bottoms, called "feet," are rough; and the filling, the main flavor-bearer, is creamy and anything you want it to be.

Macarons are a relatively new addition to the centuries-old French pastry canon, but the shells haven't changed much since they were invented. A couple of years ago, I was having dinner with Parisian pastry chef Pierre Hermé when someone asked him if he was always working and reworking his recipe for macarons. Pierre, considered the King of Macarons, said, "*Non.* I use the same recipe I was taught when I was an apprentice."

For bakers, the quest is to find a recipe for the cookies that you can rely on forever after and then change the filling any time you want. So, here's the recipe that I worked on for a long time and have been making for a long time. And so have others. This is the recipe that people tell me turned them from timid mac-makers to confident bakers. And although the recipe is long — I prefer to call it "detailed" — it's child's play. I know this because my friend Mardi Michels has taught kids to make it and has the photos to prove their success.

A word on mixing: This is a job for a stand mixer. You could make these with a hand mixer, but I don't think you'll like me much if you do.

A word on measuring: This is an example of a recipe where measuring the ingredients by weight, specifically metric weight, makes it simpler. You want equal weights of almond flour and confectioners' sugar. You'll need 160 ml of egg whites, about 5 whites — but if you just turn your glass measuring cup around to the metric side, you'll have an easy time of it. It's also easier to use the metric measure, should you have to divide an egg white in half.

Plan Ahead! The filled macarons need to soften in the refrigerator for at least 1 day. Of course you can taste them earlier, but their characteristic texture needs time to develop.

Makes about 45 sandwiched macarons

TO MAKE THE MACARONS: You'll need two baking sheets. If you're lining your baking sheets with parchment paper, you can make a template to help you get the right-size cookies: Using a cookie cutter as your guide, trace circles about 1½ inches in diameter on each piece of parchment, leaving about 2 inches between them, then flip the papers over (pencil marks down) onto the baking sheets. If you're using silicone mats, just line the baking sheets with them. Fit a large pastry bag with a plain ½-inch tip. (You can also pipe the cookies with a zipper-lock bag — fill the bag, seal it and snip off a corner.) Have a candy thermometer at hand.

Place a strainer over a large bowl and press the almond flour and confectioners' sugar through it. Please don't skip this job — it's annoying but necessary. Whisk to blend.

Put half of the egg whites in a stand mixer fitted with the whisk attachment.

Add food coloring, if you're using it, to the other half of the egg whites, stir and then pour them over the almond flour and confectioners' sugar. Using a flexible spatula, mix and mash the whites into the dry ingredients until you have a homogenous paste.

Bring the sugar and water to a boil in a small saucepan over medium heat. If there are spatters on the sides of the pan, wash them down with a pastry brush dipped in cold water. Attach a candy thermometer and cook the syrup until it reaches 243 to 245 degrees F. (This can take about 10 minutes.)

Meanwhile, beat the egg whites until they hold medium-firm, glossy peaks. Reduce the mixer speed to low and keep mixing until the sugar syrup comes up to temperature.

When the sugar is ready, take the pan off the heat and remove the thermometer. With the mixer on low speed, pour in the hot syrup, trying to pour it between the whirring whisk and the side of the bowl. You'll have spatters, but don't try to incorporate them (they'll spoil your beautifully smooth meringue). Increase the mixer speed to high and beat until the meringue has cooled to room temperature, about 10 minutes — you'll be able to tell by touching the bottom of the bowl.

Give the almond flour mixture another stir with the spatula, then scrape the meringue over it and fold everything together. Don't be gentle here: Use your spatula to cut through the meringue and almond flour mixture, bring some of the batter from the bottom up over the top and then press it against the sides of the bowl. The action is the same as the one you used to get the egg whites into the almonds and sugar: Mix and mash. Keep folding and mixing and mashing until when you lift the spatula, the batter flows off it in a thick band.

If you want to add more food coloring, do it now.

Spoon half of the batter into the pastry bag (or zipper-lock bag) and, holding the bag straight up, 1 inch above one of the baking sheets, pipe out 1½-inch rounds. Don't worry if you have a point in the center of each round — it will dissolve into the batter. Grab the baking sheet with both hands, raise it about 8 inches above the counter and let it fall to the counter. Don't worry, and don't try to cushion the blow. You need to do this to get the bubbles out of the batter and to smooth the tops. Refill the bag, pipe the second sheet and drop it onto the counter.

Set the baking sheets aside in a cool, dry place to allow the cookies to form a crust. When you can lightly touch the top of the macarons without having batter stick to your finger, you're ready to bake. (Depending on temperature and humidity, this can take 15 to 30 minutes, or sometimes more.)

GETTING READY TO BAKE: Center a rack in the oven and preheat it to 350 degrees F.

Bake the macarons, one sheet at a time, for 6 minutes. Rotate the pan and bake for another 6 to 9 minutes, or until the macarons can be carefully peeled away from the paper or lifted from the mat. The bottoms will still feel just a little soft. Slide the parchment or silicone mat off the baking sheet onto a counter and let the macarons cool.

Repeat with the second baking sheet.

Peel the macarons off the parchment or silicone and match them up for sandwiching.

TO SANDWICH THE MACARONS: Line a baking sheet with parchment paper. You can use a teaspoon or a piping bag to fill the macarons; it's up to you how much filling you'll want to use. Spoon or pipe some filling onto the flat side of a mac and sandwich it with its mate, gently swiveling the top macaron to spread the filling to the edges. Place on the baking sheet and repeat with the remaining macarons and filling. Cover the macarons with plastic wrap or pack them into a container. Refrigerate for at least 24 hours before serving.

VANILLA–BROWN BUTTER MADELEINES

2/3 cup (91 grams) all-purpose flour

3/4 teaspoon baking powder

7½ tablespoons (3¾ ounces; 106 grams) unsalted butter, cut into chunks

1/3 cup (67 grams) sugar

1 moist, plump, pliable vanilla bean or 2 teaspoons pure vanilla extract

2 large eggs, at room temperature

¼ teaspoon fine sea salt

1 tablespoon honey

1 tablespoon Scotch, bourbon, dark rum or milk

Confectioners' sugar, for dusting

STORING

The madeleine batter can be kept, covered with a piece of plastic wrap pressed against the surface, in the refrigerator for up to 2 days. The baked cookies can be kept covered at room temperature for up to 1 day; their texture will not stay the same, but their taste will. The madeleines can also be wrapped airtight and frozen for up to 2 months. Thaw, then warm briefly in a 350-degree-F oven before serving.

This very special rendition of the traditional madeleine is made with browned butter and the scraped pulp of a vanilla bean. Its flavor is reminiscent of butterscotch (when I first noticed that, I decided to play it up and included a splash of booze in the recipe). Its texture is precisely what you want in a mad: light when it's warm (the most delicious temperature for a madeleine) and much like your favorite buttery sponge cake a day later (the most wonderful texture for dunking).

While you can make madeleines in small molds of any shape, the classic molds are shell-shaped. By baking the batter in these shallow molds, you get cookies that are beautifully brown on the scalloped side and lightly golden on the plain side. Actually, the plain side isn't so plain — it's normally mounded. I say normally, because hundreds of madeleines later, I've discovered that the "bumps" can be perfidious — you can't count on them to turn up reliably. It's annoying but not tragic, since the flavor and texture are consistently as they should be despite the occasional, always puzzling flatness.

Under the theory that it's impossible to have too many choices when it comes to mads, I urge you to make these beauties, the Classics (see Playing Around) and the exotic Matcha–White Chocolate Mini Mads (page 319) too.

Makes 12 madeleines

To prepare the madeleine pan, use a pastry brush (easiest) or a paper towel to coat the molds with softened butter, then dust with flour and tap out the excess. (If you'd like, you can coat the molds with baker's spray.) Do this even if your molds are nonstick or silicone; it's good to be on the safe side. If your pan is silicone, place it on a baking sheet.

Whisk the flour and baking powder together.

Put the butter in a small saucepan and bring it to a boil over medium heat, swirling the pan occasionally. Allow the butter to bubble away until it turns a deep honey brown, 5 to 10 minutes. Don't turn your back on the pan — the

PLAYING AROUND

Classic Madeleines. Don't brown the butter. Instead, melt ¾ stick unsalted butter and set it aside to cool. Omit the vanilla bean and rub the freshly grated zest of 1 lemon into the sugar; whisk 1 teaspoon pure vanilla extract into the batter after the eggs are incorporated. Finally, use milk instead of the alcohol (or not — the classics are wonderful with a hit of dark rum).

Double-Butter Mads. One morning I was drawn into the kitchen by the scent of browning butter (an unmistakable aroma) and found my husband at the stove. He'd melted butter in a skillet, let it brown and, having split day-old madeleines in half lengthwise, was toasting them in the hot butter. Eaten right out of the skillet with a dab of jam, they were sensational. In fact, they were so good that it would be worth letting some of your mads go stale just to have them like this the next morning.

difference between brown and black is measured in seconds. And don't worry about the little brown flecks in the bottom of the pan — they're a good thing. Pour the butter into a heatproof glass or bowl and measure out 6 tablespoons, which is what you'll need for the mads (and probably exactly what you'll have).

Put the sugar in a medium bowl. If you're using a vanilla bean (if using extract, you'll add it later), slice it in half lengthwise and use the back of your knife to scrape out the soft, seedy pulp; put the pulp on top of the sugar. (You can use the pod to make vanilla sugar.) Using your fingertips, rub the ingredients together until the sugar is moist and fragrant. Add the eggs and whisk energetically for a minute. If you're using extract, whisk it in now. Whisk in the salt and honey. Still using the whisk (or switch to a spatula, if it's more comfortable for you) and a soft touch, blend in the dry ingredients. When they are completely incorporated, gently stir and fold in the melted butter a little at a time, checking the bottom of the bowl to make sure that none pools there. Stir in the alcohol or milk.

Divide the batter among the molds. Refrigerate for at least 1 hour, preferably 2 or 3 hours.

GETTING READY TO BAKE: Center a rack in the oven and place a baking sheet on the rack. Preheat the oven to 400 degrees F.

Carefully place the madeleine mold on the hot baking sheet. Or, if using a silicone mold, leave it on the baking sheet it was on. Bake for 10 to 12 minutes, or until the madeleines are puffed and browned around the edges. Remove the pan from the oven and, if it's metal, grab an end and tap the pan on the counter — the madeleines should come tumbling out. If you're using a silicone mold, turn it upside down over the counter and pull at two opposite ends until the cookies fall out. Pry out any reluctant mads with a table knife.

Dust the cookies with confectioners' sugar and serve them as soon as you can.

MATCHA–WHITE CHOCOLATE MINI MADS

Coming up with cookie names is often a problem for me. I want the name to tell you what you're going to get, but tell too much, and you risk ending up with the cookie's biography rather than its one-line resumé. And so, with these mini mads, I included the big hitters in the name and left out the little guy, the lime zest, even though it's this bit player that changes the game. The lime perks up the matcha green tea (which can be a little vegetal) and tamps down the white chocolate (which can be super-sweet). In fact, it wasn't until I added the lime that I was sure that these would make it into this collection.

While their flavor is not at all traditional, their shell shape and sponge texture are models of the genre. And, like their classic cousins (page 318), they are delicious warm and meant to be eaten soon after they're baked: Minutes after trumps hours later. Happily, you can prepare the batter ahead and then, on the day you're going to bake, fill the molds, pop them into the fridge and bake them when you're ready. Think of them as a classy convenience food.

A word on the tea and chocolate: Matcha green tea is among the most prized and expensive of Japanese teas. It is a powdered rather than leaf tea and meant to be blended into hot water with a small bamboo whisk designed especially for the job. Matcha that is right for a tea ceremony is not the matcha you want for cookies — it would be sad to mix this precious tea with anything other than water and sadder still to bake it at a high temperature. For baking and cooking, you want culinary matcha, a lower-grade tea with a much lower price tag. But what you want for the white chocolate is the best quality you can get, which might mean searching for an imported chocolate. (I use Valrhona and Guittard as my "house" whites.) Whatever you do, please don't use white chips — they won't melt properly.

Makes about 36 mini madeleines

⅓ cup (45 grams) all-purpose flour

1 teaspoon matcha green tea (see headnote)

½ teaspoon baking powder

Pinch of fleur de sel or fine sea salt

¼ cup (50 grams) sugar

1 lime

1 large egg, at room temperature

½ teaspoon pure vanilla extract

3 tablespoons (1½ ounces; 43 grams) unsalted butter, melted

1½ ounces (43 grams) best-quality white chocolate, melted and still fluid

1 tablespoon milk, at room temperature

Confectioners' sugar, for dusting

To prepare the mini madeleine pan, use a pastry brush (easiest) or a paper towel to coat the molds with softened butter, then dust with flour and tap out the excess. (If you'd like, you can coat the molds with baker's spray.) Do this even if your molds are nonstick or silicone; it's a better-safe-than-sorry thing. If your pan is silicone, place it on a baking sheet.

Whisk together the flour, matcha, baking powder and salt.

Put the sugar in a medium bowl and finely grate the zest of half the lime over it. Reach into the bowl and, using your fingertips, rub the ingredients together until the sugar is moist and fragrant. Add the egg and vanilla and whisk energetically for a minute or two — you want the egg to thicken and pale a bit. Gently whisk in the dry ingredients. Still using the whisk (or switch to a spatula, if it's more comfortable for you) and a soft touch, fold and blend in the butter, followed by the white chocolate. When they are completely incorporated, stir in the milk.

Spoon about 1 teaspoon of batter into each mold; they will be almost full. Don't worry about evening out the batter, it will spread in the oven. Scrape the remaining batter into a bowl; press a piece of plastic wrap against the surface to create an airtight seal. Refrigerate the leftover batter and the mold for at least 1 hour.

GETTING READY TO BAKE: Center a rack in the oven and preheat it to 425 degrees F.

Bake the madeleines for 8 to 10 minutes, or until they are puffed and golden around the edges. Remove the pan from the oven and, if it's metal, grab an end and tap the pan on the counter — the madeleines should come tumbling out. If you're using a silicone mold, turn it upside down over the counter and pull at two opposite ends until the little cookies fall out. Pry out any reluctant mads with a table knife.

Don't bother transferring the madeleines to a cooling rack. Just dust them with confectioners' sugar and eat them now, or minutes from now.

Repeat with the remaining batter, making certain that the molds are cool, clean, buttered and floured (or sprayed).

STRAWBERRY SHORTCAKE COOKIES

These are the kind of cookies that make you want to check that there's champagne in the fridge. Defying the natural order of things, they are both pâtisserie-perfect and a cinch to make. The base is a very French whole-egg sponge cake (called a génoise), which, when baked in a muffin tin, comes out cute as a button: a featherweight puff for a dab of strawberry compote (an optional but terrific addition), a ring of whipped cream and a crown of sliced fresh berries. These are beautiful and as good as they look.

I love serving them with sparkling wine, but they're great with homemade lemonade or tea. If you have any cut berries, compote and/or whipped cream left over, serve them alongside the shortcakes — the cakes don't need anything extra, but having the berries and cream on the table encourages people to treat their cakes like sundaes, and that's always fun.

A word on the eggs: In order for the egg-and-sugar mixture to triple in volume and develop the structure that will keep the sponge light and lovely, the eggs must be at room temperature. If your eggs are coming straight from the refrigerator, or if you're not certain that they're warm enough, put them in a bowl, turn your tap to its hottest setting and run water over them for a minute, then keep them in the hot water for another 3 to 5 minutes.

FOR THE CAKES
⅓ cup (45 grams) all-purpose flour
¼ teaspoon baking powder
Pinch of fine sea salt
2 large eggs, at room temperature
⅓ cup (67 grams) sugar
½ teaspoon pure vanilla extract
½ teaspoon pure rose extract (optional)

FOR THE WHIPPED CREAM
1 cup (240 ml) very cold heavy cream
2 tablespoons confectioners' sugar
1 teaspoon pure vanilla extract
½ teaspoon pure rose extract (optional)
1 tablespoon cold sour cream (optional)

FOR THE TOPPING
8 to 12 ounces (2 to 3 cups; 226 to 340 grams) strawberries, hulled
Strawberry Compote (page 491; optional)

Makes about 24 shortcakes

Center a rack in the oven and preheat it to 350 degrees F. Butter and flour two regular muffin tins or use baker's spray (do this even if your tins are nonstick).

TO MAKE THE CAKES: Whisk the flour, baking powder and salt together.

Working with a stand mixer fitted with the whisk attachment, or in a large bowl with a hand mixer, beat the eggs and sugar together on medium speed for about 30 seconds, then increase the speed to medium-high and beat for 3 to 5 minutes, until the mixture is pale and tripled in volume. Reduce the speed to medium and beat in the vanilla and, if you're using it, rose extract. Working

STORING

The cakes can be wrapped in plastic and kept at room temperature for up to 1 day. The shortcakes are best eaten as soon as you top them, but the génoise can be made up to 1 day ahead and kept covered at room temperature. The compote can be made up to 3 days ahead and kept covered in the refrigerator. The whipped cream can be made up to 1 hour ahead and kept tightly covered in the refrigerator.

with a flexible spatula, fold in the dry ingredients in 2 or 3 additions. Make sure to reach down to the bottom of the bowl and cut into the batter at various places — you'd be surprised how tricky the flour is; it can hide out in unexpected spots. The eggs will lose some of their volume as you fold, but be sure to fold until the dry ingredients are completely incorporated.

Divide the batter among the tins. (I use a small cookie scoop for this job, mounding the batter in the scoop.)

Bake the cakes for 11 to 13 minutes, rotating the tins after 6 minutes, or until they are golden brown and have pulled away from the sides of the molds. If you poke the tops of the cakes gently, they'll spring back. Transfer the tins to racks and let the cakes rest for 3 minutes, then, using a table knife, carefully pry them loose and transfer them to a rack to cool to room temperature.

TO MAKE THE WHIPPED CREAM: Working in a clean mixer bowl with a clean whisk, or in a large bowl with the hand mixer, beat the cream on medium speed just until it mounds softly. Beat in the sugar, followed by the vanilla and the rose extract, if you're using it. When the cream holds firm peaks, quickly beat in the sour cream, if you're using it.

TO TOP THE SHORTCAKES: The shortcakes should be assembled within an hour or two of serving and kept in the refrigerator. If you can swing it, topping them just before serving is best. Cut the berries from top to bottom into 3 or 4 slices each, depending on their size. These are going to stand up in the center of the little shortcakes, so they need to be thick enough for you to work with yet thin enough to not take up all the real estate. Fit a pastry bag with a medium open star tip and fill it with the whipped cream (or fill a zipper-lock plastic bag, seal the bag and snip off a corner).

Using the knuckle of your index finger, press down on the center of each génoise puck just a little. If you're using the compote, spoon a small amount of it (a teaspoon or less) into each indentation — you're aiming to have a dollop of compote in the center of the cake; there should be a bare border. Pipe a circle of whipped cream around the compote (or on each cake). If this is too fussy for you, you can cover the compote with cream, taking care not to make a very thick layer (½ inch high is good). Finish each shortcake by pressing 2 or 3 slices of strawberry together, fanning them out just a little and standing them, pointed end up, in the center of the cake.

PISTACHIO-BERRY SLIMS

These are among the most elegant cookies I make. They have the looks of a confection you'd find in a Viennese pastry shop; the texture of a favorite childhood macaroon (indeed, these are macaroons, classy ones); the pure taste and brilliant color of pistachios; the sweetness and glisten of raspberry jam; and the beauty and sweet-tart flavor of fresh raspberries. That they're also easy adds to their mystique. Serve them, and if you don't want to admit that you prepared them in 10 minutes, don't.

A word on the egg whites: I can't give you an exact measurement for them. In all likelihood, you'll need both whites, but just before the last bit goes into the processor, pinch the dough — if it holds together and feels as though you'll have an easy time shaping it with your hands, call it finished.

Makes about 18 cookies

Center a rack in the oven and preheat it to 350 degrees F. Use an insulated baking sheet or stack two baking sheets one on top of the other; line the (top) sheet with parchment paper or a silicone baking mat.

Put the pistachios and sugar in a food processor and pulse until the nuts are ground. There should still be a few larger pieces of nuts scattered throughout the mix; be sure to stop before you grind the mix into a paste. Pour the whites into a small bowl and stir them with a fork just to break them up. Add a bit of the whites to the processor, pulse to incorporate and then add some more. Keep doing this until you've got a dough that holds together when you squeeze it. You'll probably use all the whites, but you might need a tad less. It's better to have a moist dough than a dry one, so make a judgment call and then relax.

Scrape the dough out onto the center of the baking sheet and, using your fingers and a flexible spatula, shape it into a slender log about 14 inches long and 1¼ inches wide. Steadying the edges of the log with the fingers of one hand, use the fingers of your other to make a trench (for the jam and the raspberries) about 1 inch wide down the center of the log, leaving about ¼ inch of solid (untrenched) dough at each end. It's almost inevitable that the log will

1½ cups (210 grams) shelled pistachios (rub off any loose skins)
⅓ cup (67 grams) sugar
2 large egg whites
About ⅓ cup (108 grams) raspberry jam
About 18 fresh raspberries

It's best to keep the log intact and to cut the slims as you need them. Store the log, or the cut cookies, covered in the refrigerator, where they'll be good for up to 2 days. If you need to keep them longer, don't add the fresh berries until serving time. (Warm the jam with a little heat from a hair dryer to soften it so that you can settle the berries in securely.) These are not cookies to be frozen.

crack here and there as you press down to make the trench, but stabilizing the dough will keep it from cracking in two. When you've finished making the trench, you can push together and smooth over whatever cracks you see.

Bake the log for 16 to 18 minutes, rotating the pan after 9 minutes, or until the log feels firm; it won't color much. Transfer the baking sheet to a rack — you're going to fill the log with jam while it's still warm.

Put the jam in a small saucepan and bring it to a boil over low heat, or do this in a microwave. When the jam is hot and liquefied, carefully spoon it into the trench you made; dab away any spots of jam that dribble, as they will, on the log. Finish with a line of the fresh raspberries down the center of the jam, placing the berries one against the other. Let cool to room temperature.

Transfer the log to the refrigerator and chill for at least an hour before serving. To serve, use a long serrated knife and a gentle sawing motion to slice between the berries.

the
beurre & sel
collection

the beurre & sel story

For a brief and wonderful time, my son, Joshua, and I were the proprietors of Beurre & Sel (French for "butter and salt"), a cookie boutique. We had a mini kitchen in East Harlem and a very beautiful micro shop on New York's Lower East Side. We had some of the most gorgeous packaging in town (thanks to Joshua and graphic designer Kyle Poff), and we had cookies that often moved the small sweet into the realm of modern art.

The cookies had a very particular look. They were all exactly the same size. The ones in our signature clear tubes were 2 inches in diameter, and the individual ones in our boutique were an inch bigger. And they were all perfectly tailored, with beautifully straight sides.

Before we officially opened Beurre & Sel, Joshua and I did a series of pop-up events. To get ready for our first, I tested all the recipes at home before I had to bake them in a commercial kitchen with equipment I'd never used before and on a scale that rattled my nonmathematical mind. Everything I baked tasted great, but none of the cookies were the same size. The look was unprofessional, and it was impractical too: Some of the cookies were so big or so misshapen they wouldn't fit into our boxes.

I'd been baking for weeks, and I had to go into the commercial kitchen in a couple of days. I was near tears when I grabbed a metal circle, a baking ring that I'd used to make mini cakes when I was in my French phase. I packed the dough into the ring and baked it. Salvation! The ringed cookies were stunning. They were perfectly shaped and perfectly sized. And they were something else: different. Not only did they look different, but the act of confining the dough within the rings' boundaries changed the way the cookies baked, and it changed their texture too.

Over the next few days, I began converting my recipes, some of them favorites I'd been making for years. I learned that I couldn't use leavening — it would cause the ringed cookies to rise around the edges and sink in the middle. I learned that some of the doughs that I used to scoop were really better rolled. I discovered that thickness mattered, and that it mattered in different ways from one cookie to the next. And oven temperatures needed to change too. It was a crash course in a new way of cookie making.

Joshua called what we made "cookies for grown-ups" and, while plenty of kids walked away from our shop happily munching on sablés, jammers and chunkers, there was no question that our cookies seemed better suited to tea trays than to lunch boxes. Especially our cocktail cookies, a collection of savory cookies I created to go with wine and beer, spirits and spirited drinks. (See the Cocktail Cookies chapter.)

By the time we closed up shop, Joshua and I had been professional cookie makers on and off for about five years. When we retired, we received torrents of mail from people who had loved our cookies. And wherever I travel, even abroad, I still meet people who remember our cookies and sigh when they say their names. The word "jammer" (page 350) is spoken with the kind of joy and wistfulness I used to reserve for Paul Newman. I'm always asked if we'll do it again, and I always say, "No, but one day I'll put together the recipes so that you can make our cookies at home."

Shortly after our first pop-up, which was written about in newspapers and magazines across the country, I got a message from Tim Mazurek, the creator of the blog *Lottie & Doof,* saying that he'd hacked my Classic Jammer recipe. What Tim had done was brilliant: Lacking rings, he fitted the dough into muffin tins. For years now, I've been passing along Tim's trick, and it's what I suggest you do to make the Beurre & Sel cookies at home. Unless you have rings (which are available in kitchen supply shops and on Amazon) — there are directions for ringed cookies here too.

FRENCH VANILLA SABLÉS

2 sticks (8 ounces; 226 grams) unsalted butter, cut into chunks, at room temperature

½ cup (100 grams) sugar

¼ cup (30 grams) confectioners' sugar, sifted

½ teaspoon fine sea salt

2 large egg yolks, at room temperature

2 teaspoons pure vanilla extract

2 cups (272 grams) all-purpose flour

Sanding sugar, for sprinkling

In many ways, the sablé, the classic French shortbread cookie, was the crown jewel of the Beurre & Sel collection. I've always thought of the sablé as the perfect butter cookie, the one all shortbread strives to equal, and in this recipe I think you have the model cookie — it's rich, as it should be; sandy, as it should be; flavorful; and memorable. It's basic but in no way ordinary. The sablé was often the first cookie someone bought at Beurre & Sel, and then it brought them back to try all the others. Because of its phenomenal texture and universally beloved flavor, I found it easy to construct new flavors based on it. It was the foundation of our Classic Jammers (page 350) and of many variations after that.

Makes about 30 cookies

Working with a stand mixer fitted with the paddle attachment, or in a large bowl with a hand mixer, beat the butter, both sugars and the salt on medium speed for about 3 minutes, scraping the bowl as needed. The mixture should be smooth but not fluffy. Reduce the mixer speed to low and, one by one, beat in the yolks, followed by the vanilla. Turn off the mixer, add the flour all at once and pulse the mixer until the risk of flying flour has passed. With the machine on low, mix just until the flour disappears into the dough. Give the dough a couple of turns with a sturdy flexible spatula.

Turn the dough out onto the counter and divide it in half. Gather each piece into a ball and shape into a disk.

Working with one piece of dough at a time, roll the dough ¼ inch thick between pieces of parchment. Slide the parchment-sandwiched dough onto a baking sheet — you can stack the slabs — and freeze for at least 1 hour, or refrigerate for at least 2 hours.

GETTING READY TO BAKE: Center a rack in the oven and preheat it to 350 degrees F. Butter or spray a regular muffin tin (or use nonstick), or two tins, if you've got them. Have a 2-inch-diameter cookie cutter at hand.

Working with one sheet of dough at a time, peel away both pieces of paper and put the dough back on one piece of paper. Cut the dough and drop the

STORING

Wrapped airtight, the dough can be refrigerated for up to 2 days or frozen for up to 2 months. The cookies will keep in a tin at room temperature for about 5 days. If you don't dust them with sugar, they can be wrapped airtight and frozen for up to 2 months (the sugar would melt in the freezer).

PLAYING AROUND

Slice-and-Bake Sablés. These will be too
higgledy-piggledy to turn into Jammers
or anything else that's structured, but
they'll be delicious to enjoy any way you'd
like. Divide the dough in half and shape
each half into a log about 9 inches long.
Wrap the logs and freeze for at least
3 hours and up to 2 months. When you're
ready to bake, slice the logs about 1/3 inch
thick. Place the rounds about 2 inches
apart on lined baking sheets and sprinkle
with sanding sugar. Bake one sheet at
a time on the center rack of a 350-
degree-F oven for 17 to 20 minutes.

Ringed Sablés. If you have 2-inch baking
rings (see page 25), use the rings to cut
out the rolled dough. Bake the dough — in
the rings — on lined baking sheets just as
you would the muffin-tin cookies. Leave
the rings in place for at least 20 minutes
before lifting them off, rinsing and reusing.

rounds into the muffin tin(s). The rounds might not fill the muffin cups completely
now, but they will once they bake. Save the scraps from both pieces of dough,
then gather them together, re-roll, chill and cut. Sprinkle the tops of the cookies
with sanding sugar.

Bake the cookies for 16 to 19 minutes, rotating the tin(s) after 10 minutes, or
until they feel firm to the touch and are golden brown around the edges. Transfer
the muffin tin(s) to a rack and let the cookies rest for about 10 minutes before
carefully lifting them out onto the rack to cool to room temperature.

Continue with the remainder of the dough, using cool tins.

There is no way to describe the World Peace Cookie without resorting to what would be considered hyperbole by anyone who hasn't tasted one. They're flat-out phenomenal. And hundreds of thousands of people agree with me. Just do an Internet search for "World Peace Cookie," and you'll see — the last time I checked there were over ten million references!

WPCs, as we call them at our house, are basic chocolate sablés of the slice-and-bake variety. The dough is made with cocoa — splurge on good cocoa, it's worth it with these (I use Valrhona) — and has fleur de sel in it, enough to be truly present. And then there are pieces of chopped bittersweet chocolate. Again, splurge — this is a cookie that's all about the chocolate, so the chocolate should be great. (You could use store-bought mini chips, but I hope you won't.) I know it sounds simple and it might even sound like a cookie you've made before, but even top-of-the-pack veteran bakers shake their heads in wonder when they first encounter the WPC.

The recipe came to me from Pierre Hermé, France's most renowned pastry chef. When he taught me how to make these, sometime in the late 1990s, he called the cookie Korova, because he had created it for a restaurant of that name. I included it in my book *Paris Sweets*. A few years later, a neighbor was telling me how much he loved the cookies and how he'd changed their name. "At home," he said, "we call them World Peace Cookies." I renamed them immediately and included them with that name in my book *Baking: From My Home to Yours*.

When we baked them at Beurre & Sel, we rolled the dough ⅜ inch thick and cut cookies with our rings so that they'd be uniform and fit into our signature packaging. At home, I bake them as I did from the start: I shape the dough into logs and then slice and bake the cookies as I need them.

A word on mixing, log rolling and patience: This dough can be different from batch to batch. It always seems to turn out well no matter what, but the inconsistency can be frustrating. I've found that it's best to mix the dough for as long as it takes to get big, moist curds that hold together when pressed and then knead if necessary so it comes together. When

1¼ cups (170 grams) all-purpose flour

⅓ cup (28 grams) unsweetened cocoa powder

½ teaspoon baking soda

1 stick plus 3 tablespoons (11 tablespoons; 5½ ounces; 155 grams) unsalted butter, cut into chunks, at room temperature

⅔ cup (134 grams) packed light brown sugar

¼ cup (50 grams) sugar

½ teaspoon fleur de sel or ¼ teaspoon fine sea salt

1 teaspoon pure vanilla extract

5 ounces (142 grams) best-quality bittersweet chocolate, chopped into irregular bits

STORING

The dough can be refrigerated for up to 3 days or frozen for up to 2 months. If you've frozen the dough, you needn't defrost it before baking — just bake the cookies 1 minute longer. Packed in a container, the cookies will keep at room temperature for up to 3 days; they can be frozen, well wrapped, for up to 2 months.

you're rolling it into logs, keep checking that the logs are solid (see page 12). Again, the dough can be capricious and it may not always roll into a compact log on the first (or second or third) try. Be patient.

Makes about 36 cookies

Sift the flour, cocoa and baking soda together.

Working with a stand mixer fitted with the paddle attachment, or in a large bowl with a hand mixer, beat the butter and both sugars together on medium speed until soft, creamy and homogenous, about 3 minutes. Beat in the salt and vanilla. Turn off the mixer, add all the dry ingredients and pulse a few times to start the blending. When the risk of flying flour has passed, turn the mixer to low and beat until the dough forms big, moist curds. Toss in the chocolate pieces and mix to incorporate. This is an unpredictable dough: Sometimes it's crumbly and sometimes it comes together and cleans the sides of the bowl. Happily, no matter what, the cookies are always great.

Turn the dough out onto a work surface and gather it together, kneading it if necessary to bring it together. Divide it in half. Shape the dough into logs that are 1½ inches in diameter. Don't worry about the length — get the diameter right, and the length will follow. (If you get a hollow in the logs, just start over.) Wrap the logs in plastic wrap and freeze them for at least 2 hours, or refrigerate them for at least 3 hours.

GETTING READY TO BAKE: Center a rack in the oven and preheat it to 325 degrees F. Line two baking sheets with parchment paper or silicone baking mats.

Working with one log at a time and using a long, sharp knife, slice the dough into ½-inch-thick rounds. (The rounds might crack as you're cutting them — don't be concerned, just squeeze the bits back onto each cookie.) Arrange the rounds on the baking sheets, leaving about 2 inches between them. (If you've cut both logs, keep one baking sheet in the fridge while you bake the other.)

Bake the cookies for 12 minutes — don't open the oven, just let them bake. When the timer rings, they won't look done, nor will they be firm, and that's just the way they should be. Transfer the baking sheet to a cooling rack and let the cookies rest until they are only just warm, at which point you can munch them, or let them reach room temperature (I think the texture's more interesting at room temperature).

Bake the remaining dough on cool sheets.

PLAYING AROUND

Rolled-and-Cut World Peace Cookies. WPC dough has a mind of its own and it's hard to corral it into perfect rounds no matter how you handle it. If you're on a quest for a neater, rounder cookie, roll the dough to a thickness of ⅜ inch and refrigerate or freeze as you would for logs. If you have 2-inch baking rings, use a cookie cutter that's slightly smaller than 2 inches, cut out rounds and center the rounds in the baking rings. (Muffin tins won't work for these cookies.) Alternatively, you can cut out the dough and bake it on lined baking sheets — it's how we made the beautiful cookie in the photograph. The baking time remains the same no matter how you cut the cookies.

ESPRESSO CHOCOLATE SABLÉS

1½ tablespoons instant espresso

1 tablespoon boiling water

2 sticks (8 ounces; 226 grams) unsalted butter, cut into chunks, at room temperature

2/3 cup (80 grams) confectioners' sugar

½ teaspoon fine sea salt

Pinch ground cinnamon (optional)

¾ teaspoon pure vanilla extract

2 cups (272 grams) all-purpose flour

4 ounces (113 grams) bittersweet chocolate, finely chopped

STORING

The dough can be refrigerated for up to 2 days or frozen, well wrapped, up to 2 months; cut and bake directly from the freezer. The cookies will keep in a tin at room temperature for about 5 days or, wrapped airtight, in the freezer for up to 2 months.

My original recipe for these deeply coffee-flavored and amply chocolate-flecked cookies produced a classic shortbread with the melt-in-your-mouth texture that's the hallmark of great shortbread and the result of using only confectioners' sugar in the dough. When I adapted the recipe for Beurre & Sel and baked the cookies in metal rings, constraining their spreadability, the change was anything but subtle: The sablés were still tender, but their texture became denser and their flavor more intense.

The trick of making an espresso extract to add to the dough is a good one to know. If you want to use it for other things — a spoonful is good in brownies, chocolate sauces or even in chocolate chip cookies — make more than you need now and keep it in the refrigerator, where it will be fine for months.

Of course these are good with coffee and coffee drinks, but they're surprisingly nice with milk and not at all bad with cognac.

Makes about 40 cookies

Dissolve the espresso in the boiling water. Set the extract aside to cool to lukewarm or room temperature.

Working with a stand mixer fitted with the paddle attachment, or in a large bowl with a hand mixer, beat the butter, sugar, salt and cinnamon, if you're using it, together on medium speed for about 3 minutes, scraping down the bowl as needed, until well blended. Mix in the vanilla and espresso extract on low speed. Turn off the mixer, add the flour all at once and pulse to begin incorporating it, then mix on low speed until the flour almost disappears into the dough. Scrape down the bowl, add the chopped chocolate and mix until evenly distributed. Give the dough a few last turns with a sturdy flexible spatula.

Turn the dough out onto the counter and divide it in half. Shape each half into a disk.

Working with one piece of dough at a time, sandwich it between pieces of parchment paper and roll it to a thickness of ¼ inch. Slide the dough, still

Ringed Espresso-Chocolate Sablés. If you have 2-inch baking rings (see page 25), use them to cut out the rolled dough. Bake the dough — in the rings — on lined baking sheets just as you would the muffin-tin cookies. Leave the rings in place for at least 20 minutes before lifting them off, rinsing and reusing.

sandwiched, onto a baking sheet — you can stack the slabs — and freeze the dough for at least 1 hour, or refrigerate for at least 2 hours.

GETTING READY TO BAKE: Center a rack in the oven and preheat it to 325 degrees F. Butter or spray a regular muffin tin, or two tins, if you've got them. Have a 2-inch-diameter cookie cutter at hand.

Working with one sheet of dough at a time, peel away both pieces of paper and put the dough back on one piece of paper. Cut the dough and drop the rounds into the muffin tin(s). The dough might not fill the molds completely, but it will once baked. Save the scraps from both pieces of dough, then gather them together, re-roll, chill and cut.

Bake the cookies for 18 to 20 minutes, or until they feel firm to the touch and have some color. Transfer the muffin tin(s) to a rack and leave the cookies in the tin(s) for about 10 minutes before carefully lifting them out onto the rack to cool completely.

Continue with the remainder of the dough, if you only baked one sheet, always using cool tins.

COCONUT-LIME SABLÉS

If anyone had told me that these would develop a committed cult following, I'd have told them they'd backed the wrong sweet. Not that they aren't tasty and satisfying; they are. Not that their flavor and the memory of that flavor doesn't linger; it does. And not that their texture — flaky, crunchy and chewy at the same time — isn't fascinating; it is. It's just that they seemed a touch too simple to become a gotta-have.

Because I use some toasted and some untoasted coconut, the cookie's texture is both crisp and chewy. And there is so much lime zest that the cookie reminds some people of a piña colada. All of this comes as a surprise, since the cookie masquerades as a plain coconut-dusted shortbread.

I like to use sweetened coconut in the cookie dough for its chewiness, but I prefer the dryness of unsweetened coconut for the topping. However, it's more of a technicality — use what you've got.

Makes about 26 cookies

Whisk the flour, cornstarch and coriander together.

Put the sugar and lime zest in the bowl of a stand mixer or in a large bowl in which you can use a hand mixer and, using your fingertips, work the zest into the sugar until the sugar is moist and fragrant. If using a stand mixer, fit it with the paddle attachment. Add the butter and salt to the bowl and beat on medium speed for about 3 minutes, until smooth. Beat in the vanilla extract. Turn off the mixer and add the dry ingredients all at once. Pulse the mixer and then, when the risk of flying flour has passed, mix on low speed until the flour disappears into the dough. Add the toasted and untoasted coconut and pulse to incorporate. There will probably be some dry ingredients in the bottom of the bowl — work them in by hand with a sturdy flexible spatula.

Turn the dough out and divide it in half. Shape each half into a disk.

Working with one piece at a time, roll the dough between pieces of parchment paper to a thickness of a scant ½ inch. Slide the sandwiched dough onto a baking sheet — you can stack the slabs — and freeze for at least 1 hour, or refrigerate for at least 2 hours.

1½ cups (204 grams) all-purpose flour

¼ cup (32 grams) cornstarch

Pinch of ground coriander

⅔ cup (134 grams) sugar

Finely grated zest of 2 limes

2 sticks (8 ounces; 226 grams) unsalted butter, cut into chunks, at room temperature

¼ teaspoon fine sea salt

1½ teaspoons pure vanilla extract

⅔ cup (80 grams) shredded sweetened coconut, half toasted (see page 20)

Shredded unsweetened coconut, for sprinkling (see headnote)

STORING

The dough can be refrigerated for up to 2 days or wrapped airtight and frozen for up to 2 months. The cookies will keep for about 3 days tightly covered at room temperature or for up to 2 months, well wrapped, in the freezer.

GETTING READY TO BAKE: Center a rack in the oven and preheat it to 325 degrees F. Butter or spray a regular muffin tin, or two tins, if you've got them. Have a 2-inch-diameter cookie cutter at hand.

Working with one sheet of dough at a time, peel away both pieces of parchment and put the dough back on one piece of parchment. Cut the dough and drop the rounds into the muffin tin(s). Save the scraps from both pieces of dough, then gather them together, re-roll, chill and cut. Don't worry if the dough doesn't completely fill the cups; it will once it's baked. Sprinkle the tops with the unsweetened coconut, completely covering the rounds.

Bake the cookies for 18 to 20 minutes, rotating the tin(s) after 10 minutes, or until the cookies are a pale golden brown — they'll be a deeper color around the edges and the coconut on top will be toasted. Transfer the tin(s) to a rack and wait for 15 minutes, then unmold the cookies and allow them to cool completely on the rack.

Repeat with the remaining dough, always using cool muffin tins.

PLAYING AROUND

Ringed Coconut-Lime Sablés. If you have 2-inch baking rings (see page 25), use them to cut out the rolled dough. Place the dough — still in the rings — on lined baking sheets and sprinkle with the coconut. Bake as you would the muffin-tin cookies. Leave the rings in place for at least 20 minutes before lifting them off, rinsing and reusing.

MINT CHOCOLATE SABLÉS

2 cups (272 grams) all-purpose flour

½ cup plus 2 tablespoons (53 grams) unsweetened cocoa powder

2 sticks (8 ounces; 226 grams) unsalted butter, cut into chunks, at room temperature

1 cup (200 grams) sugar

⅓ cup (40 grams) confectioners' sugar

½ teaspoon fine sea salt

1 large egg

1 tablespoon pure peppermint oil or extract

4 ounces (113 grams) dark chocolate, coarsely chopped

My son, Joshua, and I have a thing for the mint-and-chocolate combo. In creating one for Beurre & Sel, we tried gooey cookies and chubby ones, sandwich cookies and cakey ones, and, in the end, we were surprised by our final choice: this sleek and simple sablé.

To get the fullest chocolate flavor, I add both cocoa and chopped chocolate, and the best of each. I use Valrhona cocoa and their extra-bitter chocolate, but you should use what you like most. And to get that cool mint flavor, one that's strong enough to break through chocolate's richness but not so strong that it tastes medicinal (a hazard with mint), I use pure peppermint oil (extract's fine too).

At Beurre & Sel, the cookie went out into the world naked — no sugar dusting, no icing, no glaze — and held its own. At home, I sometimes doll it up a bit by piping on either melted chocolate (dark or white) or royal icing (page 488), with or without a splash of peppermint oil or extract. If you decide to pipe, go light.

Makes about 40 cookies

Sift the flour and cocoa powder together or push them through a strainer.

Working with a stand mixer fitted with the paddle attachment, or in a large bowl with a hand mixer, beat the butter, both sugars and the salt together on medium speed until smooth, about 3 minutes; scrape down the bowl as needed. Add the egg and beat for 2 minutes, then beat in the peppermint oil or extract. Turn off the machine, add the dry ingredients all at once and pulse until the risk of flying flour has passed. Then mix on low speed only until the flour and cocoa are fully incorporated. Add the chopped chocolate and mix just to blend, or do this bit of mixing with a sturdy flexible spatula.

Turn the dough out onto the counter and divide it in half. Gather each half into a ball and flatten into a disk.

Working with one piece of dough at a time, roll the dough ¼ inch thick

STORING

The dough can be refrigerated for up to 2 days or, wrapped airtight, frozen for up to 2 months. Cut and bake the dough directly from the freezer. The cookies will keep in a tin at room temperature for up to 5 days or, wrapped airtight, in the freezer for up to 2 months.

Ringed Mint-Chocolate Sablés. If you have 2-inch baking rings (see page 25), use them to cut out the rolled dough. Bake the dough — in the rings — on lined baking sheets just as you would the muffin-tin cookies. Leave the rings in place for at least 20 minutes before lifting them off, rinsing and reusing.

between pieces of parchment. Slide the parchment-sandwiched dough onto a baking sheet — you can stack the slabs — and freeze for at least 1 hour or refrigerate for at least 2 hours.

GETTING READY TO BAKE: Center a rack in the oven and preheat it to 350 degrees F. Butter or spray a regular muffin tin, or two tins, if you've got them. Have a 2-inch-diameter cookie cutter at hand.

Working with one sheet of dough at a time, peel away both pieces of paper and put the dough back on one piece of paper. Cut the dough and drop the rounds into the muffin tin(s). The rounds might not fill the cups completely now, but they will once they bake. Save the scraps from both pieces of dough, then gather them together, re-roll, chill and cut.

Bake the cookies for 11 to 13 minutes, or until they feel firm to the touch. Transfer the muffin tin(s) to a rack and leave the cookies in the tin(s) for about 10 minutes, before carefully lifting them out onto the rack to cool completely.

Continue with the remainder of the dough, always using cool tins.

LAVENDER-WHITE CHOCOLATE SABLÉS

Lavender, so quickly recognizable as a fragrance, has a flavor that can be hard to place, in part because it's so unexpected in a cookie, and in part because the flowers tend to taste more like lemon than you'd imagine. I like the puzzle of the ingredient and really like how its cool astringency blends with white chocolate's cozy, warm vanilla flavor. They're a perfect match in this buttery shortbread.

You need to use dried culinary lavender — lavender that hasn't been sprayed — and, of course, you want it to burst with fragrance. Keep your lavender in a cool, dry place away from sunlight, which would bleach it. Smell it before you measure it: If it's lost its scent, it's lost its usefulness. Culinary lavender usually comes as whole blossoms, but the gray and purple flowers are too large to be pleasant in a cookie. Either pulverize them in a clean coffee or spice grinder or pound them into a coarse powder with a mortar and pestle.

Makes about 45 cookies

Put the sugar and lavender in the bowl of a stand mixer or in a large bowl that you can work in with a hand mixer. Using your fingers, rub the ingredients together until the sugar (and probably your kitchen as well) is fragrant. Add the flour and salt and whisk to blend. If using a stand mixer, fit it with the paddle attachment. Drop pieces of cool butter into the bowl and beat on medium-low speed until the dough forms moist, clumpy curds that look like streusel and hold together when pinched. Reaching this stage takes longer than you may think — you might have to mix for 10 minutes or more. Sprinkle in the vanilla, toss in the chopped chocolate and mix until blended.

Turn the dough out onto the counter and divide it in half. Gather each half into a ball and shape into a disk.

Working with one piece of dough at a time, roll the dough ¼ inch thick between pieces of parchment. Slide the parchment-sandwiched dough onto a baking sheet — you can stack the slabs — and freeze for at least 1 hour, or refrigerate for at least 2 hours.

½ cup (100 grams) sugar

2 teaspoons culinary lavender, measured whole and then ground (see headnote)

2⅓ cups (317 grams) all-purpose flour

½ teaspoon fine sea salt

2 sticks (8 ounces; 226 grams) unsalted butter, cut into chunks, at cool room temperature

1 teaspoon pure vanilla extract

4 ounces (113 grams) best-quality white chocolate, finely chopped

STORING

The dough can be refrigerated for up to 2 days or, wrapped airtight, frozen for up to 2 months; bake directly from the freezer, adding a few more minutes to the baking time. These cookies keep in a container at room temperature for up to 5 days or, wrapped airtight, in the freezer for up to 2 months.

GETTING READY TO BAKE: Center a rack in the oven and preheat it to 350 degrees F. Butter or spray a regular muffin tin, or two tins, if you've got them. Have a 2-inch-diameter cookie cutter at hand.

Working with one sheet of dough at a time, peel away both pieces of paper and put the dough back on one piece of paper. Cut the dough and drop the rounds into the muffin tin(s). The dough might not fill the cups completely now, but it will once baked. Save the scraps from both pieces of dough, then gather them together, re-roll and chill.

Bake the cookies for 16 to 18 minutes, rotating the tin(s) after 10 minutes, or until they feel firm to the touch. The tops will be pale but the bottoms will have some color. Transfer the muffin tin(s) to a rack and leave the cookies in the tins for about 10 minutes before carefully lifting them out and onto the rack to cool completely.

Continue with the remainder of the dough, always using cool tins.

PLAYING AROUND

Ringed Lavender–White Chocolate Sablés. If you have 2-inch baking rings (see page 25), use them to cut out the rolled dough. Bake the dough — in the rings — on lined baking sheets just as you would the muffin-tin cookies. Leave the rings in place for at least 20 minutes before lifting them off, rinsing and reusing.

CLASSIC JAMMERS

1 recipe French Vanilla Sablé dough
(page 332), rolled and chilled

About ½ cup (160 grams) thick jam, such
as blueberry or raspberry

1 recipe Use-It-for-Everything Streusel
(page 500), chilled

I have a deep and special attachment to this cookie. I literally dreamed it up in Paris, meaning that I had a dream about how this cookie would be made, what it would look like and how fabulous it would taste — and I baked it as soon as I woke up. I loved it so much that I took it to my friend, the pastry chef Pierre Hermé, and I left his atelier grinning: He loved it as much as I did.

The cookie has three components: The base is a French Vanilla Sablé, (page 332), a perfect shortbread; there's a spoonful of jam in the center; and there's a circle of streusel around the jam. It is one of the most beautiful cookies I've ever created and one of the most delicious — the play of vanilla with fruit jam and tender cookie with crumbly streusel is ideal. It was also one of our most popular cookies at Beurre & Sel and the one I riffed on over and over again.

The idea of building a cookie from three delicious elements was so compelling that I found myself coming up with new combinations more often than we could actually produce them. If you end up loving the Jammer as much as I do, try the Mulled Wine Jammers (page 362), Spiced Pumpkin Jammers (page 359) and Honey-and-Tea Jammers (page 353), and then try making a Jammer to call your own. When something's this good, there can never be too many of them in the world.

Makes about 30 cookies

Center a rack in the oven and preheat it to 350 degrees F. Butter or spray a regular muffin tin, or two tins, if you've got them. Have a 2-inch-diameter cookie cutter at hand.

Working with one sheet of dough at a time, peel away both pieces of parchment paper and put the dough back on one piece of paper. Cut the dough and drop the rounds into the muffin tin(s). Save the scraps from both pieces of

Ringed Jammers. If you have 2-inch baking rings (see page 25), use them to cut out the rolled dough. Place the dough — in the rings — on lined baking sheets and build the Jammers in the rings. Bake as you would the muffin-tin cookies. Leave the rings in place for at least 20 minutes before lifting them off, rinsing and reusing.

dough, then gather them together, re-roll, chill and cut. Don't worry if the dough doesn't completely fill the molds — it will once it's baked.

Spoon about ½ teaspoon jam onto the center of each cookie. Spoon or sprinkle streusel around the edges of each cookie — you want to cover the surface of the dough but leave the jam bare.

Bake the cookies for 20 to 22 minutes, rotating the tin(s) after 11 minutes, or until the streusel and the edges of the cookies are golden brown; the jam may bubble and that's fine. Leave the cookies in the tin(s) for about 15 minutes before transferring them to a rack to cool.

Repeat with the remaining dough, making certain that the tins are cool.

HONEY-AND-TEA JAMMERS

I made these as an Easter special for Beurre & Sel, but as spring moved into summer, and summer became fall, people still asked for them, and I couldn't take them off the menu. The base is a softish sablé flavored with honey, vanilla and crushed black tea. The jam in the center is strawberry (if you wanted to flavor it with a bit of rose extract or a splash of kirsch, Framboise or Chambord, I wouldn't stop you), and the crunch is my standard (and beloved) Use-It-for-Everything Streusel.

A word on the tea: I used Harney's Paris tea for these at Beurre & Sel. I chose it because it's flavored with vanilla, caramel and bergamot, which is lemony (and the base of Earl Grey tea), flavors that mix so beautifully with honey. Choose whatever tea you enjoy. A citrus tea is nice in these, as is a light green leaf tea. You might even look for something floral, like a rose tea, or fruity, like a berry tea.

Makes about 30 cookies

Put the sugar and tea in the bowl of a stand mixer or in a bowl in which you can use a hand mixer. Using your fingertips, rub, press and mash the ingredients together until the tea is finely crushed and the sugar is fragrant. If using a stand mixer, fit it with the paddle attachment. Toss the butter and salt into the bowl and beat on medium speed until smooth, about 3 minutes. Pour in the honey and vanilla and beat for 2 minutes, scraping down the bowl as needed. Mixing on low speed, add the yolk and beat for a minute. Turn off the mixer, add the flour all at once and then pulse to begin incorporating it. When the risk of flying flour has passed, mix on low speed, stopping to scrape down the bowl as needed, until the flour has disappeared into the dough.

Turn the dough out onto the counter and divide it in half. Gather each piece into a ball and shape into a disk.

Working with one piece of dough at a time, roll the dough ¼ inch thick between pieces of parchment. Slide the parchment-sandwiched dough onto a baking sheet — you can stack the slabs — and freeze for at least 1 hour, or refrigerate for at least 2 hours.

⅓ cup (67 grams) sugar

1 tablespoon loose tea (see headnote)

1 stick plus 1 tablespoon (9 tablespoons; 4½ ounces; 128 grams) unsalted butter, cut into chunks, at room temperature

½ teaspoon fine sea salt

3 tablespoons honey

1 teaspoon pure vanilla extract

1 large egg yolk, at room temperature

2 cups (272 grams) all-purpose flour

About ⅓ cup (108 grams) thick strawberry jam

1 recipe Use-It-for-Everything Streusel (page 500), chilled

STORING

Wrapped airtight, the dough can be refrigerated for up to 2 days or frozen for up to 2 months. The cookies can also be assembled, wrapped airtight and frozen for up to 2 months. Bake straight from the freezer; they might need another minute or so in the oven. The baked cookies will keep covered at room temperature for up to 2 days and can be frozen, well wrapped, for up to 2 months.

PLAYING AROUND

Ringed Honey-and-Tea Jammers. If you have 2-inch baking rings (see page 25), use them to cut out the rolled dough. Place the dough — in the rings — on lined baking sheets and build the Jammers in the rings. Bake as you would the muffin-tin cookies. Leave the rings in place for at least 20 minutes before lifting them off, rinsing and reusing.

GETTING READY TO BAKE: Center a rack in the oven and preheat it to 350 degrees F. Butter or spray a regular muffin tin, or two tins, if you've got them. Have a 2-inch-diameter cookie cutter at hand.

Working with one piece of dough at a time, peel away both pieces of parchment paper and put the dough back on one piece. Cut the dough and drop the rounds into the muffin tin(s). Save the scraps, combine them with the scraps from the second piece, re-roll, chill and cut. Don't worry if the dough doesn't completely fill the cups; it will once it's baked.

Spoon about ½ teaspoon jam onto the center of each cookie. Spoon or sprinkle streusel around the edges of each cookie — you want to cover the surface of the dough but leave the jam bare.

Bake the cookies for 20 to 22 minutes, rotating the tin(s) after 11 minutes, or until the streusel and the edges of the cookies are golden brown; the jam may bubble, and that's fine. Leave the cookies in the tin(s) for about 15 minutes before transferring them to a rack to cool completely.

Repeat with the remaining dough, always making certain that the tins are cool.

BLONDIES

½ cup (60 grams) coarsely chopped pecans, toasted

2 ounces (57 grams) best-quality milk chocolate, finely chopped

⅓ cup (40 grams) shredded sweetened coconut

1 stick (8 tablespoons; 4 ounces; 113 grams) unsalted butter, cut into chunks, at room temperature

¾ cup (150 grams) packed light brown sugar

¼ cup (50 grams) sugar

¼ teaspoon fine sea salt

1 large egg, at room temperature

1 teaspoon pure vanilla extract

1 cup (136 grams) all-purpose flour

STORING

You can scoop the dough out onto a lined baking sheet, pat it down, freeze until firm and then pack the pucks in an airtight container and freeze for up to 2 months. Leave the pucks at room temperature while you preheat the oven. The blondies are best eaten soon after they're baked, but they can be kept in a covered container at room temperature for up to 1 day or frozen, wrapped airtight, for up to 2 months.

The dough for these blondies is classic. It's got a generous amount of butter and more brown sugar than white — but the add-ins are new: coconut, chopped pecans and best-quality milk chocolate. The trio is made for the butterscotch flavor of brown sugar, and it adds to the blondies' chewiness. Because these are baked in mini-muffin tins, most of each little blondie is chewy, but the edges are crispy. It's like getting an edge piece of blondie (the best part) every time.

Making these Beurre & Sel cookies at home, I discovered a surprise: The dough can be scooped and baked and the blondies are awfully nice that way (see Playing Around). You don't get as much chew, but there's plenty of pleasure in each bite.

A word on add-ins: I've given you my favorites, but they're not the only possibilities for great blondies. Change the milk chocolate to white chocolate or butterscotch bits and the pecans to walnuts or peanuts, if you'd like. But I hope you'll keep the coconut, because it's a major contributor to the cookie's wonderful texture.

Makes about 30 blondies

Center a rack in the oven and preheat it to 325 degrees F. Butter or spray a mini-muffin tin, or two tins, if you've got them.

Stir the pecans, chocolate and coconut together.

Working with a stand mixer fitted with the paddle attachment, or in a large bowl with a hand mixer, beat the butter, both sugars and the salt together on medium speed until smooth, about 3 minutes. Add the egg and beat on low, scraping the bowl as needed, until you have a smooth, creamy mixture. Beat in the vanilla. Turn the mixer off, add the flour all at once and pulse a few times to start incorporating it. Then mix on low until the flour is almost fully blended into the dough. Add the pecans, chocolate and coconut, mixing just until they're evenly distributed; if you'd like, you can do the last few turns by hand with a sturdy flexible spatula.

Using a small cookie scoop, scoop out level portions of dough or use a

Blondie Drops. To make the blondies as traditional cookies, position the racks to divide the oven into thirds and preheat it to 375 degrees F. Line two baking sheets with parchment paper or silicone baking mats. Using a small cookie scoop, scoop level portions of dough or use a teaspoon to get rounded spoonfuls, dropping them onto the sheets, leaving a generous 2 inches between them — these are spreaders. Bake for 9 to 11 minutes, rotating the sheets top to bottom and front to back after 6 minutes, or until the cookies are deeply golden around the edges; the centers will still be soft. Let rest on the sheets for 3 minutes, then transfer to racks to finish cooling.

Blondie Bars. To make bars, double the recipe and scrape the dough into a buttered 9-x-13-inch baking pan. Bake on the center rack of a preheated 325-degree-F oven for about 40 minutes, until the edges of the blondies are golden and just starting to pull away from the sides of the pan; a tester poked into the center will come out clean. Let the blondies cool to room temperature on a rack before cutting them into squares.

Ringed Blondies. If you have 2-inch baking rings (see page 25), place them on lined baking sheets. Using a medium scoop (or a rounded tablespoon of dough), scoop, press and bake the blondies as you would the muffin-tin cookies. Leave the rings in place for about 15 minutes before lifting them off, rinsing and reusing.

teaspoon to get rounded spoonfuls. When all the dough is in the cups, press each mound of dough down very lightly with moistened fingertips.

Bake for 14 to 16 minutes, or until the cookies are firmly set around the edges and golden brown in the center. A tester inserted in the center of a blondie should come out clean. Transfer the tin(s) to a rack and let the blondies rest for 3 minutes, then unmold them either by turning the tin(s) over and rapping them against the counter or popping the blondies out with table knife. Transfer the blondies to the rack and serve them after they've cooled for about 10 minutes or when they've reached room temperature.

Repeat with the remaining dough, always using cool tins.

SPICED PUMPKIN JAMMERS

I think of these as proof that a good idea is the base of lots more good ideas. Once I hit on the Classic Jammer (page 350), riffing (okay, jamming) on the theme was almost inevitable. I'd look at ingredients and think, "Can I Jammer them?" Holidays would come and I'd wonder, "Can it be a Jammer day?"

And so, as you might have already guessed from the name, I made these for Thanksgiving. The cookie has the same spices you'd use in pie, the "filling" is creamy pumpkin and the streusel is speckled with pumpkin seeds. I like these so much that I make them all through what I think of as pumpkin season — they're as good for back-to-school and Halloween as they are for Thanksgiving and Christmas. (For another cookie riff on a Thanksgiving pie, see the Sweet Potato Pie Bars, page 68.)

Makes about 30 cookies

TO MAKE THE COOKIES: Whisk the flour, cinnamon, ginger and allspice together.

Working with a stand mixer fitted with the paddle attachment, or in a large bowl with a hand mixer, beat the butter, both sugars and the salt together on medium speed until smooth and creamy, about 3 minutes. One by one, beat in the yolks, beating for 1 minute after each one goes in and scraping down the bowl as needed. Beat in the vanilla. Turn the mixer off, add the dry ingredients all at once and pulse to begin blending. When the risk of flying flour has passed, mix on low speed until the flour mixture disappears into the dough.

Turn the dough out onto the counter and divide it in half. Gather each piece into a ball and shape into a disk.

Working with one piece of dough at a time, roll the dough ¼ inch thick between pieces of parchment. Slide the parchment-sandwiched dough onto a baking sheet — you can stack the slabs — and freeze for at least 1 hour, or refrigerate for at least 2 hours.

MEANWHILE, MAKE THE FILLING: Use a sturdy flexible spatula to beat the cream cheese in a small bowl until soft and smooth. Work in the pumpkin puree.

TO MAKE THE STREUSEL: Stir the pumpkin seeds into the streusel.

FOR THE COOKIES

2 cups (272 grams) all-purpose flour

1½ teaspoons ground cinnamon

1½ teaspoons ground ginger

¼ teaspoon ground allspice

2 sticks (8 ounces; 226 grams) unsalted butter, cut into chunks, at room temperature

½ cup (100 grams) packed light brown sugar

¼ cup (50 grams) sugar

½ teaspoon fine sea salt

2 large egg yolks, at room temperature

1 teaspoon pure vanilla extract

FOR THE PUMPKIN FILLING

4 ounces (½ cup; 113 grams) full-fat cream cheese, at room temperature

½ cup (113 grams) canned pumpkin puree (not pumpkin pie filling; drained if watery)

FOR THE STREUSEL

About ⅓ cup (about 43 grams) unsalted hulled pumpkin seeds (pepitas)

1 recipe Use-It-for-Everything Streusel (page 500), chilled

GETTING READY TO BAKE: Center a rack in the oven and preheat it to 350 degrees F. Butter or spray a regular muffin tin, or two tins, if you've got them. Have a 2-inch-diameter cookie cutter at hand.

Working with one sheet of dough at a time, peel away both pieces of parchment paper and put the dough back on one piece of paper. Cut the dough and drop the rounds into the muffin tin(s). Save the scraps from both pieces of dough, then gather them together, re-roll, chill and cut. Don't worry if the dough doesn't completely fill the cups; it will once it's baked.

Spoon about 1 teaspoon of the pumpkin filling onto the center of each cookie and use the back of the spoon to spread it across the cookie, leaving a slim border. Spoon or sprinkle streusel over the cookies to cover the entire surface.

Bake the cookies for 20 to 22 minutes, rotating the tin(s) after 12 minutes, or until the streusel and the edges of the cookies are golden brown. Leave the cookies in the tin(s) for about 15 minutes before transferring them to a rack to cool completely.

Repeat with the remaining dough, always making certain that the tins are cool.

PLAYING AROUND

Ringed Spiced Pumpkin Jammers. If you have 2-inch baking rings (see page 25), use them to cut out the rolled dough. Place the dough — in the rings — on lined baking sheets and build the Jammers in the rings. Bake as you would the muffin-tin cookies. Leave the rings in place for at least 20 minutes before lifting them off, rinsing and reusing.

STORING

Wrapped airtight, the dough can be refrigerated for up to 2 days or frozen for up to 2 months. The filling can be made up to 3 days ahead and kept covered in the refrigerator. The cookies can be assembled, wrapped airtight and frozen for up to 2 months. Bake straight from the freezer; they might need another minute or so in the oven. The baked cookies will keep covered at room temperature for up to 2 days and can be frozen, well wrapped, for up to 2 months.

MULLED WINE JAMMERS

FOR THE STREUSEL

2/3 cup (91 grams) all-purpose flour

1/3 cup (53 grams) yellow cornmeal

3 tablespoons sugar

1 tablespoon light brown sugar

1/4 teaspoon ground cinnamon

1/4 teaspoon fine sea salt

5 tablespoons (2½ ounces; 71 grams) cold unsalted butter, cut into small cubes

1/2 teaspoon pure vanilla extract

FOR THE JAM

Small piece of cinnamon stick (2 to 3 inches)

2 points from a star anise

2 whole cloves

1¼ cups (300 ml) fruity red wine (I like a California Syrah)

1 tablespoon honey

2 strips orange or tangerine peel (or 1 orange or tangerine slice)

1/2 cup (70 grams) plump, moist dried cherries, coarsely chopped

1/2 cup (60 grams) plump, moist dried cranberries, coarsely chopped

3 tablespoons plump, moist raisins

1/3 cup (108 grams) thick, fruity best-quality cherry jam

FOR THE COOKIE BASE

1 recipe French Vanilla Sablé dough (page 332), rolled out and chilled

There's a lot going on in this cookie, and all of it is great. You'll recognize the Classic Jammer (page 350) construction. But while the cookie is my beloved French Vanilla Sablé (such a good team player), the streusel has cornmeal and the jam is a mix of spicy mulled red wine, dried cherries, raisins and cranberries, with store-bought cherry jam to pull it all together. It is one of my all-time favorite cold-weather cookies.

A word on timing: Each of the elements in this recipe has to cool or be chilled before you can use it. Make the dough first and get it rolled out and chilled. Then move on to the streusel, pop that into the fridge and make and cool the jam. The best move — if you can swing it — is to make everything a day or two ahead. Then, on baking day, making these beautiful cookies will be quick work.

A word on quantity: You may have some of the mulled-wine jam left over — it's hard to make a smaller quantity of this — but you won't be sorry.

Makes about 24 cookies

TO MAKE THE STREUSEL: You can make the streusel by hand or in a mixer. I prefer to use a stand mixer, but fingers are fine. Whisk the flour, cornmeal, both sugars, the cinnamon and salt together in the mixer bowl or a large mixing bowl. Drop in the cubes of cold butter and toss all the ingredients together with your fingers until the butter is coated.

If you're working with a mixer, fit it with the paddle attachment and mix on medium-low speed until the ingredients form moist, clumpy crumbs. Squeeze the streusel, and it will hold together. Reaching this stage takes longer than you think it will — you might have to mix for 10 minutes or more. Sprinkle over the vanilla and mix until blended.

Or, if you're working by hand, squeeze, mash, mush or otherwise rub everything together but the vanilla until you have a bowlful of moist clumps and curds. Squeeze the streusel, and it will hold together. Sprinkle over the vanilla and toss to blend.

PLAYING AROUND

Ringed Mulled Wine Jammers. If you have 2-inch baking rings (see page 25), use them to cut out the rolled dough. Place the dough — in the rings — on lined baking sheets and build the Jammers in the rings. Bake just as you would the muffin-tin cookies, but these will probably need another minute or two in the oven. Leave the rings in place for at least 20 minutes before lifting them off, rinsing and reusing.

STORING

The mulled-wine jam will keep, tightly covered, for a few weeks in the refrigerator. The streusel can be kept for up to 2 weeks in the fridge and up to 2 months in the freezer. The cookies can be assembled, wrapped airtight and frozen for up to 2 months. Bake them straight from the freezer; they might need another minute or so in the oven. The baked cookies will keep covered at room temperature for up to 2 days and can be frozen for up to 2 months.

Pack the streusel into a covered container and refrigerate for at least 1 hour; 3 hours would be better.

TO MAKE THE JAM: First, mull the wine. Tie the spices together in cheese-cloth to make a little hobo bag. Toss the sachet into a medium saucepan, add the wine, honey and citrus (peel or fruit) and bring to a boil over medium heat. Lower the heat and let the mixture simmer gently, uncovered, for 10 minutes. Add the dried fruits and cook and stir frequently over low heat until most of the liquid evaporates, about 8 minutes. Remove the pan from the heat, pick out and discard the spice bag and the citrus and stir in the cherry jam. Scrape the mixture into a bowl and cool to room temperature (you can do this in the refrigerator, if you'd like). If you're not using the jam now, cover it tightly and refrigerate until needed.

GETTING READY TO BAKE: Center a rack in the oven and preheat it to 350 degrees F. Butter or spray a regular muffin tin, or two tins, if you've got them. Have a 2-inch-diameter cookie cutter at hand.

Working with one sheet of dough at a time, peel away both pieces of parchment paper and put the dough back on one piece of paper. Cut the dough and drop the rounds into the muffin tin(s). Save the scraps from both pieces of dough, then gather them together, re-roll, chill and cut. Don't worry if the dough doesn't completely fill the cups, it will once it's baked.

Spread about 1 teaspoon jam over the top of each cookie, leaving a slim border. Spoon or sprinkle enough streusel over each sablé to cover it (and the jam).

Bake the cookies for 20 to 22 minutes, turning the tin(s) after 11 minutes, or until the streusel and the edges of the cookies are golden brown; the jam may bubble, and that's fine. Leave the cookies in the tin(s) for about 15 minutes before transferring them to a rack to cool to room temperature.

Repeat with the remaining dough, making certain that the tins are cool.

The artist John "Crash" Matos has been a family friend for more than twenty years and an inspiration to all of us. John is a wildly talented painter (he paints on canvas, walls, Ferraris, suitcases and guitars — including Eric Clapton's), a caring friend and a true cookie lover. When Crash painted his first guitar for Clapton, it was a Fender Stratocaster, and it came to be called a Crashocaster. So when I created this cookie to celebrate a showing of Crash's work in New York City, the name Crash-O-Cookie seemed inevitable.

An almost classic soft-and-chewy oatmeal cookie with pieces of milk chocolate scattered throughout, this one recently puzzled a friend who asked what the fruit was. When I said raisins, he was incredulous. "But I hate them!" he exclaimed and asked what I'd done to make them so good. The answer: I'd put them in hot water to plump and forgot about them. The long soak made the raisins taste as if they'd been infused with wine. In fact, if you'd like to up the flavor, you can soak the raisins in red wine, brandy, cognac, rum or black tea.

Makes about 50 cookies

Position the racks to divide the oven into thirds and preheat it to 350 degrees F. Line two baking sheets with parchment paper or silicone baking mats.

Even if your raisins are moist, the flavor of these cookies will improve if you give them a soak: Toss the raisins into a bowl, cover with very hot tap water (or booze or tea; see headnote) and let them plump while you make the dough. When you're ready for the raisins, drain and pat them dry.

Whisk together the oats, flour, cinnamon and baking soda.

Working with a stand mixer fitted with the paddle attachment, or in a large bowl with a hand mixer, beat the butter, both sugars and the salt together at medium speed until smooth, about 2 minutes. One by one, add the eggs, beating for 1 minute after each one goes in, then beat in the vanilla. Scrape down the bowl. Turn off the mixer, add the dry ingredients all at once and pulse a few

1½ cups (240 grams) plump, moist raisins

3 cups (240 grams) old-fashioned rolled oats (not quick-cooking)

1½ cups (204 grams) all-purpose flour

1½ teaspoons ground cinnamon

1 teaspoon baking soda

2 sticks (8 ounces; 226 grams) unsalted butter, cut into chunks, at room temperature

¾ cup (150 grams) sugar

¾ cup (150 grams) packed light brown sugar

½ teaspoon fine sea salt

2 large eggs, at room temperature

1½ teaspoons pure vanilla extract

9 ounces (255 grams) best-quality milk chocolate, finely chopped

STORING

The dough can be wrapped well and refrigerated for up to 3 days. The cookies will keep at room temperature for at least 4 days; they can be wrapped airtight and frozen for up to 2 months.

times, then mix on low speed until they are almost blended. Add the raisins and chopped chocolate and mix on low just until blended. Give the dough its last few turns using a sturdy flexible spatula.

Using a medium cookie scoop, scoop out level portions of dough, or use a tablespoon to get rounded spoonfuls. Drop the dough onto the baking sheets, leaving 2 inches of space between the mounds. Press the dough down gently until the cookies are about ½ inch high.

Bake the cookies for about 15 minutes, rotating the sheets top to bottom and front to back after 8 minutes, or until the cookies are only slightly firm around the edges and still pokeable (and maybe even a bit wet looking) in the center. (If the dough was refrigerated and became very hard, you might have to add another minute or so to the baking time.) Place the baking sheets on racks and let the cookies rest for 3 to 5 minutes, then gently transfer them to the racks to cool completely; they'll firm as they cool.

Repeat with the remaining dough, making sure that your baking sheets are cool.

PLAYING AROUND

Mega Crash-o-Cookies. To make saucer-size cookies, scoop the dough using a large cookie scoop and leave a lot of room between the scoops. In fact, it's best if you bake just 6 cookies at a time. Bake the cookies for 17 to 19 minutes.

CHUNKERS

1 cup (5 ounces; 141 grams) plump, moist dried cherries, coarsely chopped

⅓ cup (45 grams) all-purpose flour

5 tablespoons (26 grams) unsweetened cocoa powder

½ teaspoon fine sea salt

¼ teaspoon baking powder

3 tablespoons (1½ ounces; 43 grams) unsalted butter, cut into 6 pieces

13 ounces (368 grams) bittersweet chocolate, coarsely chopped

8 ounces (226 grams) salted cashews, coarsely chopped

6 ounces (170 grams) best-quality milk chocolate, coarsely chopped

2 large eggs, at room temperature

¾ cup (150 grams) sugar

1 teaspoon pure vanilla extract

Unlike most of the cookies on the Beurre & Sel list, these are scoop-and-bake free-forms. They are chubby and chockablock with chopped-up good things that poke out of the cookies at every which angle. Famously disorderly, they are phenomenally delicious. Among the Beurre & Sel customers, they had a serious following.

There are chopped salted cashews in the mix; winey, sweet-tart dried cherries; chopped milk chocolate; and both chopped and melted bittersweet chocolate. You need a lot of chocolate — more than a pound! — and every penny that you put into buying great chocolate for these will come back to you in oohs, aahs and culinary contentment. There's no question that Chunkers are one of the world's great cookies.

A word on technique: To get the very best texture — and with these, that means that the cookie gets softer as you approach the center — give the eggs and sugar the full measure of time in the mixer, add the melted ingredients while they're still warm and fold in the rest of the ingredients as efficiently as you can. Scoop the cookies while the dough is still warm, and don't second-guess yourself — they'll look seriously underbaked when you take them out of the oven, but they'll firm to perfection on a rack.

Makes about 18 cookies

Position the racks to divide the oven into thirds and preheat it to 325 degrees F. (If your oven has hot spots, center the rack and bake one sheet at a time because it's best not to have to open the oven and take the time to rotate the sheets during the short bake.) Line two baking sheets with parchment paper or silicone baking mats. Cover the bottom of a flat-bottomed jar or glass with plastic wrap.

Put the chopped cherries in a bowl, cover with very hot tap water and let soak while you put together the rest of the ingredients. When you're ready for them, drain and pat dry between paper towels.

Whisk the flour, cocoa, salt and baking powder together.

The flattened pucks of dough can be frozen for up to 2 months. Do not defrost before baking; leave at room temperature while you preheat the oven. The cookies are at their most splendid the day they're made. In fact, nothing beats a Chunker that's just a couple of hours out of the oven. However, they'll keep, covered, at room temperature for about 2 days. And they can be frozen, well wrapped, for up to 2 months.

Put the butter in a medium heatproof bowl. Scatter over 7 ounces (198 grams) of the bittersweet chocolate and place the bowl over a saucepan of water; the bottom of the bowl should not touch the water. Bring the water to a gentle simmer and slowly melt the butter and chocolate. Stir occasionally and be careful not to overheat the mixture — you don't want the chocolate and butter to get so hot that they separate.

Toss the remaining 6 ounces (170 grams) bittersweet chocolate, the cashews, milk chocolate and cherries together in another bowl.

Working with a stand mixer fitted with the whisk attachment, or in a large bowl with a hand mixer, beat the eggs and sugar together on medium-high speed for about 5 minutes (don't skimp on the time), until the eggs are pale and the whisk leaves tracks. Beat in the vanilla. With the mixer on medium-low, scrape in the warm melted butter and chocolate and mix just until incorporated. Switch to a sturdy flexible spatula and, as gently as you can with this heavy batter, fold in the flour mixture, making certain that you get to anything that's at the bottom of the bowl. When almost all of the dry ingredients are incorporated, add the chopped chocolate, nuts and cherries, folding and stirring until they're mixed in. (Everything will be chocolate-covered except the cashews; their oil makes them somewhat resistant to coating.)

Using a large cookie scoop, scoop out level portions of the warm dough or use a tablespoon to get heaping spoonfuls, placing the mounds of dough about 2 inches apart on the baking sheets. Use the bottom of the jar to lightly press down on each mound — you're aiming to get a puck with a diameter of 2½ inches.

Bake the cookies for 10 to 11 minutes, or until the tops, which will crack, are mostly dry — the centers might look wet and unbaked. The cookies will still be very soft (don't try to budge them). Go by time, and have faith. Transfer the baking sheets to a rack and let the cookies cool and set for about 30 minutes, until you can lift them from the parchment paper. If you haven't done so, bake the second sheet.

COCONUT PATTIES

At its core, this cookie is an old-school coconut macaroon made with unsweetened coconut, egg whites and sugar, but the technique for making it is French, the untraditional shape mine and the flavoring open to fantasy. Just about any flavor that you like with coconut will go with this cookie. I'm fond of tinting it pink and adding rose extract (see Playing Around); swapping lemon zest for lime; or going heavy on vanilla (up the extract to 1 to 1¼ teaspoons). What I never want to change is the texture: I love the cookie for its light crust and its soft, chewy center.

In order to get that terrific texture, the dough is cooked in a saucepan until it is hot to the touch and then cooled before baking. Actually, what happens in the oven is less about baking than it is about drying, since the mix is already fully cooked. When it comes to shaping the dough, my preference is to form balls and then press them down. For precision, I press each ball into a baking ring and then remove the ring, but opting for a more freeform shape and flattening them with your fingertips is fine too.

A word on the coconut: You must use unsweetened coconut — sweetened shredded coconut won't absorb the sugar or blend with the whites. It will also make your cookies too sweet. I use short finely shredded coconut that I buy from the bulk bins in natural food markets.

A word on lemon oil: Pure lemon oil adds true and deep flavor to the mix. If you can't find the oil, use pure lemon extract.

Makes about 20 cookies

Put the sugar in a heavy medium saucepan, top with the zest and use your fingertips to rub the zest into the sugar until it is moist and aromatic. Using a flexible spatula, stir in the egg whites, then add the coconut, stirring until the coconut is evenly moistened — a job that takes a couple of minutes. Put the pan over medium-low heat and cook, stirring without stopping, until the mixture is hot to the touch. Plunge a table knife into the coconut — it should come out very warm. Depending on the heat, this will take 5 to 8 minutes. Scrape the

⅔ cup (134 grams) sugar

Finely grated zest of 2 limes (or lemons)

4 large egg whites

2½ cups (200 grams) shredded unsweetened coconut (see headnote)

1 teaspoon pure lemon oil (or pure lime oil or pure lemon extract)

¼ teaspoon pure vanilla extract

Sanding or granulated sugar, for sprinkling (optional)

STORING

The dough can be refrigerated for up to 3 days. Packed in a covered container, the cookies will keep at room temperature for about 1 week. Keep them longer, and they'll get a little firmer and a little drier, but they'll still find happy takers.

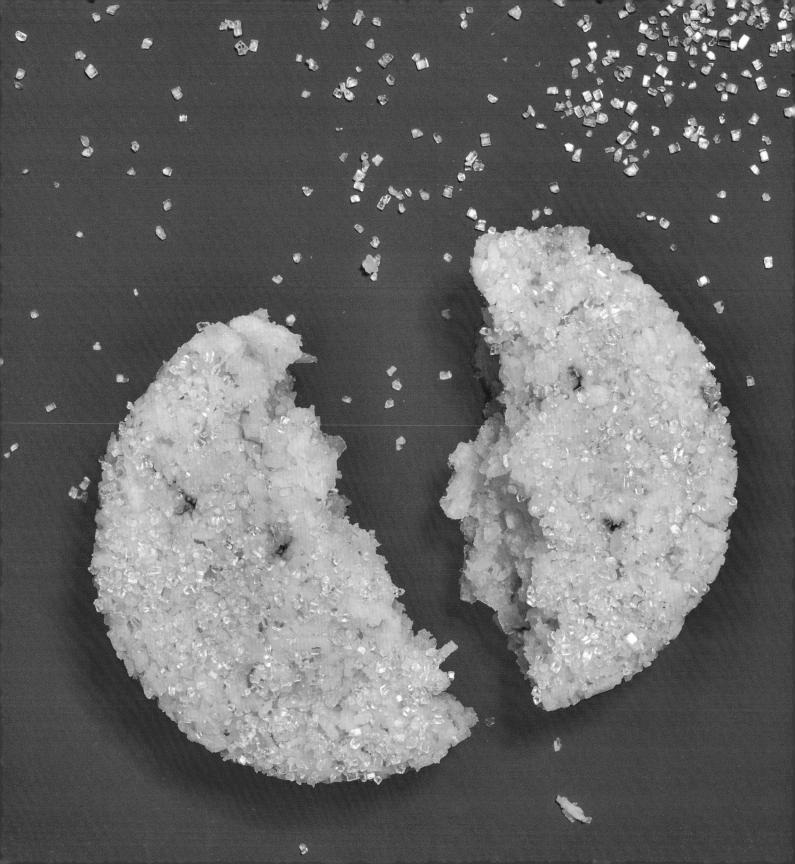

mixture into a bowl and stir in the lemon oil (or extract) and the vanilla. Press a piece of plastic wrap against the surface of the dough and refrigerate for at least 5 hours.

GETTING READY TO BAKE: Center a rack in the oven and preheat it to 300 degrees F. Use an insulated cookie sheet or stack two baking sheets one on top of the other. Line the (top) sheet with parchment paper or a silicone baking mat.

I use a medium cookie scoop to portion the dough, a 2-inch baking ring (see page 25) or cookie cutter to shape the cookies and a spice jar that fits in the ring to flatten the dough (wrap the bottom of the jar in plastic wrap). You can also use a tablespoon and shape the patties by hand. Scoop the dough out onto the baking sheet, leaving about 2 inches of space between the scoops (or rounded tablespoonfuls) of dough. If you're using a baking ring or cookie cutter, place the ring around each mound of dough, press the dough down gently with the jar (the patty will be about ¼ to ⅓ inch thick) and remove the ring. If you don't have a ring, just press the dough down. If you'd like, sprinkle the tops of the patties with sugar.

Bake for 25 to 30 minutes, or until the patties feel dry and slightly firm to the touch and are just lightly browned here and there. Transfer the baking sheet to a rack and let the patties cool completely — they're too fragile to move when they're warm.

PLAYING AROUND

Rose-Flavored Tuckers. I made these for a Mother's Day mom-and-daughter tea the fashion designer Gaby Basora held at her SoHo, New York, shop, Tucker. I wanted something pink and girly, and these were perfect for the occasion. Perfect with sparkling rosé wine too. Omit the lime zest and lemon oil and add 1 teaspoon pure rose extract (my favorite brand is Star Kay White). Do not use rose water — you won't get enough flavor. If you'd like, once the dough is cooked and flavored, stir in a couple of drops of red food coloring to turn the cookies pink. Because they will brown a tad in the oven, ballerina pink is a better choice than devilish red.

COFFEE-CARDAMOM COOKIES

If spice cookies are good alongside coffee — and they are — then wouldn't they be even better with coffee in them? That was the question I asked myself and these cookies are the affirmative answer.

These have freshly ground espresso in the dough (you can use whatever coffee you'll be drinking with the cookies or, in a pinch, instant espresso — but don't use as much: 2 teaspoons does the trick) and I love that you can see the specks in the cookies. And although there's cinnamon in the mix, it's the addition of cardamom that makes these cookies extra special. The cardamom blends so beautifully with the coffee and cinnamon that it's elusive, but it adds spice and warmth.

I bake these until they're set around the edges but still have a little give at the center. If you'd like them a bit chewier, bake them for less time. But don't bake them longer, since they crisp after a couple of days.

The glaze is optional, but I like the look and the extra bit of sweetness that it brings to the cookies.

A word on the glaze: The recipe calls for half an egg white. The easiest way to divide the white is to beat it lightly to break it up, and then measure out 15 grams. Or put it in a mini liquid measuring cup and pour off half.

Makes about 30 cookies

FOR THE COOKIES

2 cups (272 grams) all-purpose flour

1 tablespoon ground espresso or coffee beans (or 2 teaspoons instant espresso) (see headnote)

2 teaspoons ground cinnamon

½ teaspoon ground cardamom

½ teaspoon fine sea salt

1 stick (8 tablespoons; 4 ounces; 113 grams) unsalted butter, cut into chunks, at room temperature

½ cup (100 grams) packed light brown sugar

¼ cup (50 grams) sugar

1 large egg, at room temperature

1½ tablespoons unsulfured molasses

1 teaspoon pure vanilla extract

FOR THE OPTIONAL GLAZE

½ large egg white (see headnote)

¾ cup (90 grams) confectioners' sugar

1½ teaspoons unsalted butter, melted

½ to 2 teaspoons warm water, if needed

TO MAKE THE COOKIES: Whisk the flour, espresso, cinnamon, cardamom and salt together.

Working with a stand mixer fitted with the paddle attachment, or in a large bowl with a hand mixer, beat the butter and both sugars together on medium speed until smooth, about 3 minutes. Add the egg and beat until well incorporated, about 2 minutes. Beat in the molasses and vanilla; don't be concerned if the mixture curdles. Stop the mixer, scrape down the bowl and add the flour mixture all at once. Pulse until the risk of flying flour has passed, then mix on low speed just until the dry ingredients are fully blended into the dough. You'll have a thick, very moist dough.

The rolled-out dough can be refrigerated for up to 2 days or, wrapped airtight, frozen for up to 2 months. Cut and bake directly from the freezer. Covered with a piece of plastic wrap pressed against its surface, the glaze will keep at room temperature for about 4 days. Packed in a covered container, the cookies will keep at room temperature for 5 to 7 days. They'll get drier, but they'll remain delicious. Unglazed cookies can be wrapped airtight and frozen for up to 2 months.

Turn the dough out, gather it together and shape it into a disk.

Roll the dough between pieces of parchment paper to a thickness of ¼ inch. Slide the parchment-sandwiched dough onto a baking sheet and freeze for at least 1 hour, or refrigerate for at least 2 hours.

GETTING READY TO BAKE: Center a rack in the oven and preheat it to 350 degrees F. Line two baking sheets with parchment paper or silicone baking mats. Have a 2-inch-diameter cookie cutter at hand.

Peel away both pieces of parchment paper and put the dough back on one piece of paper. Cut out as many cookies as you can and place them on the lined baking sheets. Gather the scraps together, re-roll, chill and cut.

Bake the cookies one sheet at a time for 11 to 13 minutes, rotating the sheet after 6 minutes, or until they are toasty brown on both the bottoms and tops. Poke them gently — they should be firm around the edges and softer in the center. Transfer the baking sheet to a rack and allow the cookies to cool for at least 20 minutes, or until they reach room temperature, before glazing (or serving) them. Repeat with the remaining dough, always using a cool baking sheet.

TO MAKE THE GLAZE AND FINISH THE COOKIES (OPTIONAL): Working in a medium bowl, whisk the egg white until it's foamy. Pour in the confectioners' sugar and, continuing with the whisk or switching to a flexible spatula, stir, mash and mix until the sugar is thoroughly moistened. It looks like an impossible job, but a little elbow grease will get it done. You'll have a thick mass. Push the mixture down and stir in the melted butter. If the glaze looks too thick to brush, stir in a bit of water a little at time until you get a workable consistency; you'll probably need less than 2 teaspoons of water, so go slow.

You can spread the glaze over the cookies with a small icing spatula or butter knife (to get the same look as the cookies in the photo), or you can use a brush. Dip a pastry brush into the glaze, picking up ¼ to ½ teaspoon of glaze, and brush it over one cookie, brushing in one direction. Without taking any more glaze, and working perpendicular to the original direction, brush the glaze until you have a nice crosshatch pattern. Repeat with the remaining cookies. You can serve the cookies 15 minutes after they're glazed, but if you want to save them for later, place them on a lined baking sheet and allow them to air-dry for at least 1 hour before storing.

POPCORN STREUSEL TOPS

This cookie's got corn three ways: ground, kerneled and popped. I made a slightly less corny version of it for a special Beurre & Sel event, but it never went into production. The problem was never its taste, which is fabulously good, or it's texture, which is so varied and wonderful. The issue was the extra ingredients, especially the kernel corn and the popcorn, which we would've had to store in our doll house–size kitchen. "Too much, too much," was the cry. But making them at home is not too much. Rather, it's fun and not a lot of work for a cookie that's a knockout.

The base of the cookie is a cornmeal shortbread run through with corn (fresh, frozen or canned). On top of that is popcorn. And on top of that is streusel. It's a great cookie and, although it has three parts, it never seems over the top except in its deliciousness.

A word on construction: If you'd like, you can make the cookies without the topping; dust them with sanding sugar before baking — or not. You can also skip the popcorn and just use the streusel. This is a mix, match and be happy project.

Makes about 28 cookies

Position the racks to divide the oven into thirds and preheat it to 350 degrees F. Butter or spray two regular muffin tins. Wrap the bottom of a jar or glass that will fit into the muffin cups with plastic wrap.

Whisk the flour and cornmeal together.

Working with a stand mixer fitted with the paddle attachment, or in a large bowl with a hand mixer, beat the butter, sugar and salt together on medium speed until well blended, about 2 minutes. Add the egg and beat for another 2 minutes. Beat in the vanilla and scrape down the bowl. Turn off the mixer, add the dry ingredients all at once and pulse to begin blending, Then mix on low speed until they disappear into the dough. Switch to a sturdy flexible spatula and stir in the corn.

Using a medium cookie scoop, scoop out level portions of dough, or use a tablespoon to get rounded spoonfuls, and drop them into the muffin cups.

FOR THE COOKIES

1¾ cups (238 grams) all-purpose flour

¾ cup (200 grams) yellow cornmeal

2 sticks (8 ounces; 226 grams) unsalted butter, cut into chunks, at room temperature

⅔ cup (134 grams) sugar

¾ teaspoon fine sea salt

1 large egg, at room temperature

1 teaspoon pure vanilla extract

1 cup (150 grams) corn kernels (fresh or frozen or canned, thawed or drained and patted dry)

FOR THE TOPPING

About 2 cups (1 ounce; 28 grams) plain popped popcorn, with or without salt

1 recipe Use-It-for-Everything Streusel (page 500), chilled

STORING

The dough will keep in the fridge for up to 4 days and can be frozen, well wrapped, for up to 2 months. The baked cookies can be kept covered at room temperature for a day or so, but they're really at their best the day they're made.

377

THE BEURRE & SEL COLLECTION

Ringed Cookies. If you have 2-inch baking rings (page 25), place them on lined baking sheets and scoop and press the dough into them. Build and bake the cookies in the rings, baking as you would muffin-tin cookies. Leave the rings in place for at least 20 minutes before lifting them off, rinsing and reusing.

Gently press each ball of dough down with the jar until it meets the edges of the muffin cup. Put a few kernels of popcorn on each cookie, again pressing down gently, and then top them with the streusel, squeezing the streusel a little as you drop it onto the cookies so that it clumps nicely.

Bake the cookies for 22 to 24 minutes, rotating the tins top to bottom and front to back after 12 minutes, or until the edges of the cookies and the streusel are golden brown. Transfer the tins to racks and let the cookies rest for about 3 minutes, then carefully lift them out of the cups (wedge a table knife under the cookies to raise them without losing the popcorn) and onto the racks to cool completely.

cocktail
cookies

SESAME-SEA SALT COOKIES

1 cup (136 grams) all-purpose flour

¾ cup (75 grams) almond flour

⅓ cup (67 grams) sugar

1 teaspoon fleur de sel

1 stick (8 tablespoons; 4 ounces; 113 grams) cold unsalted butter, cut into small chunks

1 large egg, lightly beaten

About ¼ cup (40 grams) mixed black and white sesame seeds

Black and white sesame seeds form a great-looking op-art mosaic on this cookie, no matter how you scatter them. But the cookie's true raison d'être is the taste, texture and cocktail compatibility. The taste is slightly sweet, definitely salty and just a touch rich because of the seeds; the texture is shortbready, with a little extra crumble because of the almond flour and a little extra crunch because of the sesame seeds. The cookies' compatibility is almost limitless: Try them with any white wine or champagne or pair them with vermouth or sherry and then bring them out again with the cheese course.

Makes about 35 cookies

Put both flours, the sugar and salt in a food processor and pulse to blend. Scatter over the pieces of cold butter and pulse until the mixture forms large, moist clumps and curds — it will look like the topping for a crumble.

Turn the dough out and knead it gently. Divide it in half and pat each half into a disk.

Working with one disk at a time, place the dough between two pieces of parchment paper and roll it to a thickness of ¼ inch. Slide the dough, still between the paper, onto a baking sheet — you can stack the slabs — and freeze for at least 1 hour.

GETTING READY TO BAKE: Center a rack in the oven and preheat it to 350 degrees F. Line a baking sheet with parchment paper or a silicone baking mat. Have a 1½-inch-diameter cookie cutter at hand.

Working with one piece of dough at a time, peel away the top and bottom papers and return the dough to one piece of paper. Cut out as many cookies as you can and put them on the lined baking sheet, leaving about an inch between them. Save the scraps, then combine them with the scraps you get from the second sheet of dough, re-roll, freeze, cut and bake.

Brush a light coating of the beaten egg over each cookie and sprinkle them with sesame seeds.

STORING

The rolled-out dough can be wrapped well and frozen for up to 2 months; cut and bake directly from the freezer. The baked cookies can be kept in a covered container for up to 1 week at room temperature.

Everything Sea Salt Cookies. Instead of covering the tops of the cookies with just sesame seeds, use the Everything Seed Mix (page 499) — it has sesame seeds, poppy seeds, onion flakes, garlic powder and pepper.

Bake the cookies for 17 to 20 minutes, rotating the baking sheet after 10 minutes, or until they're golden around the edges and the bottoms are light brown. Let the cookies rest on the baking sheet for 3 minutes, then transfer them to a rack and cool completely.

Repeat with the remaining dough, making sure the baking sheet is cool.

GOAT CHEESE AND CHIVE COOKIES

Fresh goat cheese manages to be both mild and distinctive. It's a team player. In creating these cookies, I took advantage of the cheese's affinity for herbs and spices — there's sea salt, cracked pepper and snipped chives in the dough. The dough has no leavening, yet it has the look and even the feel of biscuit dough. Once baked, the tender cookies have layers, just as there are in the best biscuits.

I leave it to you to enjoy these with cheese's other best friend: wine. The cookies are nice with champagne or white wine as an aperitif. Alternatively, they're great alongside soup.

A word on the cheese and chives: The best cheese for these cookies is a soft, mashable fresh goat cheese, often sold under its French name, *chèvre*. Chives are my first choice, but if you can't find them, you can use the pale green parts of slender scallions or even the scallions themselves. See Playing Around for other ideas.

Makes about 35 cookies

Working with a stand mixer fitted with the paddle attachment, or in a large bowl with a hand mixer, beat the butter, cheese, salt, pepper and chives together on medium-low speed until light and well blended, about 2 minutes. Add the egg and honey and beat for 2 minutes. Liquid will pool on the bottom of the bowl — it's not pretty, but it's okay. Turn off the mixer, add the flour all at once and pulse to start incorporating it. Then mix on low speed only until the flour disappears and the dough comes together. If you have some dry ingredients on the bottom of the bowl, stir them in with a flexible spatula.

Turn the dough out onto a work surface, gather it together and press it into a disk.

Place the disk between pieces of parchment paper and roll ¼ inch thick. Keeping the dough between paper, slide it onto a baking sheet and freeze for at least 1 hour.

1 stick (8 tablespoons; 4 ounces; 113 grams) unsalted butter, cut into chunks, at room temperature

3 ounces (⅓ cup packed; 85 grams) soft fresh goat cheese

½ teaspoon fine sea salt

½ teaspoon cracked or coarsely ground pepper (black or white)

2 tablespoons finely cut fresh chives or minced scallion greens or scallions (see headnote)

1 large egg, at room temperature

1 teaspoon honey

1¼ cups (170 grams) all-purpose flour

STORING

The rolled-out dough can be wrapped airtight and frozen for up to 2 months; cut and bake the cookies directly from the freezer. The baked cookies are best served within hours. If you keep them overnight, warm them in a 350-degree-F oven for a few minutes before serving.

GETTING READY TO BAKE: Center a rack in the oven and preheat it to 350 degrees F. Line a baking sheet with parchment paper or a silicone baking mat. Have a 1¼-inch-diameter cookie cutter at hand.

Peel away the parchment paper from both sides of the dough and return it to one sheet. Cut out as many cookies as you can and place them on the lined baking sheet, leaving at least an inch between them. (If the dough gets soft as you're cutting, stop and put it and the already cut cookies in the freezer to firm briefly.) Gather the scraps together, flatten them into a disk, re-roll ¼ inch thick and freeze.

Bake for 15 to 17 minutes, or until the cookies are browned on the bottom, lightly golden and firm to the touch on top. As the cookies bake, you'll see butter bubbling around the tops and edges — it will settle into the cookies as they cool. Transfer the baking sheet to a rack and allow the cookies to rest for at least 5 minutes before serving, or let them cool completely.

Cut and bake the scraps, making sure the baking sheet is cool.

PLAYING AROUND

I usually use freshly ground white Penja pepper (from Cameroon), which is fairly mild, but you might want to try Sarawak white peppercorns (from Borneo), which have more kick, piment d'Espelette (ground red pepper from the Pays Basque region in southwestern France), a sweeter red pepper like Turkish Aleppo or Urfa Biber, or chili powder. Or go for a spice like ground cumin, just go light. Instead of the chives or scallions, try minced fresh parsley or parsley and cilantro, fresh thyme leaves (rub them between your fingers to bring out their flavor) or chopped fresh lemon verbena — all so nice with goat cheese.

These cookies lend themselves to being made into baby bites. Use a ¾-inch-diameter cookie cutter and bake them for just 12 to 13 minutes. You'll get more than 100 cookies, a boon for cocktail parties.

TRISCUITY BITES

4 ounces (113 grams) cold full-fat cream
    cheese, cut into 6 pieces

1 stick (8 tablespoons; 4 ounces; 113 grams)
    cold unsalted butter, cut into 6 pieces

1 cup (136 grams) all-purpose flour

¼ teaspoon fine sea salt

20 Triscuits (I prefer Original, but you can
    use another type), coarsely broken

1 large egg white, beaten with a fork (just
    to break it up)

Fleur de sel or flake salt, such as Maldon,
    for sprinkling

These cookies began with a conversation with my friend John Bennett, who said, "I've got a thing for Triscuits." I hadn't thought about those striated wheaty crackers in years, but once John mentioned them, I couldn't get them out of my mind. Cream cheese was always my favorite Triscuit-topper, and the idea of making cream cheese dough with Triscuits mixed in came to me in a nanosecond.

Cream cheese dough, best known for its role in rugelach (page 270), is rich, flaky and faintly tangy. Since it's made without sugar, it can swing sweet or savory; add crushed Triscuits, and it becomes a full-time member of the bar-snacks brigade. Roll the dough thin, cut it in a crisscross pattern, bake it with a sprinkle of salt and start mixing the cocktails or pulling the cork on some sparkling wine.

If you fall for this dough the way I did, you'll want to make the Major Grey's Roll-Ups (page 441) too.

Makes about 55 crackers

Let the pieces of cream cheese and butter rest on the counter for 5 minutes — you want them to be slightly softened but still cool. Put the flour, salt and Triscuits in a food processor and process until the crackers are crumbed. Scatter the chunks of cream cheese and butter over the dry ingredients and pulse 6 to 10 times. Once you've got everything broken up, process in long pulses, scraping down the sides of the bowl often, until the dough forms large curds — don't work it so long that it forms a ball on the blade.

Turn the dough out and gather it together. Divide it in half and shape each half into a disk.

Work with one piece of dough at a time. Lightly flour a sheet of parchment paper, set the dough on the paper, flour the top of the dough, cover with another sheet of parchment and start rolling. You're aiming for a rough round or oval that's ⅛ inch thick — it's the thickness, not the size or shape of the dough, that matters here. Slide the dough, still sandwiched between the paper, onto a

The rolled-out dough can be wrapped airtight and frozen for up to 2 months. The bites will keep in a covered container for up to 3 days at room temperature. If they lose some of their flakiness, give them a quick warm-up in a 350-degree-F oven. You can freeze them, wrapped airtight, for up to 2 months. Rewarm if needed.

baking sheet — you can stack the slabs — and freeze the dough for at least 1 hour, or refrigerate for at least 2 hours.

GETTING READY TO BAKE: Center a rack in the oven and preheat it to 350 degrees F. Have a baking sheet and a pizza cutter or knife at hand.

Working with one sheet of dough at a time, peel away the parchment paper from both sides of the dough and return it to one piece of paper. Brush the dough lightly with the beaten egg white and sprinkle with salt. Cut the dough into strips about 1 inch wide and then cut diagonally, so you end up with diamond-shaped cookies; evenness is unattainable and even undesirable. And don't worry about separating the bites — they'll do that automatically while they bake. Slide the dough, still on its parchment, onto a baking sheet.

Bake for 18 to 20 minutes, rotating the pan after 10 minutes, or until the bites are golden brown on top and bottom. Transfer the baking sheet to a rack and let the bites cool for a few minutes, or to room temperature. They're good at just about any temperature.

Repeat with the second batch of dough, using a cool baking sheet.

GARAM GRAHAMS

No sooner had I made a batch of Graham Cracker Cookies (page 209) than I thought to make a savory version flavored with garam masala. They have all the wheaty goodness and wonderful texture of graham crackers, with the surprise of exotic spices, making them delicious with red wine and really good with beer. Because these cookies are so good with drinks, they're best made small. I like cutting them into triangles, but I leave the shape and size for you to play with.

A word on garam masala: This is an indispensable spice blend in regional Indian cuisines and one that families make themselves, customizing it to their tastes. In fact, even if you buy ready-made garam masala — as I do — you will find that brands differ; there doesn't seem to be one right mix. The blend I use has ground coriander, cumin, black pepper, cinnamon, cardamom, nutmeg, mace and cloves. What it never has is chilies, which may seem paradoxical when you know that *garam* means "warming." However, in the Ayurvedic tradition, it refers to a food's capacity to increase the body's metabolism, explaining why garam masala is so popular in the colder northern reaches of India.

Makes about 100 crackers

Stir the milk and honey together in a measuring cup with a spout.

Put both flours, the garam masala, salt, cinnamon, baking soda and pepper in a food processor and pulse a few times to mix. Add the sugar and pulse to incorporate. Scatter the cold butter cubes over the dry ingredients and pulse in long spurts just until the butter is cut in and the mixture resembles coarse meal. (If you overmix and a few clumps form, it's fine.) Pour in the liquid ingredients while pulsing in long spurts, then keep pulsing until the dough comes together and starts to pull away from the sides of the bowl — you'll have large, moist curds of dough. Remove the blade and, using a flexible spatula, stir in any ingredients that might have escaped blending.

Sprinkle some flour over a sheet of parchment paper. Turn out the dough, divide it in half and place one piece on the paper. Shape the dough into a rough

⅓ cup (80 ml) whole milk

¼ cup (60 ml) honey

1¾ cups (238 grams) all-purpose flour

¾ cup (102 grams) whole wheat flour

1 tablespoon ground garam masala

1 teaspoon fine sea salt

¾ teaspoon ground cinnamon

½ teaspoon baking soda

¼ teaspoon freshly ground black pepper

¾ cup (150 grams) packed light brown sugar

7 tablespoons (3½ ounces; 99 grams) cold unsalted butter, cut into 7 pieces

Additional salt, pepper and sugar for sprinkling (optional)

rectangle, sprinkle with flour, cover with another piece of paper and roll out into a large rectangle (roughly 12 x 8 inches) that's a scant ⅛ inch thick. (The thickness is more important than the size here.) Repeat with the second piece of dough. Stack the dough, still between the paper, on a baking sheet and freeze for at least 3 hours. (Because the dough is very sticky, it needs a good chill before you can work with it.)

GETTING READY TO BAKE: Position the racks to divide the oven into thirds and preheat it to 350 degrees F. Set out another baking sheet, as well as a ruler, a pizza cutter (or sharp knife) and a table fork.

Remove one piece of dough from the freezer, peel away the parchment paper from both sides of the dough and return it to one piece of paper. Trim the edges of the dough so that they're as straight as you can get them (or, if you don't care about symmetry, leave the ragged edges). Using the pizza cutter (or knife), cut the dough into strips that are 2 inches wide (leave them on the paper). Cut the strips into 2-inch squares, then cut the squares on the diagonal into triangles, again leaving them on the paper. (Alternatively, you can cut 1-inch-wide strips and 1-inch squares.) Prick the dough all over with the fork. If you trimmed the edges, gather the scraps of dough and reserve. Slide the dough, still on the paper, onto a baking sheet and freeze (or refrigerate) while you work on the second piece of dough. (If you have dough scraps, combine them, re-roll, chill, cut and then bake them.)

If you'd like, mix together a big pinch of sugar, a medium pinch of salt and a small pinch of pepper and lightly dust the cookies with the mixture.

Bake the cookies for 20 to 23 minutes, rotating the pans top to bottom and front to back after about 10 minutes, or until deeply golden brown, lightly puffed (the lines you cut will have baked together) and only a little springy to the touch. Transfer the baking sheets to a rack and, while the cookies are still hot, recut the lines; let cool completely.

Bake the remaining dough on a cool baking sheet.

When the cookies are cool, break them apart along the lines. They are very firm and you will have to use some pressure to break them. If you have any trouble, score the cookies again, then break apart.

STORING

The rolled-out dough can be frozen, wrapped airtight, for up to 2 months; cut and bake directly from the freezer. Kept in a covered container at room temperature, the garam grahams will be good for at least a week, but if you made them when it was humid, or if it's humid when you're going to serve them, you might find that they've lost their snap. If that's the case, give them a crisping: Bake them for 3 to 5 minutes in a 250-degree-F oven before serving. The baked cookies can be wrapped airtight and frozen for up to 2 months; give them the re-crisp treatment before serving.

FRIED POTATO CRACKERS

¾ cup (102 grams) all-purpose flour

½ cup (33 grams) potato flakes (I use Hungry Jack)

½ teaspoon baking powder

1 tablespoon (14 grams) unsalted butter, at room temperature

½ teaspoon fine sea salt or ¾ teaspoon fleur de sel

1 large egg, at room temperature

About 3 tablespoons hot water

Olive oil, for deep-frying

Fleur de sel or flake sea salt, such as Maldon, for sprinkling

When Amanda Hesser was gathering and testing thousands and thousands of recipes that had appeared in the *New York Times* in order to write *The Essential New York Times Cookbook*, she came across one for Saratoga Potatoes from 1904. Records showed that the potatoes were an instant hit, and they weren't just a fad. They came, succeeded and stayed, with a slight change of name: they became what we know and love as potato chips. A hundred and five years after they'd made their initial splash, Amanda sent me the recipe and asked if I could come up with something for the *Times* that was inspired by but different from the original.

What I came up with was a crunchy, snap-at-first-bite cracker-cookie that, like the Saratoga Potatoes, is fried in olive oil. My savory treat, rolled wafer thin and cut into slender rectangles, is more substantial than a chip, packed with more potato flavor and just might be called a kitchen hack: all that flavor, much of the texture and a lot of the surprise comes from a box of potato flakes!

The crackers were just what I wanted them to be: as snackable as potato chips, but not potato chips. I love them both munched like chips and dressed up with a little crème fraîche, some salmon roe and a squirt of lemon juice. A glass of sparkling wine is optional but highly recommended.

Makes about 60 crackers

Whisk the flour, potato flakes and baking powder together.

Whisk the butter and salt together in a large bowl until smooth. Add the egg and whisk it in (ignore the fact that the mixture will look like egg drop soup). Switch to a flexible spatula, add the dry ingredients and mix, aiming to moisten the dough but knowing that there will be lumps and dry flakes. Pour 3 tablespoons hot water over the dough and mix until it comes together. If the dough still looks a bit dry, add more water drop by drop; stop when you have a soft, moist dough.

Turn the dough out, knead it a few times and divide it in half. Shape each half into a rectangle and wrap in plastic. Refrigerate for at least 1 hour.

You can make the dough up to
1 day ahead and keep it well
wrapped in the refrigerator.
Packed airtight, it can be frozen
for up to 2 months, but the
most convenient way to keep
the dough is to roll it, cut it and
freeze the cutouts; they can be
fried straight from the freezer.
The crackers are best eaten soon
after they come out of the pot.

Line a baking sheet with parchment. Flour both sides of one piece of dough and sandwich it between pieces of parchment. Start rolling, turning the dough over to roll on both sides and dusting it with more flour as needed, until it is paper-thin. I aim for a rectangle that's about 8 x 12 inches, but it's the thinness, not the perfect shape or size, that counts. Peel off the parchment from both sides of the dough and return the dough to one piece of parchment.

Using a ruler and a pizza cutter or a sharp knife, cut the dough into long strips 1 to 1½ inches wide, then cut across the strips at 2-inch intervals. (If you'd prefer, you can make long strips, triangles or squares; the yield will vary.) Cut a lengthwise slit about ¾ inch long in the center of each piece. Transfer the pieces to the baking sheet, making layers as necessary and covering each layer with a piece of paper. Roll and cut the other piece of dough and layer the pieces. Refrigerate for at least 1 hour.

When you're ready to fry the crackers, line a baking sheet with a double layer of paper towels. Pour 1 to 1½ inches of olive oil into a Dutch oven or deep skillet and heat over medium-high heat.

When the oil is hot (it should measure 300 degrees F on a deep-fat or candy thermometer), drop a few pieces of dough into the pot. You want the oil to bubble around each piece, so don't crowd the pot. When the crackers are lightly browned around the edges and golden in the center, about 2 minutes, turn and brown the other side, about 1 minute more. (It's hard to give exact times for frying, so stay close.) With a slotted spoon, lift them out of the oil, letting the excess oil drip back into the pot, and onto the lined baking sheet. Pat off the excess oil with paper towels, sprinkle the crackers with salt and keep frying.

Serve the crackers as soon as they're not burn-your-fingers hot, or wait until they reach room temperature.

CRANBERRY FIVE-SPICE COOKIES

I am obsessed with Chinese five-spice powder, a blend that includes star anise, tongue-numbing Sichuan peppercorns, cinnamon, cloves and fennel. It's the star anise that pulls me in, but the mixture is remarkable for its balance and adaptability — it's great in both savories and sweets. It's got a holiday aroma and a lovely way of adding interest to apples, pears and almost anything made with brown sugar. But I think the quintet does its best work when paired with something sharp and tangy, as it is here with fresh cranberries. The cookies bounce between warm and edgy, tender and crunchy and unexpected and familiar. And while I made these at Beurre & Sel for Thanksgiving and Christmas, their appeal continued through winter and the cool days of early spring, so stock up on cranberries in the fall and keep them in your freezer; they'll be good for at least 6 months.

Makes about 50 cookies

Mix 1 tablespoon of the sugar and the cranberries together in a bowl. Set aside, stirring occasionally.

Whisk the flour and five-spice powder together.

Working with a stand mixer fitted with the paddle attachment, or in a large bowl with a hand mixer, beat the butter, the remaining 4 tablespoons sugar and the salt together on low speed until smooth and creamy, about 3 minutes. Add the egg and mix for 1 minute. The mixture will look curdled, but it will even out when the dry ingredients are added. Turn the mixer off, add the flour mixture all at once and pulse to begin blending. When the risk of flying flour has passed, mix on low speed only until the flour disappears into the dough. Give the cranberries a last stir and spoon them into the bowl (if there's any liquid in the bowl, discard it), along with the chopped peanuts, and mix just to incorporate; or do this by hand with a sturdy flexible spatula. Either way, try to mix as little as possible so that the cranberries don't turn the dough pink.

Turn the dough out onto a counter, knead it gently and divide it in half; pat each half into a disk.

5 tablespoons (60 grams) sugar

½ cup (50 grams) fresh or frozen (not thawed) cranberries, coarsely chopped

1¾ cups (238 grams) all-purpose flour

1 teaspoon Chinese five-spice powder

1½ sticks (12 tablespoons; 6 ounces; 170 grams) unsalted butter, cut into chunks, at room temperature

½ teaspoon fine sea salt

1 large egg

½ cup (73 grams) salted peanuts, coarsely chopped

FOR THE OPTIONAL TOPPING

Finely chopped salted peanuts

Chinese five-spice powder

Sea salt

Working with one disk at a time, place the dough between two pieces of parchment paper and roll it to a thickness of ¼ inch. Slide the dough, still between the paper, onto a baking sheet — you can stack the slabs — and freeze for at least 1 hour.

GETTING READY TO BAKE: Center a rack in the oven and preheat it to 350 degrees F. Line a baking sheet with parchment paper or a silicone baking mat. Have a 1½-inch-diameter cookie cutter at hand.

Working with one sheet of dough at a time, peel away both pieces of paper and put the dough back on one piece. Cut out as many cookies as you can and put them on the baking sheet, leaving about an inch between them. Sprinkle the cookies with any or all of the optional toppings. Save the scraps, then combine them with the scraps you get from the second disk, re-roll, freeze, cut and bake.

Bake for 12 to 14 minutes, rotating the baking sheet after 7 minutes, or until the cookies are lightly golden around the edges and feel just firm to the touch. Let the cookies rest on the sheet for a minute or two, then transfer to a rack to cool completely.

Repeat with the remaining dough, using a cool baking sheet.

STORING

The rolled-out dough can be refrigerated overnight or, wrapped airtight, frozen for up to 2 months. Or, if you'd like, you can cut out the cookies and freeze the rounds. Bake them straight from the freezer; you might have to add another minute or two to the baking time. The baked cookies will keep in a container at room temperature for up to 4 days.

HOT-AND-SPICY TOGARASHI MERINGUES

2 tablespoons plus 1 teaspoon sugar

1 teaspoon cornstarch

2 large egg whites, at room temperature

¼ teaspoon cream of tartar

¼ teaspoon fine sea salt

1 teaspoon shichimi togarashi (or more to taste; see headnote)

Shichimi togarashi, also called seven-spice blend, is a culinary gift from Japan, a remarkable blend of chili pepper and spices that manages to be hot, sweet, salty, bitter, nutty and packed with umami. While the blend — and the level of heat — varies from maker to maker, the brand that I often use (S&B) includes chili pepper, dried orange peel, black and white sesame seeds, Japanese pepper, ginger and dried seaweed. Because I don't know your blend and because, as is true of just about every spice, togarashi is most potent when it's fresh, I'd suggest you make your first batch of meringues with just 1 teaspoon and then see where you want to go after that.

Whether you make them super-hot or mild, you'll want to chase the meringues with beer.

Makes about 30 cookies

Center a rack in the oven and preheat it to 250 degrees F. Line a baking sheet with a silicone baking mat or parchment paper (I prefer silicone for these). If you'd like to pipe out the meringues (I think piping works best), have a pastry bag fitted with a plain ¼-inch tip or a plastic zipper-lock bag at hand; if not, use a teaspoon.

Push 1 teaspoon of the sugar and the cornstarch through a strainer into a small bowl and stir to blend.

Put the egg whites in a stand mixer fitted with the whisk attachment or in a bowl in which you can use a hand mixer. Add the cream of tartar — if it's lumpy, push it through the strainer into the bowl — and the salt and beat on high speed until the whites turn opaque and just start to hold their shape. Add the remaining 2 tablespoons sugar, just a little at a time, whipping until you have firm, glossy whites that hold peaks. Beat in the togarashi. If using a stand mixer, remove the bowl. Sprinkle the sugar-cornstarch mixture over the whites and, working with a flexible spatula, fold it in gently, quickly and thoroughly. If you're using a pastry or plastic bag, fill it with the meringue; snip off a corner of the plastic bag.

Kept in a tin or other container — don't store these in plastic bags or wrap — away from humidity, the meringues will keep for up to 3 days. (They may keep for longer, but they're so susceptible to moisture that it's hard to say how long.)

Pipe or spoon quarter-size dabs of meringue onto the baking sheet, leaving an inch or so of space between them.

Bake for 45 minutes without opening the oven. Turn off the oven and prop the door open with the handle of a wooden spoon. Leave the meringues in the oven to dry for about 1½ hours, until (this is the important test) you can peel them off the silicone or paper; they should not be sticky. Let the meringues cool.

OLD BAY PRETZEL-AND-CHEESE COOKIES

For years, I wanted to make a cookie that would go with beer. From the start, I knew I wanted it to have pretzels and some cheese. I worked on the cookie on and off and never really got what I wanted. Then one day, when I was making a shellfish recipe that called for Old Bay Seasoning, I had that eureka moment: Old Bay was what was missing. A couple of spoonfuls of that blend, which relies heavily on celery salt, and the cookie came together. Is it good with beer? Yes. But here's the bonus: The Old Bay makes the cookies a winner with Bloody Marys too.

I've made these with many kinds of cheese (including Gouda and Emmentaler), but I keep coming back to sharp cheddar. Play around, but stick with a cheese that melts easily. As for the pretzels, choose whatever you like to snack on and either chop them with a knife or crush them with a mortar and pestle. Since I'm crazy about pretzel sticks, that's what I use. No matter what you choose, my bet is that no one will know what gives these their crunch and that hard-to-pin-down flavor.

1¼ cups (170 grams) all-purpose flour

2 teaspoons Old Bay Seasoning

½ teaspoon fine sea salt

1½ sticks (12 tablespoons; 6 ounces; 170 grams) cold unsalted butter, cut into 24 pieces

4 ounces (113 grams) cheese, such as sharp cheddar, shredded (1 cup)

2 ounces (57 grams) salted pretzels, coarsely chopped or crushed

Makes about 50 cookies

Put the flour, Old Bay and salt in a food processor and whir to blend. Scatter the cold butter over the dry ingredients and pulse in long spurts, scraping the bowl as needed, until the dough forms curds and clumps. Add the cheese and pretzels and use quick pulses to blend them in.

Turn the dough out onto a work surface and knead it briefly to bring it together. Divide it in half and shape each half into a log about 9 inches long. Don't be concerned about being too precise, but do make certain that the log is solid (see page 12 for some tips). Wrap each log well and freeze for at least 1 hour.

GETTING READY TO BAKE: Position the racks to divide the oven into thirds and preheat it to 350 degrees F. Line two baking sheets with parchment paper or silicone baking mats.

Slice the logs ⅓ inch thick. The pretzels are pesky — they're roadblocks to

precision — so if any of the slices break, just press them back together. Place the slices on the sheet, leaving an inch of space between them.

Bake the cookies for 19 to 21 minutes, rotating the sheets front to back and top to bottom after 10 minutes, or until they are firm and golden across the entire top. Transfer the baking sheets to racks and allow the cookies to rest for 5 minutes, then lift them onto the racks to cool completely. These are not meant to be eaten warm; you need to wait until they cool so that the pretzels regain their crunch and the Old Bay has time to mellow.

CHEDDAR-SEED WAFERS

½ stick (4 tablespoons; 2 ounces;
    56 grams) unsalted butter, cut into
    chunks, at room temperature

½ teaspoon fine sea salt

½ teaspoon freshly ground black pepper

4 ounces (113 grams) sharp cheddar,
    shredded (1 cup)

2 tablespoons white wine or water

¾ cup (102 grams) all-purpose flour

1½ tablespoons poppy or other seeds

I started making these in Paris with bits of leftover shredded cheese from my favorite *fromagerie* and finished by making them in Connecticut with Cabot's Seriously Sharp Cheddar from my local supermarket. Whether I serve them with French champagne or American chardonnay, they are great. They are also great alongside soup, leafy salads and starters like roasted beets in vinaigrette.

They have a break-with-a-crack crispness, the aroma of grilled cheese, the smack of freshly ground black pepper (don't skimp!) and the raggedy, each-one's-different look of something that is proudly made by hand. I shape the wafers by rolling each little piece of dough between small pieces of parchment paper until it's as thin as it can possibly be — so thin that I bake it on the sheet of parchment it was rolled on, because peeling it off borders on the impossible. You can make these aperitif size — about 4 inches long — and get about 14 of them, or you can go larger, making about 5 wafers, each big enough to stand in for the bread you might serve with a salad.

A word on the seeds: I'm partial to poppy seeds with the cheddar, but sesame seeds are nice, as are flax and chia.

Makes 5 large wafers or 14 small wafers

Position the racks to divide the oven into thirds and preheat it to 350 degrees F. If you want to make smaller wafers, cut 15 pieces of parchment paper, each about 5 x 3 inches. For larger wafers, cut 6 pieces of parchment, each about 6 x 3 inches. Have two baking sheets at hand.

You can make these in a stand mixer fitted with the paddle attachment, with a hand mixer or with a sturdy flexible spatula; if you're using a mixer, stick to low speed. Beat the butter, salt and pepper together until smooth. Add the cheese and mix to incorporate it. Pour in the wine or water and stir to blend. Add the flour all at once and work it in until almost incorporated. Add the seeds and mix until you have a smooth dough. (If you're working with a mixer, give the dough a

few last turns with a flexible spatula so you can pick up any dry ingredients lurking in the bottom of the bowl.)

Turn the dough out onto a work surface and shape it into a log about 7 inches long — a little longer is fine, but try not to go much shorter (for tips on shaping, see page 12). For small wafers, cut the log into ½-inch slices; for larger wafers, cut the log into 5 pieces. Shape each piece into a ball, then flatten it into a disk.

Lightly flour a piece of parchment, place one disk on it, lightly flour the disk, cover it with another piece of paper and roll it as thin as you can. Peel away the top piece of parchment (you'll use it to roll all of the disks) and place the wafer, still on the bottom piece of paper, on a baking sheet. Repeat with the remaining dough.

Bake the wafers for 15 to 20 minutes, rotating the sheets top to bottom and front to back after 10 minutes. The wafers will seethe and heave in the oven. When done, they'll be golden brown (a little more golden at the edges) and firm to the touch. Remove the baking sheets from the oven, lift the wafers off the paper onto racks and allow them to dry, crisp and cool before serving.

The rolled-out dough can be wrapped airtight and frozen for up to 2 months; cut and bake directly from the freezer. The baked cookies can be kept in a covered container for about 4 days at room temperature or, wrapped airtight, for up to 2 months in the freezer.

scraps, then combine them with the scraps you get from the second disk, re-roll, freeze, cut and bake.

Bake the cookies for 16 to 18 minutes, rotating the baking sheet after 9 minutes, or until they're lightly golden on top and more golden on bottom. Let the cookies rest on the baking sheet for a couple of minutes, then transfer them to a rack and cool completely.

Repeat with the remaining dough, using a cool baking sheet.

FENNEL-ORANGE SHORTBREAD WEDGES

When I first had the idea for these cookies, I was thinking something that could be nibbled daintily with a glass of wine. Whether it's afternoon or after five, it's the texture that you notice first: The cookies are flaky (the inner crumb is layered). They've got a slight crunch followed by that melt-in-your-mouth quality that you can only get with butter (a fair amount of it). And the flavors are a surprise. Orange is instantly recognizable, but there is a welcome stranger — fennel. You might not place it immediately, but you'll know there's something different about the cookie, and you'll go back for another one or two to discover what it is.

The cookies are fragile, particularly when they come out of the oven, so baby them a bit. Let them sit on the baking sheet, and when you cut them, go slow. I use a pizza wheel (should a tip or edge break, I clear away the crumbs quickly by eating them). If you'd like, you can bake these in a cake pan; see Every-Way Shortbread Fans (page 189), for directions.

Makes 12 cookies

Center a rack in the oven and preheat it to 350 degrees F. Have a baking sheet at hand.

Whisk the flour and cornstarch together.

Put the sugar and orange zest in the bowl of a stand mixer, or in a large bowl in which you can use a hand mixer, and rub them together with your fingertips until the sugar is moist and fragrant. Toss in the chopped fennel seeds and rub them into the sugar. If using a stand mixer, fit it with the paddle attachment. Add the butter, confectioners' sugar and salt to the bowl and beat on medium speed for about 3 minutes, scraping down the bowl as needed, until the mixture is smooth. Turn the mixer off, add the dry ingredients all at once, pulse a few times, then beat on low speed until you have a mixture that resembles a crumble topping. This will take longer than you think: For the first 3 minutes or so, the dough will look hopeless — more like oatmeal than anything bakeable. But keep going (scraping the bottom of the bowl a few times), and the dough will resemble curds and clumps and will hold together when pinched.

1 cup (136 grams) all-purpose flour

2 tablespoons cornstarch

2 tablespoons sugar

Finely grated zest of 1 orange or 1 tangerine

1¾ teaspoons fennel seeds, finely chopped

1 stick (8 tablespoons; 4 ounces; 113 grams) unsalted butter, cut into chunks, at room temperature

1 tablespoon confectioners' sugar

½ teaspoon fleur de sel or ¼ teaspoon fine sea salt

Fleur de sel (or kosher salt, in a pinch), for sprinkling

415

Turn the dough out and knead it gently to bring it together. Form it into a disk and sandwich the disk between pieces of parchment paper. Roll the dough into an 8-inch circle. With these cookies, ragged edges are fine. (If you're neater than I am, you can even the edges by using a baking pan as a guide to cut a clean circle.) Lift off the top piece of parchment and slide the dough, still on the bottom piece of paper, onto the baking sheet. Use the tines of a table fork to prick the dough in a spoke pattern, outlining 12 wedges. As you prick, make sure to go all the way through the dough — you should hear the tines tapping against the baking sheet. Sprinkle the dough with fleur de sel (or kosher salt).

Bake the shortbread for about 20 minutes, rotating the baking sheet after 10 minutes, just until the edges are lightly browned. Transfer the baking sheet to a rack and let the cookie rest for about 5 minutes, then very carefully use a knife or a pizza wheel to cut along the marks you made to form a dozen shortbread fans. The cookie is very tender and flaky, so work gingerly. Allow the fans to cool completely on the baking sheet.

STORING

Packed (carefully) in a container, these will keep at room temperature for 3 to 4 days. Packed airtight, they can be frozen for up to 2 months, although the salt has a way of melting into the cookies when they defrost.

COCKTAIL PUFFS

FOR THE DOUGH

1 cup (136 grams) all-purpose flour

¼ teaspoon fine sea salt

1 stick (8 tablespoons; 4 ounces; 113 grams) cold unsalted butter, cut into small pieces

½ cup (113 grams) cold plain Greek yogurt (can be low fat)

FOR THE FILLINGS (CHOOSE ONE OR SEVERAL)

Dijon mustard (about 1 tablespoon per strip)

Pesto (about 1 tablespoon per strip)

Tapenade (about 1 tablespoon per strip)

Shredded cheddar (about 2 tablespoons per strip)

Assorted seeds or finely chopped nuts

STORING

You can freeze the rolled-out dough, well wrapped, for up to 2 months; cut and bake directly from the freezer. You can also fill the puffs and freeze them; add a minute or two to the baking time. The puffs are really best eaten within minutes of being pulled from the oven. They're good at room temperature, but they're really so much better hot and fresh.

Having made doughs with cream cheese and with sour cream, I knew a dough made with yogurt would work, but I had no idea it would work so well, puff so dramatically and taste so delicious. It's wonderful! It's lighter than puff pastry and easier to make (it's rolled out, folded in half and rolled again, frozen for two hours and then it's ready — much, much faster than classic puff). And, like puff pastry, it can be used for things sweet (see Playing Around) or savory.

Here I cut the dough into strips, spreading them with pesto or tapenade or mustard or cheese, or a combination (mustard and cheese is a favorite), fold them over, cut them into puffs and let the puffs do whatever they want in the oven: Some stay sealed, some fly open and all of them are great.

Makes about 50 puffs

TO MAKE THE DOUGH: Put the flour and salt in a food processor and pulse just to blend. Scatter over the pieces of cold butter and pulse in long spurts until the butter is broken up and you have a bowlful of small clumps — the mixture will look like streusel. Add the yogurt about one third at a time, pulsing after each addition, then pulse and process until most of the dough leaves the sides of the bowl. (Actually, the mixture will look more like frosting than dough at this point.) Scrape the dough out onto a piece of plastic wrap, flatten into a disk and freeze for about 30 minutes, or refrigerate for about 1 hour.

Generously flour a piece of parchment paper. Place the dough on the paper, flour it, cover with another piece of parchment and roll, peeling the paper away from the dough frequently to prevent creases and flouring as needed, until you have a rectangle that's about ⅛ inch thick and about 10 x 12 inches. The thickness is more important than the size or shape. Fold the dough in half (in either direction) and roll it out (don't forget to peel the paper away and flour the dough as you roll) until it is once again ⅛ inch thick and a rectangle that's about 10 x 12 inches. Slide the dough, still between the paper, onto a baking sheet and freeze for at least 2 hours.

Butter-and-Sugar Puffs. Brush the strips generously with softened butter, sprinkle with the tiniest bit of fleur de sel or Maldon or other flake sea salt and sprinkle generously with cinnamon-sugar or vanilla-sugar and/or very finely chopped nuts. Fold over or don't — these are nice cut into small pieces and baked open-faced.

GETTING READY TO BAKE: Center a rack in the oven and preheat it to 400 degrees F. Line a baking sheet with parchment paper or a silicone baking mat. Have a ruler, a pizza wheel (or a sharp knife) and a pastry brush at hand.

Remove the dough from the freezer, peel away both pieces of paper and return the rectangle to one piece. Using the ruler and the pizza wheel (or knife), cut away the ragged edges of dough. In trimming, you'll discover if the dough is too cold to cut without cracking; if it is, let it sit for a few minutes. With a short end of the dough closest to you, cut it into long strips that are 2 inches wide. Spoon and brush whatever filling you've chosen over the strips. Don't go wild — you want to have a thin layer if you're using pesto, tapenade or mustard (a scant tablespoon is about right) and you don't really want too much cheese either. Lift up the long sides of one strip so that they meet in the center and pinch them closed. Lay the strip on its side and cut into 1-inch puffs. Place them on the lined baking sheet, leaving a little room between them. Repeat with the remaining strips.

Bake the puffs for 18 to 20 minutes, rotating the sheet after about 10 minutes, or until golden brown. Color is important here, because if the puffs are too pale, the insides won't be baked through. Transfer the baking sheet to a rack and let the puffs cool for 5 minutes before serving.

CHOCOLATE-OLIVE COOKIES

I can't explain why the intense flavor of cocoa powder goes so well with oil-cured black olives, but it's nice to know that life can still be mysterious. This is a cookie made for red wine and good times. It's a surprisingly delicate shortbread, hailing from the melt-in-your-mouth family, with butter and a little olive oil, seasoned with salt and pepper and studded with olives. It's a grown-up cookie — exactly what a cocktail cookie should be.

I like it plain and simple, but after you've baked it once, you might find yourself itching to add a little something more. Try a pinch or two of herbes de Provence, a dried spice mix, some fresh chopped rosemary and/or thyme or maybe some fennel seeds.

The perfect sip-along is red wine, ruby port or, if you're lucky enough to have it, Banyuls, the slightly sweet red wine from the Languedoc-Roussillon region of France.

Makes about 60 cookies

1¼ cups (170 grams) all-purpose flour

¼ cup (32 grams) cornstarch

¼ cup (21 grams) unsweetened cocoa powder

1 stick (8 tablespoons; 4 ounces; 113 grams) unsalted butter, cut into chunks, at room temperature

2 tablespoons extra-virgin olive oil, preferably a fruity one

⅓ cup (67 grams) sugar

½ teaspoon fine sea salt

¼ teaspoon freshly ground black pepper

1 large egg yolk

⅓ cup (50 grams) chopped pitted oil-cured black olives

Sift the flour, cornstarch and cocoa powder together.

Working with a stand mixer fitted with the paddle attachment, or in a large bowl with a hand mixer, beat the butter, olive oil, sugar, salt and pepper together on medium speed until smooth, about 2 minutes. Add the yolk and beat for another minute or two, scraping down the bowl as needed. Turn off the mixer, add the dry ingredients all at once and pulse to start blending, then mix on low speed until you have moist curds. After a minute or two of mixing, you might get discouraged — the dough will look dry and shaggy — but keep mixing, and it will moisten. If you reach into the bowl, squeeze some of the curds and they hold together easily, you're done. Using a flexible spatula, stir in the olives.

Turn the dough out, knead briefly to bring it together and divide it in half.

Working with one half at a time, roll the dough into a slender log that's 8 to 8½ inches long (see page 12 for log-rolling tips). Wrap the logs well and refrigerate them overnight or, if you're in a hurry, freeze for at least 1 hour.

GETTING READY TO BAKE: Position the racks to divide the oven into thirds and preheat it to 325 degrees F. Line two baking sheets with parchment paper or silicone baking mats.

Working with one log at a time, using a thin sharp knife, slice the dough into ¼-inch-thick rounds and place them on the lined baking sheets, leaving an inch (or even less) between them.

Bake the cookies for 15 to 17 minutes, rotating the sheets top to bottom and front to back after 8 minutes, or until they are just firm to the touch (don't try to lift them from the baking sheet — they're still too fragile for that) and you catch the fragrance of the olives. Leave the cookies on the baking sheets for 3 minutes, then carefully transfer them to racks to cool completely.

STORING

The dough can be shaped into logs and refrigerated for up to 2 days or frozen, well wrapped, for up to 2 months; cut the dough and bake straight from the freezer (you might have to add a minute to the baking time). The baked cookies will keep in a covered container for about 4 days at room temperature.

PARMESAN GALETTES

¾ cup (102 grams) all-purpose flour

7 tablespoons (3½ ounces; 99 grams) cold unsalted butter, cut into 14 pieces

1 cup (not packed; 85 grams) finely grated Parmesan

Fine sea salt, if needed (it depends on the saltiness of the cheese and your taste)

STORING

The log will keep in the refrigerator for up to 3 days or, wrapped airtight, in the freezer for up to 2 months. Slice and bake directly from the freezer; add a minute to the baking time. The galettes are best eaten the day they are made, and preferably soon after they are made. If you must keep them overnight, pack them in a covered container and store them at room temperature; if you'd like, warm them in a 350-degree-F oven for a few minutes before serving.

The first time I tasted these cookies was at the Manoir de Lan Kerellec, a hotel on the coast of northern Brittany; the next was when I made them myself in my Paris kitchen; and the third was a week later when I made them in the United States.

At Lan Kerellec, aperitifs are served on a terraced slope with a view of the pink granite coast and the sea. In a setting like that, anything might taste good, but these Parmesan galettes were scene-stealers. They were sharp at first, and mellow after. They were firm on the edges and softer at the center. They were remarkable.

And they seemed even more remarkable to me when the chef gave me the recipe: just Parmesan, flour and butter, with a little salt, if you'd like. The dough is rolled into a log, chilled and sliced and baked. He baked his galettes in rings, as I often do, but they're beautiful made in muffin tins and no less wonderful baked freestanding.

A word on the cheese: The volume measurement for the Parmesan is based on fine, powdery Parmesan, the texture you get when you buy it ready-grated. If you want to grate your own cheese, do, but please weigh it: You should have 3 ounces (85 grams). Also, stick to Parmesan or Grana Padano. I've made these with moister, chewier, stretchier cheeses and been disappointed. The galette was created for the dry texture (as well as the pleasant bite) of Parmesan.

Makes about 15 galettes

Put the flour and cold butter in a food processor and pulse about 5 times, just to coat the butter pieces with flour. Pour in the Parmesan and salt and process in long bursts until you have a moist curds-and-clumps dough.

Turn the dough out onto a work surface and press and gather it together. Shape it into a log about 5 inches long and a scant 2 inches in diameter (see page 12 for tips on log-rolling). Wrap the dough and freeze for at least 1 hour, or refrigerate for at least 2 hours.

PLAYING AROUND

Parmesan is an herb-friendly cheese, so think about adding minced fresh rosemary, oregano, sage or thyme. On the spice side, think about a pinch of freshly ground pepper — black, white, pink or cayenne. Or give the galettes a touch of crunch by adding chopped toasted nuts (almonds or walnuts would be good). You could even sprinkle a (very little) bit of the Everything Seed Mix (page 499) over the cookies before sliding them into the oven.

Ringed Parmesan Galettes. You can bake these in buttered or sprayed 2-inch baking rings (see page 25) on baking sheets lined with parchment or silicone baking mats. Cut the log into ⅓-inch-thick rounds and, if the cookies are bigger than the rings, use the rings to cut them to size; if they're a little smaller, don't worry, they'll grow to meet the edges of the rings. Bake the galettes for 15 to 17minutes. Leave the rings in place for 5 minutes before lifting them off, rinsing and reusing.

GETTING READY TO BAKE: Center a rack in the oven and preheat it to 350 degrees F. If you're using a muffin tin, lightly spray it (even if it's nonstick), or use two tins, if you've got them. If you're making freestanding cookies, line a baking sheet with parchment paper or a silicone baking mat.

Working with a sturdy knife, cut the log into slices about ⅓ inch thick. Place in the tin(s) or lay them out on the baking sheet, leaving at least 2 inches of spread space between them.

Bake the tinned galettes for 18 to 20 minutes or the freestanding cookies for 15 to 17 minutes, or until golden brown on top and bottom. They may seem slightly underdone in the center, but they will firm as they cool. Cool the cookies in the tin(s) or on the baking sheet until they are only just warm or until they reach room temperature before serving. Continue baking with the remaining dough, using a cool tin.

HONEY-BLUE CHEESE MADELEINES

I've always liked the combination of honey with salty, sometimes sharp blue cheeses like Roquefort and Gorgonzola. But I didn't have the idea to put these two ingredients into a cookie until I came home after having a cheese platter at a wine bar and told Michael, my husband, how nice the honey was with the Connecticut blue. That was the "bingo" moment: butter, blue cheese and honey . . . it wouldn't take much to transform the gist of that trio into a cookie, especially if I chose to build it into a buttery madeleine.

The cookie, as you'd expect, is perfect with wine, white or red, or prosecco or another sparkling wine. And, just as blue cheese is good with port, so are these.

Makes 12 madeleines

Coat the madeleine molds with softened butter (a pastry brush makes easy work of this job), dust with flour and tap out the excess (or use baker's spray). Butter and flour (or spray) the molds even if they're nonstick or silicone, and if you're using silicone, put the mold on a baking sheet.

Whisk the flour, baking powder, salt and pepper together.

Put the eggs in a medium bowl and whisk them energetically with the sugar and honey for a minute or two to be certain that the ingredients are well blended. Add the flour all at once and, working with the whisk, or with a flexible spatula, if you prefer, gently stir and fold in the dry ingredients. Add the melted butter in 3 or 4 additions and, still using a light touch, fold it in. You'll have a beautiful thick batter with a sheen. Fold in the blue cheese.

Divide the batter evenly among the molds, ignoring the fact that the batter won't be smooth and might not fill them; the oven's heat will fix everything. Refrigerate for at least 1 hour.

GETTING READY TO BAKE: Center a rack in the oven, place a baking sheet on the rack and preheat the oven to 400 degrees F.

Place the cold madeleine tin (or the silicone molds on the cold baking sheet) on the preheated baking sheet and bake for 11 to 13 minutes, or until the

¾ cup (102 grams) all-purpose flour

¾ teaspoon baking powder

¼ teaspoon fine sea salt

½ teaspoon freshly ground black pepper

2 large eggs, at room temperature

2 tablespoons sugar

2 tablespoons honey

¾ stick (6 tablespoons; 3 ounces; 85 grams) unsalted butter, melted and cooled

2 ounces (57 grams) blue cheese, such as Roquefort or Gorgonzola, crumbled or cut into bits (about ½ cup)

madeleines are puffed and golden around the edges. Remove the pan from the oven and, if it's metal, grab an end and tap it on the counter — the madeleines should come tumbling out. If you're using a silicone mold, turn it upside down over the counter and pull at two opposite ends until the little cookies fall out. Pry any reluctant mads out of the mold with a table knife.

The madeleines can be served as soon as they're cool enough to eat — a matter of minutes — or once they reach room temperature.

STORING

The filled madeleine mold can be refrigerated, covered with a piece of buttered plastic wrap or parchment, for up to 2 days. The baked cookies can be kept covered at room temperature for up to 1 day, but they're really at their peak shortly after being baked. If you'd like, they can be wrapped airtight and frozen for up to 2 months. Once they've thawed, you can warm them briefly in a 350-degree-F oven before serving.

PUFFED GRAIN AND MISO COOKIES

3¼ cups (62 grams) puffed rice

1 cup (146 grams) salted peanuts, coarsely chopped

¾ cup (18 grams) puffed barley

⅓ cup (40 grams) plump, moist dried cranberries, goji berries or raisins, coarsely chopped (optional)

¼ cup (40 grams) white sesame seeds

1 teaspoon fleur de sel or ½ teaspoon fine sea salt

⅓ cup plus 2 tablespoons (100 ml) brown rice syrup

2 tablespoons light miso paste

2 teaspoons olive oil

1 teaspoon toasted sesame oil

I guess you could call these rice cakes, but you'd be shortchanging them — no rice cake I've ever bought has delivered this much flavor. These cookies have a puffed rice base but go their own way with the addition of puffed barley (or puffed quinoa, a somewhat elusive ingredient that's worth grabbing when you see it), light (sometimes called white or yellow) miso paste, toasted sesame oil, sesame seeds and chopped salted peanuts. They're all held together with brown rice syrup, which sweetens the mix a little and plays off the miso a lot. Head to a natural foods market, and you'll be able to one-stop shop for the ingredients. Just make sure the sesame oil is toasted.

Makes about 48 cookies

Position the racks to divide the oven into thirds and preheat it to 325 degrees F. Lightly spray a regular muffin tin, or two, if you've got them. Find a jar that fits inside the molds and wrap the bottom in plastic.

Put the puffed rice, peanuts, barley, dried fruit (if you're using it), sesame seeds and salt in a very large bowl and stir to combine.

Pour the rice syrup into a small saucepan and bring just to a boil over low heat, or do this in a microwave oven. Remove the syrup from the heat and let stand for 2 minutes, then add the miso (it's best not to boil miso — heat destroys the paste's aroma), and both oils and whisk to blend. The miso may not dissolve completely and there may be little strands of it, but that's okay.

Pour the warm liquid over the dry ingredients and, using a silicone spatula, stir until every kernel of cereal, every peanut and every berry is moistened; this will take a few minutes.

Fill each mold with 2 tablespoons dough and press the mounds flat with the bottom of the jar.

Bake for 18 to 20 minutes, rotating the tin(s) after 10 minutes, or until the cookies are golden brown. Transfer to racks and cool the cookies completely before unmolding.

STORING

You can refrigerate the dough in a storage container for up to 5 days. The cookies are good keepers, as long as there's no humidity. Loosely packed in a covered container, they'll be fine for up to 3 days.

ANYTIME TARRAGON-APRICOT COOKIES

½ cup (80 grams) finely diced plump, moist dried apricots (about 12), preferably Turkish

⅓ cup (67 grams) sugar

2 tablespoons finely chopped fresh tarragon

1 stick (8 tablespoons; 4 ounces; 113 grams) unsalted butter, cut into chunks, at room temperature

1 teaspoon fine sea salt

1 large egg yolk, at room temperature

⅓ cup (80 ml) extra-virgin olive oil

2 cups (272 grams) all-purpose flour

When I first made these tender cookies, it was with the idea that they'd be cocktail cookies. And they are. They're wonderful with white wine or rosé and even better when you're sipping and savoring outdoors. But gradually the cookies insinuated themselves into afternoon teas and pick-me-ups, and soon I was serving them alongside fruit desserts, ice creams and custards. They are nothing if not delightfully adaptable.

The backbone of the cookie is a shortbread made with both butter and olive oil. It has sugar, but less than usual, and salt, a little more than usual. It's these ingredients and their off-kilter proportions that make the shortbread a sweet-savory straddler. Oh, and the tarragon, an herb that leans toward licorice; and the apricots, abundantly sweet, but with a tart flip side. It's an interesting bundle, and more important, it makes great cookies.

A word on Turkish apricots: For these cookies, I suggest you use Turkish apricots because they are softer, moister, plumper and sweeter than the California fruit: Our domestic apricot is drier and more acidic than the Turkish variety. I prefer chewy California apricots for snacking and tender Turkish apricots for baking, but you can use whichever you like most.

Makes about 60 cookies

Put the apricots in a small bowl and cover them with very hot tap water. Soak until you're ready for them, then drain and pat them dry.

Put the sugar and tarragon in the bowl of a stand mixer or in a large bowl in which you can work with a hand mixer. Using your fingers, rub the ingredients together until the sugar is moist and aromatic. If using a stand mixer, fit it with the paddle attachment.

Toss the butter and salt into the bowl and beat on medium speed for about 3 minutes, until blended. Add the egg yolk and beat for 2 minutes more. Reduce the speed to low, gradually pour in the olive oil and continue to beat until the mixture is smooth—it will look like mayonnaise. Turn off the mixer, add the flour all at once, pulse a few times then mix on low speed only until it disappears into

the dough. Turn the mixer off again, add the apricots and mix just to incorporate. Or, mix the apricots into the dough with a flexible spatula.

Turn the dough out and knead it gently to bring it together. Divide it in half and pat each half into a disk.

Working with one disk at a time, place the dough between two pieces of parchment paper and roll it to a thickness of ¼ inch. Slide the dough, still between the paper, onto a baking sheet — you can stack the slabs — and freeze for at least 1 hour.

GETTING READY TO BAKE: Center a rack in the oven and preheat it to 350 degrees F. Line a baking sheet with parchment or a silicone baking mat. Have a 1½-inch-diameter cookie cutter at hand.

Working with one piece of dough at a time, peel away both sheets of paper and place the dough on one piece of paper. Cut out as many cookies as you can and place them on the lined baking sheet an inch apart. Gather the scraps, then combine them with the scraps you get from the second disk, re-roll, freeze, cut and bake.

Bake the cookies for 15 to 18 minutes, rotating the baking sheet after 9 minutes, or until they are golden around the edges and firm to the touch. Let the cookies rest on the baking sheet for a minute or two, then transfer to a rack and allow to cool completely.

Repeat with the remaining dough, always using a cool baking sheet.

PARM TOASTS

Call these biscotti if you want, and you wouldn't be wrong — they're made and baked just like biscotti — but I like to think of them as toasts. Serve as an on-their-own cocktail nibble, make them the base for delicious tapas (they're great with a swipe of butter and a slice of ham or juicy tomato, or both, or something a little off-sweet, like pepper jelly and soft goat's- or sheep's-milk cheese) or use as croutons to float in soup or crumble into a salad. Because they're baked twice, the Parmesan turns the same rust color that the most seductive grilled cheese sandwiches do. I love their crunchy, dry-toast texture, their marvelous flavor and the scent that fills the kitchen as they bake. That they keep almost forever is a bonus.

A word on the cheese: You must use shredded Parmesan; grated doesn't bake the same way.

Makes about 44 toasts

2½ cups (340 grams) all-purpose flour

1½ teaspoons baking powder

1 teaspoon fine sea salt

½ teaspoon baking soda

¼ teaspoon freshly ground black pepper

3 large eggs, at room temperature

7 tablespoons (100 ml) extra-virgin olive oil

2 tablespoons white wine

1 tablespoon honey

1½ cups (5¼ ounces; 150 grams) shredded Parmesan

Center a rack in the oven and preheat it to 350 degrees F. Line a baking sheet with parchment paper or a silicone baking mat.

Whisk the flour, baking powder, salt, baking soda and pepper together.

Working with a stand mixer fitted with the paddle attachment, or in a large bowl with a hand mixer, beat the eggs, oil, wine and honey together on medium speed for 3 minutes; the mix will be smooth and shiny. Turn off the mixer, add the flour all at once and pulse a few times, just until the risk of flying flour is passed, then mix on low speed only until the dry ingredients are almost incorporated. Add the cheese and mix to blend — you'll have a dough that will clean the sides of the bowl. Give the dough a last few turns with a sturdy flexible spatula.

Turn the dough out and divide it in half. Put each piece a few inches away from one of the long sides of the baking sheet — leave room between the two pieces, because they'll expand in the oven. Use your fingers and a spatula to shape each piece of dough into a rectangle about 12 inches long and 1½ inches wide. Don't strive for perfection — it's unattainable.

Bake the logs for 25 minutes, rotating the baking sheet after about

15 minutes; the logs will have expanded, cracked and browned lightly. Transfer the baking sheet to a rack and let the logs rest for 20 minutes.

Reduce the oven temperature to 325 degrees F.

Using a wide metal spatula, transfer the logs to a cutting board and, with a long serrated knife, cut into ½-inch-thick slices. Some pieces will break; sadly, that's the nature of these toasts. Lay the slices cut side down on the baking sheet and bake for 10 minutes. Turn the pieces over and bake for 10 minutes more — they'll be deeply golden brown. Transfer the toasts to racks and allow them to cool completely; they'll get crisper and firmer as they cool.

Covered and stored at room temperature, the toasts will keep for about 2 weeks.

BEE'S SNEEZE NUGGETS

1¾ cups (238 grams) all-purpose flour

1 teaspoon baking powder

½ teaspoon freshly ground black pepper

⅓ cup (80 ml) freshly squeezed lemon juice (zest the lemons before you juice them)

¼ cup (60 ml) olive oil

3 tablespoons gin

1 tablespoon honey

⅛ teaspoon pure lemon oil or pure lemon extract

2 teaspoons sugar

1 teaspoon fine sea salt

Finely grated zest of 2 lemons

½ teaspoon grated fresh ginger

Honey, for dipping (optional)

The menu at Booker and Dax, a cocktail bar in New York City from the team behind the legendary restaurant Momofuku, is so interesting that you might need to have a drink — or at least a pork bun — to tide you over while you decide what you want to order. When my friend Rebekah ordered the Bee's Sneeze, I looked at the ingredient list, took a sip and immediately wanted to turn it into a cookie. While the gin wasn't obvious cookie material, everything else in the drink was: lemon, ginger, honey and black pepper. The cocktail was ferociously tart — like the best icy lemonade on a scorcher of a day — and, under the citrus, pleasantly spicy. These sturdy, flaky nuggets capture all of that. They're good with a gin and tonic. They're surprisingly good with slices of Parmesan. And they're particularly good dipped in a little honey. Just put a bowl of honey next to the Sneezes and let everyone dip and sip.

Makes about 50 nuggets

Position the racks to divide the oven into thirds and preheat it to 350 degrees F. Line two baking sheets with parchment paper or silicone baking mats.

Whisk the flour, baking powder and pepper together. Whisk the lemon juice, oil, gin, honey and lemon oil or extract together in a large measuring cup.

Toss the sugar and salt into a large bowl and add the lemon zest. With your fingertips, rub and press the ingredients together until the sugar and salt are moist and aromatic. Add the grated ginger and rub to incorporate. Add the flour and stir with a fork to mix well. Make a well in the center and pour in the liquid ingredients. Working with a fork and starting in the middle of the bowl, stir the dry ingredients into the wet. Within a couple of minutes, you'll have a soft, perhaps pockmarked dough that will seem spongy. Reach into the bowl and fold and knead the dough gently just to pull it together — don't overdo it.

Flour a work surface and turn the dough out onto it. Lightly flour the top of the dough and use your palms to pat it into a squarish shape that's ¾ to 1 inch thick. Neatness doesn't count.

These are good the day they
are made and better a day later,
when they are drier and crisper.
In a tightly covered container,
the nuggets will keep for about
2 weeks at room temperature.
They can be frozen for up to
2 months.

Using a bench scraper or a knife, cut the dough into small pieces. You can really make these any size you want, but I usually cut them about 1 inch square because their flavor is so big. Place the nuggets about an inch apart on the baking sheets.

Bake for 25 to 30 minutes, rotating the baking sheets top to bottom and front to back at the midway mark, or until the nuggets are golden on top and more golden on the bottom. Transfer the baking sheets to racks and let the nuggets cool completely.

Serve the nuggets on their own or with a bowl of honey for dipping.

I'd call these rugelach, but then you'd expect dried fruit and cinnamon-sugar and there's none of that here. (For classic rugelach, see page 270.) Although these look like rugelach and are made like rugelach, the traditional cream cheese dough harbors a surprise — Triscuit crumbs — and the filling packs some heat. It's a mix of mustard and Major Grey's chutney, a somewhat sweet, variably spicy, jammy blend of mango and ginger. (I use mild chutney, but you can go hotter, if you'd like.)

For me, these roll-ups, while a complete invention, have a certain memory-lane quality to them. When I was a teenager, Triscuits spread with cream cheese and topped with Major Grey's chutney were not only a popular canapé, but considered worldly. I can't remember the last time I had the combination, but when I began playing with a Triscuit–cream cheese dough (page 388), the hors d'oeuvre came back to me and I made this. It doesn't seem the least bit retro, though. And if it did? Well, who doesn't love "vintage"?

Makes 32 roll-ups

Let the pieces of cream cheese and butter rest on the counter for 5 minutes — you want them to be slightly softened but still cool.

Meanwhile, put the flour, salt and Triscuits in a food processor and process until the crackers are crumbs. Scatter the chunks of cream cheese and butter over the dry ingredients and pulse the machine 6 to 10 times. Once you've got everything broken up, process in long pulses, scraping down the sides of the bowl often, until the dough forms large curds — don't work it so long that it forms a ball on the blade.

Turn the dough out, gather it together and divide it in half. Shape each half into a disk.

Working with one disk at a time, lightly flour a piece of parchment paper, set the dough on the paper, flour the top of the dough, cover with another piece of parchment and start rolling. You're aiming for a circle that's 11 to 12 inches in diameter. Don't worry about getting it perfectly round — ragged edges are

Ingredients

- 4 ounces (113 grams) cold full-fat cream cheese, cut into 4 pieces
- 1 stick (8 tablespoons; 4 ounces; 113 grams) cold unsalted butter, cut into 4 pieces
- 1 cup (136 grams) all-purpose flour
- ¼ teaspoon salt
- 20 Triscuits (I prefer Original, but you can use another type), coarsely broken
- ⅔ cup (160 grams) Major Grey's chutney
- 2 teaspoons Dijon mustard, or more to taste

just fine. Slide the dough, still sandwiched between the paper, onto a baking sheet — you can stack the slabs — and freeze the dough for at least 1 hour, or refrigerate for at least 2 hours.

GETTING READY TO BAKE: Position the racks to divide the oven into thirds and preheat it to 325 degrees F. Line two baking sheets with silicone baking mats (they make removing the roll-ups easier) or parchment paper. Have a pizza wheel (or sharp knife) at hand.

Mix the chutney and mustard together. If there are large hunks of mango in the chutney, pick them out (they're hard to roll into the dough; if you'd like, you can whir the chutney in the processor to even it out).

Peel away both pieces of parchment from one sheet of dough and put the dough back on one piece of paper. Spread half the chutney over the dough. Using the pizza wheel (or knife), cut the circle into quarters and then cut each quarter into 4 wedges. Now test the dough: if you think you can roll it up, go for it; if the dough cracks, let it rest on the counter for a few minutes before doing so. Starting at the base of each wedge, roll the dough up into chubby cookies. The chutney will ooze out and be messy — that's just how it goes. Place the roll-ups on the lined baking sheet, making sure the points are tucked under. Slide the sheet into the refrigerator while you work on the second round of dough.

Bake the roll-ups for 37 to 40 minutes, rotating the sheets front to back and top to bottom after 20 minutes, or until they are beautifully golden. The chutney will have bubbled and burned around the cookies, but the bottoms will be fine. You have to lift the roll-ups off the baking sheet as soon as they come from the oven, especially if you've baked them on parchment — wait, and the chutney will glue the cookies to the paper. Transfer the roll-ups to racks and cool to just warm or room temperature before serving.

STORING

These are at their best soon after they're made. If you must keep them overnight, pack them into a container and then reheat them briefly in a 350-degree-F oven before serving. The cookies can be wrapped airtight and frozen for up to 2 months, but the best way to freeze them is unbaked, also for 2 months: Bake them directly from the freezer, adding a few extra minutes of oven time as needed.

SOUR CREAM–EVERYTHING SEED KNOTS

All-purpose flour, for dusting
½ recipe Everything Seed Mix (page 499)
½ recipe Sour Cream Puff Dough
    (page 497), chilled and ready to roll

These cookies give the everything bagel a run for its money. Built on Sour Cream Puff Dough (page 497) and shaped for snacking, these owe their bold flavor to my eleven-year-old friend Will Dodd. If Will, an adventurous kitchen DIYer, hadn't set himself the task of making everything-bagel crisps, I'd never have gotten the idea for this terrific seed and spice mix, and we'd all be missing out on something good.

The yeasted dough is treated like puff pastry: You roll it out until it's twice as long as it is wide, fold it and turn it, repeat and then repeat. And each time you roll it, you roll in the seeds, so that by the time you're ready to cut the dough, it's deeply dotted with sesame and poppy seeds and wildly aromatic — the garlic, onion and pepper are so fragrant that you might find yourself wanting to taste the dough before it even goes into the oven.

I like to cut and twist these into knots, but they're delicious no matter what you do to them. Sometimes I just cut them into bands or nuggets (see the knots' sweet sister, Caramel-Sugar Pufflets, page 267, for instructions) and sometimes I twist them, swizzle stick style. Because the dough has so much flavor and fragrance, the look, as nice as is it, is almost secondary.

A word on amounts: I'm giving you a recipe that uses half of the Sour Cream Puff Dough. If you'd like, you can use all the seed mixture and bake the full batch, or you can make Caramel-Sugar Pufflets (page 267) with the other half of the dough.

Makes about 30 knots

Clear a large rolling space and have a ruler at hand. Sprinkle the work surface very lightly with flour and more generously with some of the seed mix and place the dough on the seeds. Sprinkle some seeds and a bit of flour over the dough and roll it until it's 16 inches long and 8 inches wide, lifting it from time to time to make sure it's not sticking and sprinkling the work surface with flour and seeds as needed. (It's hard to be exact, but the closer you can come to these measurements and to having the dough be twice as long as it is wide, the more

While the dough can be kept refrigerated for up to 4 days, once you start rolling it on the seeds, you must go right through (stopping for necessary chilling if the dough gets soft) and bake the cookies within a couple of hours. The baked knots are best the day they are made.

evenly it will puff in the oven.) With a short end toward you, fold the dough in thirds, as you would a business letter (lift the bottom third of the dough over the center third, then fold the top third of the dough over so the edges meet). Give the dough a quarter turn, so that the long side that looks like the pages of a book is on your right. This is the basic technique for this dough and the one you'll repeat, always turning the dough in the same direction.

If your room is very hot and/or the dough is very soft and you think you'll have trouble rolling it, slide it onto a parchment-lined baking sheet and pop it into the refrigerator or freezer for 15 minutes. Also, if the dough gets soft and seems to tear as you roll it, patch it as best you can, sprinkling the tear with flour, and give it a chill before carrying on.

Roll, fold and turn the dough 2 more times, always rolling it out on seeds, sprinkling seeds on top of the dough and using just as much flour as you need to keep things moving. When you have completed 3 rolls, folds and turns, chill the dough until you're ready to bake it (or for up to 2 hours).

GETTING READY TO BAKE: Position the racks to divide the oven into thirds and preheat it to 375 degrees F. Line two baking sheets with parchment paper or silicone baking mats.

Sprinkle more seeds (and flour, if needed) on the work surface and dough and roll it out once more into a 16-x-8-inch rectangle. Using a bench scraper, pizza wheel or sharp knife (being careful not to mar your counter), cut the dough in half from top to bottom and then crosswise into 1-inch-wide bands.

Cut a lengthwise slit in the middle of each band, leaving ¼ to ½ inch of solid dough at each end. To make the knot, loop each end about three quarters of the way through the slit — don't tug on the ends and don't pull the ends all the way through the slit (do that, and you'll turn the dough inside out). When the dough is properly knotted, it will have a bump where it is folded on itself and it might have a few twists, which are nice. Place the knots on the baking sheets, leaving a generous inch between them.

Bake for 14 to 16 minutes, rotating the sheets top to bottom and front to back after 8 minutes, or until the knots are puffed and golden brown. Transfer the baking sheets to racks and allow the knots to rest for 3 minutes or so, then carefully lift them onto the racks and cool to just warm or room temperature.

SWEET OR SAVORY CREAM CHEESE–HONEY NUT WAFERS

It's rare that you come across a cookie that can be sweet or savory or in between and perfect in all its incarnations. Here's that rarity. It's built on a cream cheese dough, best known for its role in rugelach (page 270). Quick and easy to make and impossible to mess up, the dough is a wonder: It crisps on the bottom, layers in the middle (like puff pastry) and flakes throughout. And, because it doesn't contain sugar, it takes to additions both sweet and salty.

My basic go-with-everything topping for these elegant wafers is a honey-walnut mixture that caramelizes in the oven, forming a thin, crunchy layer that remains chewy beneath. It's sweet but only barely, and just slightly salty, so it doubles as a tea and a cocktail cookie. If you want to push it to take a stand, you can hide a bit of jam or a pat of blue cheese under the topping, as described on page 449.

A word on size: If you decide to make the wafers savory by adding blue cheese, you might want to make them smaller. Use a 1½-inch-diameter cutter, and you'll get about 45 cookies.

Makes about 30 cookies

TO MAKE THE TOPPING: Start the topping before you make the dough. Put the walnuts, flour and salt in a food processor and pulse a few times to chop the nuts. It's okay to have some larger pieces, some small bits and some powder.

Put the honey and water in a 2-cup microwave-safe measuring cup (or a bowl) and bring to a boil in the microwave. Scrape the nut mixture into the honey and stir with a silicone spatula. Set aside to cool while you make the dough. (You can make the topping up to 3 days ahead; cover and refrigerate it.) There's no need to rinse the processor bowl.

TO MAKE THE DOUGH: Let the pieces of cream cheese and butter rest on the counter for 5 minutes — you want them to be slightly softened but still cool.

Put the flour and salt in the processor and pulse to blend. Scatter over the

FOR THE HONEY NUT TOPPING

2 cups (240 grams) walnuts (whole or pieces)

1 tablespoon all-purpose flour

¼ teaspoon fine sea salt

6 tablespoons (90 ml) honey

6 tablespoons (90 ml) water

FOR THE DOUGH

4 ounces (113 grams) cold full-fat cream cheese, cut into 4 chunks

1 stick (8 tablespoons; 4 ounces; 113 grams) cold unsalted butter, cut into 4 chunks

1 cup (136 grams) all-purpose flour

¼ teaspoon fine sea salt

Jam or marmalade, for sweet wafers (optional)

Soft blue cheese, for savory wafers (optional)

cream cheese and butter and pulse 6 to 10 times, so that the flour coats the chunks, then process until the dough forms large curds — don't go past the curd stage.

Turn the dough out and gather it into a ball. Divide it in half and flatten each half into a disk. If the dough is still cool (which it probably will be), working with one disk at a time, place the dough between pieces of parchment paper and roll it to a thickness of ⅛ inch. Slide the dough, still between the paper, onto a baking sheet — you can stack the slabs — and freeze for at least 2 hours. If the dough is warm and soft, cover and chill it for about 30 minutes (or for up to 1 day) before rolling and then chilling.

GETTING READY TO BAKE: Position the racks to divide the oven into thirds and preheat it to 400 degrees F. Line two baking sheets with parchment paper or silicone baking mats. Have a 2-inch-diameter (or 1½-inch-diameter, if making blue cheese wafers) cookie cutter at hand.

Stir the honey nut topping to incorporate any liquid that might have seeped to the bottom.

Working with one piece of dough at a time, peel away both pieces of paper and place the dough on one piece of paper. Cut out as many rounds as you can and place them on the lined baking sheets, leaving an inch of space between them. If the dough softens while you're working, return it to the freezer briefly, and chill the already-cut dough as well. If you're using either jam or cheese, place a tiny bit — a scant ¼ teaspoon is about right — in the middle of each cookie. For each cookie, scoop out 1 level teaspoon of topping and place it over the jam or cheese, if you used it, or in the center of the plain wafer and very gently press it into a circle, leaving a bare border around the edges. Gather the scraps of dough together, combine with scraps from second piece of dough, press them into a disk, re-roll, chill and bake.

Bake for 13 to 15 minutes, rotating the baking sheets front to back and top to bottom after 8 minutes, or until both the topping and the bottom of the cookies are golden brown. Transfer the baking sheets to racks and let the wafers rest for 10 minutes, then lift them onto the racks and cool until they are just warm or at room temperature.

STORING

The topping can be made up to 3 days ahead and kept covered in the refrigerator. The rolled-out dough can be wrapped well and kept in the refrigerator for up to 1 day or the freezer for up to 2 months; no need to defrost before using. The baked wafers are best eaten within hours, but they can be kept in a covered container for up to 1 day; it's humidity that will do them in, so keep them in a cool, dry place (not the refrigerator). Before serving, warm the wafers in a 350-degree-F oven for 3 to 4 minutes.

COCOA-CAYENNE COOKIES

1½ cups (204 grams) all-purpose flour

½ cup (42 grams) unsweetened cocoa powder

½ teaspoon cayenne pepper

2 sticks (8 ounces; 226 grams) unsalted butter, cut into chunks, at room temperature

½ teaspoon fine sea salt

⅓ cup (40 grams) confectioners' sugar, sifted

2 tablespoons sugar

1 large egg yolk

Flake sea salt, such as Maldon, for sprinkling

At heart, this is a quintessential chocolate shortbread cookie: buttery, flaky and not too sweet — the generous amount of cocoa powder gives an edge as well as pure chocolate flavor. But the cookie's true nature is salt-and-pepper savory. There's cayenne pepper in the mix, but it's a slow reveal; it takes two bites and a few seconds before you sense the heat. And there's salt: sea salt in the dough and flake salt on the surface. Salt is the flavor booster here. It wakes up the cocoa and cayenne, enlivens the richness of the butter and makes you want to reach for cookie after cookie.

I created these cookies with red wine in mind; they're also great with sparkling Lambrusco and satisfying with port.

Makes about 50 cookies

Sift the flour, cocoa and cayenne together.

Working with a stand mixer fitted with the paddle attachment, or in a large bowl with a hand mixer, beat the butter and salt on low speed until smooth and creamy, about 2 minutes. Add both sugars and beat until thoroughly incorporated, about 2 minutes. Add the egg yolk and mix for a minute more. Turn off the machine, add the flour mixture all at once and pulse until the risk of flying flour has passed. Then mix on low speed only until the dry ingredients disappear into the dough. You'll have a very soft dough.

Turn the dough out and divide it in half. Pat each half into a disk.

Working with one disk at a time, place the dough between two pieces of parchment paper and roll to a thickness of ¼ inch. Slide the dough, still between the paper, onto a baking sheet — you can stack the slabs — and freeze for at least 1 hour.

GETTING READY TO BAKE: Center a rack in the oven and preheat it to 350 degrees F. Line a baking sheet with parchment paper or a silicone baking mat. Have a 1½-inch-diameter cookie cutter at hand.

The dough can be rolled out, wrapped well and frozen for up to 2 months; cut and bake directly from the freezer. The baked cookies can be kept in a covered container for up to 1 week at room temperature or wrapped airtight and frozen for up to 2 months.

Working with one piece of dough at a time, peel away both pieces of paper and return the dough to one piece. Cut out as many cookies as you can and put them on the lined baking sheet, leaving about an inch between them. Gather the scraps, then combine them with the scraps you get from the second sheet, re-roll, freeze, cut and bake. Sprinkle each cookie with a few flakes of salt.

Bake the cookies for about 10 minutes, rotating the baking sheet after 5 minutes, or until they feel just firm to the touch. Let the cookies rest on the baking sheet for about 3 minutes, then transfer them to a rack to cool completely.

Repeat with the remaining dough, making certain that you start with a cool baking sheet.

SMOKY HEARTS

Hot, smoky and made for Valentine's Day. Oh, and for enjoying with Scotch or Armagnac or bourbon too. Unlike almost every other cookie in the Beurre & Sel collection, these aren't round. I made them heart-shaped as a Valentine special at the store and was surprised to see how many guys came in to buy them for themselves. They are the polar opposite of the usual V-Day treat: they're unadorned, unfrilly and neither pink nor red. They've got bold flavor and light but lingering heat.

Some of the cookies' smoke comes from smoked almonds and some from smoked paprika, which can also be the source of the gently smoldering heat. I use a mild paprika, but if you want to turn it up, go for a hotter one.

Makes about 60 small cookies

1¾ cups (238 grams) all-purpose flour

½ cup (43 grams) unsweetened cocoa powder

1 teaspoon smoked paprika (see headnote)

1½ sticks (12 tablespoons; 6 ounces; 170 grams) unsalted butter, cut into chunks, at room temperature

⅓ cup (40 grams) confectioners' sugar, sifted

3 tablespoons sugar

¾ teaspoon fine sea salt

2 large egg whites

½ cup (50 grams) smoked almonds, finely chopped

Sift the flour, cocoa powder and paprika together.

Working with a stand mixer fitted with the paddle attachment, or in a large bowl with a hand mixer, beat the butter, both sugars and the salt together at medium speed until smooth and creamy, about 3 minutes. Add the egg whites one at a time, beating for a minute after each one goes in. The egg whites will curdle the batter, but the dough will come together when the dry ingredients are added. Turn off the mixer, add the flour mixture all at once and pulse the mixer until the risk of flying flour has passed. Then mix on low only until the dry ingredients disappear into the dough. You should have a thick, smooth dough, one that might ball up around the paddle or beaters. Add the almonds and mix them in on low speed or, if you'd like, use a flexible spatula.

Turn the dough out and divide it in half. Shape each half into a disk.

Working with one piece at a time, place the dough between pieces of parchment paper and roll it to a thickness of ¼ inch. Slide the dough, still sandwiched between the paper, onto a baking sheet — you can stack the slabs — and freeze for at least 1 hour.

GETTING READY TO BAKE: Center a rack in the oven and preheat it to 350 degrees F. Line a baking sheet with parchment paper or a silicone baking

mat. Have a 1½-inch heart-shaped cutter at hand. (The cutter can be whatever size or shape you'd like, but your yield might change.)

Working with one piece of dough at a time, peel away both pieces of paper and put the dough back on one piece. Cut as many cookies as you can and place about an inch apart on the lined baking sheet. Save the scraps to combine with those from the other piece of dough, chill, re-roll and bake.

Bake the cookies for 14 to 16 minutes, rotating the baking sheet after 8 minutes, or until they feel just slightly firm to the touch. Cool the cookies on the sheet for 5 minutes, then transfer them to a rack to cool completely.

Repeat with the remaining dough, making sure to use a cool baking sheet.

STORING

You can keep the rolled-out dough in the refrigerator for up to 2 days or, wrapped airtight, in the freezer for up to 2 months; cut and bake directly from the freezer. Or cut out the cookies and freeze the hearts, then bake them straight from the freezer, adding another minute to the baking time if needed. The baked cookies will keep in an airtight container at room temperature for up to 1 week.

cookie
go-alongs
and basics

VANILLA MARSHMALLOWS

About 1 cup (128 grams) potato starch or cornstarch (or a 50-50 mix of starch and confectioners' sugar)

¾ cup (180 ml) cold water

1¼ cups (250 grams) sugar

2 tablespoons light corn syrup

2 packets (5 teaspoons; about 14½ grams) powdered gelatin

3 large egg whites, at room temperature

1 tablespoon pure vanilla extract

Food coloring (optional)

Once you've made your first batch of homemade marshmallows, there'll be no stopping you — I speak from experience. You will want to make them again and again not only for s'mores, of course, and for topping the Sweet Potato Pie Bars (page 68), but also for campfires and hot chocolate parties.

Marshmallows are meringues — strong meringues made with a cooked sugar syrup (you'll need a candy thermometer) and gelatin. The mix is very sticky and needs a lot of energetic beating. This is a good recipe for a stand mixer — you'll be happy to have its strength working for you.

Traditionally, marshmallows are left to dry (there's no baking involved) on a bed of — and thickly covered with — cornstarch or potato starch. If you'd like, though, you can make a 50-50 blend of the starch and confectioners' sugar.

This recipe produces white vanilla marshmallow squares that are 1 inch high, but you can change the flavor (see Playing Around), you can tint them any color you want (add the coloring at the end of the mixing) and you can make them any height and shape you'd like. If you mold the meringue batter in an 8-inch square pan, you'll get nice tall marshmallows that are great for hot chocolate. And you can play with the shape by dipping a tall cookie cutter in cornstarch or potato starch or confectioners' sugar and using it to cut the marshmallows.

Makes about 1 pound

Line a baking sheet — choose one with a rim that is 1 inch high — with parchment paper and dust the paper generously with some of the potato starch or cornstarch (or starch and confectioners' sugar). Have a candy thermometer at hand.

Put ⅓ cup of the water, the sugar and corn syrup in a medium saucepan and bring to a boil over medium heat, stirring until the sugar dissolves. Then continue to cook the syrup, without stirring, until it reaches 265 degrees F on

Fruit Marshmallows. Use about ⅓ cup fruit puree to flavor a batch of marshmallows. Fold the fruit into the batter at the end.

Chocolate Marshmallows. Melt 3 ounces chocolate (preferably dark chocolate) and mix it with 3½ tablespoons unsweetened cocoa powder. Fold the chocolate mixture into the batter at the end.

the thermometer. This can take about 10 minutes, during which time you should work on the gelatin and meringue.

Put the gelatin in a small microwave-safe cup and pour over the remaining cold water (about 7 tablespoons); let sit for about 5 minutes, until the gelatin has expanded and is spongy. Heat the mixture in a microwave oven for 20 to 30 seconds to liquefy it.

Put the egg whites in a stand mixer fitted with the whisk attachment and beat on medium-high speed until the whites are firm and glossy — don't overbeat them, or they will go dull. Keep an eye on the syrup while you're beating!

As soon as the syrup reaches 265 degrees F, remove the pan from the heat, reduce the mixer speed to medium and add the syrup, pouring it between the spinning whisk and the sides of the bowl. (If you have spatters, as you probably will, leave them — don't try to mix them in.) Add the gelatin and beat for another 3 minutes, so that the syrup and gelatin are fully incorporated. Beat in the vanilla. Now's the time to add food coloring — a drop at a time — if you'd like.

Using a large flexible spatula, scrape the meringue onto the lined baking sheet, putting it close to a short end of the sheet. Spread the batter into the corners and then continue to spread the batter out, taking care to keep the height of the batter at 1 inch; the batter won't fill the pan. Lift up the parchment paper covering the empty part of the sheet and press it against the edge of the batter, then put something against the paper so that it stays in place (I use custard cups).

Generously dust the top of the marshmallow batter with more potato starch or cornstarch (or starch-sugar mixture) and let the marshmallows set in a cool, dry place. They'll need about 3 hours, but they can rest for 12 hours or more.

Once they are set, cut the marshmallows with a pair of scissors or a long, thin knife. Whatever you use, you'll have to wash and dry it frequently. Have a big bowl with some potato starch or cornstarch at hand and cut the marshmallows as you'd like — squares, rectangles or even strips. As each piece is cut, drop it into the bowl of starch. Once you've got 4 or 5 marshmallows in the bowl, reach in and turn the marshmallows to coat them with the starch. One by one, toss the marshmallows from one hand to the other to shake off the excess starch. Transfer the marshmallows to a serving bowl and continue until you've cut and coated the rest of the batch.

PHILLY VANILLY ICE CREAM

There are two types of ice cream in the world: French style, made with an egg custard, and Philadelphia style, which has no eggs. French ice cream wins the rich and super-creamy award and Philly ice cream gets points for purity — without the eggs, the flavors come through bright and strong. The Philly way is the quickest and easiest method: You mix the ingredients together and then churn away. The only drawback to Philadelphia ice cream is its tendency to get too hard lightning fast. But that won't happen with this version.

To prevent that, I added vodka. The alcohol lowers the freezing point and keeps the ice cream scoopable longer. (The lower freezing point also means that it might take you longer to churn the ice cream.) And to make the texture even creamier, I added powdered milk. You can make the ice cream without the vodka or the powdered milk and it will be delicious, but it will get hard fast — which is not a problem if you're planning to serve it the day it's made.

A word on the alcohol: I chose vodka because I wanted something flavorless and I wanted to create a base that I could play with (see Playing Around). But when the flavor changes, so can the alcohol — use the alcohol to bolster whatever flavor you choose.

Makes 1½ pints

Whisk all the ingredients together in a bowl until the sugar and milk powder have dissolved; this can take a couple of minutes. To test that the mixture is smooth, rub a little between your fingers — it shouldn't feel grainy.

Pour the mixture into your ice cream maker and churn according to the manufacturer's directions. You can serve the ice cream straight from the churn as a quickly melting soft-serve, or pack it into a container and freeze until you need it. It will take about 5 hours for the ice cream to reach prime scoopability.

2 cups (480 ml) heavy cream

1 cup (240 ml) whole milk

²/₃ cup (134 grams) sugar

¼ teaspoon fine sea salt

2 tablespoons vodka or other alcohol or liqueur (see headnote)

2 tablespoons powdered milk (see headnote)

1 tablespoon pure vanilla extract

STORING

Packed in an airtight container, the ice cream will retain its lovely texture for at least 1 week.

PLAYING AROUND

Crunchy Mix-Ins. Of course you're going to want to add chocolate chips, peanut butter chips, toasted nuts, toasted or plain shredded coconut, crushed cookies, brittle, candy bits or anything else you can think of (including cookie dough). Once the ice cream is churned, add up to ¾ cup of mix-ins and spin in the machine just until they're incorporated, then pack the ice cream for the freezer.

Changing the Flavor. The base for this ice cream is neutral and can take different extracts to create new flavors. I usually leave the vanilla extract in the mix and layer in other flavors. For example, for almond ice cream, use 1½ teaspoons pure vanilla extract, 1 teaspoon pure almond extract and amaretto as the liqueur; toasted almonds or crumbled amaretti make a good mix-in. For orange or lemon ice cream, use 1 teaspoon pure vanilla extract and 1½ teaspoons pure orange or lemon oil or extract; add chopped candied orange or lemon peel to the mix, if you'd like. For peppermint ice cream, omit the vanilla and use 2 teaspoons pure peppermint oil or extract; chocolate bits are great as an add-in, of course.

Steeped Fruit Add-Ins. Steep ½ to ¾ cup cut-up dried fruit in 3 tablespoons of your chosen alcohol or liqueur. Think about raisins or pineapple steeped in rum, apricots in amaretto, cherries in kirsch, cranberries in port or crystallized ginger in Grand Marnier (use ⅓ cup or less ginger — it's powerful!). Let the fruit steep for 10 minutes, then add the liquid that remains in the bowl to the ice cream mixture. Churn, and when the ice cream is ready, add the dried fruit and spin to incorporate; pack the ice cream for the freezer.

BUTTERMILK-STRAWBERRY ICE CREAM

Everyone's got their own way of determining that summer has arrived. For me, when I'm in Connecticut, it's the first basket of local strawberries. While I seem to eat most of the berries out of hand (few baskets make it back from the farm stand untouched), I always make Strawberry Short-cake Cookies (page 322), compote (page 491), fruit salads, jams and, more recently, this ice cream. I've made other strawberry ice creams but none has stayed as smooth and creamy as this one; not a rock-hard piece of berry to be found.

The keys to the superb texture are vodka, honey and powdered milk. I puree the ingredients in a blender, but if you've got a food processor, it'll do a fine job.

And if you love this ice cream as much as I do, you'll make it with other berries. The recipe will work with blueberries, raspberries or blackberries.

Makes a generous quart

Put the berries, buttermilk, sugar, honey and salt in a blender (or a food processor) and whir until the berries are thoroughly pureed. (Smoothness can take a few minutes.) Scape down the container as needed. Add the remaining ingredients and whir until the mixture is smooth again. Scrape down the container and make certain that there isn't a clump or two of milk powder lurking on the sides or bottom.

Pour the mixture into your ice cream maker and churn according to the manufacturer's directions. You can serve the ice cream straight from the churn as a quickly melting soft-serve, or pack it into a container and freeze until you need it. It will take about 5 hours for the ice cream to reach prime scoopability.

About 8 ounces (about 226 grams) fresh strawberries, hulled

1 cup (240 ml) buttermilk, shake before measuring

½ cup (100 grams) sugar

2 tablespoons honey

¼ teaspoon fine sea salt

2 cups (480 ml) heavy cream

3 tablespoons powdered milk

2 tablespoons vodka

1½ teaspoons pure vanilla extract

STORING

Packed in an airtight container, the ice cream will retain its lovely texture for about 1 week.

CHOCOLATE ICE CREAM

2 cups (480 ml) heavy cream

1 cup (240 ml) whole milk

2/3 cup (134 grams) sugar

1/3 cup (28 grams) unsweetened cocoa
powder

3 tablespoons powdered milk (see
headnote)

1/2 teaspoon fine sea salt

5 ounces (142 grams) semisweet or
bittersweet chocolate, coarsely
chopped

2 tablespoons vodka or other alcohol
(see headnote)

This Philadelphia-style ice cream is even thicker, creamier, and more vel-vety than the Philly Vanilly (page 461). Being a Philadelphia ice cream, by definition it's not custard-based; there are no eggs. But who needs custard when you've got cream and good dark chocolate? Not I. And not you either, I bet.

To give the ice cream the deepest flavor possible, I use both cocoa and semisweet (or bittersweet) chocolate. And to help keep the texture silken and scoopable, I added vodka (you could use rum, Scotch or bour-bon) and powdered milk. Because of the alcohol, it may take you longer to churn this ice cream than others — be patient. (You can omit both the vodka and the powdered milk and still have delicious ice cream — you'll just have to enjoy it faster, because it hardens quickly.)

If you'd like mix-ins, see Playing Around, page 463.

Makes a generous pint

If you want to be able to cool the ice cream mixture down quickly so that you can churn it soon after it's made, fill a large bowl with ice cubes and cold water and have a smaller heatproof bowl that you can fit into it. Alternatively, you can wait for the mixture to come to room temperature in a bowl on the counter.

Whisk the cream, milk, sugar, cocoa, powdered milk and salt together in a medium saucepan just to mix. Add the chopped chocolate. The mixture will look a lot like Rocky Road, and that's fine. Put the pan over medium heat and cook, whisking, until the chocolate melts and the mixture comes to a boil.

Standing nearby and stirring frequently, let the mixture boil for 3 minutes. Turn it out into a heatproof bowl and place the bowl in the ice-water bath or on the counter. Stir frequently until the mixture cools to room temperature. (If a skin forms on top of the mixture, remove and discard it.) Stir in the alcohol.

Pour the mixture into your ice cream maker and churn according to the manufacturer's directions. You can serve the ice cream straight from the churn as a quickly melting soft-serve, or pack it into a container and freeze until you need it. It will take about 5 hours for the ice cream to reach prime scoopability.

STORING
Packed in an airtight container, the ice cream will retain its lovely texture for at least 1 week.

MIXED CITRUS CURD

I know that this recipe makes more curd than you'll need for cookies, but if you made less, you'd be unhappy not to have leftovers for breakfast, for after school, after work or after-hours, for cupcakes and muffins, for the base of a trifle or the top of a sponge cake, for serving with berries or for using as a filling for tartlets. I could go on and if I do, you'll want to double the recipe.

This is a very simple curd to make and one that's just about foolproof because it uses whole eggs (less finicky than dealing with yolks alone, the thickener in most curds). You need no special skill to succeed except the ability to stand by the stove and stir without stopping for a few minutes.

You can use this recipe to make any kind of citrus curd, but mixing it up is my favorite way to go. I like to use equal parts lemon, lime and orange juice and to add the zest as well. Grate the zest very fine — I use a Microplane zester — and it will blend into the curd easily.

Makes about 2 cups

1¼ cups (250 grams) sugar

Enough citrus fruit to make ¾ cup (180 ml) juice; zest the citrus before you juice it (see headnote)

4 large eggs

1 tablespoon light corn syrup

1 stick (8 tablespoons; 4 ounces; 113 grams) unsalted butter, cut into chunks

Put the sugar in a medium heavy-bottomed saucepan and add the zest from the citrus. Using your fingertips, rub and press the sugar and zest together until the sugar is moist, fragrant and tinged with color. Add the eggs and, the instant they're in, start whisking energetically. (Sugar can "burn" the yolks, so you need to mix them immediately.) Whisk in the corn syrup and juice and drop in the pieces of butter.

Put the saucepan over medium heat and start whisking — make sure you cover the entire bottom of the pan, especially the edges. If you're more comfortable with a heatproof spatula or spoon, make the switch now. Cook, stirring nonstop, for 6 to 8 minutes, until the curd thickens — it doesn't thicken much, but the change is noticeable. When you see a bubble or two come to the surface and then pop, you're finished. (Be careful: You don't want the curd to boil.)

Pull the pan from the heat and scrape the curd into a heatproof bowl or a canning jar or two. Press a piece of plastic wrap against the surface to create an

STORING

Packed airtight, the curd can be
refrigerated for at least 3 weeks.

airtight seal. Let the curd cool to room temperature before using or refrigerating.
(Alternatively, if you'd like to do what the pros do to cool the curd down quickly,
scrape it into a heatproof bowl and place the bowl in a larger bowl filled with ice
cubes and cold water. Keep the curd over the ice, stirring now and then, until it's
completely cool, then pour it into jars.)

BLUEBERRY SYRUP

1½ cups (300 grams) sugar

1 cup (240 ml) water

2 cups (300 grams) fresh blueberries, at room temperature

Finely grated zest and juice of ½ lime

PLAYING AROUND

Other Berry Syrups. You can use this recipe to make cranberry or raspberry syrup. Strawberries are a bit too watery for this technique.

STORING

In tightly sealed jars, the syrup will keep for about 1 month and the jam for about 2 weeks.

It's always nice to have a surprise up your sleeve, or in your fridge, and this is a good one: blueberry syrup that's perfection over Buttermilk Blueberry Pie Bars (page 62) and Mary's Maine Bars (page 50) and lovely over ice cream, especially when that ice cream is scooped out over a cookie.

The recipe is stir-and-boil simple, but you need a candy thermometer. And it's a twofer — make the syrup, and you get a small pot of jam as a bonus.

Makes about 1½ cups syrup (plus about ½ cup jam)

Stir the sugar and water together in a medium saucepan and place it over medium-high heat. Stir until the mixture comes to a boil and the sugar dissolves. If some sugar splashes on the sides of the pan, wash it down with a pastry brush, preferably a silicone brush, dipped in cold water. Reduce the heat to medium, attach a candy thermometer to the pan and boil, without stirring, until the syrup reaches 260 degrees F. (This will take 10 minutes or more, so be patient.)

When the syrup hits the temperature, immediately remove the pan from the heat and stir in the berries and zest. (If your berries are the least bit cold, the syrup will seize and harden — don't worry, you can work that out over the heat.) Return the pan to medium heat and cook, stirring, for another minute or so, until the syrup boils and a bunch of berries pop.

Remove the pan from the heat, stir in the lime juice, cover and allow the syrup to cool to room temperature, about 1 hour.

Strain the syrup into a jar and pack the jammy berries into another jar. The syrup is ready to use when it is chilled — it will thicken a bit.

CHOCOLATE GANACHE SAUCE

14 ounces (397 grams) semisweet or bittersweet chocolate, coarsely chopped

3 tablespoons espresso, strong coffee or hot water

1 teaspoon pure vanilla extract

¼ cup (50 grams) sugar

¾ cup (180 ml) heavy cream

Pinch of fine sea salt or fleur de sel, or more to taste

STORING

Packed in a tightly covered jar, the sauce will keep in the refrigerator for at least 2 months. To reheat and bring back its pourability, place the uncovered jar in a saucepan half-filled with gently simmering water or warm it on low in a microwave; stir frequently as the sauce heats so that it melts evenly.

Julia Moskin, a longtime reporter for the *New York Times* food section and a woman who knows her way around the kitchen, gets credit for this sauce, an all-purpose hot fudge sauce meant for ice cream, but fabulous as a dipping sauce for cookies of many kinds. We worked together on a *Times* story about ganache, and this was the centerpiece recipe. I've been making it ever since.

I'm a fan of playing around, and Julia's recipe comes with playing-around choices built into it. Like all good ganaches, it can be many things. Because it firms when it's chilled, you can use it to make truffles (chill the ganache, roll scoops into balls, dredge in cocoa and serve cold); if you pour it into a baked tart shell, it will become a lovely filling that is even lovelier topped with whipped cream. While it's hot and pourable, you can use the ganache as a glaze for bar cookies — pour it over the top, chill to set and then cut into bars.

Makes about 1½ cups

Stir all the ingredients together in a medium heavy-bottomed saucepan over very low heat and cook, stirring, until the chocolate is almost but not completely melted. Alternatively, you can stir the ingredients together in a wide microwave-safe bowl and heat on low in the microwave: Heat for 2 minutes, stir and then heat in short spurts, stirring after each blast, until the chocolate is almost melted.

Remove the sauce from the heat and whisk to bring it together. If it looks curdled, whisk more and more vigorously, and it will be fine. Taste for salt. If you'd like to thin the sauce (which you might for a glaze) add hot water by the droplet.

The sauce is ready to go over ice cream. Or serve as a cookie dip when it's still hot or has cooled to warm.

CANDIED ORANGE PEEL

3 navel or other oranges with thick skins, rinsed
3 cups (720 ml) water
2 cups (400 grams) sugar

PLAYING AROUND

Sugar-Coated Candied Peel. Remove the peels from the syrup with a slotted spoon, allowing as much of the syrup as possible to drip back into the jar (save the syrup to pour over ice cream or fruit salad), and dredge in sugar, making sure that all surfaces are covered. Transfer the peels to a rack and allow them to dry overnight. Store in a covered container away from heat and humidity.

STORING

Tightly sealed, the candied peel will keep in the fridge for about 2 months. If the syrup crystallizes, as it sometimes does, warm it in the microwave.

It's a shame that it's not easy to find high-quality candied orange peel in markets, but it's nice that it's so easy to make at home. Nice, also, that it keeps almost forever, whether you store the peels in their syrup or dry them and dredge them in sugar (see Playing Around).

Don't skip the boil-and-rinse steps — they're your insurance against bitter peel. And don't be tempted to get rid of the white cottony pith attached to the rind — it's not pleasant when you eat the fruit out of hand, but it becomes soft and sweet when poached. Also, it's lovely to have a thick piece of peel to bite into.

Of course, what's good for the orange is also good for its siblings (tangerines, clementines and the rest) and its cousins (grapefruits and limes).

Makes about 2 cups

Have a clean pint jar with a tight-fitting lid at hand.

Use a paring knife to cut a slice from the top and bottom of each orange; this will give you a firm base to steady the fruit when you remove the peel. One by one, stand each orange on a cutting board and, working from top to bottom, slice off bands of peel, about 1 inch wide. Cut all the way down to the fruit — you want each strip to include all the white cottony pith (which will be luscious after it's candied) and just a sliver (about 1/8 inch) of fruit. When you've finished, the leftover oranges are yours to enjoy.

Bring a 3- to 4-quart saucepan of water to a boil. Drop in the peels and boil for 1 minute. Drain the peels in a sieve, run cold water over them and repeat this boil-drain-and-rinse process twice more, always starting with fresh water.

Rinse the pan and pour in the 3 cups water and the sugar. Bring to a boil, carefully drop in the peels, lower the heat so that the syrup just simmers and allow the peels to poach gently (without stirring) for 45 to 60 minutes, or until they are translucent.

Spoon the peels into the jar and cover with the syrup. Seal the jar and allow the syrup to cool to room temperature before refrigerating.

MILK CHOCOLATE GANACHE GLAZE AND FILLING

10 ounces (283 grams) milk chocolate, finely chopped

⅔ cup (160 ml) heavy cream

1½ teaspoons light corn syrup (if using the ganache for a glaze)

1½ tablespoons (22 grams) unsalted butter, cut into 3 pieces, at room temperature

STORING

The ganache can be covered tightly and kept in the refrigerator for up to 5 days or frozen for up to 2 months. You'll need to bring it back to the consistency you want, so leave it out at room temperature or warm it. To warm it, heat in 5-second spurts in a microwave or put it in a bowl set over a pan of simmering water. With this ganache, the bywords are low, low heat and a very light touch.

This soft ganache should be made with the best milk chocolate you can find. I prefer Valrhona Jivara or Guittard's milk chocolate. If you want to use the ganache as a glaze, add the corn syrup and pour it over the cookies as soon as it's made. Or let it set to use as a filling.

Makes about 1 cup

Put the chopped chocolate in a small heatproof bowl.

Bring the cream and corn syrup, if using, to a boil (you can do this in a microwave oven). Pour over the chocolate and let sit for 30 seconds. Then, using a whisk or small heatproof spatula, start stirring the cream and chocolate together; start in the center of the bowl, stirring in a small circle, and then, when the center comes together, work your way out in increasingly wider circles. When the ganache is smooth, add the butter one piece at a time, stirring until it is melted and incorporated.

If you are using the ganache as a glaze, use it now. If using it as a filling, refrigerate it, stirring gently but often, until it thickens.

WHITE CHOCOLATE GANACHE GLAZE AND FILLING

Like its dark chocolate sister, this is an emulsion of chocolate, cream and butter that can be used as a filling or a glaze, but it comes from the fussy side of the family. White chocolate and heat are not best friends, and so you must baby the chocolate, controlling the heat so that it's gentle (too much heat, and the chocolate will separate or burn), and you must use the best-quality white chocolate (not confectionery chocolate) you can find. My two favorite white chocolates are Valrhona Ivoire and Guittard's.

Makes about 1 cup

Put the chocolate in a heatproof bowl.

Bring the cream to a boil in a small saucepan. Pour it over the chocolate and wait for 30 seconds. Using a whisk or a flexible spatula, start stirring the ingredients together from the center of the bowl out, working in gradually enlarging concentric circles. When the ganache is smooth and shiny (and beautiful), drop in the pieces of butter one a time, stirring until each piece is blended into the mix before adding another. Be gentle — stir, don't beat.

When the ganache is smooth and shiny, cool it to a spreadable, pipable or dollopable consistency. You can do this by putting the bowl of just-made ganache in a larger bowl filled with ice cubes and cold water and stirring it until it's a good spreadable consistency. But if you do this, be eagle-eyed! The ganache goes from liquid to solid in a flash. Alternatively, you can let the ganache set at room temperature (which takes awhile) or in the refrigerator, which is the middle ground and still requires vigilance.

10 ounces (283 grams) best-quality white chocolate, finely chopped

2/3 cup (160 ml) heavy cream

1½ tablespoons (22 grams) unsalted butter, cut into 3 pieces, at warm room temperature

STORING

The ganache will keep tightly covered in the refrigerator for about 5 days. Cold, it's too hard to work with, so you need to soften it by hitting it with spurts of heat in a microwave, warming it over a pan of simmering water or leaving it on the counter. Whatever you do, be gentle. Too much heat can break the emulsion.

DARK CHOCOLATE GANACHE GLAZE AND FILLING

Ganache is both a marvel of science and a culinary delight. In technical terms, it's an emulsion of chocolate, cream and butter, a neat trick; in terms that have to do with deliciousness, it's a smooth, profoundly chocolatey mixture that can thicken to a filling (time and the refrigerator do that) or be liquid enough to enrobe a cookie in a gorgeous glaze. It is also a perfect filling for macarons (page 312). All you have to do to bring this gem into your kitchen is cook, stir and wait. The return on your investment is high here.

Makes about 2 cups

8 ounces (226 grams) semisweet or bittersweet chocolate, finely chopped

1 cup (240 ml) plus 2 tablespoons heavy cream

½ stick (4 tablespoons; 2 ounces; 56 grams) unsalted butter, cut into 6 pieces, at a warm room temperature

Put the chocolate in a heatproof bowl.

Bring the cream to a boil in a small saucepan. Pour it over the chocolate and wait for 30 seconds. Using a whisk or a flexible spatula, start stirring the ingredients together from the center of the bowl out, working in gradually enlarging concentric circles. When the ganache is smooth and shiny (and beautiful), drop in the pieces of butter one at a time, stirring until each piece is blended into the mix before adding another. Be gentle — stir, don't beat.

When the ganache is smooth and shiny, cool it to a spreadable, pipable or dollopable consistency. You can do this by putting the bowl of just-made ganache in a larger bowl filled with ice cubes and cold water and stirring it until it's a good spreadable consistency. But if you do this, be eagle-eyed! The ganache goes from liquid to solid in a flash. Alternatively, you can let the ganache set at room temperature (which takes awhile) or in the refrigerator, which is the middle ground and still requires vigilance.

STORING

The ganache will keep tightly covered in the refrigerator for about 5 days. Cold, it's too hard to work with, so you need to soften it by hitting it with spurts of heat in a microwave, warming it over a pan of simmering water or leaving it out on the counter. Whatever you do, be gentle. Too much heat can break the emulsion.

FAUXTELLA FILLING AND SPREAD

2/3 cup (80 grams) chopped nuts or pieces (see headnote)

½ cup (120 ml) heavy cream

½ teaspoon fine sea salt

¼ teaspoon ground cinnamon (optional)

Pinch of freshly grated nutmeg (optional)

½ cup (120 ml) evaporated milk

5 ounces (142 grams) best-quality milk chocolate, melted and tepid

1½ tablespoons unsweetened cocoa powder

A great filling for sandwich cookies or a slather for any solo cookie, particularly shortbread, this is a mix that delivers the pleasure of Nutella and the convenience of being able to make it at a moment's notice with a push of a blender's button.

Nutella is made with hazelnuts, and you can make your Fauxtella with hazelnuts, if you'd like. Since my husband doesn't like them, I make mine with pecans or almonds. I also add a dash of spice to the mix — one of the perks of making something yourself.

A word on texture: When the Fauxtella comes out of the blender, it will look as though you should slurp it with a straw — it needs to firm in the fridge for a couple of hours to become spreadable.

Makes about 1¼ cups

Put the nuts, cream, salt and spices, if you're using them, in a blender and whir for about 1 minute at medium speed, or until the nuts are ground, scraping down the sides of the container as needed. (Alternatively, you can do this is in a food processor, but you won't get as smooth a mix as you do with a blender.) The mixture will look like a fluffy nut paste. Add the evaporated milk and whir for 2 minutes. Scrape in the melted chocolate, add the cocoa and blend for 1 to 2 minutes more, or until smooth.

Scrape the filling into a jar, cover tightly and chill until firm, at least 2 hours.

CREAM CHEESE MACARON FILLING

This recipe comes from my friend Mardi Michels, who uses it when she teaches macaron-making classes to grown-ups and kids. As Mardi says, "It's easy to make, it's easy to work with and it tastes good." I think that covers all the important bases.

Makes about 1 cup

Working in a large bowl with a hand mixer or a sturdy flexible spatula, beat the cream cheese and butter until smooth and creamy. Add the sugar and beat until it is incorporated and the filling is smooth. Mix in the preserves. The filling is ready to use now in a cookie, such as a macaron, that will be chilled and served cold (since the filling needs to be cold to set up).

8 ounces (226 grams) full-fat cream cheese, cut into chunks, at room temperature

1 stick (8 tablespoons; 4 ounces; 113 grams) unsalted butter, cut into chunks, at room temperature

½ cup (60 grams) confectioners' sugar, sifted

2 tablespoons thick preserves or jam (without chunky fruit)

STORING

The filling will keep for up to 5 days tightly covered in the refrigerator. Stir before using to bring it back to its creamy consistency.

SALTED CARAMEL FILLING

Scant ⅔ cup (160 ml) heavy cream

¾ cup plus 2 tablespoons (175 grams) sugar

1¼ sticks (10 tablespoons; 5 ounces; 142 grams) unsalted butter, cut into 10 pieces, at room temperature

½ teaspoon fleur de sel or ¼ teaspoon fine sea salt, or more to taste

Say "salted caramel," and most people will follow you anywhere. There is something universally seductive about the thick, smooth, spreadable blend of burnt sugar, salt, butter and cream. I first made this filling to sandwich between macarons (page 312), but it's equally good as the middle layer between two cookies (particularly chocolate cookies, page 306), and in whoopie pies (page 309).

The instructions are a bit fussy — blame it on the caramel — but the work isn't hard.

Makes about 1 cup

Bring the cream to a boil in a small saucepan on the stove, or do this in a microwave oven. Remove from the heat. Have a heatproof container at hand (I use a 1-quart Pyrex measuring cup).

Choose a wide deep skillet — I prefer nonstick for this job. Pour the sugar evenly over the bottom of the skillet, place the pan over medium-high heat, grab a heatproof silicone or wooden spatula and stay nearby. As soon as the sugar starts to melt around the edges of the pan, start stirring, making small circular motions all around the edges and then, as more sugar melts, enlarging the circles until you reach the center of the pan. Cook and stir until the sugar turns a light blond color, like ale.

Turn off the heat, stand back and add 4 pats of the butter. Swirl the pan or stir as the mixture sputters and then, again standing back, add the cream a little at a time. Return the caramel to medium-high heat and cook and stir until smooth, about 1 minute. Stir in the salt.

Carefully pour the caramel into your heatproof container and cool for about 20 minutes, stirring frequently. Ideally, you want the caramel's temperature to be 140 degrees F before proceeding.

Put the remainder of the butter in a small bowl and, using a flexible spatula, stir it until it has the consistency of mayonnaise. You can incorporate the butter into the caramel with an immersion blender (my choice), a regular blender, a mini processor or the flexible spatula. Bit by bit, blend, process or beat in the butter, beating for at least 1 minute after each bit goes in and for another minute after all of the butter is incorporated. If you used a blender or processor, stir the caramel a couple of times to deflate some of the bubbles. Scrape the mixture into a container, press a piece of plastic wrap against the surface and refrigerate until chilled.

Give the cold filling a couple of turns with a spatula before piping or spreading it.

SPICED COOKIE FILLING AND SPREAD

7 ounces (200 grams; about 25) Biscoff
cookies, broken up (about 2 cups)

¾ cup (180 ml) evaporated milk

1 tablespoon honey

1 teaspoon ground cinnamon

¼ teaspoon freshly grated nutmeg

¼ teaspoon fine sea salt

1 stick (8 tablespoons; 4 ounces; 113 grams)
unsalted butter, melted

STORING

Tightly covered in the refrigerator, the spread will keep for at
least 2 weeks.

One taste of this and you'll know that I was channeling the irresistible Biscoff Cookie Spread. In fact, I use Biscoff cookies to make the spread. Is it the same as the store-bought kind? Close, but not exactly the same. The homemade spread will make you sneak into the kitchen for another spoonful, but it's not quite as sweet or as thick as the commercial one — it swirls, but it doesn't hold its swirl for long. For this reason, it makes a terrific filling when you need just a slick, and it's a wonderful add-on for simple cookies. Spread a little on your Breakfast Biscotti (page 98), and you'll start the day off happy. And if you believe that too much of a good thing is just barely enough, you might want to churn a little into your ice cream (pages 461 and 466).

While the spread is an homage to Biscoff, you can use other kinds of spice cookies, plain cookies or a mix of leftover cookies.

Makes about 1½ cups

Put the cookies, evaporated milk, honey, cinnamon, nutmeg and salt in a blender and blend on medium speed for 2 minutes, or until the cookies are pulverized; scrape down the sides of the container as needed. (Alternatively, you can do this in a food processor — just make sure to scrape down the bowl regularly.) With the machine running, slowly pour in the melted butter. Blend, scraping as needed, for 1 minute more after the last of the butter is incorporated.

Scrape into a jar, cover and refrigerate until set, at least 5 hours.

ESPRESSO FILLING AND SPREAD

You can eat this straight off a spoon and, if you love the strong flavor of espresso, you will. Meant to be spread on cookies or sandwiched between them, it's a wonderful filling for macarons or any kind of spice cookie — the mixture is built on a two-ingredient ganache. Heavy cream is steeped with freshly ground espresso (or coffee), strained and then warmed with white chocolate. As with everything you make with white chocolate, only the best will produce something lovable. Please, no chips and certainly no confectionery chocolate.

Makes about 1 cup

Put the chopped chocolate in a heatproof bowl that you can set over a saucepan.

Bring the cream and espresso to a boil in the saucepan you'll be using later as the bottom of the double boiler. Turn off the heat, cover the pan and steep for 5 minutes.

Pour the cream through a fine-mesh strainer onto the chocolate. Don't push any of the grounds through the strainer, just let the cream drip onto the chocolate and then throw away the residue. Whisk the mixture gently.

Rinse the saucepan, add a couple of inches of water and set the bowl over the pan, making sure that the water isn't touching the bottom of the bowl. Bring the water to a simmer, stirring the ganache as it heats. When the chocolate is melted — or even just before it's completely melted — remove the bowl from the pan. White chocolate is very sensitive to heat — too much, and it will burn or separate, and neither condition is reparable. Continue to stir until you have a smooth, glossy mixture.

Spoon the spread into a jar, press a piece of plastic wrap against the surface to prevent a skin from forming and refrigerate for at least 5 hours before using (overnight is better). Even though you've infused the cream with the espresso, the chocolate needs time to take in the flavor.

6½ ounces (183 grams) best-quality white chocolate, finely chopped

½ cup plus 2 tablespoons (150 ml) heavy cream

3 tablespoons finely ground espresso or coffee beans

STORING

The spread can be kept tightly covered in the refrigerator for at least 2 weeks.

DULCE DE LECHE

1 can (14 ounces; 397 grams) sweetened
   condensed milk
Flake sea salt, such as Maldon, or fleur de
   sel (optional)

Translated from the Spanish, *dulce de leche* means "sweet milk" or "milk candy," but most of us think of it as a creamy caramel spread that can be used to sandwich cookies, lift toast from the typical, up the ante in puddings or make the center of a plain cupcake or the top of a simple shortbread a surprise. Once an exotic ingredient that you had to hunt for in specialty stores, ready-made dulce de leche can now be found in supermarkets.

I usually have store-bought in the house, but I also have a can of sweetened condensed milk, just in case I've got to make dulce de leche myself. There is really nothing to making it (to say that it makes itself accurately describes the process). You cover the can of milk with boiling water and cook for 3 hours — but you must follow the one all-important safety rule: Never let the water boil away; the can must always be submerged.

Makes about 1¾ cups

Remove the label from the can of milk and put the can on its side in a tall pot. Fill the pot with hot water and place it over medium heat. Bring the water to a boil, lower the heat and simmer gently and steadily — you'll hear the intermittent tap-tap-tap of the can against the bottom of the pot — for 3 hours. You don't have to hover over the pot while the milk cooks, but you do have to check on it now and then to make sure that the can is underwater and add more water as needed. (This is your only work, but it's an important job: This process is perfectly safe *unless* the pot boils dry.)

At the end of the 3 hours, use tongs and caution to remove the can from the pot. Place the can upright on a rack and let cool to room temperature.

Open the can, mix in a large pinch of salt, if you'd like, and scrape the dulce de leche into a jar.

STORING

Tightly covered, the dulce de leche will keep in the refrigerator for up to 3 weeks.

STRAWBERRY COMPOTE

Cooking sliced strawberries very quickly makes a mixture that falls some-where between a chunky sauce and a saucy compote — one that, no matter what you call it, is great alongside cookies or as a filling for cake-cookies, like the Strawberry Shortcake Cookies (page 322).

I like to add a splash of rose extract to the compote — just enough to accentuate the berries' fragrance, but not enough to attract attention. Depending on the season, your mood and what you're serving the compote with, you might toss a sprig of rosemary or lemon thyme into the pan, add a splash of kirsch or Grand Marnier or finish the berries with a little citrus zest.

The compote is good warm, at room temperature or chilled.

Makes about ½ cup

If your strawberries are small, quarter them; if they're large, dice or coarsely chop them. You want pieces that will hold their shape when cooked but will be small enough to be eaten daintily from a spoon. Toss the berries into a small saucepan, stir in the sugar and put the saucepan over medium heat. Bring to a boil and cook, stirring, for 5 to 8 minutes, or until the juices are just slightly thickened and syrupy.

Scrape the berries and their syrup into a bowl, stir in the rose extract, if you're using it, and cool to just warm or room temperature. Or chill the compote.

8 ounces (a generous 2 cups; 226 grams) fresh strawberries, hulled

1 tablespoon sugar

½ teaspoon pure rose extract (I use Star Kay White; optional)

STORING

Tightly covered, the compote will keep for up to 3 days in the refrigerator.

DO-ALMOST-ANYTHING VANILLA COOKIE DOUGH

1 pound (454 grams) unsalted butter, cut into chunks, at room temperature

1⅓ cups (262 grams) sugar

1 teaspoon fine sea salt

2 large egg whites, at room temperature

1 tablespoon pure vanilla extract

4 cups (544 grams) all-purpose flour

Sanding sugar, for sprinkling (optional)

This is the vanilla counterpart of the Do-Almost-Anything Chocolate Cookie Dough (page 494). Like its chocolate partner, the dough is good on its own, endlessly adaptable and exceedingly easy to work with. Singly, each one is great; together, they're the Batman and Robin of baking for a crowd, capable of making you look like the host who does it all effortlessly.

While I know you'll find bunches of ways to use this dough — its full vanilla flavor and mix of crisp and sandy texture are chameleon-like in their capacity to welcome other flavors and shapes — there are four recipes in this collection to start your imagination spinning: White Chocolate and Poppy Seed Cookies (page 185); Double Ginger Crumb Cookies (page 149); Vanilla Polka Dots (page 178); and Christmas Spice Cookies (page 236).

If you'd like to ice the cookies, do it when the cookies have cooled completely.

Makes about 80 cookies

Working with a stand mixer fitted with the paddle attachment, or in a large bowl with a hand mixer, beat the butter, sugar and salt together on medium speed until smooth and creamy, about 3 minutes. Reduce the mixer speed to low and blend in the egg whites, followed by the vanilla. The dough might curdle, but it will smooth out with mixing and the addition of the flour. Still working on low speed, add the flour in 3 or 4 additions, beating only until it is almost incorporated each time before adding more; scrape down the sides and bottom of the bowl a couple of times as you work and then continue to mix until the flour has disappeared into the dough.

The dough is ready to be divided, flavored (if needed) and scooped or rolled. See the recipes mentioned above for some suggestions.

Or, if you'd like to make plain cookies, divide the dough into quarters and shape each piece into a disk. Working with one disk at a time, place the dough between pieces of parchment paper and roll it to a thickness of ¼ inch. Slide the dough, still between the paper, onto a baking sheet — you can stack the slabs — and freeze for at least 1 hour, or refrigerate for at least 3 hours.

GETTING READY TO BAKE: Position the racks to divide the oven into thirds and preheat it to 350 degrees F. Line two baking sheets with parchment paper or silicone baking mats.

Working with one disk at a time, peel away the paper on both sides of the dough and return the dough to one piece of paper. Use a 2-inch-diameter cookie cutter (choose your shape, and change the size, if you'd like, knowing that the yield will change with it) to cut out as many cookies as you can and place them on the lined baking sheets about 1½ inches apart. Gather the scraps together, then combine with scraps from the other pieces of dough, re-roll and chill before cutting and baking. If you'd like to sprinkle the cutouts with sanding sugar, now's the time.

Bake the cookies for 19 to 21 minutes, rotating the sheets front to back and top to bottom after 10 minutes, or until they are golden around the edges and on the bottom. Cool on the baking sheets for 5 minutes before transferring them to racks to cool completely.

Repeat with the remaining dough, using cool baking sheets.

STORING

Wrapped airtight, the rolled-out dough can be kept in the refrigerator for up to 3 days or frozen for up to 2 months. Cut and bake directly from the freezer. The baked cookies can be kept in a container at room temperature for about 5 days or frozen for up to 2 months.

DO-ALMOST-ANYTHING CHOCOLATE COOKIE DOUGH

4 cups (544 grams) all-purpose flour

²⁄₃ cup (56 grams) unsweetened cocoa powder

1 pound (452 grams) unsalted butter, cut into chunks, at room temperature

1¹⁄₃ cups (262 grams) sugar

1¹⁄₂ teaspoons fine sea salt

2 large egg whites, at room temperature

2 teaspoons pure vanilla extract

Sanding sugar, for sprinkling (optional)

This is one of my favorite doughs because, in addition to being deeply chocolate flavored and generally delicious, it has a wonderful texture — a cross between a snap and shortbread; an easygoing disposition — you can roll it and re-roll it or mold it between your palms and it will keep its grace; and a remarkable affinity for other flavors — with a batch of this dough in your refrigerator (or freezer), you can make as many different kinds of cookies as your imagination can conjure up. (I give you four recipes to get you started.)

One batch of dough makes about eighty 2-inch cookies. You can make a half batch if you'd like, but when you start thinking about cookie swaps and cookie plates, parties and houseguests, I think you'll be happy to make a full batch and divide it to make an assortment. You can use this dough to make: Chocolate-Pecan Cookies (page 200), Chocolate-Raspberry Thumbprints (page 180), Chocolate-Cranberry and Almond Cookies (page 137) and Cherry-Nut Chocolate Pinwheels (page 245).

And don't underestimate the appeal of these cookies standing on their own with, if you insist, a dusting of sanding sugar or a lick of icing. If you do want to ice them, do it when the cookies have cooled completely.

Makes about 80 cookies

Sift the flour and cocoa together.

Working with a stand mixer fitted with the paddle attachment, or in a large bowl with a hand mixer, beat the butter, sugar and salt together on medium speed until smooth and creamy, about 3 minutes. Reduce the mixer speed to low and blend in the egg whites, followed by the vanilla. The dough might curdle, but it will smooth out with mixing and the addition of the flour. Still working on low speed, add the flour mixture in 3 or 4 additions, beating only until the ingredients are almost incorporated each time before adding more;

scrape down the sides and bottom of the bowl a couple of times as you work, and then continue to mix until the dry ingredients have disappeared into the dough.

The dough is ready to be divided, flavored (if needed) and scooped or rolled. See the recipes mentioned on page 494 for some suggestions.

Or, if you'd like to make plain cookies, divide the dough into quarters and shape each piece into a disk.

Working with one disk at a time, place the dough between pieces of parchment paper and roll to a thickness of ¼ inch. Slide the dough, still between the paper, onto a baking sheet — you can stack the slabs — and freeze for at least 1 hour, or refrigerate for at least 3 hours.

GETTING READY TO BAKE: Position the racks to divide the oven into thirds and preheat it to 350 degrees F. Line two baking sheets with parchment paper or silicone baking mats.

Working with one disk at a time, peel away the paper from both sides of the dough and return the dough to one piece of paper. Use a 2-inch-diameter cookie cutter (choose your shape, and change the size, if you'd like, knowing that the yield will change with it) to cut out as many cookies as you can and place them on the lined baking sheets about 1½ inches apart. Gather the scraps together, combine with scraps from the other pieces of dough, re-roll and chill before cutting and baking. If you'd like to sprinkle the cutouts with sanding sugar, now's the time.

Bake the cookies for 18 to 20 minutes, rotating the sheets front to back and top to bottom after 10 minutes, or until they feel firm to the touch. Cool on the baking sheets for 5 minutes before transferring them to a rack to cool completely.

Repeat with the remaining dough, using cool baking sheets.

SOUR CREAM PUFF DOUGH

I don't know how I ended up with *1001 Dairy Dishes from the Sealtest Kitchens*, published in 1961, long before I started cooking. It's a small paperback (from a brand that hasn't existed in decades), and while it looks thumbed through, I don't think I was the one who did the thumbing. Wherever it came from — did someone mail in box tops to get it? — and however it survived on my shelves, getting this recipe makes me glad I'm constitutionally incapable of decluttering.

In addition to being buttery and rich, tangy, beautiful and light-textured, the dough is interesting. Although it's made with yeast, it's treated like puff pastry. Once chilled, it's rolled, folded and turned several times, just as puff pastry and other laminated doughs are. It's not difficult, but it does take time.

You'll love what you can do with it. Because there's no sugar in it, it can be used to make either sweet or savory cookies. I use it for Caramel-Sugar Pufflets (page 267) and Sour Cream–Everything Seed Knots (page 444), but there's lots more to be done with it. Play around!

A word on quantity: You'll get a generous packet of dough from this recipe. Because you have to work with half of the dough at a time and because the dough can be kept in the refrigerator for a few days, you can use one piece to make sweet cookies and the other to make savories.

Makes enough for about 60 cookies

1 package (2¼ teaspoons, 7 grams) dry active yeast (rapid or regular)

¼ cup (60 ml) warm water (see yeast packet for exact temperature)

3¼ cups (442 grams) all-purpose flour

1½ teaspoons fine sea salt

2 sticks (8 ounces; 226 grams) cold unsalted butter, cut into small pieces

1 large egg

¾ cup (180 grams) full-fat sour cream

Stir the yeast into the warm water and let the mixture stand at room temperature for about 5 minutes, until creamy. The yeast might not bubble, and that's fine.

Put the flour and salt in a food processor and pulse to blend. Scatter over the pieces of cold butter and pulse in long (about 10-second) spurts until the flour looks grainy.

Whisk the egg and sour cream together in a small bowl until smooth. Add the yeast and blend.

Add the liquid ingredients to the processor a bit at a time, pulsing after each addition. Then pulse until everything comes together and you've got a moist dough.

Scrape the dough out and knead briefly and lightly to form a ball. Put the ball in a bowl, cover with plastic wrap and refrigerate for at least 2 hours.

Once the dough is thoroughly chilled, it's ready to be used. See whatever recipe(s) you've chosen for directions on rolling and baking.

EVERYTHING SEED MIX

My friend Will Dodd, age eleven, created this mix so that he could make bagel crisps at home. That he was playing with the mix while I was playing around with the Sour Cream Puff Dough (page 497) was a nice moment of culinary synchronicity — it turns out his mix is perfect for my savory knots (page 444). Turns out it's also perfect on the Sesame–Sea Salt Cookies (page 382; swap the mix for the sesame seeds). Or, scatter it (very sparingly) over the Parmesan Galettes (page 424).

Makes about ⅔ cup

Put all the ingredients in a jar or plastic storage container and stir. Shake well or stir before each use.

¼ cup (40 grams) sesame seeds (white, black or a mix)

¼ cup (35 grams) poppy seeds

2 tablespoons dried onion flakes

1 tablespoon garlic powder

2½ teaspoons kosher salt or 1 tablespoon fleur de sel

2 teaspoons freshly ground black pepper

STORING

Tightly covered in the refrigerator or freezer, the mix will be good for at least 1 month. If you've stored the mix for a while, taste before using — seeds have a nasty way of going bad, even when properly stored.

USE-IT-FOR-EVERYTHING STREUSEL

¾ cup (102 grams) all-purpose flour

3 tablespoons sugar

1 tablespoon brown sugar

¼ teaspoon ground cinnamon

¼ teaspoon fine sea salt

5½ tablespoons (2¾ ounces; 78 grams) cold unsalted butter, cut into small cubes

½ teaspoon pure vanilla extract

PLAYING AROUND

Baked Streusel Crunch. Chill the streusel. Center a rack in the oven and preheat it to 300 degrees F. Line a baking sheet with parchment paper or a silicone baking mat. Scatter the streusel over the sheet. Bake for 15 to 20 minutes, stirring and breaking up the streusel once or twice, until it's golden brown. (The streusel will melt, then firm.) Transfer the baking sheet to a rack and let cool. Break into clumps when cool.

STORING

Stored in a covered container or plastic zipper-lock bag (squeeze out as much of the air as you can), the streusel will keep in the refrigerator for up to 2 weeks. Packed airtight, it can be frozen for up to 2 months; thaw in the refrigerator.

This streusel is the one we used at Beurre & Sel, and it's the one I use at home all the time. It's part of what makes a Classic Jammer (page 350) a knockout and it's part of what can set a baker on the path to inventing new sweets. You can use it to top other cookies, and you can also bake it and sprinkle it over ice cream, mousse, baked apples, fresh berries or anything else that welcomes some sweet, seriously crunchy crunch (see Playing Around)

A word on quantity: This recipe makes enough to top a batch of cookies from the Jammer family or to scatter across brownies or a cake, but because it's so versatile, I always double the recipe. The streusel keeps well and it's great to have on hand.

Makes about 1½ cups

You can make the streusel by hand or in a mixer. I prefer to use a stand mixer, but fingers are fine. Whisk the flour, both sugars, the cinnamon and salt together in the mixer bowl or a large bowl. Drop in the cubes of cold butter and toss all the ingredients together with your fingers until the butter is coated.

If you're working with a mixer, fit it with the paddle attachment and mix on medium-low speed until the ingredients form moist, clumpy crumbs. Squeeze the streusel, and it will hold together. Reaching this stage takes longer than you think it will — you might have to mix for 10 minutes or more. Sprinkle over the vanilla and mix until blended.

Or, if you're working by hand, squeeze, mash, mush or otherwise rub everything together until you have a bowlful of moist clumps and curds. Squeeze the streusel, and it will hold together. Sprinkle over the vanilla and toss to blend.

Pack the streusel into a covered container and refrigerate for at least 1 hour (3 hours would be better) before using.

index

Note: Page references in *italics* indicate photographs.

a

alcohol, adding to ice cream, 461

Alexander, Sebastian, 30

Allen, Kim, 239

all-purpose flour, 16–17

all-purpose shortbread, 192

almond flour

   almond crescents, 218–20, *219*

   Biarritz cookies, 294–96, *295*

   cocoa-almond uglies, 140–42, *141*

   French snacklettes with, 166

   fruit-and-nut sbrisolona, 95

   macarons, 312–15, *313*

   Moroccan semolina and almond
      cookies, 155–56, *157*

   salt-and-pepper sugar-and-spice
      galettes, *212*, 213–14

   sesame–sea salt cookies, 382–84, *383*

   torta sbrisolona, 93–95, *94*

almond(s)

   breakfast biscotti, 98–100, *99*

   and chocolate-cranberry cookies,
      137–38, *139*

   -cocoa uglies, 140–42, *141*

   -coco thumbprints, 288–90, *289*

   crackle cookies, 176, *177*

   extract, flavoring ice cream with, 463

French snacklettes, 165–66, *167*

friendship cookies, 270–73, *271*

fruit-and-nut sbrisolona, 95

good, better, best cookies, 161–64,
   163

hamantaschen, 283–84, *285*

kamish, 280–82, *281*

leckerli, 56–58, *57*

lucky charm brownies, 39–41, *40*

mincemeat-oatmeal bars, 79

mixed-nut gozinaki, 240

pain de Gênes buttons, 182–84, *183*

raisin bars, 77–79, *78*

and semolina cookies, Moroccan,
   155–56, *157*

smoky hearts, 453–55, *454*

snowballs, 226

Swedish dream cookies, 227–29, *228*

Swedish visiting cake bars, 87–88, *89*

toasted, adding to ice cream, 463

torta sbrisolona, 93–95, *94*

see also almond flour

amaretti

   crumbled, adding to ice cream, 463

   Lazzaroni, about, 39

   in lucky charm brownies, 39–41, *40*

amaretto

   for almond ice cream, 463

-infused dried fruit, adding to ice
   cream, 463

anise seeds, in rousquilles, 303–4, *305*

anytime tarragon-apricot cookies,
   432–34, *433*

Anzac biscuits, *158*, 159–60

apple butter bars, Maine, 52

apple(s)

   bars, crumb-topped, 59–61, *60*

   they-might-be-breakfast cookies,
      110–12, *111*

apricot(s)

   cast-iron pan chocolate chip cookie
      bars, 53–55, *54*

   chocolate saucisson, 230–32, *231*

   dried-fruit gozinaki, 240

   fruit and four-grain biscotti, 101–3,
      102

   fruit-and-nut sbrisolona, 95

   hamantaschen, 283–84, *285*

   multi-mix-in chocolate chip cookies,
      55

   Natasha's mum's fruit and walnut
      bread bars, 90–92, *91*

   steeped in amaretto, adding to ice
      cream, 463

   -tarragon cookies, anytime, 432–34,
      433

b